International Law in Antiquity

This study of the origins of international law combines techniques of intellectual history and historiography to investigate the earliest developments of the law of nations. The book examines the sources, processes, and doctrines of international legal obligation in antiquity to reevaluate the critical attributes of international law. David J. Bederman focuses on three essential areas in which law influenced ancient State relations – diplomacy, treaty-making, and warfare – in a detailed analysis of international relations in the Near East (2800–700 BCE), the Greek city-States (500–338 BCE), and Rome (358–168 BCE). Containing up-to-date literature and archeological evidence, this study does not merely catalogue instances of recognition by ancient States of these seminal features of international law: it accounts for recurrent patterns of thinking and practice. This comprehensive analysis of international law and State relations in ancient times provides a fascinating study for lawyers and academics, ancient historians and classicists alike.

DAVID J. BEDERMAN is Professor of Law at Emory University's School of Law in Atlanta, Georgia. His previous publications cover such diverse subjects as international legal theory and history, the law of the sea and international environment, the law of State responsibility and international claims, US constitutional law of foreign relations, and maritime law.

CAMBRIDGE STUDIES IN INTERNATIONAL AND COMPARATIVE LAW

This series (established in 1946 by Professors Gutteridge, Hersch Lauterpacht and McNair) is a forum for high quality studies in the fields of public and private international and comparative law. Although these are distinct sub-disciplines, developments since 1946 confirm their interrelationship. Comparative law is increasingly used as a tool in the making of law at national, regional and international levels. Private international law is now often affected by international conventions, and the issues faced by classical conflicts rules are frequently dealt with by substantive harmonisation of law under international auspices. Mixed international arbitrations, especially those involving state economic activity, raise mixed questions of public and private international law, while in many fields (such as the protection of human rights and democratic standards, investment guarantees, and international criminal law) international and national systems interact. National constitutional arrangements relating to "foreign affairs", and to the implementation of international norms, are a focus of attention.

Professor Sir Robert Jennings edited the series from 1981. Following his retirement as General Editor, an editorial board has been created and Cambridge University Press has recommitted itself to the series, affirming its broad scope.

The board welcomes works of a theoretical or interdisciplinary character, and those focusing on new approaches to international or comparative law or conflict of law. Studies of particular institutions or problems are equally welcome, as are translations of the best work published in other languages.

General Editors	James Crawford
	David Johnston
Editorial Board	Professor Hilary Charlesworth *University of Adelaide*
	Mr John Collier *Trinity Hall, Cambridge*
	Professor Lori Damrosch *Columbia University Law School*
	Professor John Dugard *Director, Research Centre for*
	International Law, University of Cambridge
	Professor Mary-Ann Glendon *Harvard Law School*
	Professor Christopher Greenwood *London School of*
	Economics
	Professor Hein Kötz *Max-Planck-Institut, Hamburg*
	Professor D. M. McRae *University of Ottawa*
	Professor Onuma Yasuaki *University of Tokyo*
Advisory Committee	Professor D. W. Bowett QC
	Judge Rosalyn Higgins QC
	Professor Sir Robert Jennings QC
	Professor J. A. Jolowicz QC
	Professor Sir Eli Lauterpacht QC
	Professor Kurt Lipstein
	Judge Stephen Schwebel

A list of books in the series can be found at the end of this volume

International Law in Antiquity

David J. Bederman

CAMBRIDGE
UNIVERSITY PRESS

PUBLISHED BY THE PRESS SYNDICATE OF THE UNIVERSITY OF CAMBRIDGE
The Pitt Building, Trumpington Street, Cambridge, United Kingdom

CAMBRIDGE UNIVERSITY PRESS
The Edinburgh Building, Cambridge CB2 2RU, UK
40 West 20th Street, New York, NY 10011-4211, USA
10 Stamford Road, Oakleigh, VIC 3166, Australia
Ruiz de Alarcón 13, 28014 Madrid, Spain
Dock House, The Waterfront, Cape Town 8001, South africa

http://www.cambridge.org

First published 2001

Printed in the United Kingdom at the University Press, Cambridge

Typeset in Swift 10/13 in QuarkXPress™   [SE]

A catalogue record for this book is available from the British Library

ISBN 0 521 79197 9 hardback

For my Father,
who sets the highest standards

Contents

Acknowledgments

This book has been over a decade in the making. It began its life as my dissertation for a PhD in Laws at the University of London. In that stage of development, I was grateful to Professor (now Judge) Rosalyn Higgins and Professor Patricia Birnie at the London School of Economics, who both provided valuable guidance at the early, planning stages of this project. At the conclusion of writing, I was given significant direction by Professor William E. Butler of University College London, and by Professor James Crawford of Cambridge University.

I have also immensely profited from countless conversations with scores of colleagues and scholars, drawn from the international law, classics, ancient history, and political theory disciplines. It would be impossible for me to credit all of these contacts, but I would particularly acknowledge the advice of such people as Robert Bauslaugh, Hal Berman, Michael Broyde, Herbert Hausmaninger, Mark Janis, David Kennedy, Martti Koskenniemi, Benedict Kingsbury, Charles Reid, Cees Roelofsen, Alan Watson, and John Witte.

I owe a special debt of gratitude to Professor Aldo Lupi of Georgia State University, who took such especial care in checking and correcting my Latin and Greek usages, and to Professor Michael Broyde, of Emory University School of Law, who reviewed my ancient Hebrew terminology.

The dauntingly broad scope of this work placed heavy burdens on the many reference librarians that I have been privileged to be associated with in my career. I owe a substantial debt to the librarians of the Peace Palace Library in The Hague; the University of Virginia School of Law Library; and, most of all, to my colleagues at the Emory University School of Law, Robert W. Woodruff, and Pitts Theological Libraries.

I should also point out that an early version of what is now Chapter 3 of this volume appeared in a collection of essays entitled *The Influence of Religion on the Development of International Law* (Mark W. Janis, ed. 1991 & 1999).

Finally, I must acknowledge the sacrifices of my wife and daughter. Any scholar's commitment to a project of this sort comes always at a substantial cost to one's family. I just hope that the costs have been modest enough, and compensated (to some degree) with my attention, respect, and love.

As always, I fully accept responsibility for the errors and omissions found in this volume. Despite my best efforts, I am sure many will be identified. Interdisciplinary scholarship is always a risky undertaking, and a book of this scope and thrust is perhaps even more fraught with reputational danger. I can only hope that a gentle and patient reader will find it a useful contribution to our understanding of ancient peoples and their engagement with a rule of law for international relations.

Abbreviations

AJIL	*American Journal of International Law*
AJP	*American Journal of Philology*
ARMT	*Archives Royales de Mari*
BASOR	*Bulletin of the American Schools of Oriental Research*
BYIL	*British Yearbook of International Law*
CP	*Classical Philology*
CQ	*Classical Quarterly*
Eastern JIL	*Eastern Journal of International Law*
GRBS	*Greek, Roman and Byzantine Studies*
Indian JIL	*Indian Journal of International Law*
Indian YBIA	*Indian Yearbook of International Affairs*
JAOS	*Journal of the American Oriental Society*
JHS	*Journal of Hellenic Studies*
JNES	*Journal of Near Eastern Studies*
Netherlands ILR	*Netherlands International Law Review*
PCPhS	*Proceedings of the Classical Philology Society*
RCADI	*Recueil des Cours de l'Academie de Droit International de la Haye*
REG	*Revue des Etudes Grecques*
RGDIP	*Revue Generale de Droit International Public*
RIDA	*Revue Internationale des Droits de l'Antiquité* (ser. 3)

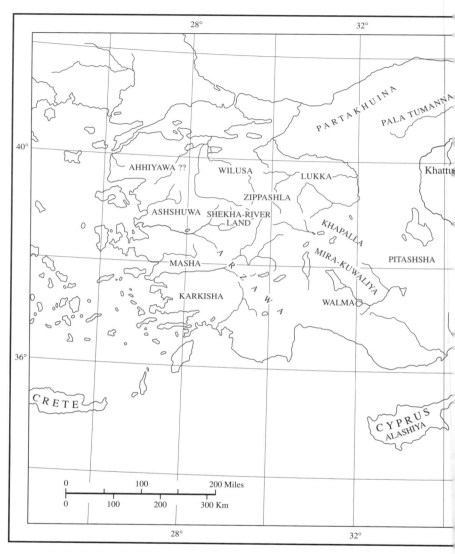

Map 1 Ancient Near East (reproduced from the *Cambridge Ancient History*, volume 2, Part 2, 3rd edn, 1975)

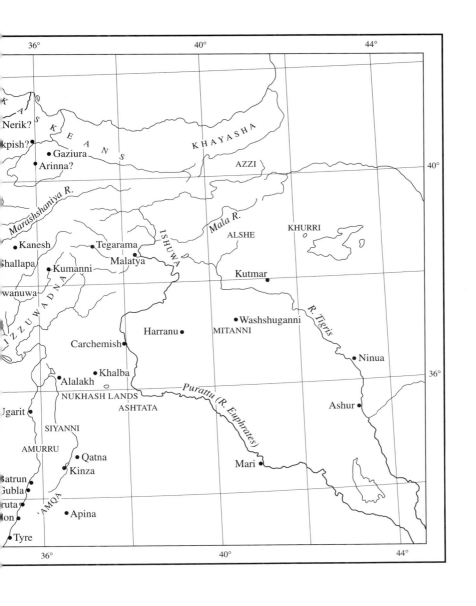

Nerik?

kpish?•

• Gaziura

• Arinna?

Marashshaniya R.

• Kanesh

hallapa

• Kumanni

wanuwa

ZIZZUWADNA

Tegarama•

Malatya

Carchemish•

• Khalba

• Alalakh

NUKHASH LANDS

ASHTATA

Ugarit•

SIYANNI

AMURRU

• Qatna

Batrun

Kinza

Gubla•

uta•

'AMQA

on•

• Apina

•Tyre

KHAYASHA

AZZI

ISHUWA

Mala R.

ALSHE

KHURRI

Kutmar•

•Washshuganni

Harranu •

MITANNI

R. Tigris

Ninua

Purattu (R. Euphrates)

Ashur •

Mari •

36°   40°   44°

40°

36°

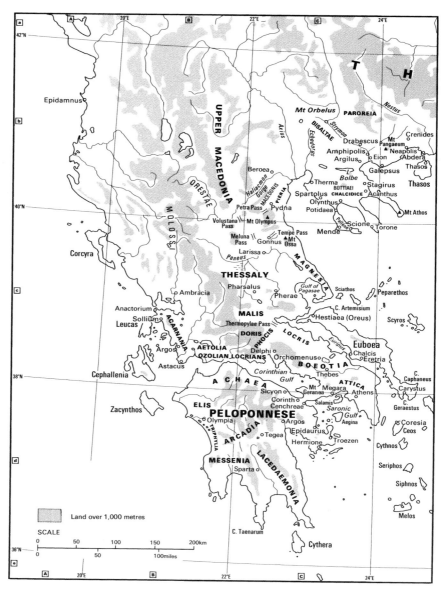

Map 2   Greece (reproduced from the *Cambridge Ancient History*, volume 5, 2nd edn, 1992)

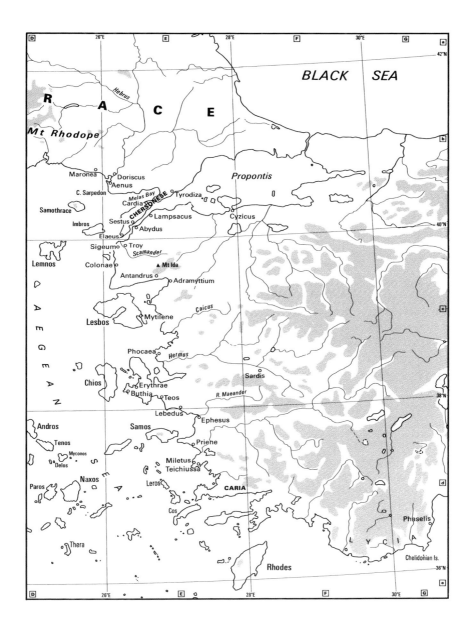

BLACK SEA

R   A   C   E

Mt Rhodope

Propontis

Maronea
Doriscus
Aenus
C. Sarpedon
Melas Bay
Cardia
CHERSONESE
Tyrodiza
Samothrace
Imbros
Sestus
Lampsacus
Cyzicus
Abydus
Elaeus
Sigeum
Troy
Scamander
Lemnos
Colonae
Antandrus
Adramyttium
Mt Ida
Caicus
Mytilene
Lesbos
Phocaea
Hermus
Sardis
Chios
Erythrae
Buthia
Teos
R. Maeander
Lebedus
Andros
Samos
Ephesus
Tenos
Priene
Myconos
Delos
Miletus
Teichiussa
Naxos
Leros
CARIA
Paros
Cos
Phaselis
Thera
LYCIA
Chelidonian Is.
Rhodes

A E G E A N

S E A

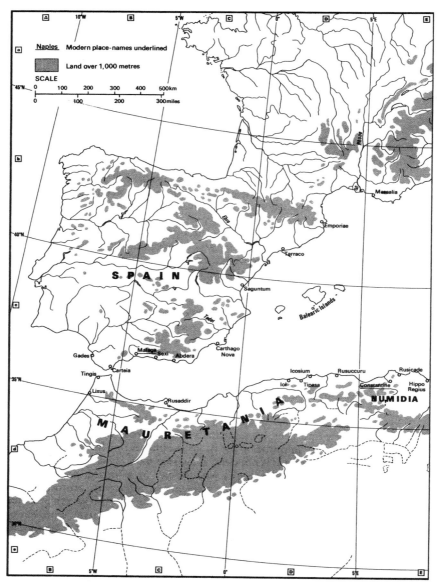

Map 3   Roman expansion (reproduced from the *Cambridge Ancient History*, volume 7, Part 2, 2nd edn, 1989)

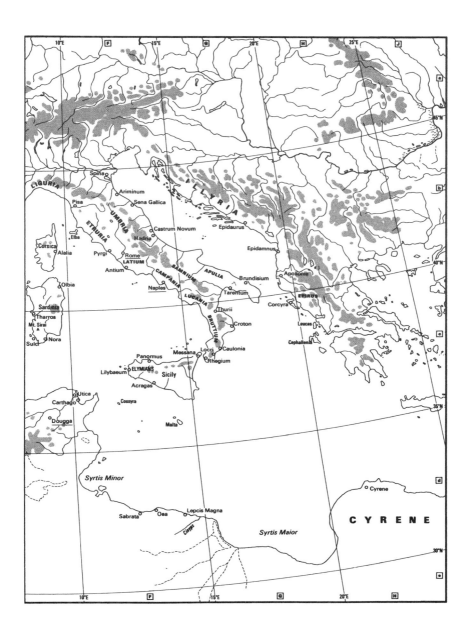

45°N

40°N

35°N

30°N

10°E · 15°E · 20°E · 25°E

LIGURIA

Spina

Ariminum

Pisa

Elba

Sena Gallica

ETRURIA

UMBRIA

Castrum Novum

Hadria

Corsica

Alalia

Pyrgi

Rome

LATIUM

Antium

CAMPANIA

SAMNIUM

APULIA

Naples

LUCANIA

BRUTTIUM

Olbia

Sardinia

Tharros

Mt. Sirai

Nora

Sulci

Panormus

ELYMIANS

Lilybaeum

Sicily

Acragas

Utica

Carthago

Cossyra

Dougga

Malta

I·L·L·Y·R·I·A

Epidaurus

Epidamnus

Brundisium

Apollonia

Tarentum

Corcyra

EPIRUS

Thurii

Croton

Leucas

Caulonia

Cephallenia

Messana

Locri

Rhegium

Syrtis Minor

Cyrene

Sabrata

Oea

Lepcis Magna

Cinyps

Syrtis Maior

C Y R E N E

1 A methodological introduction: this study and its limitations

This is a study of the intellectual origins of international law. This volume combines techniques of intellectual history and historiography in order to account for the earliest developments in the sources, processes and doctrines of the law of nations. This combination of methods is not only essential for considering the earliest formation of ideas of international law, but also for beginning an understanding of the manner in which those ideas have been received by modern publicists and the extent to which they have been recognized in the modern practice of States.

My book will thus critically examine what has become an article of faith in our discipline: that international law is a unique product of the modern, rational mind. I argue here that it is not. While this volume charts the intellectual impact of the idea of ancient international law, it purposefully ignores the appreciation of this subject by historians, political scientists and internationalists. My study, moreover, confines itself to the single inquiry of whether the ancient mind could and did conceive of a rule of law for international relations. I certainly do not attempt to argue or suggest here that modern principles or doctrines of international law can be traced to antiquity. Nor do I pronounce judgment on the exact manner in which the ancient tradition of international law was received in early-Modern Europe or after. These inquiries must be left for later research and discussion. I confront here, therefore, an ancient law of nations on its own terms. By doing so, I am making a start on a broader vision of the intellectual origins of our discipline.

Intellectual history is, after all, the story of ideas. International law, even when considered as an historical subject, is typically conceived as a collection of rules motivated by international relations. Rarely is it viewed as a cogent theory of State relations. One thrust of this book will test such a theory against the historical circumstances of the ancient world. In order to do this, my study accepts the notion that international law is impossible without a system of multiple States, each conscious of its own sovereignty and the choice between relations being premised on order or on anarchy.[1]

Times and places

As a consequence of these conceptual limitations, this volume will be limited to three general periods of antiquity. They are (1) the ancient Near East including the periods subsuming the Sumerian city-States, the great empires of Egypt, Babylon, Assyria and the Hittites (1400–1150 BCE), and a later, brief period focusing on the nations of Israel and their Syrian neighbors (966–700 BCE); (2) the Greek city-States from 500–338 BCE; and (3) the wider Mediterranean during the period of Roman contact with Carthage, Macedon, Ptolemaic Egypt, and the Seleucid Empire (358–168 BCE). I am mindful, of course, that the temporal and geographical scope of this study is huge. But it is not insuperable. I have chosen with care the times and places in antiquity for review; in each one there is an undisputed, and authentic, system of States in place. The evidence for this proposition will be detailed in Chapter 2.

By the same token, I do acknowledge that there is some arbitrariness in the dates and localities selected for research in this book. As Professor Wolfgang Preiser wrote in his recent abstract of the history of international law in antiquity:

We accept that writers of history of international law must . . . be allowed to apply the intellectual principle of order called categorization by period which is utilized by all historians, irrespective of specialization, when they perceive their task to be the comprehension respectively of an uninterrupted flow of events. It is regrettable that a living process should be thus divided into chronological and locational sections; yet, taking our limited powers of absorption into consideration, it cannot be avoided.[2]

This defense of historiographic method is especially pertinent in my study, attempting (as it does) to trace the patterns of State practice amongst different peoples and State organizations at very different times in antiquity.

---

[1] See Vilho Harle, *Ideas of Social Order in the Ancient World* 91–100, 165–68, 171–74 (1998); Georg Schwarzenberger, International Law in Early English Practice, BYIL 52, 52 (1948).

[2] Wolfgang Preiser, History of the Law of Nations: Basic Questions and Principles, in 7 *Encyclopedia of Public International Law* 126, 131 (Rudolph Bernhardt ed. 1984).

It is precisely because I believe that there is an essential unity in the nature of State behavior in ancient times that I am willing to adopt this comparative approach for this study. My selection of times and places for in-depth analysis has a very important aspect. The "uninterrupted flow of events" in ancient times in the Near East and Mediterranean meant that the traditions of statecraft that were developed at an early time by the Sumerian city-States and their Akkadian conquerors, and reformulated by the Assyrians and Hittites, were transmitted to later cultures through the Egyptians and Israelites and Phoenicians, and thence to Greece, Carthage, and Rome.

It is for this reason that I do not survey the great international law traditions of India and China in this book. The literature available on the political cultures and international societies of ancient India (from the post-Vedic period until 150 BCE)[3] and the Eastern Chou and Warring States Periods in China (770–221 BCE)[4] is large and of generally high quality.

[3] For general treatises, see, e.g., Chacko, India's Contribution to the Field of International Law Concepts, 93 RCADI 117 (1958-I); Chacko, International Law in India, 1 Indian JIL 184, 589 (1960–61); 2 ibid. at 48 (1962); Hiralal Chatterjee, International Law and Inter-State Relations in Ancient India (1958); Nawaz, The Law of Nations in Ancient India, 6 Indian BIA 172 (1957); Pavithran, International Law in Ancient India, 5 Eastern JIL 220, 307 (1974); 6 ibid. at 8, 102, 235, 284 (1975); Nagendra Singh, History of the Law of Nations – Regional Developments: South and South-East Asia, in 7 Encyclopedia of Public International Law 237 (Rudolph Bernhardt ed. 1984); Nagendra Singh, India and International Law (1969); S. V. Viswanatha, International Law in Ancient India (1925). For considerations of the general theory of international relations in ancient India, see C. H. Alexandrowicz, Kautilyan Principles and the Law of Nations, 41 BYIL 301 (1965); Derett, The Maintenance of Peace in the Hindu World: Practice and Theory, 7 Indian YBIA 361 (1958); Mahadevan, Kautilya on the Sanctity of Pacts, 5 Indian YBIA 342 (1956); Modelski, Kautilya: Foreign Policy and International System in the Ancient Hindu World, 58 American Political Science Review 549 (1964); Ved P. Nanda, International Law in Ancient Hindu India, in The Influence of Religion on the Development of International Law 51 (Mark W. Janis ed. 1991); Pavithran, Kautilya's Arthasastra, 7 Eastern JIL 193, 243 (1976); 8 ibid. at 16 (1977); Ruben, Inter-State Relations in Ancient India and Kautilya's Arthasastra, 4 Indian YBIA 137 (1955); Sastri, International Law and Relations in Ancient India, 1 Indian YBIA 97 (1952); Nagendra Singh, The Machinery and Method for Conduct of Inter-State Relations in Ancient India, in International Law at a Time of Perplexity: Essays in Honor of Shabtai Rosenne 845 (Yoram Dinstein ed. 1989). For reviews of specific doctrinal issues, see Armour, Customs of Warfare in Ancient India, 8 Grotius Society Transactions 71 (1922); Bedi, The Concept of Alliances in Ancient India, 17 Indian JIL 354 (1977); Palaniswami, Diplomacy of the Ancient Tamils, 10 Eastern JIL 17 (1978); Palaniswami, International Law (War) of the Ancient Tamils, 8 Eastern JIL 41 (1977); Pavithran, Diplomacy in Kautilya's Arthasastra, 8 Eastern JIL 163, 245 (1977); Poulose, State Succession in Ancient India, 10 Indian JIL 175 (1970); L. Rocher, The "Ambassador" in Ancient India, 7 Indian YBIA 344 (1958).
[4] See, e.g., Britton, Chinese Interstate Intercourse Before 700 BC, 29 AJIL 616 (1935); Shih-Tsai Chen, The Equality of States in Ancient China, 35 AJIL 641 (1941); Frederick Tse-Shyang Chen, The Confucian View of World Order, in The Influence of Religion on the

Nevertheless, there is simply no historical evidence to suggest that there was any substantial diplomatic contact between Indian and Chinese cultures, nor between these great Asian international systems and those of the Near East and Mediterranean. This is surprising in view of the extensive economic and religious contacts between all of these culture centers in the ancient world. Without that essential element of contact and continuity, I believe it prudent to exclude from the wider consideration of this volume Indian and Chinese contributions to the development of international law.[5]

I am mindful, of course, that this decision exposes me to the criticism directed against much modern international law scholarship: that it ignores or perverts non-European, non-Western traditions of international relations. I actually concur with this critique. But there is the obvious point that ancient cultures (whether from the Near East or Greco-Roman tradition) should not be enlisted for some modern historiographic conflict between East and West, developed versus developing worlds. I certainly make no claim here of historic continuity between the ancient and modern worlds, and absolutely eschew the notion that "modern," "Western" doctrines of international law derive any extra legitimacy by being traced back to ancient sources – assuming such could be proved (which I seriously doubt).

Comparison and relativism

Even so, that leaves a significant question about the propriety (and, indeed, even the intellectual legitimacy) of the kind of comparative study of ancient international law I wish to undertake here. I take as a starting-

Footnote 4 (cont.)
> Development of International Law 31 (Mark W. Janis ed. 1991); Te-hsu Ch'eng, International Law in Early China (1122–249 BC), 11 Chinese Social and Political Science Review 38, 251 (1927); Iriye, The Principles of International Law in View of Confucian Doctrine, 120 RCADI 1 (1967–I); W. A. P. Martin, Traces of International Law in Ancient China, 14 International Review 63 (1883); Shigeki Miyazaki, History of the Law of Nations – Regional Developments: Far East, in 7 Encyclopedia of Public International Law 215 (Rudolph Bernhardt ed. 1984); Richard Louis Walker, The Multi-State System of Ancient China (1953).

[5] For much the same reasons, I also excluded considerations of African State systems and the international relations of the Byzantine empire. For more on these, see T. O. Elias, History of the Law of Nations – Regional Developments: Africa, in 7 Encyclopedia of Public International law 205 (Rudolph Bernhardt ed. 1984); T. O. Elias, Africa and the Development of International Law (1972); A. K. Mensah-Brown, Notes on International Law and Pre-Colonial Legal History of Modern Ghana, in African Legal History 107 (UNITAR 1975); Stephen Verosta, International Law in Europe and Western Asia Between 100 and 650 AD, 113 RCADI 484 (1964–III).

point for this caveat Professor Preiser's exegesis on comparative international legal history, which is worth quoting at length:

General legal history is, for good reasons, concerned with all legal developments
of the past, regardless of where or when they appeared, and also of whether or
not they prevailed over the longer term. The history of international law has no
reason for proceeding otherwise . . . The historian of international law, for his
part, will see his task in gaining command over the international legal developments of the period in question and placing them in their correct context . . . The
comparative law approach as such is nothing new for the history of international
law . . . However, until now the comparison has been restricted almost entirely to
different epochs in the history of European international law. Once research into
the unexplored areas of international law has advanced sufficiently far to banish
the danger of premature generalizations, this approach will be able to draw on
an abundance of new and in part no doubt fascinating and exotic material. We
may hope to see the appearance of new questions and answers . . . The ultimate
aim of all conceivable comparative work in the area of the history of international law is not the comparison of individual phenomena, whatever their intrinsic importance, but the comparison of entire epochs. This means comparing
above all those periods of time for which the claim can be made . . . for the existence of a legally ordered inter-State system which on its own merits persisted
over a long period of time alongside the mere use of force. Put differently, what
is here at issue is a comparative examination of independently developed, functional international legal orders which helped influence the legal character of
their respective eras.[6]

Putting aside the attractions of "exotic material," and the extraordinary
intellectual hazard of treating any subject as "different" or "other" than
established norms (a common thrust of the Orientalism of the nineteenth
century), Preiser offers an intelligible methodology for my project. The
validity of any comparative exercise in studying ancient international law
depends on the selection of historical evidence concerning authentic
State systems and placing it in its "correct context," to use Professor
Preiser's words, while taking care to avoid "premature generalizations."
"Correct context" means, I would suppose, that statements made about
notional rules of State conduct in international relations are weighed
against the available historical record of State behavior in antiquity. It is
not enough, of course, that States may have *said* that they observed a particular rule of international law. It is quite another matter to see whether
they, in fact, did so. My survey will attempt, wherever possible, to ascertain the actual observance of these norms of State conduct.

[6] Preiser, *supra* note 2, at 128–29.

Likewise, taking care to avoid "premature generalizations" is in large part a matter of reminding oneself, as Professor Shabtai Rosenne has observed, that while "there is a marked similarity in the problems that have been faced [in different State systems], and in the solutions reached . . . they start from different underlying premises and different general philosophies of law and the place of the law in the social system."[7] One cannot be misled by supposed similarities in "detailed rules of law"[8] developed in State systems separated by great time and distance.

This study scrupulously avoids any such conclusion that there was a single, cohesive body of international law rules recognized by all States in antiquity. Such an assertion would be folly, based (as it must be) on the same ruinous reasoning that compels some writers to suggest that modern doctrines of international law can trace their lineage directly back to ancient times. The point I am making here is, at once, more subtle and more consequential. This study will seek to understand not whether there was a common set of rules of State behavior in antiquity, but whether there was a common *idea* or *tradition* that international relations were to be based on the rule of law.

Sources, process, and doctrines

The organizing principle of this book will be to examine whether an ancient law of nations had the paradigmatic attributes of modern international law. I believe that it did not. Yet, that does not make the law of nations in antiquity any less relevant or worthy of study. We conceive of international law today as a network of sources, processes, and doctrines, forming a web of obligation, though without explicit sanction. The ancient mind, I will suggest here, could not distinguish the process elements of rules for State behavior from the sources of those obligations or their content.[9] For that reason alone, ancient international law was a primitive legal system, as that concept was understood and defined by Sir Henry Maine.[10]

---

[7] Shabtai Rosenne, The Influence of Judaism on the Development of International Law, 5 Netherlands ILR 119, 121 (1958).   [8] *Ibid.*

[9] See H. L. A. Hart, *The Concept of Law* 89–96 (1961).

[10] See Sir Henry Maine, *Ancient Law* (1861) (1986 ed.); Sir Henry Maine, *International Law* 13 (1894). Other writers have developed the notion of international law as a primitive legal system: see Michael Barkun, *Law Without Sanctions: Order in Primitive Societies and the World Community* (1968); E. Adamson Hoebel, *The Law of Primitive Man* 331 (1954); Roger D. Masters, World Politics as a Primitive Political System, 16 *World Politics* 595 (1964); Yoram Dinstein, International Law as a Primitive Legal System, 19 *New York University Journal of International Law and Politics* 1 (1986).

The initial place to test that hypothesis is not, as some have supposed,[11] to examine the manifestations of international law doctrines in the ancient documents and materials. Instead, I take as my point of departure a comprehension of the sources of international legal obligation in antiquity. These will be very carefully considered in Chapter 3. What I hope to make clear is that other primitive aspects have been wrongly attributed to an ancient law of nations. For example, the sources of standards for State behavior were not, as has been supposed, exclusively religious. Reason and experience mattered in ancient international relations, just as today. To understand the sources of rules of State relations is the first step in comprehending whether those rules had content, whether they were perceived as being legitimate, and how they were given sanction.

Likewise, the doctrinal norms of international antiquity, though small in number, were broad in importance and capable of eliciting certainty and security of expectation. This will be shown for a range of restraints on State behavior, including (1) the conduct of embassies, immunities granted to envoys, and protections afforded to foreigners; (2) the sanctity given to treaties and alliances; and (3) the constraints of a nation declaring war and the limits on the actual conduct of hostilities.

These doctrines have been selected with the view of capturing the broadest spectrum of normative values in State relations. The reception, treatment, and functions of ambassadors (for example) implicated an essential inquiry: the capacity of the ancient State in placing its relations with its neighbors on a footing of friendship. A corollary of this problem was the ability of ancient States to develop statuses and relationships that would eliminate particularism. Likewise, the negotiation, ratification, enforcement, and termination of treaties was a vital aspect of ancient State relations. Some scholars (following an Austinian view of law)[12] have suggested that the only basis of a law of nations in antiquity was the positive act of one State making faith with another. Review of this assertion will be a consistent theme of this study.[13] But there is also the narrower

---

[11] This would be my single, methodological criticism of the pioneering works on this subject written in the late nineteenth and early twentieth centuries. As with any study of this sort, one must acknowledge that one is standing on the shoulders of giants. In my case, the leviathans are Coleman Phillipson's two-volume work, *The International Law and Custom of Ancient Greece and Rome*, published in 1911, the first two books of F. Laurent's earlier, multi-volume set, *Histoire de droit des gens* (1850–70), and Michael Rostovtseff, International Relations in the Ancient World in *The History and Nature of International Relations* (E. Walsh ed. 1922).

[12] See John Austin, *The Province of Jurisprudence Determined* 127, 141–42 (1832) (H. L. A. Hart ed. 1954).

[13] See Chapter 2, pp. 31–41 below; Chapter 3, pp. 51–59 below; and Chapter 5.

question of the manner in which the ancient mind was competent to interpret and enforce rules of State behavior contained in written agreements. Lastly, there is a recognition that armed conflict was a constant reality of international life in ancient times, as today. The conditions under which nations believed they had rights under international law, rights that had to be vindicated by the declaration of war against another nation, were significant choices made by ancient States. In the same fashion, the exercise of restraint in making war was surely one of the most important manifestations of the rule of law in ancient State relations.

Each of these doctrinal fields was the subject of at least some consideration by each of the civilizations studied in this volume.[14] As they are discussed in turn – diplomacy and friendship in Chapter 4, treaty-making in Chapter 5, and the initiation and conduct of war in Chapter 6 – it is important to remember that the emphasis of these chapters will not be merely to catalogue instances where ancient States apparently recognized these doctrinal features of an ancient law of nations. Instead, the object is to establish recurrent patterns of thinking and practice concerning these doctrines. This is what I intend in explicating a tradition of international law in antiquity.

Texts and sources

Intellectual history is largely a matter of close textual analysis. Such a study is, of course, only as good as the texts it relies upon. It is no surprise, therefore, that the greatest challenge for fashioning an intellectual history of international law in antiquity is the sparsity of the historical record. In researching this study I recognize that only fragments of that record, containing only limited memorializations of State practice, have found their way to the present. Some of those extant texts, one must

---

[14] The practice of international arbitration amongst the Greek city-States has been a popular subject of scholarly attention for many years. See, e.g., V. Bérard, *De arbitrio inter liberas Graecorum civitates* (1894); Victor Martin, *La Vie internationale dans la Grèce des cités* (1940) (reprinted 1979); A. Raeder, *L'Arbitrage international chez les Hellènes* (1912); J. H. Ralston, *International Arbitration from Athens to Locarno* (1929); Michel Revon, *L'Arbitrage international* 62–105 (1892); M. N. Tod, *International Arbitration Amongst the Greeks* (1913); W. L. Westermann, International Arbitration in Antiquity, 2 *Classical Journal* 197 (1906–07). Nevertheless, arbitration does not appear to have been practiced to any great degree in the ancient Near East or by the Romans and their rivals. See Louise E. Matthaei, The Place of Arbitration and Mediation in Ancient Systems of International Ethics, 2 *Classical Quarterly* 241 (1908). For that reason, arbitration – which could have been a putative element of third-party settlement of international disputes based on a rule of law – will not be considered in this book.

realize, have been degraded in transmission to the point that they are nearly useless for historical inquiry.

It is worth remembering, though, that today's record of customary international law, the uncodified practice of States, is also incomplete, and there continue today to be strong methodological problems in piecing together a complete picture of State practice. The problem today is not, of course, the historical distance of events, but, rather, the difficulty in determining which examples of modern practice are relevant, and which are not. The problem with antiquity is that the modern researcher is unaided by any contemporary treatment of the subject of rules governing State behavior in ancient times. We know, for example, that there were a few texts written in Greek and Latin (including those by Aristotle, Demetrius of Phaleron, and Varro) on subjects of statecraft that subsumed matters involved in the law of nations, such as rules for declaring war and the conduct of embassies.[15] None of these texts survived to the present day, and we have no reliable information from other classical writers as to the contents of these treatises. Our situation is aptly described by H. B. Leech in an essay he wrote in 1877:

If, in the centuries to come, the special treatises upon modern Public Law were to disappear, and the student of European civilisation in the nineteenth century should be obliged to have recourse to purely historical works for light on this subject, he would find there but scanty information upon the principles and working of the present International Code. This is our position with regard to the Public Law of ancient times.[16]

While there is a paucity of systematic treatments of the subject of the law of nations in antiquity, our task has been made easier by notable advances in classical historiography. The first among these has been in more sophisticated treatments and understandings of the literary evidence that does survive from ancient times. Greater refinement in Biblical scholarship[17] and the handling of epic or archaic texts (whether from Sumer or from early Greece)[18] have allowed for more certainty in dating the historical events narrated in these writings, as has strong archeological evidence.

[15] See H. B. Leech, *An Essay on Ancient International Law* 22–23 (1877), for a consideration of these texts. See also Sir Frank Adcock and D. J. Mosley, *Diplomacy in Ancient Greece* 183–85 (1975).   [16] Leech, *supra* note 15, at 60.

[17] See Prosper Weil, Le Judaïsme et le développement du droit international, 151 RCADI 253, 266–72 (1976–III).

[18] See Michael Gagarin, *Early Greek Law* 20 (1986) ("[M]ost scholars now feel that the [epic poems of Homer] do reflect fairly accurately Greek society during the century or so preceding their final composition"); 1 Phillipson, *supra* note 11, at ix.

This study takes exceptional care with its treatment of classical literary evidence bearing on State practices and rules of State conduct in international affairs. I suppose the preeminent caution exercised in this book is the refusal to regard any single piece of literary evidence (standing alone) as being dispositive of any proposition concerning broader patterns of practice by ancient States. Aside from that vital methodological caveat, I have appreciated a number of standard approaches to literary texts, developed by historians and philologists after long years of study.

One of these is the recognition that not all classical historians, and the histories they relate, are to be treated equally.[19] In the Greek historical canon,[20] the history of Thucydides (460–400 BCE) remains preeminent in its fidelity to historical truth. The history of Herodotus (c. 480–430 BCE), though criticized for many lapses, has at least been praised for its literary presentation. The works of Xenophon (411–362 BCE) and the later Polybius (c. 198–144 BCE) are also highly regarded. On the other hand, the histories of such writers as Diodorus Siculus (Diodorus of Sicily) (fl. 60–30 BCE) are not so well respected, being largely a pastiche of other commentators. Among the Latin histories, that of Livy is regarded as among the best (despite charges that he was writing to pander to Augustan political values); the later writings of Tacitus are somewhat less esteemed.[21] Likewise, there are many works of statecraft, biography, and political philosophy written in Greek and Latin, all of divergent probative value.

The second tactic I adopt in this study is the careful cross-reading of literary texts. Not only do I attempt to ascertain the internal coherence and integrity of all literary sources used in this study,[22] I have tried to ensure the accuracy of historical evidence of State practice by relating the information found in these texts to the available archeological evidence, the most important of which are inscriptions of significant State decrees, treaties, proclamations, and other newsworthy events. The increased availability of this inscription evidence, particularly from earlier periods of

---

[19] See generally, Adcock and Mosley, *supra* note 15, at 123–27.

[20] See generally, John Bagnell Bury, *The Ancient Greek Historians* (1909); Charles Norris Cochrane, *Thucydides and the Science of History* (1929); A. W. Gomme, *The Greek Attitude to Poetry and History* (1954); J. E. Powell, *The History of Herodotus* (1939).

[21] See Alan Watson, *International Law in Archaic Rome: War and Religion* xii–xiii and n. 5 (1993).

[22] Wherever possible, all Latin and Greek sources are cited to the authoritative Loeb Classical Library Editions. I will also provide a pin-point page cite to the volume of the relevant work and also a standard indication of the passage from which the extract is drawn. I will follow the apparent convention of referring to the specific document or fragment by name, and then including the book number (in Roman numerics), followed by the section and line (or passage) numbers.

ancient Near Eastern history, is the most signal development of the new historiography on ancient statecraft.[23] And while this inscription evidence must also be used with care, in view of possible textual corruption or political bias of the authority erecting the inscription,[24] it serves as a ready way to confirm or deny the conclusions drawn from other sources.

Throughout most of this book, I try to let ancient writers and texts speak for themselves. Although Chapter 2 – which provides an abbreviated precis of ancient State relations – is deliberately devoid of ancient voices, Chapter 3 is structured around four textual fragments, which I use to explicate the nature of international obligation in ancient times. The remaining chapters, although heavily-laden with examples (and citations to yet more) of State practice in antiquity, also feature deep analysis of significant "canonical" texts – whether Homeric epics regarding envoys (in Chapter 4), the Egyptian–Hittite Treaty of 1280 BCE and the Punic–Macedonian Treaty of 215 BCE (in Chapter 5), or the Melian Dialogue (in Chapter 6). I do see these texts (whether literary or inscription material) as the primary sources of a law of nations in antiquity.

The nature of sources on ancient State relations thus represents the single most important conditioning factor for this study. One could, I suppose, despair of the poverty of the historical record, the unreliability of texts, and the uncertainty in any conclusions reached. My approach in this study is, instead, to embrace the doubt in this intellectual exercise and to proceed with well-accepted historiographic methods.

The modern critique of ancient international law

That leaves one very important point to be considered. That is the charge that ancient international law, like all ancient law, is primitive, and it is only in the recognition of its primeval character that serious scholarship can be undertaken in international legal history of this period. This notion, already mentioned in this Introduction,[25] not only demands that this study consider the sources, process, and doctrines of ancient international law, it also fundamentally challenges the idea that there even could have been a respect for a rule of law in international relations in ancient times.

The study of a law of nations in antiquity suffers, in essence, from a

---

[23] See Georges Ténékidès, Droit international et communautés fédérales dans la Grèce des cités, 90 RCADI 469, 478–85 (1956-II).
[24] See Adcock and Mosley, *supra* note 15, at 123.
[25] See *supra* note 10 and accompanying text.

double blight. First, there is the perception that *all* law in ancient times was primitive. Ancient law was formalistic,[26] dominated by fictions,[27] had a limited range of legal norms,[28] and was based solely on religious sanction.[29] In short, it lacked the essential characteristics of a modern, rational jurisprudence. Although this critique has been largely disproved by modern scholarship that has either emphasized new, empirical research,[30] or has adopted an anthropological attitude of moral relativism in legal relations,[31] it remains a potent school of thought. If all of this was not enough, there is the second, and as yet largely unquestioned, belief that international law, even today, is a primitive legal order.[32]

The confluence of these two intellectual forces has meant that the study of ancient international law has had, of late, few advocates. Those doing serious scholarship on ancient legal systems have evinced little interest in exploring such an abstract area as legal restraints on inter-State relations. The attitude of legal historians towards ancient international law has thus been one of indifference.

Alas, the same cannot be said of contemporary international law publicists writing on the subject of a law of nations in antiquity. Indeed, one can say that the opinion of a majority of modern international lawyers is that ancient States were incapable of observing a law governing their international relations. Consider the views of a few leading publicists. In Lassa Oppenheim's well-respected manual on international law, he noted that: "International law as a law between sovereign and equal states based on the common consent of those states is a product of modern Christian civilization, and may be said to be about four hundred years old."[33] Modern writers have insisted that ancient States did not possess a notion of sovereignty[34] and that there was no sense of universal community,[35]

---

[26] See 1 Sir Paul Vinogradoff, *Outlines of Historical Jurisprudence* 364 (1920).
[27] See Maine, *supra* note 10, at 25.   [28] See Hoebel, *supra* note 10, at 286–87.
[29] See *ibid.* at 258, 268–74.   [30] See, e.g., A. S. Diamond, *Primitive Law Past and Present* (1971).
[31] See Lyons, Ethical Relativism and the Problem of Incoherence, 86 *Ethics* 107, 109 (1975–76) ("[A]n act is right if, and only if, it accords with the norms of the group"). For elaborations of this in the context of international law, see Friedrich V. Kratochwil, *Rules, Norms and Decisions* 252–53 (1989); Fernando Tesón, *Humanitarian Intervention: An Inquiry into Law and Morality* 36 (1988).
[32] See Dinstein, *supra* note 10. See the sources cited at *supra* note 10.
[33] 1 Lassa Oppenheim, *International Law* 68 (Hersch Lauterpacht 7th ed. 1948).
[34] See, e.g., James Brierly, *The Basis of Obligation in International Law and other Papers* 20 (Hersch Lauterpacht and H. Waldock eds. 1958) (1977 reprint); C. Vergé, Introduction to G. F. de Martens, *Précis du droit des gens moderne* viii (Paris 1864).
[35] See, e.g., 1 James Kent, *Commentaries on American Law* 4 (5th American ed. 1844); 2 Laurent, *supra* note 11, at 190; 3 *ibid.* at 117; Malcolm Shaw, *International Law* 14 (2nd ed. 1986); Enrico Besta, Il Diritto Internazionale nel Mondo Antico, 2 *Comunicazione e studi dell' Istituto di Diritto Internazionale e Straniero dell' Università di Milano* 9, 10 (1946).

and without these two elements the idea of international law in antiquity was a nullity. Other writers have emphasized putative features of an ancient law of nations that one would instantly recognize as being somehow associated with any "primitive" legal system: the emphasis on religious (and not legal) sanctions,[36] the inability to develop consistent, customary rules of State conduct,[37] and the belief that there could never be a condition of peace between ancient States.[38]

This modern critique of the intellectual soundness of referring to a law of nations in antiquity has served many purposes. One, of course, is to provide an acceptable story for the emergence of international law, not only as a cluster of legal doctrines, but also as a learned study. The inability of some modern scholars to perceive an international law prior to its Grotian origins has been discussed elsewhere,[39] and need not be repeated here. There is also a reproach here, which I readily credit, that antiquarian pursuits in tracing international law doctrines to some origin shrouded in the mists of time, is a silly and (ultimately) distracting exercise. The strong reaction that contemporary publicists have held to the idea of international law in antiquity may, in part, be explained as a reaction to those earlier writers who "inordinately extoll[ed] antiquity to the disadvantage of the modern age."[40] Even worse, there were those who attempted to use ancient authorities in the pursuit of some instrumental historiography, particularly those who were advancing strong, Eurocentric characteristics for modern doctrines.[41]

In large part, this entire study is structured as a response to the detractors of an ancient law of nations. Starting with first principles, I examine in Chapter 2 the notion of sovereignty within ancient States and the existence of authentic systems of States in antiquity. Chapter 3, on the sources of obligation in ancient international law, answers those who argue that ancient international law was fatally infected by religion as the basis of sanction. When I examine (in Chapter 4) the ways in which diplomats were protected from interference, and foreigners screened from reprisals, one object is to see how ancient States were able to overcome ethnic and

[36] See A. W. Heffter, *Das Europäische Völkerrecht der Gegenwart* 12 (F. H. Geffcken ed. Berlin 1881); Vergé, *supra* note 34, at 60.
[37] See 3 A. Maury, *Histoire des religions de la Grèce antique* 401–02 (Paris 1859).
[38] See Francois Guizot, *L'église et la société chrétiennes en 1861*, at 101 (Paris 1861).
[39] See David W. Kennedy, Primitive Legal Scholarship, 27 *Harvard International Law Journal* 1 (1986); Preiser, *supra* note 2, at 127.
[40] 2 Phillipson, *supra* note 11, at 166. See also Leech, *supra* note 15, at 4.
[41] See Nawaz, *supra* note 3, at 173; Rostovtseff, *supra* note 11, at 32–33; Hans-Ulrich Scupin, History of the Law of Nations: Ancient Times to 1648, in 7 *Encyclopedia of Public International Law* 132, 132–33 (Rudolph Bernhardt ed. 1984).

cultural particularism and achieve conditions of peace. In making positive acts of faith (the subject of Chapter 5), were not ancient States also testing the strength of international legal obligation? And, finally, in examining the classical restraints on the initiation and conduct of hostilities in Chapter 6, I believe that we move closer to an appreciation of the ancient mind's understanding of humanity and universality in State relations.

For these reasons, it is with some reluctance I have titled this book as a treatment of *international law* in antiquity, and not of an ancient *law of nations*. As the reader may well be aware, "international law" is itself a relative neologism, an outgrowth of nineteenth-century legal positivism as applied to international relations.[42] It may not even be the preferred term-of-art today to describe international relations under a rule of law. But "international law" connotes a number of intertwined ideas: (1) a conceptual framework of States, State sovereignty, sovereign equality, and consent in an international legal order; (2) a recognition of the techniques of government, modes of statecraft, and the scale of interactions characteristic of the current international system; and (3) a sense that States are not the only actors (or subjects) of the international system, and that individuals, collectivities of States, and transnational businesses may also have international rights and duties. Because of these proper connotations, "international law" may not consistently convey the sense of international relations in antiquity.

Of course, I also understand that no measure of care in diction or terminology can inoculate me from the criticism that this project suffers from a false essentialism of equating modern (if not current) concepts to events transpiring two to three millennia ago. But I can see no alternative but to refer here to "States," "sovereignty," "treaties," "custom," and the like. But (as I have already indicated), I try also to let ancient people speak in their own voice, and to make sense of what the ancient mind conceived as its expression for these ideas.

Why bother, one may still wonder, with the idea of international law in antiquity? The exercise attempted in this study is more than what Professor Jan Verzijl caricatured as a fatal intellectual attraction:

And what legal historian would be able to escape the rare charm emanating from . . . the treasures in the Assyro-Babylonian hall of the British Museum where one

---

[42] See Jeremy Bentham, *An Introduction to the Principles of Morals and Legislation* 296 (Burns and Hart eds. 1970); Marc W. Janis, Jeremy Bentham and the Fashioning of "International Law," 78 AJIL 405 (1984).

can read, albeit only from the explanatory labels, of frontier treaties and arbitrations, ambassadors and territorial cessions from those long flown centuries? Or who would not smile at perusing the narratives of the . . . water-clock, occasionally closed by a thumb during the hearing of evidence, which was used in arbitral proceedings between the city states of ancient Hellas with the object of imposing silence on all too long-winded lawyers? . . . However, have not all those individual roads of the law of nations appeared to be blind alleys?[43]

This study perhaps is about traversing blind alleys and about opening some doors of historical and legal inquiry. But it is also about closing some avenues of discussion. In investigating our understanding of the origins of modern international law, I am compelled to accept the ancient law of nations on its own terms, knowing that "[t]he ancient world is distant in time and hence the analyst is not drawn into the emotion-laden game of cheering for the good guys and booing the villains."[44] This approach accords nicely with the supposed moral neutrality of international law. It also allows me to question how we now conceive of international law. That means examining the essential components of State systems and the sources, process, and doctrines for constructive interaction between sovereigns. Antiquity is a good place to begin such a study.

---

[43] 1 Jan H. W. Verzijl, *International Law in Historical Perspective* 403–04 (1968).
[44] Barry S. Strauss and Josiah Ober, *The Anatomy of Error: Ancient Military Disasters and Their Lessons for Modern Strategists* 8 (1990).

2   State relations in ancient civilizations

The primary assumption of this study is that there existed at certain times and places in antiquity authentic systems of States which were disposed, through their interactions, to conceive of rules of state behavior, norms that we might call today the law of nations or international law. This assumption has been debated quite extensively. Indeed, it goes to the heart of my thesis – that ancient peoples were able to envision exogenous limits on State conduct in international relations. This chapter provides a cursory, and by no means exhaustive, answer to the question whether State systems and international relations existed in the three times and places considered in this book: the ancient Near East (from 1400 to 1150 BCE and 966 to 700 BCE), the Greek city-States (from 500 to 338 BCE), and the wider Mediterranean during the period of Roman expansion (from 358 BCE to 168 BCE). My primary goal here is to trace the outlines of a defensible posture concerning the existence of authentic State systems in antiquity, while, at the same time, giving an overview of the historiographic literature on this subject. Although most of this material will be familiar to students and scholars of ancient and classical history, it is less familiar to international lawyers, and, anyway, it is necessary to cover this ground before any intelligble observations can be made regarding the nature of a law of nations in antiquity.

The concepts of State and State system and their relevance to antiquity

I take as my working definition of a State system Professor Hedley Bull's formulation in *The Anarchical Society*:

A society of states (or international society) exists when a group of states, conscious of certain common interests and common values, form a society in the sense that they conceive themselves to be bound by a common set of rules in their relations to one another, and share in the working of common institutions.[1]

Implicit in this definition is that political entities are organized and think of themselves as States, and that it is possible to discern "common interests and . . . values" in deciding whether those States deal with each other on a "conscious" basis. Both inquiries – the existence of States and the identification of conscious value systems – are essential in the context of antiquity.

   The prevailing trend in legal literature has been to dismiss sharply the existence of authentic State systems in ancient times.[2] One consistent point made by these writers is that ancient States lived in a perpetual condition of war and conflict, incapable of sharing any sense of international community. Michael Rostovtseff, considering the views of Mommsen,[3] made this observation:

The fundamental conceptions of international relations in the ancient and in the modern world are utterly different. The modern world considers the natural condition of life in our society to be the state of peace. War is nothing but a temporary suspending of this natural condition and is regarded as an abnormal state. Free intercourse between different nations is normal; restrictions and limitations of the rights of foreigners are abnormal and require serious reasons . . . But in the ancient world, generally, the natural attitude of one state towards another was that of potential and actual enmity.[4]

Although this view has been criticized as being ahistorical and unrealistic,[5] its persistence is notable,[6] particularly in the continuing debate about the nature of balance-of-power politics in the ancient world.[7] David Hume did acknowledge that this ordering principle of international relations could be dated to antiquity,[8] and Rostovtseff said as much when he

---

[1] Hedley Bull, *The Anarchical Society: A Study of Order in World Politics* 13 (1977). See also Martin Wight, *International Theory: The Three Traditions* (Gabriele Wight and Brian Porter ed. 1992).
[2] This point has typically been made as an adjunct to the wider proposition, considered above (see Chapter 1, above), that international law is the unique product of the modern, Enlightenment mind and could not have been present in antiquity.
[3] See, e.g., Theodor Mommsen, *Römische Geschichte* (W. P. Dickson transl. 1894).
[4] See Michael I. Rostovtseff, International Relations in the Ancient World, in *The History and Nature of International Relations* 35 (E. Walsh ed. 1922).
[5] See Emil Seckel, *Über Krieg und Recht in Rom* (1915).
[6] See Malcolm Shaw, *International Law* 14 (2nd ed. 1986) (contending that ancient societies had no conception of universal community, with its ideal of world order).
[7] For more on the notion of balance of power theory as a modern, Enlightenment construct, see Edward Vose Gulick, *Europe's Classical Balance of Power* 3–91 (1955); Martin Wight, *Power Politics* 168–85 (2nd ed. 1986).
[8] David Hume, On the Balance of Power, in 1 *Essays* 348 (T. H. Green and T. H. Grose eds. 1875).

noted that "periods of the balance of power [in antiquity] were great creative periods in all domains, including the domain of international relations and international law."[9]

The critique of the notion of State systems in antiquity has taken a different turn of late. Some legal writers, largely influenced by Maine's work on ancient law,[10] have looked closely at issues of ethnic, religious, and social particularism found in ancient States and wondered whether such openly atavistic polities could ever have achieved a level of cooperation with their diverse neighbors. Nawaz makes the point nicely when he wrote that "[ancient] societies lived in isolation from each other, separated by geographical factors and racial considerations. Besides, common international interests of the modern type did not exist in the past to unify them."[11]

These factors of cultural particularism, especially as they manifested themselves in cultural identities and religious differences, were quite important in conditioning the ancient State's response to the demands of international relations. The next chapter in this study will examine this point in reference to the supposed sources of a law of nations in antiquity. But it is important to note here that many scholars believe that ancient States were able to overcome this obstacle. The point that is most often made in the literature is that an ancient State, once it had "become aware of its own corporate existence, found itself by the necessities of international intercourse obliged to accord recognition to the same quality in other communities."[12] Most recently, Vilho Harle has powerfully argued that ancient States were sovereign and territorial, and they embraced community as the basis of a peaceful, international social order.[13]

The crucial element to the assumption of ancient State systems in antiquity is that there were polities that could justly be called States in ancient times. The sociological, anthropological, and historical literature on this

[9] Rostovtseff, *supra* note 4, at 38.
[10] See Sir Henry S. Maine, *Ancient Law* (1861) (1965 reprint). See also Lord Arundell of Wardour's work, *Tradition Principally with Reference to the Mythology of the Law of Nations* (1872), where he noted that "in ancient times the comity of nations was virtually restricted to groups of cities or nations of kindred descent, or which had become confederate by reason of contiguity." *Ibid.* at 379.
[11] Nawaz, The Law of Nations in Ancient India, 6 Indian YBIA 172, 173 (1957). To a similar effect is Enrico Besta, Il Diritto Internazionale nel Mondo Antico, in 2 *Comunicazione e studi dell' Istituto di Diritto Internazionale e Straniero dell' Università di Milano* 9, 10 (1946).
[12] Thomas A. Walker, *A History of the Law of Nations* 31 (1899). See also J. Galtung, Social Cosmology and the Concept of Peace, 18 *Journal of Peace Research* 183 (1981); H. B. Leech, *An Essay on Ancient International Law* 4 (1877).
[13] Vilho Harle, *Ideas of Social Order in the Ancient World* 91–94, 165–68, 171–74 (1998). But see N. D. Fusetl- Coulanges, *The Ancient City* (1955).

subject is broad and deep.[14] One strand of writings, extending back to the political theories of Machiavelli, Hobbes, Vico, Rousseau, and Locke,[15] had its full expression in the works of Friedrich Engels,[16] as glossed and interpreted by Karl Marx and his followers.[17] The thrust of this line of scholarship was to ascribe the early development of the State in antiquity to the need to protect private property ownership. Engels did acknowledge the importance also of applications of military force, and of war and conquest, to the process of State formation.[18] The primary application of Engels' and Marx's theories was, of course, in justification of a theory of societal evolution, but they are notable in expounding the hypothesis that early forms of State organization displayed certain universal features.[19] Whatever its political agenda, all of this scholarship was strongly evolutionist in tone and went largely out of favor later in the twentieth century.[20] The emerging study of sociology in the late nineteenth century produced a different line of scholarship on the question of the early State. Emile Durkheim's[21] notions of cohesion in primitive societies and Max Weber's[22] theories of legitimate authority combined to emphasize the network of allegiances and responsibilities that are the basis of any complex social organization. Other writers tended to emphasize certain motive factors in the development of ancient states. Franz Oppenheimer's "conquest" theory (*überlagerungstheorie*), first propounded in 1909,[23] conceived of the ancient State as an oppressive instrument designed to perpetuate hegemony by a dominant ethnic, cultural, or religious elite over a population.[24] Other, more

---

[14] For theoretic overviews of the literature, see Henri J. M. Claessen and Peter Skalník, The Early State: Theories and Hypothesis, in *The Early State* 3 (Henri J. M. Claessen and Peter Skalník eds. 1978); Lawrence Krader, *Formation of the State* (1968); Elman R. Service, *Origins of the State and Civilization: The Process of Cultural Evolution* 21–46 (1975).

[15] For a criticism of early Enlightenment theories of the State, see Claessen and Skalník, *supra* note 14, at 5–6; Service, *supra* note 14, at 21–31.

[16] See especially *Der Ursprung der Familie, des Privategentums und des Staats* (1884). See also Lewis H. Morgan, *Ancient Society* (1877).

[17] See Claessen and Skalník, *supra* note 14, at 8–9; Morton H. Fried, *The Evolution of Political Society* (1967); Krader, *supra* note 14; Service, *supra* note 14, at 31–36.

[18] See Maurice Godelier, Preface, in *Sur les sociétés précapitalistes* 100–02 (Maurice Godelier ed., 1970); Krader, *supra* note 14, at 150, 274–75.

[19] See Claessen and Skalník, *supra* note 14, at 9; Krader, *supra* note 14.

[20] But see Marvin Harris, *The Rise of Anthropological Theory* (1968).

[21] Emile Durkheim, *Division of Labor in Society* (1933).

[22] Max Weber, *The Theory of Social and Economic Organization* 310–406 (A. M. Henderson and Talcott Parsons transl. 2nd ed. 1947).

[23] Franz Oppenheimer, *Der Staat* (1909). See also the second edition of the book published in 1932.

[24] See Claessen and Skalník, *supra* note 14, at 9–11. But see the strong criticism of Oppenheimer by Robert H. Lowie, *The Origin of the State* (1927).

recent, writers suggest that the mere threat of war with an outside polity served as a catalyst for State-building.[25]

Emphasis on security and warfare as the motive forces for State creation in antiquity has been met by a new line of scholarship which has carefully examined other, internal drives. These have included the need for irrigation for agriculture, and control of water often has been concentrated in the hands of an elite class of people within a society.[26] A more neutral explanation would consider the natural tendency of human beings to congregate in larger and larger settlements. Urbanization[27] and population expansion,[28] with their attendant effects on an agricultural economy, may have the most potent explanation for the development of nation-States in antiquity. Finally, some writers have hinted that spiritual concerns, often manifested in burial rituals,[29] had an impact on State formation.

The entire debate about the origins of the early State has been conditioned by a single, socio-economic inquiry.[30] One group of scholars believes that the political institution of the State was conceived as a social contract among consenting adherents in order to address pressing internal or external needs or threats. Another school sees the ancient State as "organized for the regulation of social relations in a society that [was] divided into two emergent social classes, the rulers and the ruled."[31]

It is neither essential nor necessary for this study to take a position in this controversy. Nor is it necessary to hold that the ancient State was formed and conditioned by the needs of an international community. Ancient States in Mesopotamia, the Near East, and the Mediterranean

---

[25] See Ronald Cohen, The Evolution of Hierarchal Institutions: A Case Study from Biu, Nigeria, 3 *Savanna* 153, 173 (1974); David Webster, Warfare and the Evolution of the State: A Reconsideration, 40 *American Antiquity* 464, 467 (1975).

[26] See Julian H. Steward, *Theory of Cultural Change* (1955); Karl A. Wittfogel, *Oriental Despotism: A Comparative Study of Total Power* (1957). But see the vigorous critique of irrigation theory in Henri J. M. Claessen, Despotism and Irrigation, 129 *Bijdragen tot de Taal-, Land-, en Volkenkunde* 70 (1973).

[27] See *The City-State in Five Cultures* (Robert Griffeth and Carol G. Thomas eds. 1981); Robert McC. Adams, *The Evolution of Urban Society* (1966); Robert Redfield, *The Primitive World and its Transformations* (1968); 1 Ralph Turner, *The Great Cultural Traditions: The Ancient Cities* (1941); V. Gordon Childe, The Urban Revolution, 21 *Town Planning Review* 3 (1950).

[28] See Fried, *supra* note 17; Robert L. Carneiro, A Theory of the Origin of the State, 169 *Science* 733 (1970); M. J. Harner, Scarcity, the Factors of Production, and Social Evolution, in *Population, Ecology and Social Evolution* 123 (Steven Polgar ed. 1975).

[29] See Ian Morris, *Burial and Ancient Society: The Rise of the Greek City-State* (1987); 1(2) *Cambridge Ancient History* 103 (3rd ed 1971).

[30] See Claessen and Skalník, *supra* note 14, at 16; Service, *supra* note 14, at 36–102.

[31] Claessen and Skalník, *supra* note 14, at 21.

basin, were formed by a variety of conditions, not all of which were trace-able to the demands of political organization in the face of diplomatic or military menaces. The phenomenon of States may have preceded the crea-tion of an authentic *system* of States, the logical requisite for the idea of a law of nations at the heart of this study. But modern scholarship has accepted both the fact of the existence of the ancient State and the reality of international relations in antiquity.[32]

The following parts of this chapter will provide a brief historical over-view of the ancient States and State systems which form the subject of this study. The goal is to trace in barest outline an international history for the ancient Near East, the Greek city-States, and the period of Roman expan-sion. It helps to show that in each of the times and places considered in this study there existed States conscious of their own status and sove-reignty, actually conducting international relations along predictable pat-terns which emphasized the necessity of diplomatic relations, the sanctity of agreements, and controls on the initiation and conduct of war. While each of these is a subject of its own chapter, the broad patterns of State behavior in antiquity, as well as the nature and sources of international legal obligation, can be addressed here.

The ancient Near East: Mesopotamia, Syria, and Egypt

Many historians of the ancient Near East would consider the time period between the formation of the first Sumerian city-States or the Old Kingdom Nile cultures in Egypt (c. 2800 BCE)[33] as the beginning of their study and the conquests of Alexander the Great (323 BCE) to be the end. The geographic scope of their inquiry would stretch from the Libyan desert and the farthest reaches of Egyptian power in North Africa, up to the Hellespont and Anatolia and the Caucasus, and in the East all the way into what we would call Central Asia and the farthest expansion of Persian power. Twenty-five hundred years of human history and a region encom-passing the entirety of western Asia and northeast Africa is formidable, and this study makes no attempt to recount the international history of this time and space.

---

[32] See Roberto Ago, The First International Communities in the Mediterranean World, 53 BYIL 213, 214 (1982); and Bruno Paradisi, L'amitié internationale: les phases critiques de son ancienne histoire, 78 RCADI 325, 355–56 (1951–I).

[33] Throughout this book, references to the period Before the Common Era will be indicated simply as "BCE."

Sumer and Mesopotamia

Rather, this study examines three specific time periods and regions where there existed authentic States and State systems. The first of these is a period of a few hundred years where there was a small network of Sumerian city-States in Mesopotamia, until their conquest by the Akkadian empire. These cities, including Adab, Eridu, Kish, Larsa, Lagash, Nippur, Shuruppak, Umma, Ur, and Uruk, flourished in the period 2600–2350 BCE, the transition between what Sumeriologists have called the Dynastic and Imperial periods.[34] This time of inter-city relations between Sumer polities was ended with the complete conquest of the region by Sargon the Great, the leader of northern, Semitic peoples, and the creation of the Akkadian Empire.

The city-States of Sumer have been called theocratic polities and this fact largely conditioned their internal political structure,[35] and their relations with one another. "Unified by language and culture," one scholar has written of the Sumerian cities, "they were destined for incessant rivalry and warfare."[36] The city of Kish, under the kingships of Etana and Mesilim, was the first to gain supremacy over its neighbors (c. 2800–2700 BCE). Kish was then challenged by Uruk, which reached its zenith under the rule of Gilgamesh (c. 2700–2600 BCE). Then followed a period of outside rule under the Elamites, who, in turn, were ousted by Lugalannemendu, ruler of Adab, who succeeded again in unifying Sumer for nearly 200 years (c. 2500 BCE). What followed was a long civil war in which Lagash finally triumphed under the kingship of Lugalzaggesi (c. 2450–2360 BCE). Lagash's hegemony ended with the Akkadian conquest in about the year 2350 BCE.

Leonard Woolley, the great political historian of Sumer, has considered the contradictory forces of city-State relations in ancient Mesopotamia.[37] The first desire was for centralization, natural for any region which shared a common language and ethnic identity, as well as a regional loyalty to strengthen a single economy, a common resource (in the form of water husbanded by irrigation works), and a common security against outside

---

[34] See Samuel Noah Kramer, *The Sumerians* (1963); William H. MacNeill, *The Rise of the West* 41–43 (1963); Service, *supra* note 14, at 209–22; Turner, *supra* note 27, at 133–38; Robert McC. Adams, Developmental Stages in Ancient Mesopotamia, in *Irrigation Civilizations: A Comparative Study* (1955).

[35] See Kramer, *supra* note 34, at 308–20; Geoffrey Evans, Ancient Mesopotamian Assemblies, 78 JAOS 1 (1958); Thorkild Jacobsen, Primitive Democracy in Ancient Mesopotamia, 2 JNES 159 (No 3) (1943). See also 1(2) *Cambridge Ancient History* 103–05 (3rd ed. 1971).

[36] Song Nai Rhee, Sumerian City-States, in Griffeth and Thomas, *supra* note 27, at 23.

[37] See C. Leonard Woolley, *The Sumerians* (1965).

threats.[38] "In a region where all spoke the same language, observed the same laws and customs, and worshipped the same pantheon of deities, it was tempting for an ambitious ruler to bring about political unification and centralization."[39] On the other hand, there was also a strong tendency towards fragmentation and disruption, in which localized interests, expressed in devotion to city deities,[40] produced centrifugal effects among the Sumerian city-States.

During periods of dynamic State relations, the Sumer cities participated in patterns of diplomacy that we would probably consider today as balance-of-power politics. Wolfgang Preiser[41] and Jacques Pirenne[42] have examined these relations and concluded that the city-States of Mesopotamia "were certainly sovereign structures" within the modern understanding of State organization.[43] Lagash, Umma, Kish, and their neighbors concluded treaties, had rules concerning diplomatic immunities, and maybe also norms on the conduct of war.[44]

It seems, moreover, that these patterns of behavior were not substantially disrupted during periods when one city and its ruler was overlord (*lugal*) in the Sumer world. The *lugal* enforced political unity among other cities by imposing substantial tribute payments, although strictly local affairs were left to the discretion of city rulers (*ensi*).[45] Strong feudatory relationships between lord and underling were not, apparently, a characteristic feature of Sumerian international relations in the period prior to the Akkadian absorption. Thereafter, however, the city ceased to be the applicable unit and organizing principle of State relations in Mesopotamia. Akkadian rule began this process, which transformed relations from co-equal city-States into more feudal patterns between overlord and territorial governor.[46]

---

[38] See *ibid.* at 323–24.   [39] Rhee, in Griffeth and Thomas, *supra* note 27, at 25.

[40] See generally Adam Falkenstein, *The Sumerian Temple City* (Maria deJ. Ellis transl. 1974). See also 1(2) *Cambridge Ancient History* 103 (3rd ed. 1971).

[41] Wolfgang Preiser, Zum Völkerrecht der vorklassischen Antike, 4 *Archiv des Völkerrecht* 257 (1954).

[42] Jacques Pirenne, L'Organisation de la paix dans le Proche-Orient aux 3ᵉ et 2ᵉ millénaires, 14 *Recueil de la Société Jean Bodin* 200 (1962).

[43] See Preiser, *supra* note 41, at 269. But see Hans-Ulrich Scupin, History of the Law of Nations: Ancient Times to 1648, in 7 *Encyclopedia of Public International Law* 132, 133 (Rudolph Bernhardt ed. 1984) ("The lively mutual dealings between the Sumerian City-States in Mesopotamia did indeed provide the external conditions for an international legal order to come into existence: however, the instability of these relations and above all the lack of a developed sense of legal rights and obligations meant that . . . the evolution of an international legal order did not progress beyond an early stage").

[44] See Ago, *supra* note 32, at 215.

[45] See Kramer, *supra* note 34, at 60; Woolley, *supra* note 37, at 72–73; 1(2) *Cambridge Ancient History* 104 (3rd ed. 1971).   [46] See Rhee, in Griffeth and Thomas, *supra* note 27, at 26.

This phenomenon continued even with the restoration of Sumerian power in the Third Dynasty of Ur, begun in 2050 BCE and lasting until 1950 BCE. Sumer was unified in this period and conducted relations with the Elamites and the king of Mari. Wars with the Elamites finally overwhelmed this recrudescence of Sumerian civilization, and even though there were brief moments of political and cultural renewal under the reigns of Gudea of Lagash (c. 2000 BCE) and Rim-Sin of Larsa (1758–1698 BCE),[47] the focus of power in the entire region between the Euphrates and Tigris shifted north and west into upper Iraq and Syria.

The great Near Eastern empires, 1400–1150 BCE

The most dynamic period of State relations in the ancient Near East, and the one that has produced the bulk of literary and inscription evidence surveyed in this book,[48] was the time of the ascendancy of five great empires: Egypt, Babylon, the Hittites, the Mitanni, and the Assyrians. Hans-Ulrich Scupin has briefly recounted the international history of this period:

These two and a half centuries were by no means free from military conflicts, but the predominant impression is one of a varied international life, ranging from extensive trade and cultural contacts to frequent close links between the rulers and families and to many legal ties. A close network of international relations came into existence, supported by a uniform international language, Akkadian, and included a number of States of lesser importance in addition to the principal powers.[49]

It is worth sketching the history of the empires which flourished in the Near East from the fifteenth to twelfth centuries BCE. Although this is not the place to trace the early history of the Egyptian State which grew up on the banks of the Nile in northeastern Africa,[50] it is worth noting that the Egyptians were largely isolated from foreign influences in the Old and Middle Kingdoms (c. 2850–1650 BCE).[51] This changed with the invasion of

[47] See 1(2) *Cambridge Ancient History* 446–63, 635–43 (3rd ed. 1971).
[48] Archeologists have discovered caches of diplomatic documents and archives attributed to the Egyptian dynasties at Al-'Amarna, for the Amorite kings at Mari, and for the Hittite Kingdom at Bogazköy. See Lorton, *supra* note 52, at 177; Ago, *supra* note 32, at 216; J. M. Munn-Rankin, Diplomacy in Western Asia in the Early Second Millennium BC, 18 *Iraq* 68, 109–10 (1956).   [49] Scupin, *supra* note 43, at 133.
[50] For more on this, see Service, *supra* note 14, at 225–37; Turner, *supra* note 27, at 174–214; Jac J. Janssen, The Early State in Ancient Egypt, in Claessen and Skalník, *supra* note 14, at 213–34. See also 1(2) *Cambridge Ancient History* 145–206, 230–33, 464–530 (3rd ed. 1971).
[51] See Service, *supra* note 14, at 235; Ago, *supra* note 32, at 216 n. 6; Scupin, *supra* note 43, at 133.

Egypt by the Hyksos, a group of Semitic peoples who, through significant military technology (including the use of cavalry and chariots), were able to conquer Egypt although they also quickly conformed their ways to Egyptian culture.[52]

When the Hyksos were finally driven out of Egypt in 1570 BCE, and the New Kingdom was inaugurated, the Egyptian State began to expand into the upper reaches of the Nile and into Libya. Most important of all to Egypt's perceived national security, was control of Palestine and Syria, which was the strategic quarter from which any other power could threaten Egypt. Pharaoh Thutmosis III (1480–1448 BCE) extended Egyptian power as far as the Euphrates in pursuit of these geopolitical objectives, winning also the Battle of Megiddo against a Syrian–Palestinian coalition.

The Egyptian occupation of Syria placed it in inevitable diplomatic and military competition with the other great powers in the region. Syria and Palestine were the great geopolitical prizes of international relations in this period.[53] The Assyrians, under their Middle Empire (1375–1047 BCE), also vied for this region. The Assyrians were the logical successors to Hammurabi's Babylon state, which had reached its zenith in 1728–1686 BCE by forming a strong coalition with the smaller powers of Mari and Larsa.[54] Babylonian hegemony had been ended by the Hittites, when their ruler, Mursili I, sacked Babylon in 1531 BCE. Babylon, as well as Egypt, had formed a strong centralized State system, largely in response to outside pressures. Until Egypt's penetration into Syria, no Great Power (Egypt, Babylon, Mitanni, or Assyria) was able to gain dominance over the other.[55] Some writers have suggested, though, that Babylonian influences over the conduct of international relations persisted even beyond the time that its territory was absorbed successively by the Assyrians and Hittites. Munn-Rankin has written that Akkadian (the Babylonian official language) and its legal terminology used in State relations was widely adopted,[56] maybe even by the rival Egyptians.[57] Coalitions in the period of Babylonian dominance and rivalry with Egypt were unstable, "owing to a lack of sustained common purpose among their members."[58]

---

[52] See David Lorton, *The Juridical Terminology of International Relations in Egyptian Texts through Dyn XVIII*, at 177 (1974). See also 1(2) *Cambridge Ancient History* 824–75 (3rd ed. 1971); 2(1) *Cambridge Ancient History* 354–64, 289–310 (3rd ed. 1973).

[53] See 2(1) *Cambridge Ancient History* 417–555 (3rd ed. 1973); 2(2) *Cambridge Ancient History* 1–20, 98–107, 217–73 (3rd ed. 1975).

[54] See Rostovtseff, *supra* note 4, at 40–41; 2(1) *Cambridge Ancient History* 1–41, 176–226 (3rd ed. 1973).

[55] See *ibid.* at 41; Lorton, *supra* note 52, at 177; Ago, *supra* note 32, at 216 n. 6.

[56] See Munn-Rankin, *supra* note 48, at 109–10.   [57] See Lorton, *supra* note 52, at 177.

[58] Munn-Rankin, *supra* note 48, at 110.

The Assyrians, an atavistic power during its Middle Empire, were not known for intensive diplomatic activity. Despite being neighbors to Egyptian and Hittite domains, with only the small Mitanni kingdom as a buffer, there is very little evidence of Assyria engaging in "Great Power" diplomacy during the period 1400–1150 BCE. Dennis McCarthy has suggested a simple explanation for this: "Assyria did not treat, it conquered."[59] More recent archeological evidence indicates that the Assyrians did, in fact, have a system of tributary treaties with their colonies and dependent powers.[60] It does not appear that this system of international agreements, even if it was feudal in character, was the product only of times that Assyrian central power was weak.[61] Assyrian tributaries had, it seems, a legal status and character separate from the central Empire.[62]

The last remaining party in the State system that existed in the Near East of the thirteenth and twelfth centuries BCE was the Hatti kingdom concentrated in Anatolia and Upper Syria. Hittite diplomatic activities of this period are well documented; information about them rivals the Egyptian New Empire, and far outstrips our knowledge of the bellicose Assyrians and mysterious Mitanni. Most scholars agree that the Hittites conceived of relations with other political entities as being definitively ordered.

The Hatti State was structured as a confederacy, with a complex and quite successful network of feudatory allegiances leading from local leaders to regional governors to the institution of the Great King.[63] The Hatti recognized a political status of an alliance among States of equal power; they also understood the status of a country in a state of war with their own. The primary innovation of Hittite practice was, however, in the development of a definitive legal treatment for dependent political

---

[59] Dennis J. McCarthy, *Treaty and Covenant* 68 (1963). Professor McCarthy did not, however, consider a later treaty between Assyria and the new Babylonian Empire in 823 BCE. See *ibid.* at 68 n. 3. Babylon was the dominant power in the agreement. *Ibid.* See also Georges Contenau, *La Civilisation d'Assur et de Babylon* (1937); Bruno Meissner, *Babylonien und Assyrien* (1920–25); A. T. Olmstead, *History of Assyria* (1923).

[60] See Mogens Trolle Larsen, *The Old Assyrian City-State and its Colonies* (1976); Louis Lawrence Orlin, *Assyrian Colonies in Cappadocia* (1970).   [61] See McCarthy, *supra* note 59, at 68.

[62] See Larsen, *supra* note 60, at 333–53; Orlin, *supra* note 60, at 114–38. See also 2(2) *Cambridge Ancient History* 21–44, 274–98, 443–77 (3rd ed. 1975).

[63] See Georges Contenau, *La Civilisation des Hittites et des Mitanniens* (1934); A. E. Cowley, *The Hittites* 10–14 (1926); Louis Dellaporte, *Les Hittites* (1936); McCarthy, *supra* note 59, at 84; Scupin, *supra* note 43, at 134. The debate about whether the Hittite State marked a definitive break from previous patterns of divinely mandated kingship rule is beyond the scope of my study. For some sources, see Henri Frankfort, *Kingship and the Gods* (1948); McCarthy, *supra* note 59, at 84 n. 14. See also 2(1) *Cambridge Ancient History* 235–55 (3rd ed. 1973) (on the Old Hittite Kingdom).

units.[64] With the modern literature begun in Dennis McCarthy's path-breaking book, *Treaty and Covenant*,[65] the typical characterization of this type of relationship has been vassalage.[66] The Hatti used vassalage agreements not only as a recognition of military conquest but also – and this was hitherto unknown in the ancient Near East[67] – as an arm of peaceful diplomacy. The Hittites developed a category of *kuirwana*, ranking between a co-equal ally and a vassal, a sort of privileged protectorate.[68]

The Hittite construct of international relations and diplomacy largely conditioned the State system of the time.[69] The reason was that the Hittites controlled the balance of power in the region. Under the New Kingdom, established under Shuppiluliuma (1380–1346 BCE), Hittite power increased. The first victim was Mitanni independence, destroyed by a combined Assyrian and Hittite assault in the years 1360–1350 BCE. The next target was northern Syria, then in Egypt's sphere of influence, as had been recognized in treaties between Egypt and the Hittites in 1354 and 1312 BCE.[70] Under two dynamic kings, Mursilis II (fl. 1300–1287 BCE) and Hattusili (fl. 1285–1270 BCE), the Hittites were set on a collision course with Egypt.[71]

This conflict culminated in the Battle of Kadesh on the Orontes River in Syria in the year 1288 BCE. An Egyptian expedition into northern Syria was met by a huge coalition under the Hatti Confederacy, led by the Great King Muwatalli.[72] The results were bloodily inconclusive.[73] While the Egyptian host defeated the Hittite army in the field, it had suffered such losses that it was unable to proceed to oust the Hittites from their control of the city

---

[64] It is important to note that forms of dependent relations – as expressed in international agreements – were in use among the ancient Egyptians. See Lorton, *supra* note 52, at 177; McCarthy, *supra* note 59, at 83.   [65] See McCarthy, *supra* note 59.

[66] See *ibid.* at 83–84; Scupin, *supra* note 43, at 134. See also 2(2) *Cambridge Ancient History* 117–30, 268 (3rd ed. 1975).   [67] See McCarthy, *supra* note 59, at 83–84.

[68] See Pirenne, *supra* note 42; Scupin, *supra* note 43, at 134.

[69] The impact of Hittite treaty forms on neighboring states was notable, and constitutes a central issue in formulating a common law of nations tradition transmitted from the ancient Near East to the Mediterranean polities of Greece and Rome. See Lorton, *supra* note 52, at 177 (for Hatti influence on Egypt); McCarthy, *supra* note 59, at 92 (for impact on New Assyrian Empire); Preiser, *supra* note 41, at 272–80. See also *supra* note 64 and accompanying text.

[70] See Cowley, *supra* note 63, at 12; John Garstang, *The Land of the Hittites* 324–40 (1910).

[71] See Cowley, *supra* note 63, at 12–14; Garstang, *supra* note 70, at 341–51.

[72] See Gaston Maspero, *The Struggle of Nations, Egypt, Syria and Assyria* 390–400 (1897); A. H. Sayce, *The Hittites* 26 (3rd ed. 1903). See also 2(2) *Cambridge Ancient History* 252–73 (3rd ed. 1975).

[73] See James Henry Breasted, *The Battle of Kadesh* (1903); Maspero, *supra* note 72, at 392–400; W. Max Müller, *Asien und Europa* 216 (1893).

of Kadesh and surrounding areas in northern Syria. Both sides sued for peace and secured a truce, one which resulted in a *de facto* splitting of Syria and Palestine into two zones of influence, the north dominated by the Hatti, the south controlled by Egypt. It was this state of affairs that was recognized in the famous treaty of 1280 BCE,[74] between Rameses II of Egypt and Hattusili of the Hittites, an agreement which is analyzed in this study as being emblematic of treaties between equals in the ancient Near East.[75]

This period of dynamic State relations, which flourished in the thirteenth and twelfth centuries BCE, was characterized by two features. The first was a definitive system of Great Power relations, largely played out by the Egyptians, Hittites, and Assyrians. This has been called by recent scholars "a balance and genuine concert of the principal Powers."[76] Superimposed on this network of parity treaties was a vast system of feudal and tributary arrangements, largely expressed through vassal agreements. Most of the documentary evidence of international relations of this period is of these vassalage treaties (whether concluded by Egypt, the Hatti, or the Assyrians),[77] and not of parity agreements.

Syria and Palestine, 966–700 BCE

The third authentic State system in the ancient Near East subsisted only in a narrow geographical range – the strategic zone of Syria and Palestine – and over a fairly short time period of two centuries. The earlier State system dominated by the Egyptians, Hittites, and Assyrians was utterly destroyed by the incursions of the Sea Peoples, Indo-European tribes that penetrated all of western Asia and most of Europe, as well. By 1200 BCE they had devastated the Hatti Confederation and the early proto-States of Achaean Greece.[78] Likewise, the Sea Peoples attacked Egyptian diplomatic and economic dominance in the eastern Mediterranean, and collapsed the large centers of power that had been acquired by the cyclical dynasties of the Middle Assyrian Empire and Kassite-dominated Babylon. As one writer has noted, this period saw

---

[74] This treaty has been variously dated to 1278 BCE (Ago, *supra* note 32, at 216 n. 8), 1271 BCE (Garstang, *supra* note 70, at 391) and to 1270 BCE (Scupin, *supra* note 43, at 134).

[75] See Chapter 5, pp. 146–50 below. See also Gunther Roeder, *Ägypter und Hethiter* (1919); Preiser, *supra* note 41, at 282–83.

[76] Ago, *supra* note 32, at 216 (citing Preiser, *supra* note 41, at 272; Rey, Relations internationales de l'Egypte ancienne du XVe au XIIIe siècle avant Jésus-Christ, 48 RGDIP 35 (1941–45)).   [77] See Scupin, *supra* note 43, at 134.

[78] See Ago, *supra* note 32, at 217 n. 11.

[t]he central power [of the State] weakened; large areas escaped its control and split up again into a plethora of virtually independent cities or principalities. In the general decline of civilization the major monarchies ceased to keep up diplomatic relations or, more generally speaking, to have any stable legal ties.[79]

When a stable system of State relations was restored it was, as just noted, narrowly localized in the area of Syria and Palestine. Instead of following earlier geopolitical patterns in which this strategic area was exclusively competed for, and dominated by, great outside Powers, the period beginning with the ninth century BCE saw the emergence of two indigenous State cultures: Israel and Phoenicia.[80] The Israelite state was unified from a collection of tribal entities under Saul (in c. 1010 BCE), governed by kings David and Solomon (1006–926 BCE), and then split into two parts, Israel in the north and Judah in the south, in about the year 926 BCE.[81] The Phoenicians, a very loose grouping of autonomous city-States on the Syrian coast (including Aradus, Byblos, Beirut, Sidon, and the dominant city, Tyre), established themselves about the year 1000 BCE. After the Sea Peoples receded, the Phoenicians filled the economic vacuum left by the destruction of Egyptian trading interests and the death of the Minoan civilization on Crete and the decline of Mycenaean culture on the Greek mainland.[82]

Records are extant of State relations between the Jewish states and the Phoenician cities, as well as with outside powers (most notably the Egyptians and the New Assyrian Empire). King David imposed vassal treaties on the nations around Syria, while Solomon entered into a parity treaty with Tyre.[83] The hill tribes in Syria were also known to carry on

---

[79] *Ibid.* at 217.
[80] See *The Haverford Symposium on Archaeology and the Bible* 2 (Elihu Grant ed. 1938); McCarthy, *supra* note 59, at 51; A. T. Olmstead, *A History of Palestine and Syria to the Macedonian Conquest* (1931); Turner, *supra* note 27, at 247.
[81] See Prosper Weil, Le Judaïsme et le Développement du Droit Internationale, 151 RCADI 253, 264–66 (1976–III). See also 2(2) *Cambridge Ancient History* 562, 573, 583–84 (3rd ed. 1975); 3(2) *Cambridge Ancient History* 322–409 (2nd ed. 1991). For comprehensive histories of the formation of Israel as an ancient State, see Gösta W. Ahlström, *The History of Ancient Palestine* (1993); Robert B. Coote and Keith W. Whitelam, *The Emergence of Early Israel in Historical Perspective* (1987); Frank S. Frick, *The Formation of the State in Ancient Israel* (1985); J. Maxwell Miller and John H. Hayes, *A History of Ancient Israel and Judah* (1986).
[82] See N. G. L. Hammond, *A History of Greece to 322 BC*, at 24–71 (2nd ed. 1967); Turner, *supra* note 27, at 214, 233–34, 247–48.
[83] See J. A. Thompson, *The Ancient Near Eastern Treaties and the Old Testament* 11–12 (1964) (citing 2 Samuel 8:6, 14 and 10:10, as well as 1 Kings 4:21 and 5:12). See also Walker, *supra* note 12, at 34. See also Judges 11:12–28 (dispute between Jephthah and King of Ammon).

diplomacy and make treaties in this period,[84] as were individual Phoenician towns.[85]

Most academic attention has been focused on the State relations of the Jewish polities in Palestine during this period. Arising from older currents of Bible scholarship, this area of study was galvanized by George Mendenhall's 1955 book, *Law and Covenant in Israel and the Ancient Near East*,[86] which advanced the thesis that the scriptural construct of the covenant between Yahweh and his chosen people of Israel was largely modeled on the patterns, forms, and even the syntax of Hittite and Assyrian vassal treaties. This theory has spawned an enormous literature[87] that, at least until recently, has commanded the discourse on ancient State relations. If Mendenhall's covenant thesis is true, it would mean that Jewish State relations may have been rather less particularistic than had previously been conjectured.[88] Yet, even after the division of Israel into two kingdoms, there appeared to be a sharp division between intra-Jewish relations and arrangements made with outside powers.[89]

In any event, this brief period of a regional State system in the ancient Near East, localized with few State actors, could not have persisted. Egypt and the New Assyrian Empire grew more powerful and more menacing towards the independent states of Syria and Palestine. Following a time in the seventh century BCE when Palestine was under Assyrian domination, Sargon II of Assyria laid siege and sacked Samaria in 722 BCE; all of Phoenicia (except for Tyre) was conquered by the Assyrian King Sargon III by the year 701 BCE.[90] Later rulers, Sennacherib and Esarhaddon, expanded Assyrian rule.[91] After an ill-fated alliance with Egypt, Judah under Hezekiah submitted to Assyrian rule in 700 BCE. Henceforth, no autonomous State system subsisted in the region. Nor did a great transnational

---

[84] See Thompson, *supra* note 83, at 12.

[85] See Aristide Théodoridès, Les relations de l'Egypte pharaonique avec ses voisins, 23 RIDA 87, 103 (1975). See also 3(2) *Cambridge Ancient History* 461–72 (2nd ed. 1991).

[86] George Mendenhall, *Law and Covenant in Israel and the Ancient Near East* (1955).

[87] See, eg., F. Charles Fensham, Common Trends in Curses of the Near Eastern Treaties and *Kudurru*-Inscriptions Compared with Maledictions of Amos and Isaiah, 75 *Zeitschrift für die Alttestamentliche Wissenschaft* 155 (1963); Delbert R. Hillers, *Treaty Curses and the Old Testament Prophets* (Rome 1964); Dennis J. McCarthy, *Treaty and Covenant* (1963). See also 2(2) *Cambridge Ancient History* 563–64 (3rd ed. 1975). A thorough review of this theory is made in Chapter 5.

[88] See Walker, *supra* note 12, at 31–32 ("The Israelites are, in the view of their historians and teachers, a Chosen Race of brother tribes clearly marked off from the surrounding Heathen. This fact colours all of their international dealings."); Weil, *supra* note 81, at 273–76.

[89] See Mendenhall, *supra* note 86, at 38; Walker, *supra* note 12, at 31–32.

[90] See 3(2) *Cambridge Ancient History* 86–102 (2nd ed. 1991).   [91] *Ibid.* at 103–41.

State system, such as the one that had existed some centuries before, replace it. This was the period of great, successive empires. Assyrian dominance yielded to a new Babylonian regime, which in turn submitted to Medean and Persian dominance, which was only finally vanquished by the conquests of Alexander the Great.

It would be a grave mistake to suppose that the tradition of State relations in the ancient Near East was utterly extinguished by these events. Patterns of State relations, reflected in diplomatic, treaty, and warmaking practices, continued to be transmitted and remembered, to be resuscitated whenever new, authentic State systems arose. One line of transmission was into the western Mediterranean with the founding of the Phoenician colony at Carthage.[92] The other was through contacts with the emerging Greek culture,[93] and it is to the State system of the Greek city-States that I will now turn.

The Greek city-States, 500–338 BCE

Greek civilization traced its roots back to the Cretan and Mycenaean Bronze-age cultures centered on the islands of the Aegean and surrounding land areas.[94] The political organization of the Mycenaean state was premised on kingship and domination over subject populations. Political authority was projected from fortified settlements, called *poleis*.[95] Compared with the structure of the Greek city-States of the later, Classical period, Mycenaean models were unitary and remarkably extensive.

The strong, centralized states of the Mycenaean period came to an end around the year 1200 BCE. The wave of migrations which figured so prominently in the fundamental transformation of the ancient Near East in the twelfth century BCE also had its impacts on the Greek periphery. The Ionian and Dorian invasions of that century swept away the last vestiges of power of the Mycenaean kings. This began a very unsettled period, called by some scholars the Dark Age of Greek history.[96] Populations declined dramatically, and many settlements became isolated from one another.

---

[92] See Ago, *supra* note 32, at 218–19.
[93] See *ibid.* at 219–20; Rostovtseff, *supra* note 4, at 60.
[94] See J. Chadwick, *The Mycenaean World* (1976); J. T. Hooker, *Mycenaean Greece* (1976); 2(1) *Cambridge Ancient History* 627–57 (3rd ed. 1973).
[95] See Morris, *supra* note 29, at 171–200; Carol G. Thomas, The Greek Polis, in Griffeth and Thomas, *supra* note 27, at 32–34.
[96] See V. R. d'A. Desborough, *The Greek Dark Ages* (1972); A. M. Snodgrass, *The Dark Age of Greece* (1971); 2(2) *Cambridge Ancient History* 658–710 (3rd ed. 1975).

This trend was reversed in the eighth and ninth centuries BCE which saw explosive Greek colonization into all parts of the Mediterranean littoral. Ionian colonies were established in the Black Sea, the shore of Asia Minor, and along the Italian and Sicilian coasts in the central Mediterranean. Dorian colonies, with Corinth, Thera, and Megara as their founders, were established on the Epiran coast, in North Africa, in southern Italy, and in Byzantium. By the end of the sixth century BCE, at the conclusion of the archaic period, Greek colonial expansion was complete.[97] In the year 500 BCE, the heart of the Mediterranean was within the Greek culture area, challenged only by Carthage in the western Mediterranean, by Etruria (and later Rome) in Italy, and most ominously by the immense, unitary and powerful Persian empire in the east.

The year 500 BCE also marks the beginning of most studies of Greek diplomacy and international relations. As Mosley has explained:

little documentary or detailed literary evidence survives from [the archaic] periods. The details of diplomatic practices emerge for the first time . . . from the history of Classical Greece at the time the city-state was at its zenith . . . [A]s far as Ancient Greece is concerned, the historian of diplomacy cannot derive much from the period before the Persian Wars of the fifth century.[98]

Greek civilization was not, of course, politically unified. The basic unit of social organization was the city-State or *polis*, the same name given to the Mycenaean castles which had dominated Greek political life nearly eight centuries before.

The simplest description of a *polis* would be a city State, developed from urban settlements and their communal lands. The *polis* was characterized by internal and external independence and economic self-sufficiency.[99] The form of government of a *polis* could be a monarchy, aristocracy, or democracy. The nature of government did not, in fact, define the *polis*. Rather, it was the character of a "community of people and of place."[100] It is important to remember that the *polis* was also a religious entity and

[97] See L. Jeffrey, *Archaic Greece: The City-States c. 700–500 BC* (1976); Raphael Sealey, *A History of the Greek City-States. ca. 700 – 338 B.C.*, at 10–33 (1976); 2(2) *Cambridge Ancient History* 773–803 (3rd ed. 1975).
[98] D. J. Mosley, *Envoys and Diplomacy in Ancient Greece* 1 (1973). But see Eugène Audinet, Les traces du droit international dans l'Iliade dans l'Odyssée, 21 RGDIP 29 (1914), and T. Sorgen-Grey, *De vestigiis iuris gentium homerici* (1871) who examine the attributes of international law in epic Greece.
[99] See M. I. Finley, *Economy and Society in Ancient Greece* (1981); M. I. Finley, *The Ancient Economy* (1973).   [100] Thomas, *supra* note 95, at 43.

institution, for as Victor Ehrenberg has noted, "There was no real community among the Greeks that was not also a religious community."[101] The identification of gods and *polis* occurred by the city's fostering of specific cults and by vesting religious responsibilities in officials of the State. By the same token, the *polis* was also a military complex. The Greek city-State was dependent for its defense on well-tended fortifications and on a citizen army largely comprised of *hoplites*, armored soldiers who campaigned and battled together as a single, cohesive unit.[102]

Greek *poleis,* even in their later forms of more extensive city-States, still tended to be territorially small and compact. Corinth, one of the most important States during the entire period under review in this study, occupied only 340 square miles. Perhaps only a dozen Greek city-States had over 10,000 citizens or in excess of 50,000 residents all told.[103] Only Athens and Sparta reached populations of more than a quarter of a million souls in the fifth century.[104] Social stratification was deep. A tiny class of citizens dominated the political, economic, and social life of Greek cities and held many rights and privileges denied to residents and, of course, to slaves.[105]

The relatively small size of Greek city-States led invariably to a singular paradox of Greek relations. Intensely strong feelings of loyalty towards one's *polis* conflicted with an identification towards the superiority of Greek culture and the inferiority of other peoples. Coleman Phillipson, writing in 1911, commented that "Patriotism and keen jealousy of interference [by other cities] occasioned mutual distrust and an unbending spirit of opposition, which frequently led to keen strife and obstinate wars . . . The Greeks as Greeks cherished aspirations for unity, but as citizens their constant aim was decentralization."[106] Later sociologists have referred to the same phenomenon, but with a different argot, speaking of the Greek *polis'* "overwhelming sense of attachment to [its] territory,"[107] manifested both in mythological reverence to local landmarks[108] and

---

[101] Victor Ehrenberg, *The Greek State* 16 (1960). See also 1 James Brown Scott, *Law, the State and the International Community* 43–60 (1939).

[102] W. K. Pritchett, *The Greek State at War* (1971–79).   [103] See *ibid.*

[104] See A W. Gomme, *The Population of Athens in the Fifth and Fourth Centuries BC* 26 (1933).

[105] See Ehrenberg, *supra* note 101, at 39–43; M. I. Finley, *Politics in the Ancient World* 1–23 (1983); Sealey, *supra* note 97, at 134–68.

[106] 1 Coleman Phillipson, *The International Law and Custom of Ancient Greece and Rome* 32–33, 37 (1911). See also 2 F. Laurent, *Histoire du droit des gens* 18 (1850–70); Peter Karavites, *Capitulations and Greek Interstate Relations* 20–22, 117–20 (1982).

[107] Thomas, *supra* note 95, at 44.

[108] See H. Bengtson, *Introduction to Ancient History* 36 (6th ed. transl. R. I. Frank and F. D. Gilliard 1970) (discussing Helmut von Moltke's definition of locale).

intense concern for the demarcation of boundaries.[109] One might justly consider the virulent form of local patriotism practiced by the inhabitants of ancient Greek city states as particularism.[110]

Whatever we might call it, modern scholars have been wrestling with this conundrum in ancient Greek relations. Thomas A. Walker, writing in 1899, began the debate with his incendiary comment that the "International Law of such a people [as the Greeks] could . . . be hardly more than an intermunicipal law."[111] This was the view of Laurent in his enormously influential work, *Histoire du droit des gens*, published between 1850 and 1870.

Many writers replied to this charge of the narrow, limited nature of international law conditioned by ancient Greek particularism. Coleman Phillipson considered the characterization of Greek relations as "intermunicipal" as being only an epithet. The Greek cities, he contended, had a well-conceived notion of sovereignty and this was the essential element in any State system which purported to develop rules of behavior for independent political entities.[112]

Indeed, with a bit of intellectual *jujitsu*, Phillipson was able to subvert entirely Walker's and Laurent's thesis. He did so by pointing out the obvious: Greek State relations were not, in fact, premised on perpetual warfare or on universal centralization. The truth lay somewhere in between – a system of city-States, sharing common values but also a firm sense of their independence and sovereignty. "Neither universality nor particularity," Phillipson concluded, "obliterates or even diminishes the international character of rules and practices when . . . such rules are regularly insisted on."[113] Hans-Ulrich Scupin, in his discussion on the subject, comments:

Doubt cannot be cast on the existence of ancient Greek international law either on the ground that this was an instance of relations between the subjects of the same nationality, or even of one "Hellenic" nation, or because of the small scale of the relationships. The Greeks never formed a single nation in the political sense, for all their consciousness of their cultural unity; the fact that they had a common heritage never prevented them from treating subjects of other Greek States in exactly the same way as non-Greeks, or from forming alliances with non-Greek

[109] See G M. Ténékidès, *La Notion Juridique de l'Independance et la Tradition Hellénique* 167–70 (1954); D. J. Mosley, Crossing Greek Frontiers under Arms, 21 RIDA 161, 163 (1973).
[110] See Thomas, *supra* note 95, at 45.   [111] Walker, *supra* note 12, at 38.
[112] See 1 Phillipson, *supra* note 106, at 31.
[113] *Ibid.* at 62–63. To the same effect is Sir Paul Vinogradoff, Historical Types of International Law, in 1 *Bibliotheca Visseriana Dissertationum ius internationale illustrantium* 1, 13 (1923).

powers against their fellow Greeks. The undeniably small scale of all the relationships [does not tend] to exclude the possibility of an international legal system governing relations between equals . . . the only criterion is the legal structure of the system in question, not its size.[114]

Scupin's observation leads to a consideration of three other aspects of the ancient Greek State system prevailing between 500 and 338 BCE. The first question is the manner in which members of the system built coalitions and alliances for inter-Hellenic conflicts. The overriding dynamic of shifting combinations of Greek city-States was the maintenance of what we would today regard as a balance-of-power system. As Adcock and Mosley noted in their preeminent work on Greek diplomacy: "The most common source of conflicts of interest was territorial ownership and rights of access. The result was that frequently the bitterest relations existed between neighbouring rather than distant states."[115] This meant that two competing neighbors often sought to build alliances with more remote cities in order to counter-balance the power of their adversary.[116] These arrangements could accrete into pan-Hellenic coalitions, such as the Athenian and Spartan alliances during the Peloponnesian War (431–404 BCE).

These coalitions were rarely premised on the sovereign equality of their members.[117] The typical pattern was, instead, hegemony exercised by one lead city. Preeminence given to one *polis* was a natural outgrowth of the earlier patterns of colonization in the ancient Greek world. The mother-city was bound to exercise a prevailing influence over her colonies.[118] Likewise, the great powers of ancient Greece – Athens, Sparta, and Thebes – tended to dominate their smaller neighbors, a process that was extensively documented by Greek historians like Thucydides and Herodotus, as well as by modern scholars.[119] Hegemony had its natural effect of limiting the autonomy of smaller *poleis*.[120]

---

[114] Scupin, *supra* note 43, at 134–35. See also Ago, *supra* note 32, at 222–23; Wolfgang Preiser, Die Epochen der antiken Völkerrechtsgeschichte, 23–24 *Juristenzeitung* 737 (1956); R. Purnell, Theoretical Approaches to International Relations: The Contribution of the Greco-Roman World, in *Approaches and Theory in International Relations* 19, 21 (T. Taylor ed. 1978) ("international relations in terms of coexisting multiple sovereign units was . . . transcended in the Greco-Roman world.").

[115] Sir Frank Adcock and D. J. Mosley, *Diplomacy in Ancient Greece* 128 (1975).

[116] See Henry Wheaton, *History of the Law of Nations in Europe and America* 16 (New York 1845).

[117] See M. Amit, *Great and Small Poleis* 7 (1973) (Collection Latomus No. 134).

[118] See Ehrenberg, *supra* note 101, at 105.

[119] See generally, Amit, *supra* note 117; G. E. M. de Ste Croix, *The Origins of the Peloponnesian War* (1972); J. A. O. Larsen, *Greek Federal States: Their Institutions and History* (1968).

[120] See Ehrenberg, *supra* note 101, at 106, 112–20.

The Greeks developed an extensive lexicon describing different characters of unequal relations between cities. It is, as Robert Bauslaugh has noted, that: "Classical Greek diplomacy was far more sophisticated than a simple dichotomy of friends and enemies."[121] Not only were different degrees of power relationships acknowledged, but so was the concept of neutrality in which "the option of abstention [from conflict] was clearly enough defined and widely enough accepted to provide protection against belligerent hostility."[122] There were also periodic initiatives for federations of a number of Greek city-States. The Second Athenian League of 377 BCE and the Macedonian-inspired Corinthian League of 337 BCE were both notionally international associations of free, autonomous, and equal cities. More localized unions of cities were also common, whether in the form of non-interference agreements (*symbola*), grants of full citizenship rights (*isopoliteiai*), offensive and defensive alliances (*symmachiai* and *epimachiai*), or religious institutions (*amphictyones*).[123] Greek international organization was spectacular in its complexity.

The second problem presented in Greek international intercourse was a manifestation of Hellenic particularism and its impact on relations with non-Greek peoples. We are forced to confront, then, Plato's comment in *The Laws* that: "Every state is [in] a natural state of war with every other, not indeed proclaimed by heralds, but everlasting."[124] This was a view espoused by fifth-century tragedians and fourth-century philosophers,[125] and repeated as late as Greece's absorption into Macedonian control when Philip's ambassador to the Aetolians declaimed that: "With foreigners, with barbarians, all Greeks have and ever will have eternal war, which is always the same, and not from causes which change with the times."[126]

This Greek rhetoric of particularism, combining intellectual and cultural superiority[127] with the notional refusal to treat with foreign powers on a footing of sovereign equality,[128] was a direct outgrowth of the trauma of the Persian Wars of 500–479 BCE. Prior to 500 BCE, Greek cities carried on

---

[121] Robert A. Bauslaugh, *The Concept of Neutrality in Classical Greece* 36 (1991).   [122] *Ibid.*

[123] See generally, Ehrenberg, *supra* note 101, at 103–31. These classifications are considered in Chapter 4, pp. 120–24 below, and in Chapter 5, pp. 154–71 below.

[124] 1 Plato, *Laws* 7 (R. G. Bury transl. Loeb Classical Library reprint 1984) (passage i (626a)).

[125] See Wolfgang Preiser, History of the Law of Nations: Basic Questions and Principles, in 7 Rudolph Bernhardt, *Encyclopedia of Public International Law* 126, 130–31 (1984).

[126] See 5 Livy, *History of Rome* 77–79 (B. O. Foster transl. 1929) (Loeb Classical Library reprint 1982) (passage xxi. 27).

[127] See Adcock and Mosley, *supra* note 115, at 144 and n. 285; Arthur Nussbaum, *A Concise History of the Law of Nations* 5 (rev. ed. 1954); Walker, *supra* note 12, at 38.

[128] See Preiser, *supra* note 125, at 130–31; Scupin, *supra* note 43, at 135.

amicable and constructive relations with Persian communities in Asia Minor, Carthaginian outposts in Sicily, and Roman and Etrurian cities in Italy.[129]

This all changed when the Greek cities had to withstand the loss of their colonies in Asia Minor and the Ionian islands, and then in 490 BCE, and again in 480–479 BCE, two concerted invasions by Persian forces, incursions that were only repulsed at the battles of Marathon, Thermopylae, Salamis, Plataea, and Miletus. Athenian ascendancy was assured after the creation of the Delian League in 477 BCE[130] and the re-establishment of Greek control in Asia Minor after the Persian defeat at Eurymedon in 465 BCE. Renewed Athenian colonial expansion brought her into conflict with Persia in the east, Carthage and Etruria in the west, and, most ominously of all, with its closest rival, Sparta. It was imperative for the Athenians to prevent Persian alliance-building within the Hellenic community, and the rhetoric of particularism was designed primarily as a propaganda instrument against the inevitable alliance that would be formed by Sparta, her allies, and Persia against Athens,[131] the conditions which led to the beginning of the Peloponnesian War in 431 BCE.

The reality of Hellenic international relations was that the Greeks were perfectly prepared to deal with alien powers on terms of complete equality, so long as such an alliance comported with the needs of the balance of power. The number of peace treaties concluded between Greek and non-Greek powers was large.[132] By the fourth century BCE, once memories of the Persian Wars had receded and the demands of containing local hegemons were more imperative, Greek "State practice, in a fundamental manner, openly and irrevocably ceased following [a] theory [of exclusion] and demonstrated that it had long evolved its own theory according to which it was prepared to act."[133] The ultimate proof of this was the constitution of the Second Athenian Naval League in 377 BCE, designed to counter both Spartan and Theban ambitions, which expressly allowed for membership by both Hellenes and barbarians.[134]

Despite the suggestions of a few modern commentators that the rules of international law did not extend at all beyond Greece,[135] the consensus

---

[129] See Adcock and Mosley, *supra* note 115, at 145 and nn. 286–88 (citing 1 Herodotus, *Histories* 25–29, 83–85, 181 (A. D. Godley transl. 1920) (Loeb Classical Library reprint 1969) (passages i.22–24, i.69, i.141)).   [130] See Adcock and Mosley, *supra* note 115, at 145.

[131] See *ibid.* at 150. See also Karavites, Capitulations, *supra* note 106, at 35–36.

[132] See Ago, *supra* note 32, at 223 and n. 29.   [133] Preiser, *supra* note 125, at 130–31.

[134] See Adcock and Mosley, *supra* note 115, at 145 and n. 289; Scupin, *supra* note 43, at 135.

[135] See 1 Bruno Paradisi, *Storia del diritto internazionale del Medio Evo* 71 (1940); Stadtmüller, *Geschichte des Völkerrechts* 24 (1951).

appears to be that Greek city-States conducted relations on the basis of equality during most of their international history, with the possible exception of Persia during its invasions in the fifth century BCE.[136] As Ago noted in his writings, classical Greek international relations were largely characterized by tolerance and pluralism; non-Hellenes may have been deemed *xenoi*, strangers, but that did not necessarily convey the contempt that Plato and Philip's ambassador implied by calling them *barbaroi*.[137]

That leaves one remaining issue in the Greek conception of State relations under a rule of law. It is the basic inquiry of whether the Greeks embraced a concept of binding rules of state behavior, a law of nations. There has been extraordinarily divisive scholarship on this point. Classical philologists have noted a plethora of terms in ancient Greek to describe a conception of a law of nations. References were consistently made in Greek literary sources to "the laws of the Hellenes" or the "common law of Hellas" or the "laws common to men."[138] But even the philologists have been split on the provenance and usage of phrases implying a Hellenic *agraphos nomos* – an unwritten, customary rule of law in interstate relations.[139]

Much ink has been spilt on close textual analysis of the leading Greek historians' and philosophers' views on this subject. G. E. M. de Ste Croix's controversial work, *The Origins of the Peloponnesian War*, published in 1972,[140] devotes many pages to this exercise, offering what has been considered an unorthodox reading of Demosthenes, Isocrates, Aristotle, and Thucydides. Each of these writers sought to advance his own views on the dilemma of might versus right in international relations.

De Ste Croix characterizes Demosthenes' speech *On the Liberty of the*

---

[136] Evidence strongly suggests that most – but not all – of Greece was united against the Persian invader. Thessaly and Thebes may have made separate peaces with the Persians. See Adcock and Mosley, *supra* note 115, at 145. See also Chapter 6, at note 47 and accompanying text.   [137] See Ago, *supra* note 32, at 222–23 and nn. 28 and 31.

[138] See 1 Phillipson, *supra* note 106, at 57–58 (who collects these references). For particular occurrences of these phrases, see 1 Thucydides, *History of the Peloponnesian War* 7, 195 (C. F. Smith transl. 1919) (Loeb Classical Library reprint 1980) (passages i.3, i.118); 2 *ibid.* at 379 (passage iv.97.2); 1 Polybius, *The Histories* 191, 259, 383 (W. R. Paton transl. 1922) (Loeb Classical Library reprint 1975) (passages i.70.6, ii.8.12, ii.58.4–5); and 2 *ibid.* at 313, 461 (passages iv.6.11, iv.67.4).

[139] See 1 A. W. Gomme, A. Andrewes and K. J. Dover, *A Historical Commentary on Thucydides* 172 (1948–81); Martin Ostwald, *From Popular Sovereignty to the Sovereignty of Law* 119 (1986); Martin Ostwald, *Autonomia: Its Genesis and Early History* 3 (1982); M. Ostwald, Was There a Concept of *agraphoi nomoi* in Classical Greece? in *Exegesis and Argument: Studies in Greek Philosophy Presented to Gregory Vlastos* 70 (E. N. Lee, A. P. D. Mourelatos and R. M. Rorty eds. 1973); George A. Sheets, Conceptualizing International Law in Thucydides, 115 *American Journal of Philology* 51 (1994).   [140] See de Ste Croix, *supra* note 119.

Rhodians[141] as an affirmation that in inter-State disputes (*en tois Hellenikois dikaiois*) "the strong simply coerce the weak."[142] The question debated in that speech was whether Athens should have declared war on Rhodes when the Rhodians had given no offense. Demosthenes spoke in favor of war, but in doing so he acknowledged that there was a question of conforming Athenian conduct to some notion of international "legality,"[143] a position consistent with ones taken earlier by the orator.[144] Similarly, Isocrates' statement in *On the Peace*, a speech intended to influence Athenian policy during the Social War of 357–355 BCE (marking the breakup of the Second Athenian Naval League created in 377 BCE), was a ringing endorsement of a rule of law in international relations. "We recognized the principle," Isocrates wrote, "that it is not just for the stronger to rule over the weaker."[145]

De Ste Croix reserved his harshest commentary for Thucydides' account of the Peloponnesian War. He characterized Thucydides' opinion with the view that "all States . . . always do what they believe, rightly or wrongly, to be in their own best interests, and in particular they rule whenever they can."[146] This is merely the modern echo of Plato's remark in the *Laws* that his imaginary lawgiver would condemn the "stupidity of the majority of mankind" for failing to perceive that every State "is in a natural state of war with every other."[147]

One passage in Aristotle's *Politics* has also been enlisted in the debate on might versus right in Greek international relations. Aristotle wrote:

When it comes to politics most people appear to believe that mastery is the true statesmanship; and men are not to be ashamed of behaving to others in ways which they would refuse to acknowledge as just, or even expedient, among themselves. For their own affairs, and among themselves, they want an authority based on justice: but when other men are in question, their interest in justice stops.[148]

[141] 1 Demosthenes, *Collected Works* 419–20, 429 (J. H. Vince transl. 1930) (Loeb Classical Library reprint 1989) (*On the Liberty of the Rhodians*, passages 15, 28–29)).
[142] de Ste Croix, *supra* note 119, at 17.
[143] 1 Demosthenes, *supra* note 141, at 417 (passages 9–10).
[144] See Bauslaugh, *supra* note 121, at 48 n. 24.
[145] 2 Isocrates, *Orations* 49–51 (George Norlin transl. 1929) (Loeb Classical library ed. 1982) (*On the Peace*, passage 69). This passage has been glossed by de Ste Croix, *supra* note 119, at 17; J. de Romilly, Fairness and Kindness in Thucydides, 28 *Phoenix* 95, 100 (1974).
[146] de Ste Croix, *supra* note 119, at 22.
[147] 1 Plato, *Laws*, *supra* note 124, at 7 (passage i (626A)). See also James Brown Scott, *supra* note 101, at 68–84.
[148] Aristotle, *Politics* 545 (H. Rackham transl. 1932) (Loeb Classical Library reprint 1990) (passage vii.2.8 (1324b32–36)).

But, once again, the context reveals a different meaning to Aristotle's words. He was being intensely critical of polities which did not conduct their foreign relations on the basis of justice, likening such behavior to barbarism.[149] If there was any doubt on this point, one might recall Aristotle's statement in the *Rhetoric*: "There is naturally a common idea of justice and injustice (*koinon dikaion kai adikon*) which all men intuitively understand in some way, even if they have neither communications nor treaty (*syntheke*) with one another."[150]

This assertion was important and relevant in understanding the nature of ancient Greek State relations. Aristotle spoke of "a common idea of justice" intuitively understood within the Hellenic community. International justice meant that there were commonly shared expectations of behavior, understood and respected even though they were not the subject of diplomatic adjustment or codification in a treaty. As Robert Bauslaugh has noted;

these interstate rules did not evolve into a written international law, but due to mutual respect born of shared culture . . . they exerted a surprisingly powerful hold over the thinking and actions of the classical Greeks . . . The authority of the *agraphoi nomoi* of interstate relations was, by necessity, grounded in the moral consciousness of those involved.[151]

The ancient Greek conception of an unwritten, customary law of interstate relations[152] was not without its inconsistencies and these have been vigorously revealed by historians of such note as Martin Ostwald, de Ste Croix, D. J. Mosley, and Peter Karavites.[153] Nonetheless, the Greek city-States of the fifth and fourth centuries BCE overall satisfy the criterion for an authentic State system, which, as one modern international lawyer has specified, means that "independent and sovereign states can live, and are in reality compelled to live, in a community which provides a law of international relations to the member-states, provided there exist some common interests and aims, which bind these states together."[154]

Ultimately, outside forces disrupted the classical Greek inter-state

---

[149] See *ibid.* at 611 (passage vii.13.14 (1333b35–1334a2)) ("Training for war should not be pursued with a view to enslaving men who do not deserve such a fate."). See also James Brown Scott, *supra* note 101, at 85–91; W. von Leyden, *Aristotle on Equality and Justice: His Political Argument* 84–90, 102–03 (1985).

[150] Aristotle, *The Art of Rhetoric* 139–41 (J. H. Freese transl. 1926) (Loeb Classical Library reprint 1982) (passage i.13 (1373b6–9)).   [151] Bauslaugh, *supra* note 121, at 36, 52.

[152] See also Ago, *supra* note 32, at 222.

[153] For the latter, see Mosley, *supra* note 98, at 93; Karavites, *supra* note 106, at 9–11.

[154] 1 Lassa Oppenheim, *International Law* 71 (7th ed. Hersch Lauterpacht 1948). This is substantially the same test as enunciated by Hedley Bull: see *supra* note 1.

system. Just as the Persian Wars of the fifth century were the defining moment in the creation of a Greek international consciousness, and gave spirit to an extraordinarily rich (if fractious) international life to the Greek city-States, so too did the accretion of power by Macedon, on the Greek northern border, spell the end of Greek independence. Once the Macedonian tribes were united under Philip II's dynamic leadership, beginning in 359 BCE, it was inevitable that Macedon would meddle in, and then dominate, Greek internal disputes.

Macedonian power crept south, with the conquest of Thessaly in 352 BCE and Thrace in 342 BCE. Too late, the Greek cities realized that Macedon formed a more potent threat than Persia; their Hellenic League was vanquished in 338 BCE at the battle of Chaeronea. Greece was absorbed into the Macedonian kingdom, while (at the same time) utterly Hellenizing their ostensible protectors. When Alexander the Great marched against Persia in 334 BCE, he was as much leading a Macedonian invasion and creating a vast empire, as he was Hellenizing the entire eastern Mediterranean and all the Near East. Thereafter, the independence and autonomy of the Greek *poleis* was largely a fiction and an authentic State system ceased to exist in Greece.

In any event, not much of a State system would exist in the eastern Mediterranean and the Near East for several centuries. City-States gave way to great empires. After Alexander the Great's death in 323 BCE, his empire was divided among his successors (*Diadochi*) with their power centers in Antigonid Macedon, Ptolemaic Egypt, and Seleucid Syria and Persia.[155] The shifting relations between the successor kingdoms had more in common with the dealings of warlords and thieves, than with the State systems that had persisted earlier in the Near East or in Greece. To identify another State system in the ancient world, it is necessary to look westwards.

Rome and its competitors, 358–168 BCE

The last ancient State system to be reviewed in this study is, in many respects, the least problematic. Roman history is well documented in both literary and inscription sources. Its international relations followed established patterns, culminating in a period (the one reviewed here) that has all of the hallmarks of a dynamic (though ultimately, unstable) system of

---

[155] See Peter Green, *Alexander to Actium: The Historic Evolution of the Hellenistic Age* 1–51, 119–34 (1990).

States. For a brief time, Rome was neither a weak Italian city-State nor a great and sprawling empire. During that intermission it was an aggressive nation State competing with like-minded polities not only proximately in the Italian peninsula, Sicily, and North Africa, but also, later, in Greece, Egypt and the rest of the eastern Mediterranean.

For the three centuries after its founding in 750 BCE, Rome carried on relations with its neighbors on a "restricted regional framework,"[156] chiefly with other members of the Latin League and the Etruscan cities. This was a significant time, if for no other reason than that a strong alliance between Carthage and the Etruscans managed successfully to resist Greek penetrations of influence in southern Italy and Sicily. But for this confluence of interests, central Italy (and subsequent Roman power) would have been smothered at its birth. In any event, by the fourth century BCE, Rome was the leading power in central Italy, after its victory in the Second and Third Samnite Wars (326–304 and 298–290 BCE).[157]

By virtue of that status, Rome began entering into a wider ambit of diplomacy with other, more far-flung States. Documented treaties between Rome and Carthage are extant from 500, 348 and 306 BCE. A Roman–Carthaginian alliance (or at least a non-aggression pact) figured prominently in the Roman defeat of Pyrrhus, a Greek Epirot mercenary commander who had pretensions of domination in central Italy.[158] The war against Pyrrhus and the Hellenized city-State of Tarentum (282–272 BCE) brought Rome into direct contact with Greek methods of diplomacy and international relations. One commentator has suggested that:

[i]n th[is] first period of her history, when Rome was one of several Italian petty states, there was room for the adoption by the Romans of some such conceptions of international obligation as those which prevailed amongst the Hellenes ... [T]he practice of Rome in her international relations during this period reveals features similar to those distinguishable in the international practice of the Hellenic commonwealths.[159]

The war with Pyrrhus brought Rome into the orbit of Greek influence and, in the words of Roberto Ago, "completed a process of the formation of a

---

[156] Ago, *supra* note 32, at 226. See also H. H. Scullard, *A History of the Roman World, 753–146 BC*, at 92–114 (3rd ed. 1961).

[157] See Scupin, *supra* note 43, at 136–37 (who attributes Roman expansion in central Italy to the reduction of class strife and internal reforms). See also Andreas Alföldi, *Early Rome and the Latins* (1964); Einar Gjerstad, *Early Rome* (1954–73); Jacques Heurgon, *The Rise of Rome* (1973); E. T. Salmon, *Roman Colonization* (1969); E. T. Salmon, *Samnium and the Samnites* (1967); J. W. Spaeth, *A Study of the Causes of Rome's Wars from 343 to 265 BC* (1926).

[158] See P. Levêque, *Pyrrhos* (1957).   [159] Walker, *supra* note 12, at 44.

common international law as between all of the peoples of the Mediterranean."[160] Many scholars take the year 358 BCE as the date when Rome entered a community of States in Italy and the wider Mediterranean littoral.[161]

Rome joined a State system that included as its Great Powers Carthage and the *Diadochi* states of Macedon, Syria, and Egypt. Also included in the system were smaller States such as Syracuse (in Sicily), the residuum of the independent Greek cities, the powerful naval republic of Rhodes, and the kingdoms of Pergamos, Bithynia, Cappadocia, Pontus, and Paphlagonia. Together these States formed a "true International Circle, a distinct society of civilised states of very considerable extent."[162] As a community, they had a very conscious sense of dealing with one another as equals and within a system that regarded each as being "civilized" and not barbaric.[163]

The State system of this period had a greater potential for stability than any that had existed hitherto in antiquity. Unlike the shifting coalitions of the Greek city-States or the ponderous "super" powers of the ancient Near East, the Mediterranean world of the third and second centuries was multi-polar and explicitly premised on balance-of-power notions. The States were large enough to comprise large populations and powerful enough to project force in more than one direction. As it turned out, coexistence and stability was impossible and the dynamic character of Roman expansionism posed an insuperable threat to the balance of power.[164] Ultimately, a stable, multi-polar system broke down into a war of coalitions, a conflict that one side was bound to lose.

These events placed Rome on a collision course with its great regional rival, Carthage. Indeed, the period of the Punic Wars (264–146 BCE) was the high-water mark of the Mediterranean State system of this period. The first Punic War (264–241 BCE) was largely a naval conflict in which no outside powers intervened. The result was that Carthage lost its control

---

[160] Ago, *supra* note 32, at 227 n. 46. See also 1 Jacques Pirenne, *Les Grands Courants de l'histoire universelle* 219–22 (1959); Bruno Paradisi, Due aspetti fondamentali nella formazione del diritto internazionale antico, in 1 *Civitas Maxima, Studi di storia del diritto internazionale* 173 (1974).   [161] See Scupin, *supra* note 43, at 136–37.

[162] Walker, *supra* note 12, at 51. See also Ago, *supra* note 32, at 229.

[163] The historian Polybius, writing in Greek but resident in Rome during the period 168–144 BCE, commented extensively on this subject. See 1 Polybius, *supra* note 138, at 175–77, 257–59 (passages i.65, ii.8), 2 *ibid.* at 411–13 (passage iv.45), 3 *ibid.* at 229–31, 249–51 (passages v.95 and 104), 4 *ibid.* at 165–79, 239–41 (passages x.27–31, xi.5), 5 *ibid.* at 131–33 (passage xviii.22). See also Wheaton, *supra* note 116, at 18.

[164] See Arnaldo Momigliano, *Alien Wisdom: The Limits of Hellenization* 15 (1975); 1 Pirenne, *supra* note 160, at 226.

over Corsica, Sardinia, and Sicily, but was compensated by a Roman-recognized sphere of influence in Spain. The Second Punic War began with Carthaginian encroachments in northern Spain in 219 BCE, ostensibly violating the earlier agreement with Rome. Rome demanded the return of Saguntum and the surrender of the Carthaginian commander, Hannibal. What ensued was a life-and-death struggle between the two States, on both land and sea, and over a sphere of operations covering the entire western Mediterranean. Fortune at first favored Carthage, with Hannibal crossing the Alps, and his destruction of the Roman armies at Trebia and Cannae in 218 and 216 BCE.[165]

It was at this moment that outside powers chose to intervene, and a treaty of alliance was signed between Philip V of Macedon and Carthage in 215 BCE. Immediately, Ptolemaic Egypt sided with Rome and together they subverted the allegiance of the Greek city-States, chafing under Macedonian domination since 338 BCE. With Egypt arrayed against Macedon, the Seleucid Empire based in Asia Minor and Syria was compelled to join Macedon and Carthage. Within a few years, the entire Mediterranean was at war. It was a clash that the Romans were destined to win, not in concert with allies, but alone for their own imperial ambitions.[166]

The first step was to vanquish Carthage. This took many years of a bloody and inconclusive Roman strategy of attrition. Ultimately, the Romans were able to carry the war into North Africa, defeating Hannibal at Zama in 202 BCE. A rump Carthaginian state remained, but with only a sphere of influence in North Africa, and even this was ended with the punitive Third Punic War of 149–146 BCE. The Romans also turned their sights to punishing the Macedonians for their intervention. The Second Macedonian War of 200–197 BCE allowed Egypt and Rome to combine with the vacillating Greek cities to crush Macedon. Antiochus III of the Seleucid Empire had made gains against Egypt in Syria (still a region of bitter competition), but these were reversed when Rome invaded Asia Minor in 192 BCE. After the Roman victory at Magnesia in 190 BCE, Antiochus sued for peace, forswore a naval presence in the Mediterranean

---

[165] For more on the Punic Wars, see J. F. Lazenby, *The First Punic War* (1996); T. A. Dorsey and D. R. Dudley, *Rome Against Carthage* (1971); Gilbert Charles Picard and Colette Picard, *The Life and Death of Carthage* (1968); H. H. Scullard, *Scipio Africanus and the Second Punic War* (1930).

[166] See R. Malcolm Errington, *The Dawn of Empire: Rome's Rise to World Power* (1972). See also *Rome and the Greek East to the Death of Augustus* 1 (Robert K. Sherk ed. 1984) (text of treaty between Rome and Aetolian League, 212 BCE).

and suffered the expansion of two buffer states, Rhodes and Pergamon, both favorably disposed to Rome.[167]

By 168 BCE, with the end of the Third Macedonian War and the total destruction of the Macedonian kingdom, Rome was the supreme power of the Mediterranean. Carthage and Macedon were gone. The Seleucids were weakened and land-locked in Asia Minor and the Syrian hinterland. Only Egypt, a steadfast ally of Rome, was unaffected. But it alone could not challenge Rome. That is why the year 168 BCE marks the end of this last, authentic State system in antiquity. As Wolfgang Preiser has written:

> [T]he first requirement for international law as the law of inter-State coordination is now missing [in 168 BCE]: the simultaneous existence of several States which, free of one another's power of command, mutually respect each other as independent entities of equal rank. Instead, in place of an equality long grown precarious, there arose a subordination of all under a dominating empire. The fact that the traditional forms of international law were still maintained for a while longer, in a limited fashion, rested on the victor's free will and ability to afford the appearance of generosity; in reality they signify nothing.[168]

The period after 168 BCE is marked by Roman imperialism and the creation of dependent states, *clientelae*.[169] Disputes between Roman clients or even between those polities on the periphery were based on Roman dominance,[170] even as Roman citizenship came to be more broadly extended to tributary peoples.[171]

That still leaves the question, at least for the period under consideration here, whether the Romans could actually deal with their neighbors on a basis of sovereign equality. The consensus of historiographic opinion has shifted on this subject with time, as with other aspects of the debate about ancient States and their international relations. Well-regarded scholars of the nineteenth century were adamant that Roman particularism, as manifested in the Roman State's imperialism, precluded any Roman adoption

---

[167] For more on this period of Roman expansion, see 3 Max Cary, *History of the Greek and Roman World: 323 to 146 BC* (2nd ed. 1963); G. Colin, *Rome et la Grèce de 200 à 146 avant J. C.* (1908); David Magie, *Roman Rule in Asia Minor* (1950); E. Pais, *Stori di Roma durante le grandi conquiste Mediterranee* (1931); Hatto H. Schmidt, *Rom und Rhodos* (1957); F. W. Walbank, *Philip V of Macedon* (1940).

[168] Preiser, *supra* note 41, at 131–32. See also Scupin, *supra* note 43, at 137.

[169] For more on which, see E. Badian, *Foreign Clientelae (264–70 BC)* (1958); E. Badian, *Roman Imperialism in the Late Republic* (1967); T. Frank, *Roman Imperialism* (1914); Stephen Verosta, International Law in Europe and Western Asia Between 100 and 650 AD, 113 RCADI 484, 543–45 (1964–III).   [170] See Walker, *supra* note 12, at 58–59.

[171] See A. N. Sherwin-White, *Roman Citizenship* 126–63 (1939). See also Finley, *supra* note 105, at 84–96.

of the principles of international law.[172] The Romans may have suffered equal relations with other polities, but the notion of sovereign equality was thought, by these scholars, to be alien to a political culture that was so juridically exclusive.[173]

A more realistic attitude toward Roman strength is called for, at least during this early, critical period of Roman expansion. Rome was not all-powerful at this time. The Roman State had to deal with other polities as equals, because that is what the balance-of-power diplomacy of fourth-century Italy required and the second-century Mediterranean demanded.[174] Complete reciprocity in diplomatic relations and treaty-making were substantially recognized by Rome during this period. "The desire for self-assertion . . . in the early centuries of the Roman Republic, was in no way directed at obtaining unrestricted power," Scupin has written; "it did not prevent the States with which the Romans came into contact, whether friendly or hostile, from being considered as independent subjects of the law of equal rank, with which legal relations were thus possible on the basis of equality."[175]

As a consequence of this willingness to carry on diplomacy based on the rule of law, the Romans had well-developed views about which foreign polities were worthy of equal treatment. Rome refused to have relations with entities that did not possess a high level of political organization and cohesion.[176] It was only with free and independent nations that Rome extended the basic indicia of membership in an international community: the sending and reception of ambassadors, the conclusion of *sponsiones* or *foedera*, and the proper formalities for initiating conflict.[177]

These attitudes were confirmed in extracts collected in the post-classical *Digest* of Justinian, and although great care needs to be taken in referring to this source (because of its very late appearance after the period in question and uncertain provenance of certain collected fragments), it at least speaks to the question of how the Romans regarded legal relations with foreign nations. One noteworthy point gleaned from the *Digest* is that, from a very early stage, the Romans did not recognize a perpetual state of war with their neighbors: "If with certain nations we have

---

[172] See 1 Phillipson, *supra* note 106, at 106–07 (quoting M. Revon, *L'arbitrage international* 101 (1892)).   [173] See H. Bonfils, *Manuel de droit international public* 35 (1905).

[174] See Scupin, *supra* note 43, at 139. See also 1 Phillipson, *supra* note 106, at 103–04.

[175] Scupin, *supra* note 43, at 139.

[176] See Cicero, *De Re Publica* 65 (Clinton Walker Keyes transl. 1928) (Loeb Classical Library reprint 1988) (passage i.25). See also 4 *The Digest of Justinian* 886 (Theodor Mommsen and Paul Kruger eds., Alan Watson transl. 1985) (49.15.7.1; Proclus, *Letters* 8).

[177] See 1 Phillipson, *supra* note 106, at 110–11.

no connection of friendship or hospitality and no treaty concluded in order to establish friendship, the men of these nations are not our enemies."[178] This position was in sharp distinction to unorganized and uncivilized peoples the Romans called *alienigeni*, barbarians. According to the *Digest*, the property of barbarians was *res nullius*, subject to acquisition without formality or declaration of war; individuals could be subjected to slavery, their burials desecrated.[179]

Roman practice thus continued Greek notions of distinguishing polities within a community of nations (whose relations were subject to the rule of law) and those peoples outside the pale of civilization. The Romans certainly inherited the forms and styles of Greek international relations.[180] It is also important to remember that Rome dealt with non-Hellenized cultures, most particularly the Carthaginians. The international relations of Ptolemaic Egypt and Seleucid Syria, successor kingdoms of Alexander the Great's conquests, retained some aspects of ancient Near Eastern practices, tracing their lineage back to Hittite diplomatic language and treaty forms, and perhaps back even to Akkadian and Sumer styles.

We have, in essence, two traditions of ancient State practice. The feudal empires of the Near East created their special diplomatic argot, one that was transmitted (by contacts through the Egyptians, Phoenicians, and Israelites) to the later political cultures of the Mediterranean basin. The second heritage was produced by the querulous relations of the Greek city-States. Roman statecraft was a mixture of these two manners. How these two traditions came to define the ancient conception of a law of nations remains to be discussed in the following chapters. What needs to be reiterated here is that there were special times and places in antiquity where political entities coalesced as States and related with like-constituted polities on the basis of independence, sovereign equality, and a respect for rules in the conduct of international relations.

---

[178] 4 *Digest*, *supra* note 176, at 886 (4915.5.2; Pomponius, *Quintus Mucius* 37). See also Rostovtseff, *supra* note 4, at 62–63.
[179] See 4 *Digest*, *supra* note 176, at 786 (4712.4; Paul, *Praetor's Edict* 27), 886 (49.15.5.2; Pomponius, *Quintus Mucius* 37).
[180] See Ago, *supra* note 32, at 228–29; H. B. Leech, *An Essay on Ancient International Law* 22 (1877); Momigliano, *supra* note 164, at 14.

3 Religion and the sources of a law of nations in antiquity

International law has been called a primitive legal system. A review of the literature developing that assertion is made elsewhere in this study,[1] and it does provide the initial premise for this chapter. International lawyers will go to any lengths to defend their discipline against the charge that it is anything less than "real" law. Yet they will readily concede that State relations in the ancient world were unprincipled, devoid of any sense of legal obligation, and without effective sanctions. In short, they acknowledge for antiquity what they deny for the modern law of nations. This chapter critically reviews this concession by examining the sources of a law of nations, and of international legal obligation, in ancient times.

A number of characterizations have been attributed to primitive legal systems.[2] Some of these describe the contents of primitive legal doctrines, most notably the lack of certainty and security of expectation, the limited range of norms, and the use of retaliation (rather than social sanction) as the decisive element of enforcement.[3] Other characterizations describe what might be called the "process" elements of primitive law. Legal fictions, which transformed doctrines by subtly changing their underlying assumptions as social demands required, competed with formalism

---

[1] See Chapter 1. See also Hersch Lauterpacht, *The Function of Law in the International Community* 434 (1933) (for a vigorous denial of this metaphor for state relations); Yoram Dinstein, International Law as a Primitive Legal System, 19 *New York University Journal of International Law and Politics* 1, 2 (1986) (for an outstanding synthesis for this proposition). The primary source for the notion that international law, at least in antiquity, was a manifestation of a primitive legal system is Henry Maine, *Ancient Law* (1861) (1986 reprint), who discussed the Roman conception of the *ius gentium* in the context of natural law principles. *Ibid.* at 36–93. See also *infra* notes 179–186 with text.

[2] For more on the attributes of primitive law, see A. S. Diamond, *Primitive Law Past and Present* (1971); R. W. M. Dias, *Jurisprudence* 390 (5th ed. 1985); Max Gluckman, *Politics, Law and Ritual in Tribal Society* (1965); Edwin S. Hartland, *Primitive Law* (1924); E. Adamson Hoebel, *The Law of Primitive Man* (1954).   [3] See Dinstein, *supra* note 1, at 2–8, 11–15.

which exalted form (the integrity of ritual) over substance (the adaptability of rules).[4]

Moreover, the very sources of legal obligation can be called "primitive." Two phenomena have been observed in this respect. First, there is the importance of custom in determining the content of norms. It is axiomatic that "[l]aw begins everywhere with custom,"[5] and it seems especially so with international law. We take it as an article of faith that the modern law of nations derives its legitimacy from the consent of States. We have completely accepted the notion that custom is a form of positive law. To call international law "primitive," because its sources of obligation are rooted in custom, is no insult. Indeed, we regard the customary character of international law as one of its signal strengths.

The second attribute for primitive legal sources has not been as well received. That characteristic is the pervasive influence of religion on law. In tribal cultures, the enforcement of social order has been linked to magic.[6] In slightly more developed societies, religion was the decisive motive force for law.[7] Only when law was entirely divorced from religious belief was it considered distinctively rational, which is nothing more than saying it was unambiguously "modern."[8] Publicists have thus vigorously maintained that modern international law has entirely shed any religious foundation for the sense of obligation which exists between sovereign States.[9]

The law of nations in antiquity has been dismissed because of its allegedly religious character.[10] This feature is supposedly what made it a primitive legal system. To propose that an ancient law of nations was primitive assumes that religious belief provided the principles of State behavior, as well as the sanctions for the enforcement of those norms. It is this premise that will be critically reviewed in this chapter, while two distinct ques-

---

[4] See *ibid.* at 22–29.   [5] 2 J. Bryce, *Studies in History and Jurisprudence* 640 (1901).
[6] See Hoebel, *supra* note 2, at 268–74.
[7] See Dinstein, *supra* note 1, at 16–17. Professor Dinstein, citing the work of E. Adamson Hoebel, *supra* note 2, suggested that the ties between law and religion were manifested in a number of ways, including (1) the sanctification of a code or legal system to an ascribed deity, (2) the interpretation of law by priests, (3) the ritualization of legal transactions, (4) the taking of oaths, and (5) the backing of religious sanctions with secular force. This study accepts these manifestations of religion in primitive law, and will consider them in reference to the sources of ancient international law.
[8] Cf. Maarten Bos, *A Methodology of International Law* 37–38 (1984) (for a discussion of the role of reason in modern legal life).
[9] See Dinstein, *supra* note 1, at 17–18 ("The present development of international law is devoid of any religious contents").
[10] See, e.g., 1 Coleman Phillipson, *The International Law and Custom of Ancient Greece and Rome* 43 (1911).

tions are considered. First, was religion the sole source of ancient international law? Secondly, even if it was, did that diminish the principles it espoused, or compromise the effectiveness of its sanctions?

It matters whether religion was ostensibly the sole source of antiquity's law of nations. It seems essential to the "primitive" hypothesis that religious belief provided the only terms of reference of an ordered international system of States. The working hypothesis of this entire study is that other intellectual phenomena, including elemental notions of custom and sharpened instincts for rhetoric, also had an impact on State behavior. This conclusion accords, moreover, with the very characteristics that primitive legal systems are supposed to exhibit. As noted already, primitive law also embraced custom as a source for norms of behavior. Religion and custom can act as complementary forces in a society, but they can also compete with each other, with custom acting as an antidote to the particularistic strictures of belief and ritual.

Examining the intellectual sources of an ancient law of nations nicely illustrates this dynamic. It shows that ancient societies were aware of something that publicists today take for granted: the distinction made between the doctrinal contents of a norm of State behavior, and the available sanctions for its enforcement. The law of nations in ancient times seemed to appreciate this dichotomy, although implicit in its acceptance was the sure and certain knowledge that belief could not guarantee predictable and acceptable State behavior. As doctrine developed separately from sanctions, an all-encompassing role for religion in international relations was partially repudiated.

The first part of this chapter will discuss the metaphysics of ancient international law. By "metaphysics" nothing more is meant than essential, or at least irreducible, propositions. I will suggest that the law of nations in antiquity had two of these. First, the essential principle which international law sought to preserve in State relations was good faith. Secondly, good faith had to be guaranteed by an oath invoking some form of sanction in case of non-compliance.

What is of interest for modern publicists is not what good faith may have meant in antiquity, but how promises of State behavior were enforced. Ancient people conceived of three different kinds of sanctions applicable in international relations. They correspond, I argue, with distinctive sources of obligation, each of which will be the subject of its own part in this chapter. The first was divine sanction, based on a fear of direct punishment by the god or gods invoked in an international undertaking. The source of this compulsion was religion. Secondly, there was a social sanction enforced through the rituals, institutions, and political legitimacy of the ancient State, and manifested by a fear that the national god or gods would abandon that State to its enemies. Custom was the source of this penalty. The third was an intellectual sanction, developed through legal argumentation and rhetoric, motivated by fear only of being deprived of a moral right and freedom of action. Its source was reason.

It would be a mistake to regard these three sources of international legal obligation as discrete impulses in the ancient mind. Religion fused with custom and with reason to produce different combinations of sanctions in ancient international relations. This should come as no surprise since even in modern societies these constraints on human behavior combine in sometimes surprising ways. It is rare that a religious tradition, which at its inception can purely articulate commands for conduct, can long withstand forces which ritualize belief and make it serve as a form of political legitimacy. Religion and custom may also, after a time, become secularized. The sources of an ancient law of nations experienced each of these transformations.

This chapter attempts to correlate some substantive doctrines of ancient international law with their sources of legal obligation. Discussion here of treaty formalities is intended to illustrate the form of oaths. In the same way, the institution of envoys and of the declaration of war show how ritual and custom provided another source of sanction. Detailed consideration of these doctrinal convolutions and the intricacies of international legal norms will otherwise be reserved for the next chapters. Nonetheless, the relationship between doctrines and sources is important in another way, since it reveals the most fundamental difference between ancient and modern international law: antiquity's complete elimination of process as an essential link between sources and substance. Ancient international law was not a primitive legal system because of its doubtful dependence on religious belief. It was primitive because the ancient mind could not conceive of norms of State behavior apart from the admittedly diverse sanctions for non-compliance with those rules.

The metaphysics of ancient international law

Good faith and breaking faith

Before there was religion, even before there was right, there was force and terror and lawlessness. Before there was law, no matter how primitive, there was anarchy. Some modern writers have suggested that an ancient law of nations never even progressed to the stage of a primitive legal system, according to this definition. "[I]nternational law," wrote Michael

Rostovtseff in 1922, "supposes a kind of general agreement on some principles, be they of legal or of moral and religious nature. This was not the case in the [ancient] world. The sole deciding force was might."[11] This statement elaborates a dichotomy between legal and religious sources of obligation, even as it concedes that either can provide the basis for principles of State behavior. The conclusion reached by Rostovtseff was that the law of nations in antiquity had failed to establish any principled means of conducting international relations.

It is true that the ancient mind struggled to legitimize the use of force between States. Only one principle was capable of providing a credible alternative to the constant recourse to war in settling disputes. This was good faith. As an idea, it was adopted by nearly all ancient civilizations as a means of recognizing the integrity of promises made both within a social order and in the international realm. Implicit in the idea was sovereignty. States had no obligation to make promises; but once they did, they were compelled to keep them.

In Western civilization, the idea of good faith in personal and international relations has been transmitted through the Roman notion of *bona fides*. "The basis of all relationships, of all obligations was conceived to be sincerity and good faith."[12] This is merely a restatement of a *sine qua non* in modern legal culture: that there can be no right without a corresponding obligation, and that promises are enforceable only between those who have consented to be bound. In a sense, this is a rather simplistic solution to the problem of legitimizing force in State relations. If nations, like people, can forswear violence, then such promises should be enforceable. Free will was raised as the supreme value of personal and international affairs, but the Roman solution, for example, purposefully ignored community interests, whether they were of a society of nations or a collectivity of individuals. These were not considered because they were assumed. The interests of the State always prevailed over those of the individual, or of the nation's neighbors, allies, and enemies.

The Roman principle of *bona fides* was qualified by a definitively nationalistic vision of good faith. This was manifested in its corollary use as an invective. The duplicity, dissimulation, and infidelity of foreign nations was a consistent subject of reproach.[13] When a Roman spoke of *punica fides*

---

[11] Michael Rostovtseff, International Relations in the Ancient World, in *The History and Nature of International Relations* 43 (E. Walsh ed. 1922).

[12] 1 Phillipson, *supra* note 10, at 68.

[13] See *ibid.* at 68–69. The Greeks also had similar expressions. See *ibid.* at 118–19. See also M. Merten, *Fides Romana bei Livius* (PhD dissertation, Johann Wolfgang Goethe Universität, 1965).

or *graeca fides* it was no compliment to his enemies. Good faith was a jingoistic notion for the Romans.

Good faith thus found many different voices in ancient international relations. As first principles go, good faith was certainly the only common denominator in relations between disparate cultures. The only thing many could agree on was that if they could agree on something, that agreement would be binding.

Of course, as soon as ancient people invented good faith, they were faced with the problem of what to do when faith was broken. Penalties were inevitable. Historians have been nearly unanimous in their pronouncement that this sanction was solely religious. Henry Wheaton, in his classic *History of the Law of Nations*, published in 1845, wrote that "[w]ith the ancient nations of Greece and Italy, law, both public and private, so far as depending on penal sanctions, was exclusively founded on religion."[14] Likewise, Rostovtseff later noted that "[t]he sanction of all treaties was a religious one."[15]

Other writers have emphasized that ancient law and religion had their own special synergy. Indeed, "the commission of an offense against the one was usually met by penalties prescribed by the other, in addition to those laid down by itself."[16] What was obvious to the ancient mind was that "to commit an infraction of the law [was] to commit an offense against the gods, who must be duly appeased."[17] For an ancient nation to break faith was also to invite supernatural retribution.

Writers of many intellectual persuasions have disagreed sharply over the nature of that retribution, and also whether the religious character of an ancient law of nations somehow compromised the effectiveness of its sanctions. This second concern, however, is unimportant. As Coleman Phillipson observed nearly ninety years ago:

[a]s to the argument that because a certain code of conduct in international relations draws its sanction from religion, it cannot therefore be described as possessing the character of *international law*, the answer is that it is of no consequence at all where the sanction lies; since the fundamental question is whether there is a generally admitted rule regulating certain international relationships, and whether there exists any potent sanction whatever similarly recognized as enforcing the observance of that rule. The religious sanction did not impair but added force to the legal and political sanction . . . The juridical nature of ancient rules obtaining between States is attested by their consciousness of being bound by the

---

[14] Henry Wheaton, *History of the Law of Nations in Europe and America* 3 (New York 1845).
[15] Rostovtseff, *supra* note 11, at 47. See also Georg Busolt and Heinrich Swoboda, *Griechische Staatskunde* 2 (1926).   [16] 2 Phillipson, *supra* note 10, at 302.   [17] 1 *ibid.* at 43.

obligations implied, by their regarding the due observance thereof as just, and violation unjust and punishable.[18]

What needs to be considered further, though, is exactly what forms sanctions in the ancient law of nations took. It is not enough, as Phillipson believed, to know that the sanction existed somewhere in the intellect of the ancient mind. He was content merely in positioning it squarely in the domain of religion.

In so doing, Phillipson deftly turned the arguments of those who suggested the law of nations in antiquity had no real juridical character. Yet, he also commented that "[a]ncient [international] law is an embodiment of categorical commands without assigning reasons therefor. It is an imposition of unquestioned sovereign authority which sees no need for elucidation by argument or comment in preambles or otherwise; and this sovereign authority ultimately lies with the gods."[19] This damns the international law of antiquity with faint praise. More importantly, however, it is also an incomplete statement of the sources of international legal obligation in the ancient world.

Four fragments

A clearer vision of these sources starts in ambiguity, but should end with revelation. The ambiguity lies in the literary quality of the accounts of ancient international relations which have been transmitted to us. To the modern reader, these materials seem more like fables with the inevitable moral at the end. Consider the following stories, but remember that the factual predicates of these tales (their accounts of State behavior) must be separated from their moral content.

The plague prayers of King Mursilis[20]

In the second half of the 14th century BCE, the realm of the Hittites, whose center lay in Asia Minor, was visited by a tenacious plague which depopulated the country. An oracle traced the epidemic back to malfeasances committed by the father and predecessor of the reigning king, which included the breach of an inter-State treaty which was placed under the protection of the gods by means of a

---

[18] 1 *ibid.* at 51 (original emphasis).   [19] 1 *ibid.* at 43.

[20] See 2(2) *Cambridge Ancient History* 85 (3rd ed. 1975); S. Langdon and A. H. Gardiner, The Treaty of Alliance Between Hattusili, King of the Hittites, and the Pharaoh Rameses II of Egypt, 6 *Journal of Egyptian Archaeology* 179, 197 (1920); Wolfgang Preiser, History of the Law of Nations: Basic Questions and Principles, in 7 *Encyclopedia of Public International Law* 130 (Rudolph Bernhardt ed. 1984), which draw this fragment from the so-called "plague prayers" of King Mursili.

mutual oath. The deity, offended by this breach of oath, now revenged itself on the transgressor's descendants.

The fable of Fabius[21]

The great misfortunes which befell [Rome] from the Gauls, are said to have proceeded from the violation of . . . sacred rights. For when the barbarians were besieging Clusium, [the Roman] Fabius Ambustus was sent [as] ambassador to their camp with proposals of peace [on behalf of the Clusians, who were Roman allies]. But receiving a harsh answer, he thought himself released from his character as an ambassador, and rashly taking up arms for the Clusians, challenged the bravest man in the Gaulish army. [Fabius won the combat, but the Gauls] sent a herald to Rome to accuse Fabius of bearing arms against them, contrary to the treaties and good faith, and without a declaration of war. Upon this the [*fetials*] ordered the Senate to deliver him up to the Gauls, but [Fabius] appealed to the people [and he was] screened from the sentence. Soon after this, the Gauls marched to Rome, and sacked the . . . city.

Darius' heralds[22]

When King Darius of Persia sent his heralds to Athens and Sparta in 491 BCE to demand earth and water as tokens of submission, the Athenians threw them into prison, and the Spartans dropped them into a well, inviting them to take their earth and water there. Divine vengeance was wrought upon the Spartans and they were for long unable to obtain favorable omens at their sacrifices. This wrath was only later assuaged when the Spartans sent two nobles to Darius' heir, Xerxes, as a sacrifice for their previous misdeed, a sacrifice which the Persian king declined.

Greek historians disagreed about the punishment which befell Athens. Herodotus doubted any connection between the mistreatment of Darius' envoys and the destruction of their city ten years later. Pausanias suggested that the punishment fell upon the house of one man, Miltiades, son of Cimon.

The speech of the Plataean deputies[23]

During the Peloponnesian War, the city of Plataea was nominally allied with Athens, but sought to remain neutral. Thebes, a Spartan ally, attacked Plataea. The

---

[21] 1 Plutarch, *Lives* 307, 349–51 (B. Perrin transl. 1914) (Loeb Classical Library reprint 1968) (*Numa*, passage xii.7), also quoted in Lord Arundell, *Tradition Principally with Reference to Mythology and the Law of Nations* 397 (1872).

[22] This fragment is drawn largely from 3 Herodotus, *Histories* 435–39 (A. D. Godley transl. 1920) (Loeb Classical Library reprint 1969) (passage vii.133–36). See also D. J. Mosley, *Envoys and Diplomats in Ancient Greece* 85 (1973) (for a textual examination of these passages).

[23] This account comes from 2 Thucydides, *History of the Peloponnesian War* 91–125 (C. F. Smith transl. 1919) (Loeb Classical Library reprint 1965) (passage iii. 52–68). See also N. G. L. Hammond, Plataea's Relations to Thebes, Sparta and Athens, 112 JHS 143 (1992).

Plataean garrison capitulated and placed themselves at the mercy of Sparta. A hearing was held to decide their fate, with Spartans as judges.

Among the Plataean submissions were: "[the Thebans] came not only in time of peace, but at a holy season, and attempted to seize our city; we righteously and in accordance with universal law defended ourselves and punished the aggressor . . ." and "[b]efore you pass judgement, consider that we surrendered ourselves, and stretched out our hands to you; the custom of Hellas does not allow the suppliant to be put to death."

The Thebans replied that they had been invited to liberate the city and that the Plataeans had been guilty of slaying those to whom quarter had been granted. They called for the Spartans to "[m]aintain . . . the common Hellenic law which [the Plataeans] have outraged, and give to us, who have suffered contrary to law, the just compensation of our zeal in your cause."

The Spartans condemned the Plataeans and the garrison was put to death.

These extracts have both a literary and historical quality. They are unified by one theme: they each purport to show how a sanction was applied for a violation of a standard of international behavior. In the account of the plague prayers, the story is sad and straightforward enough. The breaker of a treaty was visited with a pestilence sent by the angered god who acted as surety for that agreement. In this fable, the connection between infraction and punishment was direct, inexorable, and made manifest to the party who broke faith. In fact, it was that last element, an oracle or religious authority tracing the misfortune to an earlier violation, which gave this religious sanction its tragic and terrible tenor.

The tale of Fabius shows a very different kind of fear. In that story, the Roman envoy broke faith by engaging in combat against the Gauls. The Gauls took no action against him, but instead sought his extradition from Rome. The extract makes reference to the decision of the *fetials*, an essentially secular institution which was created to determine if war was to be declared and to settle questions of diplomatic immunities and treaty formalities.[24] The college of *fetials* ordered that Fabius be delivered up to the Gauls, but the Senate overruled this decision. As a consequence, the Gauls

---

[24] For more on the *fetials*, see 1 Phillipson, *supra* note 10, at 115–16 (for a consideration of their religious and secular character); G. Fusianto, Dei feziali e del diritto feziale, in 13 *Atti della Reale Accademia dei Lincei* (ser. 3) (1883–84) (for the earliest study of the *fetials'* legal role in ancient Rome); Lord Arundell, *supra* note 21, at 374–75 (on the creation of the College); Tenney Frank, The Impact of the Fetial Institution, 7 CP 335 (1912).

The *fetial* institution is discussed in more detail later in this chapter, pp. 76–79 below; in Chapter 5, pp. 194–202 below; and in Chapter 6, pp. 231–41 below.

proved victorious in the ensuing war against Rome and the city itself was sacked.

It was apparent that the penalty for Rome's malfeasance was not exactly inspired by divine forces, at least not in the same way as King Mursilis' plague. Instead, the sanction combined both religious and social components. It was undoubtedly rooted in the belief that improper behavior would result in the nation's gods abandoning the State to its enemies.[25] Unlike the Hittite king's violation, the faith that Fabius broke was not guaranteed by an oath or a declaration, but rather by some customary notions of the proper comportment of envoys and of the correct commencement of hostilities.

The social sanction was revealed by the role of the *fetials* in the affair. The *fetial* college's primary duty was to preserve the political legitimacy of the Roman state in its international affairs. It was its prerogative to indicate when an enemy had given such offense as to make war *ius belli*, and thus secure for Rome the victory it sought. It was also within the power of the *fetials* to administer the oaths that would bind the Roman state. The *fetials* condemned Fabius because he had usurped their authority. This fable shows how, in ancient societies, religious ritual was transformed into institutional and political power. The source of this sanction was really a kind of custom, which depended on the political legitimacy of the State being preserved by quasi-religious institutions.

The tale of Darius' heralds tells of the same belief held in the account of the plague prayers and in Fabius's fable. What is curious in this fragment is that Athens and Sparta suffered different fates for the same unlawful act: the murder of Persian envoys. The Spartan experience was much like that of the Hittite king. They were unable to gain favorable auguries whenever they made a sacrifice at the temple of Talthybius, a Homeric figure who was the herald of Agamemmnon, and whose descendants provided Sparta's hereditary class of envoys.[26] The *talthybiadai* were a prototype of Rome's *fetials*, although lacking in the same institutional authority. They were powerful enough, it seems, to have demanded that Sparta expiate this misdeed by sending two envoys to Xerxes as a sacrifice. The Persian king refused to accept them, and Talthybius' wrath went unassuaged until sixty years later, in 430 BCE, when the Athenians intercepted a Spartan embassy to Persia and executed them.[27] An additional irony was

---

[25] See Wheaton, *supra* note 14, at 3. See also 2(2) *Cambridge Ancient History* 14 (3rd ed. 1975) (describing Mitanni King's death as a judgment of the Gods), 287 (Kassite ruler, by breaking treaty with Assyria by invading that country, was condemned to defeat).

[26] See Mosley, *supra* note 22, at 87.   [27] See *ibid*.

that the murdered envoys were the sons of the two Spartan heralds that Xerxes had earlier pardoned. As in all Greek tragedy, the Spartans suffered the fate they were due.

Strangely enough, the Athenians escaped their punishment by refusing to acknowledge that it was coming to them. Herodotus took pains to disclaim any connection between Athens' later sack and the treatment of Darius' envoys. The essential connection between violation and retribution was thus denied, and a religious basis for the sentence was refuted. A customary ground of punishment was undermined also by the legend that a single Athenian family bore the blame for the act, even though that was ultimately the form the punishment took for Sparta. There was no link between an institution within the city-State, such as the Spartan *talthybiadai*, and atonement for the crime committed. Without that link, proper expiation of an international wrong was impossible. In short, Athens evaded condemnation by shifting its international duty from religion and from custom.

The plea of the Plataean deputies illustrated the opposite danger of making contentions in favor of legal constraints separate from religion. This extract was also a fine example of Greek legal rhetoric, for Thucydides purported to recount the exact arguments used by Plataea and Thebes in their submissions to Sparta. This was no arbitration, though. The Plataeans had been vanquished, and their fate was decided by their foe's ally. Plataea emphasized Greek customary law concerning the outbreak of hostilities and the conduct of warfare. Custom would have spared the Plataean garrison from death. Thebes also cited custom, the "common Hellenic law," in their submissions. Yet, no reference can be found in this exchange to any deity, nor to any sanction that would be directly or implicitly delivered by a god. The Plataeans only reminded the Spartans of the infamy they would incur if they condemned the city.[28] The Plataeans relied primarily on reason as the source of the international legal obligations they wished to be respected. The custom they cited was very different from that feared by Sparta when the *talthybiadai* warned that sacrifices would be inauspicious, or by Rome when their city was sacked by the Gauls. The fate of the Plataeans was obviously a setback for reason, but it was enough that it informed their sense of international law.

In rendering these four fragments it becomes manifest that religion, custom, and reason were not discrete and separate compartments in the

---

[28] See 2 Thucydides, *supra* note 23, at 101–05 (passage iii.57–58). See also Peter Karavites, *Capitulations and Greek Interstate Relations* 68–70 (1982) (for a full account of this incident).

ancient mind, at least not as it was concerned with the sources of international legal obligation. The plurality of those sanctions – divine, social, and intellectual – gave a depth of meaning to the moral contained in each of the stories. That moral is nothing more than the metaphysic described above. The obligation of good faith, just like the punishment for breaking faith, could arise from an oath or by an institutional prerogative or by the force of intellect. The balance of this chapter surveys the contours of religion, of ritual and custom, and of reason and rhetoric in the ancient conception of the sources of a law of nations.

Religion

Nationalism and universalism

Religion brought ancient nations together and separated them. The concept of nationalism in antiquity invariably embraced national religions, while multinational empires were typically governed by universal sects. Although some Enlightenment writers bemoaned the fact that ancient societies came too early to embrace that most universal of creeds, Christianity,[29] later publicists realized that inherent in a common religion was a common political order, and thus the extinction of international law itself. Nationalistic and universal tendencies in ancient religions together conspired to produce a problematic influence on the development of inter-State relations.

Ancient religions worshipped national gods. This meant that the "gods of the different oriental monarchies were friendly to their nation only and enemies of all other nations."[30] National gods were sometimes "shared" between different States, often as a sign of alliance or a token of political submission, but, more typically, ancient States held the view that nothing was more destructive to local religion than foreign ceremonies.[31]

The God of the Israelites was the paradigmatic national god of antiquity. Not only was he the one god of a tribe of people, exclusive and jealous, but his divine providence attached to a particular domain. "I am the Lord that

---

[29] See 1 Robert Ward, *An Enquiry into the Foundation and History of the Law of Nations in Europe* 172–73 (London 1795).

[30] Rostovtseff, *supra* note 11, at 44. See also Mikhailovich Kapustin, *Mezhdunarodnoe Pravo* [International Law] 7 (1873); 1 Le Baron Michel de Taube, *Istoriya Zarozhdeniya Sovremennovo Mezhdunarodnovo Pravo* [The History of the Conception of Contemporary International Law] 19 (1899). See also 1(2) *Cambridge Ancient History* 103 (3rd ed. 1971) (for the notion of Gods "owning" cities in Sumer).

[31] See Norman Bentwich, *The Religious Foundations of Internationalism* 39, 49–50 (2nd ed. 1959).

brought thee out of Ur of the Chaldees," he told his people. "To give thee this land to inherit it . . . [and] he made a covenant with Abraham saying, Unto thy seed have I given this land."[32] That land was inalienable, "for the land is mine: for ye are strangers and sojourners with me."[33] The religion of ancient Israel was not only virulently nationalistic, it was decidedly territorial.[34]

Later cultures also expressed similar fears of defilement by foreigners. Livy reported that after the Gauls were defeated in 390 BCE, the Senate decreed that those temples that were in the possession of the enemy had to be resanctified and due expiations made for them.[35] Likewise, when the Persians were vanquished by the Spartans and Athenians in 479 BCE, the Delphic Oracle instructed that all sacrificial fires in Greece be extinguished, because they had been polluted by the presence of the barbarians. A new, cleansed flame was brought from the common hearth at Delphi.[36]

This last account says much of the Greek conception of national religion. The Greeks disdained foreigners, called them barbarians, and held them to be outside of the Hellenic compact, as those who had not poured out libations to their gods.[37] This compact was based on a common religion, language, and ethnicity.[38] To be Greek was to be within the pale of civilization, and thus bound to tacitly peaceful relationships. Even though peace was not often the norm between Greek city-States, that was because of hostility generated not by religion, but by political and economic rivalry.

Religion could, however, unify nations even where common interest could not. The Greek *amphictyones* were established among city-States with shared altars, hearths, and temples. Common rites were observed, and the same anniversaries and games were celebrated. Examples of these religious federations abounded in ancient Greece.[39] The most famous, and influential, was that established for the Delphic Oracle. While scholars

---

[32] Genesis 15:7, 18.   [33] Leviticus 25:23.

[34] See Deuteronomy 19:14 ("In the inheritance which you will hold in the land that the LORD your god gives you to possess, you shall not remove your neighbor's landmark, which the men of old have set."). See also Vilho Harle, *Ideas of Social Order in the Ancient World* 76–81, 183–91 (1998); Martin Sicker, *Judaism, Nationalism and the Land Borders of Israel* (1992).

[35] See 3 Livy, *History of Rome* (B. O. Foster transl. 1922) (Loeb Classical Library reprint 1967) (passage v.50); see also 1 *The Digest of Justinian* 353 (Theodor Mommsen and Paul Krueger eds., Alan Watson transl. 1985) (11.7.36; Pomponius, *Quintus Mucius* 26) (requiring expiatory ceremonies for all places and objects that had in any way been in contact with the enemy).   [36] See 2 Plutarch, *supra* note 21, at 211, 277 (*Aristides*, passage xx.4).

[37] See Wheaton, *supra* note 14, at 5. See also Harle, *supra* note 34, at 179–83.

[38] See Arthur Nussbaum, *A Concise History of the Law of Nations* 9 (rev. ed. 1954).

[39] See Robert A. Bauslaugh, *The Concept of Neutrality in Classical Greece* 39–41 (1991); 2 Phillipson, *supra* note 10, at 2–4. See also 1(2) *Cambridge Ancient History* 103 (3rd ed. 1971) (for a similar concept in Sumer).

have disagreed whether the purposes of this, the Amphictyonic Council, were primarily religious, or also political,[40] there is no doubt that its object was to preserve the sacred precincts of the temple from aggression or defilement, to extend immunities to officials carrying out its business, to arbitrate disputes among its members, and to protect those rendered helpless in wartime.[41] The Amphictyonic Council even went to war on two occasions to punish those members who had infringed on the privileges of the Delphian temple.[42]

Religion thus legitimized a system of independent and sovereign States in antiquity. Outside the Greek realm were barbarians and lawlessness, sacrilege and endless war. The Hellenic civilization never aspired to empire, having already attained a satisfactorily universal religion among their constituent political entities. It was the Romans who envisioned universal empire and its inclusion of alien peoples and national religions.[43] As with the Greeks, these cultures observed formalities in their relations with other States, and the chief of these was that most solemn and religious act of a nation swearing its good faith with a pledge.

Making and breaking oaths

Oaths implicated the most religious of compulsions, the intervention of the guarantor god or gods against the party that broke faith. Ancient treaties were, as a matter of definition, an exchange of oaths. A mere promise made without the appropriate religious formula was not held to be binding on the parties.[44] What is even more important to understand is

[40] Compare Wheaton, *supra* note 14, at 15 (who argues that it was chiefly a religious institution, and largely ineffective), with 2 Phillipson, *supra* note 10, at 11 ("[I]t is clear that the Delphic amphictyony . . . exercised a great influence directly or indirectly in the promotion of international comity, and in the regularization of, and insistence on, many principles of interstatal practice.").

[41] See 2 Phillipson, *supra* note 10, at 5–7 (for more on the composition of the Council and its purposes); see also, Victor Martin, *La vie internationale dans la Grece des cités* (1940); Georges Ténékidès, Droit international et communautes federales dans la Grèce des cités, 90 RCADI 469, 583–96 (1956–II).   [42] See 2 Phillipson, *supra* note 10, at 8–9.

[43] See Bentwich, *supra* note 31, at 66. See also Alan Watson, *International Law in Archaic Rome: War and Religion* 66–67 (1993), who comments that "Roman state religion very early lost its mythology . . . It became, at an early stage, a religion of observance, not of belief or theology . . . It became a matter of keeping man – especially man in his public function – in proper contact with the gods." *Ibid.* at 66. For more on the nature of Roman religion, see Georges Dumézil, *Archaic Roman Religion* (1970); Alan Watson, *The State, Law and Religion: Pagan Rome* (1992).

[44] An example of this was provided by the same Plataeans who suffered at the hands of the Thebans. Earlier, in 431 BCE, the Plataeans were victorious and, it seems, they were not gracious winners. After promising to grant quarter to Theban prisoners, they reneged

that there was a tradition of covenant-making that was common to all of antiquity. There was not only a commonality of terminology in oath-making, traced back to Akkadian and Hittite origins and transmitted then to Egyptian, Greek, Carthaginian, and even Roman models,[45] but also a singularity in the idea that what secured good faith in agreements made between nations was some form of an oath.

Ancient Near Eastern oath-taking

In the ancient Near East, it was a strongly held view that "gods were the ultimate rulers of states."[46] Therefore, when ancient States made faith with each other, it was logical to believe that such an act involved divine direction and guidance.[47] In the parable of King Mursilis and his plague prayers,[48] the punishment visited upon the State for treaty breach was a direct sanction of the deity which served as guarantor for the covenant.[49]

The structure and phrasings of ancient Near Eastern treaty oaths is particularly well documented.[50] Although our information is largely confined to agreements between a suzerain and a subordinate political entity (what we might call "vassalage" treaties), there is enough evidence suggesting the ways in which peoples of the ancient Near East guaranteed good faith. The single, consistent theme from Sumerian, Babylonian, Hittite, Assyrian, Israelite, and Egyptian practices is that oaths were exchanged in a ceremony accompanied by elements and formalities that enunciated the penalties of non-performance. Many recent scholars (including Peter Karavites and others) have ably argued that this ancient Near Eastern tradition of oath-taking was transmitted to Homeric and

Footnote 44 (*cont.*)
and said that they had not sworn an oath to that effect. See 1 Thucydides, *supra* note 23, at 267–69 (passage ii.5). This act of perfidy featured in the Theban submissions to the Spartan tribunal which decided later the Plataeans' unhappy, but perhaps richly deserved, fate. See *supra* note 28.

[45] See M. Weinfeld, Covenant Terminology in the Ancient Near East and its Influence on the West, 93 JAOS 190, 197–98 (1973). See also Delbert R. Hillers, *Treaty Curses and the Old Testament Prophets* 6 (1964); Samuel Mercer, *The Oath in Babylonian and Assyrian Literature* (1927); Erich Ziebarth, Der Fluch im griechischen Recht, 30 *Hermes* 57 (1895).

[46] J. M. Munn-Rankin, Diplomacy in Western Asia in the Early Second Millennium BC, 18 *Iraq* 68, 72 (1956). For more on this supposition, see 2 G. R. Driver and John C. Miles, *The Babylonian Laws* 11 (1960); T. Jacobsen, 2 JNES 171 (1943).

[47] See Munn-Rankin, *supra* note 46, at 72–74.   [48] See *supra* note 20 with text.

[49] See Dennis J. McCarthy, *Treaty and Covenant* 93–94 (1963).

[50] For a discussion of the manner in which these treaty inscriptions have been transmitted, see McCarthy, *supra* note 49, at 19–20.

epic Greece, and became part of a Mediterranean tradition of treaty-making. This line of transmission was supplemented by a vector from Palestine (including Israel and Phoenicia).

Among the earliest Sumerian city-States the stated penalty for non-performance of a treaty may have been a simple statement by the oath-taker that his life would be forfeit if he broke his promise.[51] Or, in the later practice of Hammurabi of Babylon, he touched the "tablet of the life of the gods," containing the treaty text, and then "touched his throat" while a calf was slaughtered, symbolically declaring the penalty for perjury in a divine oath.[52] In other Mesopotamian cultures, there were other kinds of sacrifices made; puppies and goats figured prominently in quite a number of States' covenant ceremonials.[53]

Covenant practice reached its zenith in the ancient Near East with the vassal treaties made by the Hittites and Assyrians. The structure of a Hittite covenant followed very predictable forms and structures.[54] These included a preamble, a historical prologue on the relations between the parties, the substantive stipulations of the agreement, provisions for deposit of the instrument in a temple and periodic readings, a list of gods serving as witnesses, and, finally, the enunciation of curses falling upon the party that failed to heed the treaty and the blessings that would accrue if they did.[55] As has been well documented, the form of promises in Hittite vassal treaties was apodictic. The typical promise and oath was structured as "Thou shalt not do X" or "Thou shalt do Y."[56] The obvious parallel to the covenant form in Israelite practice is what sparked contemporary scholarly interest in ancient Near Eastern treaty-making.

In vassalage treaties made by the Hittites, the gods of the subordinate party enforced the agreement;[57] the suzerain only rarely assumed any liability for failure of performance. By contrast, in parity agreements, both the stipulations (enforced through oaths) and penalties (expressed through curses) were reciprocal. Later Assyrian treaties, including the

---

[51] See Le Baron Michel de Taube, L'inviolabilité des traités, 32 RCADI 292, 301–02 (1930–II).

[52] See Munn-Rankin, *supra* note 46, at 84–91 (glossing 2 *Archives Royales de Mari: Lettres Diverses* (C. F. Jean transl. 1950) (passages 37.6–9, 62.9 and 72.24) (hereinafter "2 ARMT")).

[53] See George E. Mendenhall, Puppy and Lettuce in Northwest-Semitic Covenant Making, 133 BASOR 26 (February 1953); M. Held, Philological Notes in the Mari Covenant Ritual, 200 BASOR 39 (1970); Klaus Baltzer, *The Covenant Formulary* 9–38 (D.E. Green transl. 1971).

[54] For the scholarly literature on the forms of Hittite treaties, see Hillers, *supra* note 45; McCarthy, *supra* note 49; George E. Mendenhall, *Law and Covenant in Israel and the Ancient Near East* (1955).   [55] Mendenhall, *supra* note 54, at 32–35.

[56] See McCarthy, *supra* note 49, at 34–37.

[57] See *ibid.* at 47–48; Mendenhall, *supra* note 54, at 34.

vassal treaty between Esarhaddon and Baal of Tyre in 672 BCE,[58] followed very similar patterns. So, too, did Egyptian treaties.[59] Some differences did develop with time, including changes in covenant terminology and the order and significance given to various elements of the international agreement.[60]

The main difference between Hittite covenant forms and both earlier (Sumerian) and later (Assyrian and Israelite) practices was the place of ceremony and ritual in the covenant institution. Hittite practice was virtually devoid of ceremony; the vassal merely swore to the treaty in public. There were no rites involving animal sacrifice, nothing to give form and substance to the curses uttered for breach of faith.[61] As Howard Jacobson has noted: "It is important to remember that ritualistic dramatization is a regular component of treaties and oaths in the ancient Near East. But the dramatization serves not to symbolize the agreement, but rather to concretize the curses which accompany the oath."[62]

As for those curses, they reflected an extraordinarily diverse and imaginative mind, and most were implicated in the treaty-ratification ritual. One Assyrian underling would thus be compelled in a vassal treaty with his master to utter "this head is not the head of a ram, it is [my] head" and "just as the ram's head is torn off . . . so may [my head] be torn off" if the terms of the covenant were not obeyed.[63] These simile curses show a connection between treaty ceremony and ancient magical practice, "for they employ common magical techniques of analogy and substitution."[64] The curse acted as a magical spell to replace the object being distressed for the party swearing the oath.[65]

Other curses were not so complicated, being simple maledictions in which the "oath-breaker is threatened with an evil fate, but no god is invoked and there is no simile."[66] Some scholars have catalogued

---

[58] For more on which, see McCarthy, *supra* note 49, at 197–98; D. J. Wiseman, *The Vassal-Treaties of Esarhaddon* (1958). See also 3(2) *Cambridge Ancient History* 125–26 (2nd ed. 1991).

[59] See David Lorton, *The Juridical Terminology of International Relations in Egyptian Texts through Dyn. XVIII*, at 82, 132 (1974) (for derivations of Egyptian terms for "swearing an oath").

[60] For a discussion of these differences, see Michael L. Barré, *The God-List in the Treaty Between Hannibal and Philip V of Macedon* 44–45 (1983); McCarthy, *supra* note 49, at 53–55, 98–104.

[61] See McCarthy, *supra* note 49, at 53–55. See also Paul Guggenheim, Contribution à l'Histoire des Sources du Droit des Gens, 94 RCADI 1, 55–56 (1958–II).

[62] Howard Jacobson, The Oath of the Delian League, 119 *Philologus* 256, 256–57 (1975).

[63] See Hillers, *supra* note 45, at 19.

[64] *Ibid.* at 20. See also A. Goetze, *Kleinasien* 154 (2nd ed. 1957).

[65] For more on animal sacrifice in treaty rites, see McCarthy, *supra* note 49, at 39–40, 55–56. See also Peter Karavites, *Promise-Giving and Treaty-Making: Homer and the Near East* 63–64 (1992) (on historical tradition of animal sacrifice as part of treaty ceremonial).

[66] See Hillers, *supra* note 45, at 26. See also McCarthy, *supra* note 49, at 124.

maledictions of this sort used in the Hittite vassal treaties. They were known generally as *kudurru* (the Babylonian name for boundary stones upon which some curses were inscribed), and were especially intended to protect the domains of the suzerain by "extensive curse-formulae in the name of various gods."[67] The maledictions covered such points as the transgressor being killed and having no progeny, being afflicted by various illnesses, being exposed after death, being condemned to wander after the destruction of his dwelling place, and his lands being overtaken by natural calamities.[68] It was a *kudurru* of this sort that was visited upon King Mursilis.

As has been the subject of extensive scholarship, the treaty practices of the ancient Israelites closely followed the patterns of their Semitic neighbors and their Assyrian conquerors.[69] Israelite covenant practice was deeply rooted in both the apodictic and casuistic character of ancient Jewish law.[70] The Bible's old testament featured many cases of the Israelites making treaties with their neighbors, and the consequences of oath-making. The Hebrew terminology for making a covenant has etymological similarities to Hittite and Akkadian forms.[71] Covenants were "surrounded by oaths and religious symbols, such as the holy number seven and the sacrificing of animals."[72]

The Bible recounts only a handful of circumstances in which God directly punished the Jews for failing to observe a pact with another nation.[73] In the parable of the Gibeonites,[74] the fear of divine wrath was both implicit and explicit. In that story, the Lord had earlier instructed his

---

[67] See F. Charles Fensham, Common Trends in Curses of the Near Eastern Treaties and *Kudurru*-Inscriptions Compared with Maledictions of Amos and Isaiah, 75 *Zeitschrift für die Alttestamentliche Wissenschaft* 155, 157 (1963). For a possible link between *kudurru* and the Greek concept of *horkia* and *horkos*, see Karavites, *supra* note 65, at 59.

[68] See *ibid.* at 158–70. See also J. Kohler and A. Ungnad, *Assyrische Rechtsurkunden* 16, 19 (1913); D. J. Wiseman, *The Alalakh Tablets* 28, 59–62, 87 (1953); Karavites, *supra* note 65, at 109–15 (cataloguing such curses in Homer).

[69] See J. A. Thompson, *The Ancient Near Eastern Treaties and the Old Testament* 28–29 (1964).

[70] The first to present this thesis was Albrecht Alt in *Die Urspruenge des Israelitischen Rechts* (1934). See also Mendenhall, *supra* note 54, at 6–7. For more on the covenant lawsuit in ancient Jewish law, see H. Gunkel and J. Begrich, *Einleitung in die Psalmen* (1933); Thompson, *supra* note 69, at 30–31; Herbert B. Huffman, The Covenant Lawsuit in the Prophets, 78 *Journal of Biblical Literature* 285 (1959).

[71] See Weinfeld, *supra* note 45, at 196–97; M. Weinfeld, The Covenant of Grant in the Old Testament and in the Ancient Near East, 90 JAOS 184, 188–89 (1970).

[72] Nussbaum, *supra* note 38, at 3; see also Genesis 21:22–32, and Isaiah 8:9 (for the forms and character of promises made by the Israelites). See also Thompson, *supra* note 69, at 24–26; Weinfeld, Grant, *supra* note 71, at 196–99.   [73] See 2 Samuel 21:1–6.

[74] See Joshua 9:3–18.

people to make peace with the submissive cities "very far off from thee ...
But of the cities of these peoples that Jehovah thy God giveth thee for an
inheritance, thou shalt save alive nothing that breatheth."[75] The
Gibeonites tricked the Jews into believing that they had come from far
away, so Joshua "made peace with them, and made a covenant with them,
to let them live: and the princes of the congregation swore unto them."[76]
The fraud was discovered, but "all the princes said unto the congregation,
We have sworn unto them by Jehovah, the God of Israel: now therefore We
may not touch them."[77]

The princes of the congregation had a disagreeable choice to make.
They could have defied the Lord's territorial imperative to obliterate those
enemy nations within the "Israelite inheritance," or, instead, they could
have broken faith with the Gibeonites. At least in Joshua, the sworn
promise prevailed over the divine instruction. Whether the sanction for
breaking their oath with the Gibeonites seemed more terrible to the congregation, we will never know. But it seems that the decision to observe
their treaty obligation was motivated by a concern to respect the rituals
and forms of the promise, rather than its content and purposes.[78]

But later, in Samuel, we are told that in the Kingship of Saul, some
Gibeonites were executed. As a consequence, "there was a famine in the
days of David for three years, year after year."[79] The only way to expiate this
occurrence was the sacrifice of seven of Saul's descendants.[80] In a scenario
reminiscent of the consequences of the murder of Darius' envoys, the
breach of covenant was only cured by the later death of the descendants
of the perpetrator or guarantor of the oath.

The parallels between ancient treaty oaths and the Israelite covenant
with their God are notable and significant. They depend on one assumption: that the ancient Israelites viewed themselves in some sense as in a
fealty relation with their God.[81] This issue is obviously beyond the scope
of this study. What needs to be noted here is that the ancient Near Eastern
tradition of oaths and curses had an essential unity and continuity.
Moreover, the nature of obligation arising from the exchange of oaths and
the articulation of treaty curses was religious in only a particular way. To
the extent that maledictions were invoked – that bad things would
happen if the terms of an international agreement were not kept – it was

---

[75] Deuteronomy 20:15–17.   [76] Joshua 9:3–15.   [77] Joshua 9:17–19.
[78] See Shabtai Rosenne, The Influence of Judaism on the Development of International
Law, 5 *Netherlands International Law Review* 119, 141–42 (1958) (discussing later examples of
treaty observances, cited by Josephus in his *Antiquities*).   [79] 2 Samuel 21:1.
[80] See 2 Samuel 21:3, 6.   [81] See McCarthy, *supra* note 49, at 172–73.

not always clear that it would be a deity who would oversee the punishment. Sometimes this was implied, but in some cases the ancient mind understood that the consequences of bad faith would follow without a necessary divine intervention. Likewise, in the fashioning of treaty ritual, the act of substitution, and the playing out of sacrifices or destructions, had more the character of magic than of religion.[82] There was a subtle tension at work here between religion and ritual, one that continued in the practices of the Mediterranean cultures considered in this book.

Greek and Roman oaths

Substantial dispute persists about the origins and character of the idea of good faith in both ancient Greece and Rome. We do know that oaths served to solidify the institution of friendship between individuals in different clans and localities. In ancient Greece, ritualized friendship was based on the concept of *pistis*, roughly translated as fidelity. Those who swore an oath to friendship exchanged lances or spears (known in Greek as *pista*) and thus became *pistoi* to each other.[83]

What is unclear is the extent to which the oath really was significant to this act.[84] As Everett Wheeler has noted, "[o]aths . . . not only validated agreements but also guaranteed them, for oaths were taken in the name of the gods who were thought to punish the perpetrators of perjury, bad faith, and oath breaking as well as their families and descendants."[85] Early in Greek history, it was believed that one who broke faith "waged war against the Gods."[86]

This belief can be seen in the development of a highly refined treaty ceremonial. Attic Greek had many phrases describing the process of

---

[82] See Elias J. Bickerman, Hannibal's Covenant, 73 AJP 1, 10–11 (1952).

[83] See Gabriel Herman, *Ritualised Friendship and the Greek City* 50 (1987); 1 Phillipson, *supra* note 10, at 391–92; Ténékidès, *supra* note 41, at 526–27. Closely allied to the notion of *pistoi* was the principle of *dexia*, the pledge of friendship, manifested by the symbolic handshake or embrace. See *ibid.* at 50–54.

[84] For a historiography on this question, see Michael Gagarin, *Early Greek Law* 43 (1986); Louis Gernet, *Anthropologie de la Grèce antique* 241–47 (1968) (transl. 1981); Kurt Latte, *Heiliges Recht* 5–47 (1920). See also Rudolf Hirzel, *Der Eid: ein Beitrag zu seiner Geschichte* (1902).

[85] Everett L. Wheeler, Sophistic Interpretations and Greek Treaties, 25 GRBS 253, 253 (1984). See also Martin, *supra* note 41, at 401–03.

[86] See 1 Xenophon 233 (Carleton L. Brownson transl. 1921) (Loeb Classical Library reprint 1932) (*Hellenica*, passage iii.4.11); 2 *ibid.* at 387 (*Anabasis*, passage ii.5.7). See also Joseph Plescia, *The Oath and Perjury in Ancient Greece* 3–4 (1970); Ténékidès, *supra* note 41, at 561–64. See also David Cohen, Horkia and Horkos in the Iliad, 27 RIDA 49 (1980).

making faith with another nation, as well as special names for the gods serving as surety.[87] Early in the Greek heroic age, the main proceedings of the treaty ritual were established. In the third book of the *Iliad*, a solemn agreement was made between the Trojans and Argives to give Helen to the winner of a combat between Menelaus and Alexander.[88] A preliminary announcement was made by the heralds for a truce, so that the treaty could be concluded.[89] Then this invocation was made to the gods to bear witness to the transaction:

Father Zeus, that rulest from Ida, most glorious, most mighty, and thou Sun that beholdest all things, and hearest all things, and ye Rivers and thou Earth, and ye that in the underworld punish men deceased, whosoever has taken a false oath; be ye witnesses, and watch over the faith-ensuring pledges.[90]

Oaths were then exchanged, the conditions of the treaty were recited, and a sacrifice made.[91] Finally, a libation of wine was poured, hands were joined, and this warning was made for the parties to keep true to their oaths: "Zeus, most glorious, most mighty, and ye other immortal gods! Whomsoever shall first commit wrong contrary to their pledges, may their brains and their children's be dispersed on the ground, like this wine, and may their wives prove faithless."[92]

The essential elements of Homeric oath-making were the summoning of the gods as witnesses, the recital of conditions, the oath exchange, a symbolic act of solemnity (an animal sacrifice, libation, or joining of hands), and the final stipulation of a punishment for breaking faith.[93] Treaty engagements, and the oaths securing them, were kept distinct and separate in the religious conception of the ceremonial. As more secular formalities were developed in ancient Greece, including rules on publication, ratification, and periodic renewal of obligations,[94] the sense of obligation became more and more ingrained in the terms of the compact.

Consider, for example, the justly famous oath of the *hieromnemones*, the

---

[87] See Weinfeld, *supra* note 45, at 196–99. See also 1 Phillipson, *supra* note 10, at 391–94.

[88] See 1 Homer, *The Iliad* 137–39 (A. T. Murray transl. 1921) (Loeb Classical Library reprint 1971) (passages iii.268–301). For an extended discussion of this passage from *The Iliad*, as well as the influence of ancient Near Eastern treaty practices on Homeric events, see Karavites, *supra* note 65, at 22–25, 34, 41–44.

[89] See *ibid.* at 137 (passage iii.268–70) (where "the lordly heralds brought together the faith-ensuring pledges of the gods, and mingled the wine in a bowl, and poured water over hands of the princes").   [90] *Ibid.* (passage iii.276–80).   [91] *Ibid.* at 137–39 (iii.281–91).

[92] *Ibid.* at 139 (iii.298–301). See also Karavites, *supra* note 28, at 22.

[93] See Eugène Audinet, Les traces du droit international dans l'Iliade et dans l'Odyssée, 21 RGDIP 29, 31–32 (1914); Karavites, *supra* note 65, at 82–107.

[94] See Mosley, *supra* note 22, at 11, 26; 1 Phillipson, *supra* note 10, at 413–15.

representatives of Greek city-States deputized before the Amphictyonic Council:

I swear never to destroy any of the villages forming part of the amphictyony nor turn the bed so as to prevent the use of the running waters, either in time of peace or war, and if any people violates this rule I shall declare war against it and will destroy its towns. That if anyone pillages the property of the gods or in anywise becomes the accomplice of those who touch sacred things or aids them by his counsel, I will employ in avenging my feet, my hands, my voice, and all my strength.[95]

Because of its "archaic simplicity and brevity"[96] this oath, transcribed by the orator Aeschines, has been attributed to an early age of Greek history. In the oath itself, no imprecation is made for divine intervention. Only later, when the Council was forced in 585 BCE to take action against Cirrha, was a mighty oath sworn and that city's lands held forfeit to the gods.[97] In a similar vein was the c. 427 BCE treaty between Athens and Colophon, where the parties swore that "if I transgress this oath, may I utterly be destroyed, both myself and my family for all time, but if I keep my oath may there be an abundance of good things for me."[98]

Some writers have suggested that as belief in the very existence of the gods waned in ancient Greece, under the influence of the sophists, oaths in general (but particularly in international undertakings) lost their previous authority.[99] And it seems clear that Greek rational thought did not usually entertain the notion of divine retribution for breaches of international faith.[100] The only exception to this development is that the Greeks

---

[95] The English translation of this oath is drawn from J. H. Ralston, *International Arbitration from Athens to Locarno* 155 (1929) (citing A. Raeder, *L'arbitrage international chez les Hellenes* 165 (1912) (quoting Aeschines, *Speeches* 245–47 (Charles Darwin Adams transl. 1919) (Loeb Classical Library reprint 1988 reprint) (*De falsa Legatione*, passage 115))).

[96] H. B. Leech, *An Essay on Ancient International Law* 26 (1877). See also P. Bibikov, *Ocherk Mezhdunarodnaya Prava v Gretsii* [The Features of International Law in Greece] 44–45 (1852); D. B. Levin, *Istoriya Mezhdunarodnovo Prava* [A History of International Law] 15 (1962).

[97] See 1 Phillipson, *supra* note 10, at 388 (quoting Aeschines, *supra* note 95, at 393 (*Contra Ctesiphontem*, passage 109)).

[98] 1 *Translated Documents of Greece and Rome: Archaic Times to the End of the Peloponnesian War* 109–10 (Charles W. Fonora ed. transl. 2nd ed. 1983) (fragmented text corrected). See also Sir Frank Adcock and D. J. Mosley, *Diplomacy in Ancient Greece* 216–19 (1975) (collecting other examples); Ténékidès, *supra* note 41, at 521–23.

[99] See Hirzel, *supra* note 84, at 79–104; Plescia, *supra* note 86, at 86–87. For opposing views, see Raoul Lonis, *Les usages de la guerre entre grecs et barbares* 130 (1969); Raoul Lonis, *Guerre et religion en Grèce à l'époque classique* 50–57 (1979); 3 W. Kendrick Pritchett, *The Greek State at War* 2–10 (1979).

[100] This belief was firmly rooted in epic period or archaic Greece. See Peter Karavites, Diplomatic Envoys in the Homeric World, 34 RIDA 41, 74–75 (1987); Martin P. Nilsson, *Greek Folk Religion* 3–41, 102, 120 (1961).

continued to believe that the gods would directly punish infractions of their own interests, such as the defilement of a temple[101] or an offense against a herald or envoy (as occurred in the case of Darius' emissaries).[102] As will be reviewed in greater detail in Chapter 5,[103] the ancient Greeks developed secular means of ensuring good faith, including experiments with anti-deceit clauses in treaties and the exchange of hostages.[104]

It is important to indicate here that the oath did not disappear in Greek city-State relations. In later compacts, oaths were exchanged and deities invoked, but the actual sanction was either completely secular or left in doubt. In the treaty of alliance between Elis and Heraia, concluded sometime between 588 and 572 BCE according to the inscription found at Olympia,[105] a fine of a talent of silver was imposed against a party who failed to come to the aid of the other, or who defaced the record of the treaty.[106] In the alliance entered into between Athens and the Argive confederacy in 420 BCE, an oath was required to be taken over "full-grown victims" and with the formalities "deemed the most binding" by those States.[107]

The reference to "victims" has been hotly disputed by classicists. One theory holds that it meant that hostages were exchanged by the parties.[108] Another theory suggests that it was merely a confirmation of the practice of animal sacrifice, begun in the heroic age.[109] The treaty's requirement that it be ratified in the most solemn form by the contracting parties was completely consistent with its provision which specified the actual wording of the oath: "I will be true to the alliance, and will observe the agreement in all honesty and without fraud or hurt: I will not transgress it in any way or manner."[110] Likewise, in the oath sealing the Delian League of 478 BCE, a perpetual alliance against Persia, masses of iron were thrown

---

[101] See 1 Herodotus, *supra* note 22, at 23–25 (passage i.19–22) (Lydian ruler, Alyattes, raided the temple of Athena at Miletus, and was punished by divinely sent illness which was cured only when he agreed to rebuild the temple).

[102] See *supra* note 22 with text. See also Mosley, *supra* note 22, at 85–87.

[103] See Chapter 5, notes 241–272 and accompanying text.

[104] See also Lonis, *supra* note 99, at 108–11, 133, 139, 150. See also Raoul Lonis, Les otages dans les relations internationales en Grèce classique, in *Mélanges offerts à Léopold Sédar Senghor* 215 (1977).

[105] See Sir Paul Vinogradoff, Historical Types of International Law, in 1 *Biblioteca Visseriana Dissertationum ius internationale illustrantium* 1, 20 (1923).

[106] See Leech, *supra* note 96, at 27.   [107] 3 Thucydides, *supra* note 23, at 95 (passage v.47.8).

[108] See Vinogradoff, *supra* note 105, at 20.

[109] See *supra* notes 88–92 and accompanying text. Human sacrifice has never been seriously suggested, which is fortunate, since an ancient law of nations could hardly withstand the charge that that kind of ceremony was the source of its legal obligation.

[110] 3 Thucydides, *supra* note 23, at 95 (passage v.47.8).

into the sea and the incantation uttered that the oaths were to hold until the metal rose to the surface, that is, for all time.[111]

The Romans likewise believed that oaths were guaranteed by their gods. As Plutarch said of Roman practice, "Every oath ends in a curse on the perjurer."[112] The Roman notion of *fides* was, as already suggested in this chapter,[113] strongly related to the Greek principle of *pistis*. Both ideas involved a pledge of good faith.[114] Some scholars have suggested, however, that "the Greeks had greater freedom to interpret oaths than the Romans."[115] The reasoning behind this suggestion, made first by Rudolf Hirzel,[116] was that the Romans had already conceptualized in their law strong penalties punishing perjury,[117] known generically as the formulas of *dolus malus* or *sine dolo malo*.[118]

The basic structure of Roman oath-making likewise followed Greek and ancient Near Eastern patterns,[119] but the symbolism did diverge.[120] Some oaths and curses used by the Romans had Greek origins,[121] but reciprocity, or duality of obligation, was the essential underpinning of Roman oaths. Oaths were exchanged in a ceremony called the *sponsio*, which

---

[111] See 2 Plutarch, *supra* note 21, at 289 (*Aristides*, passage xxv.1). See also 20 Aristotle, *The Athenian Constitution* 73 (H. Rackham transl. 1935) (Loeb Classical Library reprint 1981) (passage xxiii.5). For a similar oath, sworn by the Phocaeans, see 1 Herodotus, *supra* note 22, at 207 (passage i.165). For glosses on the oath of the Delian League, see J. A. O. Larsen, *Representative Government in Greek and Roman History* 49–50 (1955); Martin, *supra* note 41, at 152 n. 1; R. Meiggs, *The Athenian Empire* 46 (1972); Jacobson, *supra* note 62, at 256. For a suggestion that the iron-sinking metaphor had earlier, Near Eastern origins, see Jacobson, *supra* note 62, at 257–58 n. 6.

[112] 4 Plutarch, *Moralia* 75–76 (Frank Cole Babbitt transl. 1936) (Loeb Classical Library reprint 1972) (*Quaestiones Romanae*, passage 44).   [113] See *supra* note 12 with text.

[114] Compare 4 Herodotus, *supra* note 22, at 105 (passage viii.105) (*pistis* as "full trust") with 3 Livy, *supra* note 35, at 427–29, 439–43, 449–50 (passages viii.21, 25 and 27). See also Hirzel, *supra* note 84, 137–41; 1 Phillipson, *supra* note 10, at 393–94 (collecting appearances of the term *fides* in Latin literature).   [115] Wheeler, *supra* note 85, 169, at 266.

[116] See Hirzel, *supra* note 84, at 22, 41, 48. Professor Hirzel was primarily glossing 21 Cicero, *De Officiis* 387 (Walter Miller transl. 1913) (Loeb Classical Library reprint 1990) (passage iii.29.108), and 5 Livy, *supra* note 35, at 375 (passage xxii.53.11).

[117] See 4 Digest, *supra* note 35, at 803 (48.4.4; Scaevola, *Rules* 4).

[118] See Wheeler, *supra* note 85, 169, at 266–67 and n. 53.

[119] See 1 Phillipson, *supra* note 10, at 415–18.

[120] See 1 *ibid.* at 394–96; Watson, *supra* note 132, at 8–9, 31–33 (discussing the use of the peculiarly Roman symbolism of the twig or herb held by the *fetial*, called the *verbena*).

[121] For example, the Romans modified the metaphor of sinking iron ingots as symbolic of a perpetual peace. Instead, the dominant metaphor was ostracism and removal, symbolized by the casting out of the rock or stone. See 2 Polybius, *infra* note 126, at 61 (passage iii.25.7–9) (treaty of 279 BCE between Rome and Carthage); 4 Plutarch, *supra* note 21, at 357 (*Sulla*, passage x.4) (oath imposed by Sulla on Cinna). See also *infra* note 127 and text.

marked the conclusion of a treaty.[122] Not surprisingly, Janus is said to have been the protector of alliances, "his double face symbolizing the two peoples united by the treaty of peace."[123]

There was also a double character to the sanctions invoked in Roman oaths. In the twelfth book of the *Aeneid*, Aeneas makes a treaty with Latinus, and the latter swore:

by Earth, Sea, Sky and the twin brood of Latona and Janus the double-facing, and the might of nether gods and grim Pluto's shrine: this let our Father hear, who seals treaties with his thunderbolt. I touch the altars, I take to witness the fires and the gods between us; no time shall break this peace and truce in Italy, howsoever fortune fall; nor shall any force turn my will aside, not if it dissolve land into water in turmoil of deluge, or melt heaven in hell . . .[124]

The penalty alluded to here was the direct, divine intervention that we have seen before. The malefactor would be struck down by Jupiter's or Zeus' thunderbolt. In other treaties, the fear of being punished by the gods was made even more explicit. Livy reported that a member of the college of *fetials*, when solemnizing a treaty, would declare that if the Romans were "the first to violate [any of the conditions of the agreement] deliberately by public concert, then on that day, O Jupiter, do thou strike down the Roman people, as I shall here strike down this pig; and do thou strike them all the more as thou are more powerful."[125]

When the Romans made treaties with Carthage a very different metaphor for retribution was used. The Carthaginians preferred, apparently, to swear by the gods of their fathers.[126] So when the first peace treaty was made between the two nations, in the fifth century BCE, the oath made, according to Polybius, was:

---

[122] See Hans-Ulrich Scupin, History of the Law of Nations: Ancient Times to 1648, in 7 *Encyclopedia of Public International Law* 132, 138–39 (Rudolph Bernhardt ed. 1984).

[123] 1 Phillipson, *supra* note 10, at 389 (citing Servius, *Ad Aeneida Commentarii*, passage xii.198).

[124] Virgil, *Aeneid* 278 (J. W. Mackail transl. 1908) (passage xii.197–205).

[125] 1 Livy, *supra* note 35, at 85 (passage i.24.6–9). The provenance of the oath that Livy narrates has been hotly disputed. See R. M. Ogilvie, *A Commentary on Livy, Books 1–5*, at 109–10 (1965).

[126] See 2 Polybius, *The Histories* 61 (W. R. Paton transl. 1922) (Loeb Classical Library reprint 1975) (passage iii.25). See also Barré, *supra* note 60, at 90, 101 (who is at slight variance with this conclusion since the Carthaginians swore oaths to their national deities and also spirits in nature). Professor Barré reaches the conclusion that Carthaginian treaty oaths held more in common with Hittite and Assyrian models, and were uninfluenced by Roman forms. See *ibid.* at 101–02. See also Bickerman, *supra* note 82, at 3–5. For more on the differences between Roman and Carthaginian oath-taking, see Louise E. Matthaei, On the Classification of Roman Allies, 1 CQ 182, 202 (1907).

If I abide by this oath may [Jupiter] bless me; but if I do otherwise in thought or act; may all others prosper in their countries, under their laws, in their livelihood, and preserve their household gods and tombs: may I alone be cast out, even as this stone is now.

Whereupon the officiating *fetial* hurled a stone from his hand.[127] This oath emphasized social ostracism, but not divine vengeance. In this pledge, as in that made between Rome and Carthage, the inventoried items, the symbols of prosperity, were actually present at the solemnization of the treaty. They were very real signifiers for the bounties of peace and of society, as well as the hazards that came with war, and with breaking faith. These metaphors for good faith and oath-taking appear to have formed a common tradition in the ancient world.

Ritual and custom

In ancient Israel, Greece, and Rome, two distinct forms of oath-making were common. In some, the guarantor of the treaty was an angry god. In others, it was the fear of chaos. This second class of pledges was evidence of what I call the "social" sanction in an ancient law of nations. The rituals described were made to reinforce a punishment that was not immediately connected with divine intervention. Instead, the implicit fear was that the gods would abandon the State to its enemies, and that all that the nation held dear – its lands, its livelihood, its particular social order – would be lost.

Rituals give symbolic validation to States and their rulers. Thomas Franck has suggested that:

[i]n the modern state system, ritual and other kinds of symbolic validation play much the same role as in ancient and medieval societies, integrated by inclusion and exclusion, seducing subjects into obeying rules and rulers, validating the exercise of power and generally contributing to the legitimization of the institutions and rules of the society.[128]

Although international society is "underendowed with such symbolic validation,"[129] it does attempt to legitimize itself through rituals.

This was especially true for the law of nations in antiquity, where rituals were nothing more than an expression of custom. More than that, rituals which strengthened the sense of international legal obligation

---

[127] 2 Polybius, *supra* note 126, at 61 (passage iii.25).
[128] Thomas Franck, Legitimacy in the International System, 82 AJIL 705, 729–30 (1988).
[129] *Ibid.* at 730.

were invariably connected with powerful institutions in ancient civilizations. The custom of antiquity should not, however, be confused with the
"customary international law" of today. Although Pindar's maxim, that
"custom is the king of all things,"[130] may have been respected by Greek
rhetoricians and Roman jurists, there is little evidence of an appreciation
by ancient peoples of custom as an external *source* of the law of nations.
Instead, custom provided the institutional basis for the formalism of
ritual,[131] and that, in turn, gave an additional strength to international
undertakings. Custom and ritual in international life were internal to the
ancient State.

In antiquity there were two kinds of ritual institutions concerned with
the law of nations. First, there were priesthoods charged with the keeping
of sacred texts. These writings, after consultation and interpretation, provided guidance for the conduct of relations with other States. The Biblical
scriptures of the Israelites were, of course, the preeminent instance of a
priestly caste responsible for the promulgation of the divine law. That law
concerned every aspect of human life, but only peripherally did it carry
instructions on the proper behavior of States. The custom which was
detailed in those writings was inaccessible without the work of priests
and jurists.

We have already seen manifestations of the second kind of ritual institution. The Spartan *talthybiadai* and the Roman *fetials* were sacerdotal colleges, tightly organized groups of functionaries given both sacred and
secular duties.[132] Their holy rites included regular observances of sacrifices and festivities. Their secular responsibilities involved participation
in three ceremonies that critically defined the ritual character of an
ancient law of nations: the reception of ambassadors, the making of treaties, and the declaration of war.

The customs surrounding the titles, powers, and privileges of envoys

---

[130] This was quoted by 2 Herodotus, *supra* note 22, at 51 (passage iii.38).
[131] See 1 Phillipson, *supra* note 10, at 68.
[132] For a sampling of the literature concerning the origins of the *fetial* institution, see K.
Latte, *Römische Religionsgeschichte* 121–24 (1960); Theodor Mommsen, *Römische Staatsrecht*
(1899) (rep. 1952); Ogilvie, *supra* note 125, at 100–12, 127–36; Alan Watson, *International
Law in Archaic Rome: War and Religion* 1 (1993); T. R. S. Broughton, Mistreatment of
Foreign Legates and the Fetial Priests: Three Roman Cases, 41 *Phoenix* 50, 58–62 (1987);
Frank, *supra* note 24, 147, at 335–42; F. W. Walbank, Roman Declarations of War in the
Third and Second Centuries, 44 *CP* 15 (1949); Thomas Wiedemann, The Fetials: A
Reconsideration, 36 *CQ* 480, 486–88 (1987). For more on the selection of individuals
serving as *fetials*, see Watson, *supra* note 132, at 8 (citing 1 Dionysius of Halicarnassus,
Roman Antiquities 521–27 (Ernest Cary and Edward Spelman transl. 1937) (Loeb Classical
Library reprint 1990) (passage ii.72)).

"are among the oldest of symbols and rites associated with the conduct of international relations."[133] In the law of nations of antiquity, ambassadors were the embodiment of the secular State. The dispatch and reception of envoys was the ultimate symbolic act of State equality and of peace. To offend an ambassador was an insult to the sending nation, and was an invitation for war.[134]

In Greece, the institution of envoys was traced back to the earliest recorded history, and beyond into the realm of myths and legends. The Greek heralds were said to be of divine stock, descended from Hermes, and they adopted his serpent staff as their emblem.[135] Gradually, the mythic inspirations for ambassadors gave way to more pragmatic and secular roles. Also in Greece, the office of herald became responsible for purely ceremonial transactions.[136] Nevertheless, diplomacy was impossible without the heralds, because without them safe conducts could never have been arranged and treaties never concluded. Ambassadors, appointed officials charged with carrying messages and concluding nego- tiations, were also dependent on the privileges and immunities that were accorded to heralds. The most important of these protections was the right to relay an unpleasant message, and to be spared punishment. This immunity was secured in ancient Greece by the fiction that the envoy was sent not by men, but by the gods.[137]

For ancient diplomacy, ritual and custom played a key part in maintain- ing a stable State system. The practice of receiving ambassadors had its origins in the belief that the envoy was the personification of the sending State and its gods. The ritual of accepting an envoy was the same as for accepting a foreign god. Because of the particularistic impulses of ancient religions, it was an extraordinary concession to admit a representative of a foreign nation into the sacred precincts of the State. In its earliest expres- sions, diplomacy was a rejection of nationalistic religions. In actuality, the restraint that ancient nations showed in respecting the privileges and immunities of ambassadors was not really religious. Instead, the ritual institutions of the State provided the "internal" source of that compulsion.

---

[133] Franck, *supra* note 128, at 733.
[134] See 2 Samuel 10 (where King David responded to an insult, made by Hannun, King of Ammon, to his ambassadors, by waging a violent war); Rosenne, *supra* note 78, at 141 (describing a later incident, told by Josephus, of Jewish ambassadors being killed by nomadic tribesmen and of the resulting conflict).
[135] See D. J. Mosley, *supra* note 22, at 87–88.   [136] See *ibid.* at 88–89.
[137] See 1 *The Iliad*, *supra* note 88, at 29 (passage i.334) (where Achilles addresses Agamemnon's ambassadors: "Hail, heralds, messengers of Zeus and men").

In contrast, the declaration of war by one ancient State against another was a reaffirmation of nationalist impulses in religion. Whereas the reception of ambassadors symbolically indicated accommodation and peace, the ritual for opening hostilities was a celebration of exclusion and superiority. All ancient civilizations had ceremonies for the proper sanctioning of war, involving the two kinds of ritual institutions already mentioned: the interpreters of sacred texts and the sacerdotal colleges. These customs centered around two distinct, but obviously interrelated, tasks. The first was to decide if war would be sacred, good, and just or if it would be profane, evil, and unjust. Their second duty was to oversee the rites that would invoke the gods' support for war, and to ensure victory.

No ritual in ancient international relations was as solemn or as significant as the decision to initiate hostilities. That choice was immediately confirmed or denied by the nation's own deities. If the war was just, and the formalities proper, then triumph would be forthcoming. If not, defeat and despair would visit the State. For the Israelites, the choice of war was dictated by priestly reference to divine texts.[138] As will be remembered from the tale of the Gibeonites,[139] the Jews were commanded in the Pentateuch to wage a religious war (*mitzvah*) against the seven Canaanite nations and against Amalek.[140] All other wars were "optional," in the sense that they could be engaged in for territorial expansion or for other reasons. The only legal distinction made in the Bible between religious and optional wars concerned the conduct, and not the commencement, of hostilities.[141]

In both Greece and Rome, no scriptural text provided explicit guidance for when war would be just or unjust. The custom for declaring war was a ritual intended for any set of factual circumstances. This sometimes gave the proceedings a very formalistic flavor. In epic Greece, the primary concern was that satisfaction for injuries be correctly sought before the conflict began.[142] For the Greeks, the justification for war was important, particularly where there was a violation of a sacred duty owed by a State.

For Rome, it was the ritual that mattered and not the gravity of the

---

[138] See Alfred P. Rubin, The Concept of Neutrality in International Law, 16 *Denver Journal of International Law and Policy* 353 (1988).

[139] See *supra* notes 74–77 and accompanying text.   [140] See Deuteronomy 7:11, 25:19.

[141] But see Deuteronomy 20:10–12 (which prescribes for *mitzvah* that a besieged city be allowed to surrender); see also Rosenne, *supra* note 78, at 139–40 (for more on the distinction between religious and optional war).

[142] See e.g., 1 Homer, *The Iliad*, *supra* note 88, at 131, 181, 253 (passages iii.205; iv.384; and v.803).

offense that gave rise to the declaration of war.[143] The Romans craved regularity, and they fashioned a fabulously sophisticated ceremonial for declaring war. Like the Greeks, the essence of the rite was the demand for reparations from the foreign state, the *rerum repetitio*.[144] According to Livy, the *pater patratus*, the leader of the delegation of the *fetial* college, appeared at the frontiers of the offending nation, and said:

Hear, O Jupiter, hear, ye territories [naming the country in question], let the law of heaven hear. I am the state envoy of the Roman people; I come, as their ambassador, in all justice and piety, and let my words gain credence. [Whereupon the specific request for reparation was made.] If I unjustly or impiously demand those persons or those things to be given up to me [in cases of a request for extradition or cession of territory], as the messenger of the Roman people, then never permit me to enjoy my native country.[145]

After a period of grace had passed, the *pater patratus* reappeared at the frontier and remonstrated with the defaulting nation and called on Jupiter and Janus to bear witness to the injustice of the other state's refusal.[146]

The traditional view of classicists has been that the Roman formula for declaring war was an oath.[147] The *fetial* swore it, not only in his individual capacity but also as the personification of the nation. The sanction for making an unfounded request for reparation was individual privation for the messenger and, implicitly, defeat for Rome in the ensuing conflict.[148] The *fetial* who bore false witness in these solemn ceremonies invited the anger of the gods, whilst Rome would have to fear the disorder that defeat

---

[143] But cf. Scupin, *supra* note 122, at 138 (who suggests that Cicero, *De re Publica* 213 (Clinton Walker Keyes transl. 1928) (Loeb Classical Library reprint 1988) (passage iii.23–35), maintained that both the formalities and the *iusta causa* had to be proper).

[144] See 2 Phillipson, *supra* note 10, at 329. See also William V. Harris, *War and Imperialism in Republican Rome, 327–70 BC*, at 169–71 (1979); Louise E. Matthaei, The Place of Arbitration and Mediation in Ancient Systems of International Ethics, 2 CQ 241, 248–50 (1908).

[145] 1 Livy, *supra* note 35, at 115–17 (passage i.32.6–14).

[146] See *ibid.* at 117 (passage i.32.10). For other aspects of the curious *fetial* ritual for declaring war, see Harris, *supra* note 144, at 171; Christiane Saulnier, Le rôle des prêtres fetiaux et l'application du "ius *fetiale*" à Rome, 58 *Revue historique du droit français et étranger* 171, 186–87 (1980).

[147] See Warde Fowler, *The Religious Experience of the Roman People* 128–30 (1911); Max Kaser, *Das römische Zivilprozessrecht* 18 (1966); Dieter Nörr, *Aspekte des römischen Völkerrechts: Die Bronzetafel von Alcántara* 13 (1989); Tenney Frank, The Import of the Fetial Institution, 7 CP 335, 337–40 (1912). For an historiography of this position, see Watson, *supra* note 132, at 10–20.

[148] See Matthaei, *supra* note 144, at 248–50. See also Jean Bayet, *Histoire politique et psychologique de la religion romaine* 165 (1969); Georges Dumézil, *La religion romaine archaïque* 208–45 (1966); Saulnier, *supra* note 146, at 186–87.

in war brought. For these reasons, the prevailing view has been that the *fetial* institution and its war-declaring ritual acted as a means to counter Roman wars of aggression.[149]

This view of the role of the *fetials*, as a social institution in mediating religious impulses and the demands of international relations, has been sharply challenged of late. After examining the historical record of Roman expansion, more recent writers have pungently noted that the *fetial* ritual must have been designed to assuage guilty feelings surrounding the Roman initiation of unjustified wars of aggression, as well as serving mystificatory and propaganda functions.[150] Thomas Wiedemann's recent scholarship has softened this skepticism somewhat, correctly emphasizing the archaic ritual of *fetial* procedures for war-declaration and likening them to early, private law methods of dispute settlement.[151]

The most recent review of the Roman ritual for declaring war was made by Alan Watson in his book, *International Law in Archaic Rome*.[152] Watson's thesis is simple, but has broad implications for an understanding of the nature and sources of international legal obligation in antiquity. He suggests that in the *fetial* procedure for declaring war, captured in the incantation of the *pater patratus* rendered above,[153] the *fetial* did not invoke the Roman gods as witnesses of the *bona fides* of Rome's grievances. Instead, the gods served as *judges* of the correctness of Rome's just war (*iustum bellum*).[154] Watson reaches this interpretation based on the similarity between the terms used by the *pater patratus*, as narrated by Livy, and archaic Roman private law forms of action, including the *legis actio* (initiating a law-suit) and the *legis actio per manus iniectionem* (used to enforce a judgment).[155]

Watson thus concludes that:

[t]his approach to the declaration of war has important consequences. First, the Romans have the psychological advantage of knowing that, even before the fighting begins, they have the verdict of the gods. Their war is just. Second, this conclusion is not shaken even by a Roman defeat. A defeat in the just war shows that the Romans were unable to execute the god's judgment. Execution of judgment is not the affair of the gods.[156]

---

[149] See Tenney Frank, *Roman Imperialism* 9 (1914); H. H. Scullard, *From the Gracchi to Nero* 2 (1959).

[150] See Harris, *supra* note 144, at 171; J.-M. Michel, *L'extradition du général en droit romain*, 39 *Latomus* 675 (1980); Saulnier, *supra* note 146, at 186–87.

[151] See Wiedemann, *supra* note 132, at 485–88.   [152] See *supra* note 132.

[153] See *supra* note 145 and accompanying text.   [154] See Watson, *supra* note 132, at 10–11.

[155] See *ibid.* at 20–27.   [156] *Ibid.* at 27–28.

It is important to remember in this context that the *pater patratus*, when demanding restitution, calls down the wrath of Jupiter upon himself if his demands are unjust. He does not seek divine vengeance on the opposing State if they fail to make the needed reparations.[157] Likewise, the *fetials* "have no role to play in the conduct of the [ensuing] war,"[158] either by accepting the surrender of a defeated community or in overseeing the vows of a military leader seeking victory in the conflict.

Elsewhere in his volume, Watson decides that the Roman gods did not really serve as direct guarantors for treaties concluded under a *fetial* procedure.[159] His observation is also that the *fetial* process for declaring wars and sealing treaties was "remarkably unreligious."[160] Watson acknowledges that this flies in the face of the sacred character of the *fetials* as an institution and the oaths and formulas they administered. "But," Watson notes, "the end envisaged for the oath is entirely secular, the protection from breach . . . which itself has no religious content."[161] The process of making treaties and declaring war was stripped, at least in Roman practice, of its religious aspects and was transformed into social institutions. This was consistent with the wider transformation of Roman state religion into a system "of observance, not of belief or theology . . . of keeping man – especially man in his public function – in proper contact with the gods."[162]

Declaring war, receiving envoys, and making treaties were institutions which depended, for their sense of obligation, on the rituals that preserved the ancient State against chaos. This distinctive "social" sanction came, over time (and especially in the practices of Mediterranean cultures), to dominate the thinking of those concerned with the enforcement of good faith in international relations.

Reason and rhetoric

But might the *pater patratus* have feared anything else when he made his declaration? Or the Spartans when, over the objections of the *talthybiadai*, they put Darius' envoys to death? Or the Israelites when they honored

---

[157] See *ibid.* at 53.   [158] *Ibid.*   [159] See *ibid.* at 31–34.
[160] *Ibid.* at 42. See also A. Mishulin, Obyavleniye Voini i Zaklucheniye Mira oo Drevnik Rimlyan [The Declaration of War and the Conclusion of Peace in Ancient Rome] 10–11 *Historical Journal* 106, 108–09 (1944).
[161] *Ibid.* But see Karl-Heinz Ziegler, Das Völkerrecht der römischen Republik, in 1 *Aufstieg und Niedergang der römischen Welt* 68, 70 (H. Temporini ed. 1972) (who takes the opposite view).   [162] See Watson, *supra* note 132, at 66.

their pact with the Gibeonites? The received wisdom is that ancient peoples respected their international legal obligations only when the religious command of obedience prevailed. I have suggested here that that command could be muted, to become only a quiet whisper of duty. What remained in those instances was a no less forceful observance of the rituals and customs which gave regularity, structure, and success to an ancient State's international life. These rites were fashioned by ancient people's need for social order. Custom, as distinct from religion, was a decisive motivation for keeping faith.

Was reason, as distinct from religion or ritual, also a significant impulse for State behavior? My answer is "yes," but it is a proposition most difficult to prove. One problem is in defining the ancient conception of reason. If reason was just an intellectual negation of religious belief, the absence of a fear of divine retribution and social disintegration, then the modern political philosopher has an easy task. Ancient States obviously conducted themselves out of self-interest, ambition, and greed. They were no different in this respect from today's nations. To believe otherwise would be a perverse interpretation of human nature.

Yet, that is not enough for the intellectual historian. What remains is to answer the other, thornier, question: did ancient peoples see the law of nations (with its essential obligation to keep faith) as an idea whole and complete without reference to belief? If there had been no gods to guarantee an ancient State's promise, and no social order that had to be preserved by that guarantee, what other reasons would have persuaded that State to keep its word? The question is not whether the obligation, itself, would always have been respected. That asks too much of the ancient law of nations, just as it demands too much of modern international law. Instead, the emphasis should be on the rhetoric of ancient international law, the arguments that were made, irrespective of their success, to convince a State to keep faith or break faith.

Most of these arguments had nothing, of course, to do with law, or even morality. They were about power: the power to break treaties with impunity, or to violate the rights of ambassadors, or to begin a war without notice. The plea of the Plataean deputies[163] was delivered in the face of the overwhelming power of their Spartan and Theban victors. The arguments used by the Plataean deputies were, as noted above, virtually devoid of religious references. Instead, they said that their conduct comported with the "universal law" of Greece, while that of the Thebans did not. The only

---

[163] See *supra* notes 24 and 28 with accompanying text.

sanction they invoked against the Spartans, when they found against them and executed their garrison, was the indignity of mankind.[164] No lightning bolts from Zeus. No later defeat traced back to the act of infamy. Just unfavorable public opinion.[165]

Consider a similar tableau laid in 433 BCE. Years earlier, war-weary Athens had concluded a truce with Sparta. One of Sparta's allies, Corinth, was waging a war against a former colony, Corcyra, and was about to launch a renewed attack. Corcyra sent envoys to Athens seeking an alliance, which would have placed Athens in violation of the earlier truce.[166] The Corcyraeans argued that it was expedient and necessary for Athens to break the truce and come to their aid. The Corinthians also sent a delegation to Athens. "Do not say to yourselves," they contended, "that one thing is just, but that in the event of war another thing is expedient; for the true path of expediency is the path of right ... [T]he material advantage generally accrues to him whose conduct is least open to moral obliquity."[167] The Athenians adopted a prudent course by making a defensive alliance only with Corcyra, but were later drawn into the war with Corinth. The following year, an Athenian envoy in Sparta was called upon to explain his country's violation of the truce. He concluded his discourse on the virtues of might with this rhetorical flourish: "Did justice ever deter anyone from taking by force whatever he could?"[168]

A fundamental premise of today's international law is that no matter how lawless a State's conduct, it can never be justified by utility or by overweening power. The rule of law means, if nothing else, that defenses of State behavior must, at least, *appear* neutral, principled, and consistent. The statements of the Corcyraean and Athenian envoys give credence to the conclusion that an ancient law of nations, when not enforced by religious beliefs, had no sanction at all.

This conclusion is, however, belied by the actual practice of ancient peoples, who were fully aware of the risk of breach of faith in any aspect of international relations, whether in the reception of envoys, the conduct of hostilities, or the making of agreements. The Greeks especially

---

[164] See 2 Thucydides, *supra* note 23, at 101 (passage iii.57).

[165] For the role of indignation in public opinion as being a force shaping international legal obligation in ancient Greece, see Bauslaugh, *supra* note 39, at 52–54 (discussing Greek terms for justice (*dikaion*), reasonableness (*to eikos*), and expedience (*to sympheron*)); Martin, *supra* note 41, at 404–12 (extensively glossing Thucydides). See also Karavites, *supra* note 28, at 114–17 (on Greek virtue of *aretē*, helping the weak to "claim ... justice in interstate relations").

[166] See 1 Thucydides, *supra* note 23, at 57–59 (passage i.32).

[167] *Ibid.* at 75–77 (passage i.42).   [168] *Ibid.* at 129–31 (passage i.76).

understood the difficulties in treaty enforcement, recognizing the dangers not only of the very act of making faith but in the legal exercise of subsequently interpreting the terms of an agreement. Attic Greek even had a term for unscrupulous, or sophistic, constructions of treaties,[169] and the Romans came close to replicating such concerns.[170] The use of sophistic interpretation was, nevertheless, an accepted means of circumventing obligation under an (arguably) ambiguous treaty text, while also avoiding a charge of perjury in violation of a divinely guaranteed or socially sanctioned oath.[171] What is significant, though, is the extent to which ancient peoples responded to the intellectual phenomenon of chicanery in the legal interpretation of international obligations by adopting legal antidotes, including anti-deceit clauses in treaties.[172]

What modern publicists also forget is that the same intellect which could extol might over right, was at least liberated from religion to the extent that it could also exalt justice over expediency. Being freed from the fear of divine retribution or of social disintegration meant that the ancient mind could choose to keep faith for the intrinsic value of the promise. Having that choice made State relations the province of humankind, and not the domain of deities.

International arbitration, as practiced in the Greek and Roman civilizations, was an excellent example of this transformation. The institution of settling disputes by the decision of a third party was begun, reputedly, by the Olympian gods.[173] These legends were a potent metaphor for relations between city-States. Their mythical character reinforced the practice and legitimized it as a means of resolving quarrels between sovereign and equal political entities. This was the religious aspect of arbitration.

The next step was to ritualize dispute settlement into an institutional context, partly religious and partly secular. The Oracle of Delphi, at least in Greece, played this role. Not only was it a sacred precinct, a place for putting questions to the god Apollo, it was also the *raison d'être* for an intergovernmental organization, the Amphictyonic Council previously men-

---

[169] See Wheeler, *supra* note 85, 169, at 259 (citing Eustathius, *ad Od.* xix.396). See also Hirzel, *supra* note 84, at 75–79; Plescia, *supra* note 86, at 84–85; Luitgard Camerer, *Praktische Klugheit bei Herodot* 67 (1965).

[170] See 21 Cicero, *supra* note 116, at 35 (*De Officiis*, passage i.10.33) ("calumnia quadam et nimis callida, sed malitiosa iuris interpretatione"); 3 Tacitus, *Histories* 77–79 (John Jackson transl. 1931) (Loeb Classical Library reprint 1979) (passage iv.41.2) ("trepidis et verba iuris iurandi per varias artes mutantibus").

[171] See Hirzel, *supra* note 84, at 43–45; Marcel Detienne and Jean-Pierre Vernant, *Cunning Intelligence in Greek Culture and Society* 29 and n. 3 (J. Lloyd transl. 1978). See also Wheeler, *supra* note 85, 169, at 269–74 (for a catalogue of classical references to treaty deceit).

[172] See generally, Wheeler, *supra* note 85, 169.

[173] See 2 Phillipson, *supra* note 10, at 129–30 (for examples cited by Pausanias).

tioned in this chapter.[174] The Oracle was, however, an abominable arbitrator. Difficult questions were often evaded, and it often suggested that an individual be selected to decide the matter.[175] When awards were rendered they typically lacked the clarity and precision needed to settle the matter authoritatively. For example, Clazomenae and Cyme disputed the ownership of a temple located in a territory nearly equidistant between the two cities. The Pythia gave possession to that city "which should be first to sacrifice at [the temple]: but each must start from their own territory at sunrise on the same day, which should be fixed by common agreement."[176] The Oracle's solution was to invite the disputants to make a mad dash to the temple steps.

The Greeks did not find this kind of award to be intellectually satisfying. So, as we might expect, arbitrations became a largely secular, and reasoned, process. Yet, ceremony was never abandoned. It was used only to strengthen the integrity of the institution. Consider, for example, the arbitration held between Calymna and Cos in the second or first century BCE. Cos had espoused the claim of two of its citizens whose ancestors had, many years before, lent money to Calymna.[177] The Cnidians were appointed as arbitrators, and the members of the tribunal took this oath:

I swear by Jupiter, the Lycian Apollo, and by the earth that I will judge in the case between the parties under oath as will appear to be most just. I will not judge according to one witness if this witness does not appear to me to tell the truth. I have not received any present with relation to this suit, neither myself nor any other for me, man or woman, nor by any detour whatsoever. May I prosper as I adhere to my oath, but unhappiness to me if I perjure myself.[178]

This oath confirmed not only the impartiality of the judges, but also participation in a very detailed arbitral process, specified in the inscription which the Cnidians raised when they rendered an award for Calymna.[179]

Records of Greek arbitrations also offer a glimpse of what ancient jurists considered to be evidence of State practice. In making submissions before international tribunals, parties were known to have offered records of previous treaties or decisions, maps and charts, the writings of historians, interpretations of myths and legends, archeological evidence, and even eye-witness testimony.[180] Greek orators were fairly indiscriminate in selecting material intended to persuade a tribunal. Usually, historic and

---

[174] See *supra* notes 39–42 with text.   [175] See 2 Phillipson, *supra* note 10, at 133.
[176] M. N. Tod, *International Arbitration Amongst the Greeks* 95 (1913).
[177] See *ibid.* at 49.   [178] J. H. Ralston, *supra* note 95, at 161.
[179] See Tod, *supra* note 176, at 120–22.
[180] See Ralston, *supra* note 95, at 163–64; Tod, *supra* note 176, at 132–52; 2 Phillipson, *supra* note 10, at 162–63.

mythic evidence supporting one party's territorial claim was successfully rebutted by the other litigant's use of more contemporaneous records showing prescriptive rights.[181]

The evidence used in Greek arbitration illustrated the reasoned character of the awards, which was essential for their legitimacy and enforcement. As a method of dispute settlement, arbitration did not rely on divine authority for its sanction, or even on the institutional power of an oracle or *amphictyony*. Awards were respected because they were the product of a rhetorical exchange where the interested parties could marshal whatever arguments or forms of persuasion they wished. The choice was not mandated by an oracle or by a god. By placing the decision in the hands of a third party, the parties knew that awards could be dictated by reason or by passion, knowledge or folly, fairness or prejudice. Which was nothing more than saying that the matter was decided by other men.

One point that remains on the subject of the role of reason in the development of ancient international law is the concept of *ius gentium* under Roman law.[182] The modern historiographic jurisprudence of the *ius gentium* is extensive, beginning with Sir Henry Maine's thesis that it represented the totality of customs and usages practiced by Rome and her Latin neighbors in the conduct of their international and commercial relations.[183] This view was, of course, a restatement of Savigny's assertion[184] that the *ius gentium* was strictly a private law phenomenon in Rome, a view which has prevailed to this day.[185] And, indeed, a careful reading of the Roman law sources[186] makes clear that the *ius gentium*, as a branch of law distinct from the *fetial* procedure[187] and even from equity,[188] was viewed as a rational collection of unwritten laws or customs.[189]

---

[181] See Adcock and Mosley, *supra* note 98, at 185 (Athens' 346 BCE submissions to Macedon for a claim to Amphipolis); Tod, *supra* note 176, at 150–51.

[182] See 1 Phillipson, *supra* note 10, at 70–76.

[183] See Maine, *supra* note 1, at 86. See also Sir Henry Maine, *Village Communities in the East and West* 193–94 (1871). Maine's discussion of *ius gentium* was intended primarily as a rebuttal to the notion that it was later transformed into the modern law of nations. See Maine, *supra* note 1, at 43–44, 80–83. For the same view, see Wheaton, *supra* note 14, at 26.

[184] See 1 F. C. von Savigny, *System des heutigen römischen Rechts* book i, ch. iii, § 22 (1840).

[185] See 1 Phillipson, *supra* note 10, at 72–76.

[186] See 1 *Digest*, *supra* note 35, at 14 (1.3.35; Hermogenian, *Epitome of the Law* 1); 4 *ibid.* at 922 (50.7.18(17); Pomponius, *Quintus Mucius* 37). See also Watson, *supra* note 132, at 87–88 n. 12.

[187] See Edward Poste, *Gaii Institutiones juris civilis* 358 (1890); A. Chauveau, Le droit des gens dans la rapports de Rome avec les peuples de l'antiquité, 4 *Nouvelle Revue historique de droit français et étranger* 393, 409 (1891).

[188] See Sallust, *The Jugurthine War* 212 (J. C. Rolfe transl. 1921) (Loeb Classical Library reprint 1985) (passage xxxv.7). The incident discussed in this passage is considered in Chapter 4, at notes 187–189 and accompanying text.

[189] See Cicero, *supra* note 116, at 339 (*De Officiis*, passage iii.17).

But if the *ius gentium* is understood in a more generic, and less technical (or juristic) sense, it does provide a useful coda to this discussion of the ancient mind's engagement with international legal obligation. Just as the Greek concept of *nomoi Hellenes* or *agraphoi nomoi*[190] conveyed a sense of a binding set of customary norms on international behavior in the Greek world, the *ius gentium* – when extended to the *fetial* law and procedure – may have indicated a similar understanding on the part of the Romans. But custom in this sense is different from the form of sanction that arises when one polity fears social disintegration for the failure to observe some stricture of international obligation. Custom as an unwritten law of nations was the primary means by which ancient polities undertook obligations.[191] To the extent they made written treaties, they regarded the written documents (as David Lorton has suggested) as "only evidentiary, and not as dispositive."[192] This reasoned compliance with standards of international conduct provided its own enforcement mechanism.[193] And, in any event, "compliance in the preponderance of instances is a better criterion for 'law' than the existence of an enforcement mechanism."[194] In these expressions and usages, a reason-based construction of obligation in the ancient law of nations was merged and fused with custom and social sanction, religion and fear of divine punishment.

Conclusion

An ancient law of nations was, at its heart, sanctioned by belief, but its first principles were governed by ritual, by custom and by reason. The belief in enforcing good faith was not, however, exclusively religious. This chapter argues that the people of antiquity imagined three different sources of international legal obligations. Their fear of direct, divine retribution was plainly religious. Their concern for maintaining social order was motivated more by a dread of chaos, than of drawing the anger of their gods. Lastly, rules of State behavior were conditioned also by pragmatism, reasons that were not attributable to a fear either of divine vengeance or abandonment.

Religion was not, as many have supposed, the sole source of international legal obligation in ancient times. Instead, religion and ritual and rhetoric mixed to produce an idea of obligation which was premised on the first principle of an ancient law of nations: breaking faith brought punishment, whether divine or human, immediate or delayed, terrible or trivial. As two scholars have eloquently noted:

[190] For more on this concept, see Chapter 2, at notes 138–139 and accompanying text.
[191] See Adcock and Mosley, *supra* note 98, at 183–85.   [192] Lorton, *supra* note 59, at 178.
[193] See *ibid.* at 178–79.   [194] *Ibid.*

Ancient like modern scruples were often based on moral and humanitarian grounds . . .; the guardians of general morality might be involved in such matters, but only at a remove. Even more apparently blatant religious phenomena such as omens and auspices were probably seen not as reflexions of divine wishes but as part of the natural world, of which note should be taken, as with signs of the weather: but prayers to the gods to send better omens showed a belief that gods could alter nature within the limits of Fate, although in the meantime it was foolish rather than impious to ignore the signs.[195]

Religion, ritual, and reason were all part of the common effort of early civilizations to "create order (a cosmos) out of chaos, an effort which extended from mythopoeic cosmology to the ordering of the state."[196]

This being settled, there remains the mooted question, first posited by Coleman Phillipson, whether it would have made any difference had ancient international law been really religious in character. This inquiry only matters to those who see the contemporary law of nations as the unique product of the modern, Enlightenment mind. The question is important, I think, because of its unstated assumption that a religious (non-rational) basis for international law is somehow defective and dangerous. That returns us to the proposition critiqued already in this study, that ancient international law was a primitive legal system precisely because religion supplied the sense of compulsion for States.

For those who espouse this view, the chief distinction of the law of nations in antiquity has gone unnoticed. It is not that religion may or may not have pervaded that law. Rather, it was that the ancient mind saw the law of nations as indistinct from State behavior. International law was not a set of objective rules. It was cause and effect: breaking faith brought punishment. As Phillipson also noted, "[t]he ancients judged the results by the law; the moderns judge the law by the results."[197] Ancient people could not separate the act of breaking faith from the inevitable, if sometimes delayed, event of retribution. To the extent that the gods were parties to the sanction, mighty States were not immune when they broke faith. "[R]ight or wrong were defined irrespective of whether a power stood behind it or not; the Gods punish the wrongdoing when men are lacking to do it."[198]

There was an intellectual intermediary between the sense of obligation

---

[195] A. J. Holloday and M. D. Goodman, Religious Scruples in Ancient Warfare, 36 CQ 150, 151–52 (1986).   [196] Lorton, *supra* note 59, at 179.

[197] 1 Phillipson, *supra* note 10, at 46.

[198] Stephen Verosta, International Law in Europe and Western Asia Between 100 and 650 AD, 113 RCADI 484, 502 (1964–III).

– the act of making faith – and the substance of that duty, and the consequences of its violation. There was no way to rationalize expediency with
justice. Nor was there recourse to doctrines or exceptions, to principles or
policies. The moral right won by keeping faith was an absolute virtue in
the ancient world. It may not have always been observed, but it was always
prized.

4 Making friends: diplomats and foreign visitors in ancient times

The reception and protection of diplomats and embassies

Some general concepts

Fundamental to the idea of a law of nations in ancient times was the proper respect and protection to be accorded to the official representatives of other sovereigns. Two ancient States might have been in a condition of distrust or competition, and yet diplomatic contacts were constantly promoted and reinforced between them as long as they were not actually at war. The principles of diplomatic intercourse were surely seen as rules to be followed save in the most grievous breach. The international law of diplomats and diplomatic protection was fundamental, because without it the simplest forms of negotiation between independent polities would have been impossible. The rules of diplomatic conduct were, therefore, motivated by the highest demands of necessity. Before launching into the more specific ideas surrounding the functions of diplomatic personnel in antiquity – including their reception and protection from harm – some significant general concepts of diplomatic practice should be noted.

Each of the ancient cultures surveyed in this study held strong notions of hospitality and the proper courtesies and facilities to be extended to strangers from afar. In a world of imperfect and dangerous communications and means of transport, where even modest distances posed incredible obstacles and difficulties for travelers, hospitality was more than a merely desirable institution of personal favor. Rather, in each of the State systems considered here, hospitality was sanctioned and ritualized. It undoubtedly possessed a private aspect: one family or household extending hospitality to a traveler from abroad. The legal aspects of this will be considered in the second part of this chapter. Of concern here is how beliefs regarding private hospitality became institutionalized and ritualized into patterns of *State* practice.

Again, there seems no doubt that notions of hospitality and friendship were sanctioned on a religious basis and formalized by social institutions having the legal power to compel obedience. In Rome, the relationship between a patron and client, or between a host and guest, had a special character. Violation of a host's duty to a visitor invoked the imprecation of a *sacratio capitis*.[1] Even more significant, the institution of private hospitality was hereditary. The lawful heirs of both the host and guest had the duty to extend all of the honors and benefits of ritualized friendship.[2] This surely made sense in antiquity. In this fashion, long-distance relationships were formed between families, clans, and larger social groupings. In the well-organized societies examined in this book, ritualized friendship quite literally made possible long-distance trade and communications. A well-chanced visit, linked with an extension of kind and sincere hospitality, could mean the difference between prosperity or ruin for two trading houses for generations to come. It also permitted the full realization of social and cultural contacts between people of otherwise seemingly disparate religious and ethnic backgrounds.

The enormous implications of this ancient institution will be seen throughout this study: in the treatment of aliens living abroad, in the peaceful settlement of certain kinds of disputes, and even in the conduct of hostilities between two warring nations. It is of note that the principle of private hospitality was quickly transformed into an essential feature of

---

[1] See 1 Coleman Phillipson, *The International Law and Custom of Ancient Greece and Rome* 224 (1911) (quoting the provision of the Twelve Tables prescribing: "Patronus si clienti fraudem fecerit, sacer esto."). In Greek mythology, murder of a guest was a breach of the Olympian Gods' laws of hospitality. One notable breach was when Heracles murdered his houseguest, Iphitus, for his horses, permissible because no bond of kinship existed between the two, and Iphitus had no relatives (thus preventing the initiation of a blood-feud). See 2 Homer, *The Odyssey* 307 (A. T. Murray transl. 1919) (Loeb Classical Library reprint 1919) (passage xxi.24–30). See also Baron Michel de Taube, Les Origines de L'Arbitrage International: Antiquité et Moyen Age, 32 RCADI 1, 32–33 (1932–IV). For more on Greek practice, see Gabriel Herman, *Ritualized Friendship and the Greek City* (1987). See *ibid.* at 53 and n. 36 (glossing Xenophon and Aeschines in their condemnations of those individuals who broke faith with their guests).

[2] According to Livy, the *hospitium privatum* was a reciprocal undertaking, involving rights and duties of mutual assistance and protection, whether in peace or in war, devolving upon the sons or other heirs of the respective parties. See 6 Livy, *History of Rome* 411 (Frank G. Moore transl. 1922) (Loeb Classical Library reprint 1967) (passages xxv.18) and 12 *ibid.* 41 (Evan T. Sage and Alfred C. Schlesinger transl. 1938) (Loeb Classical Library reprint 1979) (passage xl.13). See also Herman, *supra* note 1, at 50–54; Ihering, Die Gastfreundschaft im Altertum, in *Deutsche Rundschau* 357–97 (June 1887) (for the origins of hospitality in commercial activities).

inter-State relations. This transformation occurred quite early. Friendship and diplomacy were always inextricably linked. Strong personal relationships undoubtedly facilitated diplomatic contacts even between potentially belligerent nations. In the fourteenth century BCE, the Hittite king was vexed because one of his vassals, one Piyamaradu, was raiding his territories. The Hittite king complained to a neighbor, the king of Ahhiyawa, whose protection Piyamaradu had sought when militarily confronted by the Hittites. The Hittite king then asked the ruler of Ahhiyawa for Piyamaradu's extradition. The bearer of this message was a prominent individual well known to the king of Ahhiyawa. The historical record indicates that the well-born messenger had previously participated in diplomatic contacts between the houses of Hatti and Ahhiyawa. The selection of this envoy was apparently critical to the Ahhiyawa king's favorable consideration of the Hittite request: Piyamaradu was bound-over to the Hatti;[3] this, despite the fact that Piyamaradu was owed hospitality by his host. The selected envoy was privileged in his functions precisely because of the bond of friendship and hospitality that had been formed.[4] Likewise, Livy relates the incident where ambassadors were dispatched by King Perseus of Macedon to Rome in 171 BCE. This was apparently a delicate mission, and the only reason Perseus felt comfortable enough to send the embassy was that a bond of private hospitality existed between him and one of the current consuls in Rome, Marcius, a tie that had been formed between their fathers.[5]

These examples of "personal diplomacy" are hardly surprising. The concept of private hospitality and friendship, extended between individuals of different nationalities, surely acted as a critical facilitation of diplomacy. Even more significant was the manner in which the hereditary aspect of private hospitality was transmuted into the concept of perpetual peace between sovereigns. As seen in the examples of Roman and Hittite practice,[6] the initiation of diplomatic relations acted, in effect, as the formation of a bond of public friendship between two States. This fiction was probably intended as an antidote to the religious particularism of many ancient nation-States.[7] The very act of receiving a foreign nation's

---

[3] See J. T. Hooker, *Mycenaean Greece* 124 (1977).

[4] See Peter Karavites, Diplomatic Envoys in the Homeric World, 34 RIDA 41, 85 (1987). See also Eugène Audinet, Les traces du droit international dans l'Iliade et dans l'Odyssée, 21 RGDIP 29, 33 (1914) (regarding the institution of hospitality in ancient Greece).

[5] See 12 Livy, *supra* note 2, at 405 (passage xlii.38) ("legati a Perseo rege venerunt, privati maxime hospitii fiducia, quod ei paternum cum Marcio erat").

[6] See *supra* notes 3–5 and text. See also V. Korosec, Hethitische Staatsverträge: Ein Beitrag zu ihrer juristichen Wertung, 60 *Leipziger Rechtswissenschaftliche Studien* 23 (1931).

[7] See Chapter 3, text at notes 30–43.

ambassadors was seen as an acceptance of an alien religion and its national gods. The concept of perpetual peace was seen as a very public form of ritualized hospitality between two nations.[8]

The analogue between the forms and functions of private hospitality (on the one hand) and official diplomacy (on the other) was imperfect and certainly had its limits. International diplomacy could not have proceeded on the same basis, with the same assumptions of human nature, as the laws of private hospitality and comradeship. There was simply too much at stake. The fortunes of nations could be risked on a diplomatic interchange or negotiation. Envoys could be feckless. Or, worse still, they could take advantage of the rules of hospitality to deceive a host. So ancient peoples had an alternative to seeing the rules of diplomatic conduct as the extension of the dictates of private hospitality. This choice was reflected in their substantial concern in establishing the trustworthiness of diplomatic personnel. The Greeks were preoccupied with this. Many Greek cities established laws to punish envoys found guilty of distortions or fabrications in the course of their official acts.[9] In a prequel to the correspondence between the Hittite and Ahhiyawa kings, related above,[10] relations between the two countries became so bad that one Hittite king suggested to his Ahhiyawa counterpart that the poor relations between the two countries could be blamed on their respective messengers. He proposed that they put an end to the ugly affair by cutting off the heads and mutilating the bodies of the ambassadors responsible for the misunderstanding.[11] There is no indication whether this proposition was acted upon.

One technique for assuring the integrity of visiting envoys was to hold them personally liable for their transgressions or those of their masters.

---

[8] See Bruno Paradisi, L'amitié internationale: les phases critiques de son ancienne histoire, 78 RCADI 325, 346 n. 1 (1951-I).

[9] See 10 Plato, *Collected Works* 475 (R. G. Bury transl. 1926) (Loeb Classical Library reprint 1926) (*Laws*, passage xii.1. 941A). See also 2 Homer, *The Iliad* 119 (A. T. Murray transl. 1921) (Loeb Classical Library reprint 1929) (passage xv. 158) (where Zeus commanded Iris not to prevaricate in relaying a message). Nonetheless, the "difficult position of envoys away from home was officially recognized when a proviso was made in the terms of the foundation of the Hellenic League in 302 [BCE] that if an individual state considered a decision of the League unacceptable, punishment should not be meted out as a result by that state to its representatives." D. J. Mosley, *Envoys and Diplomacy in Ancient Greece* 94–95 (1973). See also H. B. Leech, *An Essay on Ancient International Law* 45–46 (1877) (noting the case of the Mylasans who "not only submitted to the execution of its ambassador by the prince to whom he was sent, but ratified the sentence by inflicting the further penalty of confiscation of his property in favour of that prince").   [10] See *supra* note 3 and text.

[11] Karavites, *supra* note 4, at 98 n. 85 (citing Denys Lionel Page, *History and the Homeric Iliad* 12 (1959)).

This seemingly conflicted with every civilized principle of diplomatic immunity, and yet it was not really viewed as a contradictory practice by ancient peoples. Diplomats were often held as privileged sorts of hostages, particularly in Greece.[12] Envoys who violated their own *bona fides* were subjected, under Roman law, to noxal surrender to an enemy.[13] Other examples abound of personal coercion being applied against the official representatives of foreign States, all for the purpose of preventing deception or trickery in the process of international relations.

The ancient reconciliation of diplomatic immunity with sanctioned retribution is one of the subjects of this chapter. Suffice it to say here, though, that such duress rarely achieved much success. One example is enough. In the winter of 478 BCE, Athens began rebuilding the city's fortifications destroyed in the earlier Persian invasion. Athens' neighbors fretted about this development, and sought Spartan help to dissuade the Athenians from what might have been perceived as an aggressive move. The Athenians needed to buy some time, pending the completion of their works. This they accomplished with a diplomatic stratagem. Athens dispatched to Sparta one Themistocles, a leading citizen, but extraordinarily well regarded and well trusted by the Spartans. He assured the Lacedaemonians that no such aggression was intended and allayed their fears of a new round of Athenian imperial expansion. Reports of continued building on the walls found their way back to Sparta. Themistocles assured his Spartan hosts that the accounts should not be believed, and that, instead, a high-level Spartan delegation be sent to Athens to investigate in person. But Themistocles had secretly arranged that when that Spartan embassy arrived in Athens it would be detained to act as security for his own safety, once his own fraud was discovered, which it inevitably was. Thucydides reported that, since the eminent Spartans were in the hands of the Athenians, the Lacedaemonian authorities had no choice but to accept Athens' *fait accompli* and release Themistocles.[14]

---

[12] See 5 Plutarch, *Lives* 405 (B. Perrin transl. 1917) (Loeb Classical Library reprint 1968) (*Pelopidas*, passage xxvi.4) (Macedonian nobility resident in Thebes, held hostage). See generally, M. Amit, Hostages in Ancient Greece, 98 *Rivista di Filologia e di Istruzione Classica* 129 (1970).

[13] See J. W. Rich, *Declaring War in the Roman Empire in the Period of Transmarine Expansion* 109 (1976) (Collection Latomus No. 149); F. de Visscher, *Le Régime Romain de la Noxalité* (1947).

[14] See 1 Thucydides, *History of the Peloponnesian War* 149 (C. F. Smith transl. 1919) (Loeb Classical Library reprint 1980) (passage i.89–92). The same story is recounted in 4 Diodorus Siculus, *History* 229–40 (C. H. Oldfather, C. L. Sherman, C. Bradford Welles and F. R. Walton transl. 1946) (Loeb Classical Library reprint 1989) (passage xi.39.2); and 2 Plutarch, *supra* note 12, at 53–55 (*Themistocles*, passage xix).

This story says much about the mutual expectations of diplomatic relations by ancient States. Some level of trickery and dishonesty was acceptable, perhaps even required. What is noteworthy, however, is the extent to which the rules of diplomacy were so widely observed. Because the international law of diplomacy was inextricably linked with each of the authentic State systems considered in this book, a polity's acceptance of diplomatic niceties was often considered a *sine qua non* for its participation in the international system of State relations. There were a few, basic rules of diplomatic intercourse: (1) foreign envoys would be treated as guests; and (2) although tolerable levels of personal coercion were permitted, the diplomats would otherwise be immune from sanctions in the host State. These basic rules were respected by nearly all of the States existing *within* the three time periods of international relations pondered here. The content of the rules was, moreover, remarkably consistent throughout the entirety of antiquity and throughout the ancient world. The universality of diplomatic law was a signal feature of its success.

A consistent theme of historic narratives from antiquity is the extent to which even peoples and States on the periphery of "civilization" still followed the dictates of diplomatic practice. So it was that Polybius could express surprise that the mercenary leaders of Libyan tribes observed all of the correct rituals (at least by Greco-Roman standards) in their relations with the Carthaginians in 238 BCE.[15] In the same fashion, Indian sources reported successful diplomatic initiatives with the Hellenistic States established by Alexander the Great on the Indian periphery, as well as with Rome centuries later.[16]

In the same vein, the historical evidence is strong that Persia conformed its international conduct and behavior to Greek diplomatic standards, even as Persian kings attempted to conquer Greece in the fifth century BCE. The use of envoys to secure permissions to cross neutral territories was a consistent feature of Persian practice.[17] As will be seen later, Persian forces often respected the immunities of religious sanctuaries, and Persian authorities were willing to submit certain kinds of local disputes

---

[15] See 1 Polybius, *The Histories* 229–31 (W. R. Paton transl. 1922) (Loeb Classical Library reprint 1975) (passage i.85).

[16] See Singh, History of the Law of Nations – Regional Developments: South and South-East Asia, in 7 *Encyclopedia of Public International Law* 237, 241 (Rudolph Bernhardt ed. 1984) (citing Strabo, xv.4.73, on the Indian mission to Rome in 20 BCE, as well as many other instances).

[17] See 2 Herodotus, *Histories* 7, 115, 405 (A. D. Godley transl. 1920) (Loeb Classical Library reprint 1969) (passages iii.4 and 88, iv.203) and 4 *ibid.* 159 (passage ix.1). See also D. J. Mosley, Crossing Greek Frontiers Under Arms, 20 RIDA 161, 164–65 (1973).

to third-party arbitration.[18] Robert Bauslaugh has noted that "[f]rom their earliest agreements with Greek city-States, the Persians demonstrated a surprising readiness to respect and use Greek diplomatic institutions."[19] One explanation is that these institutions (or at least some aspects of them) were not exclusively Greek at all. The conduct of diplomacy and the observance of diplomatic rules were not, therefore, particular practices of different cultures and polities.

That leads one to consider the last general concept which motivated the development of the ancient practice and organization of diplomacy. This was the notion of sovereign equality. The power to dispatch and receive ambassadors, the right of legation, was typically seen as an incident of power and political independence.[20] The Romans were particular sticklers on this point: they would not receive ambassadors from a less than free and autonomous political entity. This was codified in later Roman law,[21] but even in the time of Roman transmarine expansion, as Polybius recorded, Roman authorities would not receive embassies from defeated peoples. When the town of Aegina fell to Roman forces in 208 BCE, the inhabitants who had not escaped the city begged Publius, the pro-consul, to allow them to send envoys to the cities of their kinsmen to obtain a ransom. At first, Publius denied the request. "The time for sending ambassadors," he said, "was when they were their own masters, not when they were slaves or captives." Publius later relented, giving the Aeginetans leave to send envoys to procure ransom, "since that was the custom of their country."[22] Unspoken in this account is that the Aeginetans could have, obviously, attempted to send emissaries to their kinsmen, but

---

[18] See 3 Herodotus, *supra* note 17, at 187–89, 249 (passages vi.42.1 and vi.97) (temple at Delos spared in 490 BCE); but cf. 3 *ibid.* at 123, 253–55 (passages v.102 and vi.101) (Didyama destroyed in revenge for the burning of the temple of Cybele at Sardis). See also Robert A. Bauslaugh, *The Concept of Neutrality in Classical Greece* 38–43, 91 and n. 10, 94 (1991); 1 L. Piccirilli, *Gli arbitrati interstatali greci: dalle origini al 338 aC* at § 11 (1973).

[19] Bauslaugh, *supra* note 18, at 91.

[20] For an example from the ancient Near East, see 2(2) *Cambridge Ancient History* 258 (3rd ed. 1975), where the King of Ashur self-anointed himself as a "Great King," and so addressed himself to the Hittite ruler, who responded pungently: "As my [father] and grandfather did not write to the King of Ashur [about brotherhood], even so you must not write about Great-Kingship to me." *Ibid.* See also *ibid.* at 278–79.

[21] See 4 *The Digest of Justinian* 920 (Theodor Mommsen and Paul Krueger ed., Alan Watson transl. 1985) (50.7 (de legatione).2.pr; Ulpian, *Opinions* 2) ("Legatus contra rem publicam, cuius legatus est, per alium a principe quid postulare potest"); *ibid.* at 921 (50.7.16; Modestinus, *Rules* 7) ("Is, qui legatione fungitur, libellum sine permissu principis de aliis suis negotiis dare non potest").

[22] 4 Polybius, *supra* note 15, at 97 (passage ix.42) (as recited in 1 Phillipson, *supra* note 1, at 310–11).

without Roman assurances there was no guarantee that their safety would be respected. In short, the privileges and immunities of diplomats came as part and parcel of the right of legation.

It made sense surely to regard those diplomatic practices as an essential part of a system of States. Envoys, as already noted, were seen as the personification of the sending State. Any offense to an ambassador was an offense against a coequal sovereign. It was also possible to see the entire system of diplomatic privileges and immunities as an outgrowth of the recognition that certain classes of entitled individuals were subject only to their own sovereign's authority, even when they traveled into the territorial realm of another ruler. Diplomatic privileges, as an outgrowth of extraterritorial immunities, were a very real way that political entities avoided conflict.

Taken together, the general principles that guided the ancient practice of diplomatic law had a profound impact on the manner in which envoys operated and the extent to which they were protected. Ritualized hospitality was balanced carefully with concerns over the probity of an envoy and that of his master. The universality of rules of diplomatic comportment was qualified by the principle that only legitimate States had the right to send and receive embassies. Despite these contradictions, the overall picture of the international law of diplomacy in antiquity was remarkably stable and predictable. We begin with the actual modalities of international relations: the terminology used to describe the different sorts of diplomatic officials and their functions, the general manner in which embassies were dispatched and received, and the way diplomatic missions were continued or terminated.

The formalities of diplomacy

Terminology and types

Some of the ancient State systems considered in this study elaborated sophisticated distinctions between the different sorts of individuals engaged in communications between nations. Others did not. Among this latter group were the peoples mentioned in the Old Testament. Modern scholars have concluded that there does not appear to be any distinction made between the use of two terms appearing in the Septuagint.[23] "The

---

[23] See Karavites, *supra* note 4, at 80 n. 70 (citing Genesis 32:1; Numbers 20:14–21, 21:21, 22:5; Deuteronomy 2:26–36, 3:1–6; Judges 7:24, 9:31; 1 Samuel 11:3).

Hebraic word for messenger is sometimes translated in the Old Testament as 'ambassador' but appears to indicate a messenger at the court."[24]

If the typology of early Near Eastern ambassadors was preoccupied with the relative power and authority they possessed, the ancient Greek city-States were more concerned with the very different functions of heralds and envoys.[25] "A variety of words was used by the Greeks to describe those who were despatched on diplomatic missions. Heralds (*kerykes*), envoys (*presbeis*) and messengers (*aggeloi*) are all found [in Greek literature], and the main distinction is between heralds and the others."[26] Adcock and Mosley speculate that *aggeloi* was the most generic term, although as a literary reference it most often referred to the envoys of foreign, barbarian peoples.[27] *Presbeis* began as a word without diplomatic nuance, meaning simply an elder in the community.[28] Scholars have been in sharp disagreement about the etymology of these terms. Some believe strongly that *kerykes* and *aggeloi*, as used in both archaic and epic texts, refer equally to the heraldic institution, and not to envoys as a diplomatic office.[29] Other writers have simply held that the textual evidence is too thin, at least on the question of the origin of these words.[30]

Greek heralds were deemed to have mythic beginnings. The first herald, Keryx, was the son of the god Hermes and Pandrosus, the daughter of Cecrops.[31] Hermes, along with Iris, served as Zeus' divine messenger. Keryx's descendants had the duty to announce Zeus' festivals. In primitive and archaic Greek society, "heralds followed a recognized calling or profession which gave them a specific and honourable status in society. They

---

[24] Ragnar Numelin, *The Beginnings of Diplomacy* 295 (1950). See also 1(2) *Cambridge Ancient History* 540–41 (3rd ed. 1971); John T. Greene, *The Role of the Messenger and the Message in the Ancient Near East* 8–43 (1989) (reviewing Sumerian, Babylonian, Assyrian, Hittite, Ugaritic, and Egyptian terminologies for messengers).

[25] The Greek cities also had rules distinguishing envoys based on their power and authority. These will be considered in more detail at *infra* notes 67–76 and accompanying text.

[26] Sir Frank Adcock and D. J. Mosley, *Diplomacy in Ancient Greece* 152–53 (1975).

[27] See *ibid.*   [28] See *ibid.*

[29] See Michael Ventris and John Chadwick, *Documents in Mycenaean Greek* 123, 385, 396 (1956).

[30] See H. G. Buchholz, *Erwähnen die Pylostafeln Herolde? Festschrift für Friedrich Matz* 25–31 (1962); C. J. Gadd, *Ideas of Divine Rule in the Ancient East* 62 (1948); L. R. Palmer, *Interpretation of Mycenaean Greek Texts* 141 (1963).

[31] See Pollux iv.91, as cited in Karavites, *supra* note 4, at 44–45. See also Mosley, *supra* note 9, at 87–88. From Diodorus we learn that when Hermes acted as an emissary of the gods he earned the title Hermes Koinos. See 3 Diodorus, *supra* note 14, at 301 (passage v.75.1). In ancient Greek, *koinos* implied impartiality, and so it was that heralds "divinely facilitated common good [and were] impartial to either party and therefore equally beneficial to both." Bauslaugh, *supra* note 18, at 37–38.

performed a variety of tasks which ranged from acting as convenors of political meetings to pouring out the wine in the halls of the Homeric kings and princes."[32] Heralds carried the staff of Hermes, which, according to Thucydides, was a polished stick with a snake entwined at each end.[33] An aspect of primitive diplomacy, indeed of all primitive political organization, the scepter was an essential symbol for heralds in almost all of their roles.[34]

Heralds figured prominently in the Homeric poems. They appear in order to make sacrifices and offer libations.[35] They also had a role in "pronounc[ing] agreements and the prayers which accompanied the agreements loudly enough so that everybody would hear them and nobody would remain ignorant of the stipulations or the curses that attended the breach of the agreement."[36] When a declaration of war was made in Homer's poems, it was a herald who went around and aroused the warriors for the battlefield.[37] But surely the chief role for heralds in epic Greece was their task in escorting diplomatic missions. As already mentioned,[38] the hero Achilles acknowledged the divine origin and sacrosanct status of Agamemnon's heralds who accompanied Briseis.[39] Odysseus called upon a herald to guide two of his comrades into the land

---

[32] Adcock and Mosley, *supra* note 26, at 152–53. See also Mosley, *supra* note 9, at 88.

[33] See 1 Thucydides, *supra* note 14, at 91 (passage i.53.1). See also Dio Chrysostom 247 (H. Lamar Crosby transl. 1951) (Loeb Classical Library reprint 1985) (*On Law*, lxv.9) (suggesting that the staff itself "is a symbol of the law").

[34] See F. J. De Waele, *The Magic Staff or Rod in Graeco-Italian Antiquity* (1927); K. Murawaka, "Demiurgos," 6 *Historia* 385 (1957); Peter Karavites, *Promise-Giving and Treaty-Making: Homer and the Near East* 30 (1992).

[35] See 1 Homer, *The Odyssey*, *supra* note 1, at 11 (passage i.110) (heralds pouring wine for the suitors of Penelope).

[36] Karavites, *supra* note 4, at 53 (citing 1 Homer, *The Iliad*, *supra* note 9, at 137 (passage iii.266–77)).

[37] See 1 Homer, *The Iliad*, *supra* note 9, at 83 (passage ii.437, 446). For those instances in which heralds made a formal declaration of war, see Donald Lateiner, Heralds and Corpses in Thucydides, 71 *Classical World* 97, 103 (1977) (noting six occurrences in 1 Thucydides, *supra* note 14, at 255, 259, 261, 281, 395 (passages i.146, ii.1, ii.2.4, ii.12.3, ii.74.1), 3 *ibid.* 239 (passage vi.32.1)). One such case was Melesippus' statement, at the commencement of the Ten Years War in 413 BCE, that "[t]his day will be the beginning of great evils for the Hellenes." 1 Thucydides, *supra* note 14, at 281 (passage ii.12.3). Interestingly, Melesippus is the only herald actually named in Thucydides. See G. T. Griffith, Some Habits of Thucydides when Introducing Persons, 187 PCPhS 21 (1961). See also 5 Dio Chrysostom, *supra* note 33, at 247 (*On Laws*, xv.9) ("the herald who is dispatched from one's bitterest foes the law protects and guards"). The role of heralds in the declaration of war in ancient Greece will be considered in Chapter 6.

[38] See Chapter 3, text at note 134.

[39] See 1 Homer, *The Iliad*, *supra* note 9, at 29 (passage i.334) (where Achilles addresses Agamemnon's ambassadors: "Hail, heralds, messengers of Zeus and men").

of the Lotus-eaters.[40] "Clearly, the purpose of the escorting heralds was to bestow sacrosanctity on the mission, thereby providing protection to the delegates in an unknown land."[41]

If the social privileges of being a herald in epic Greece were considerable, so too were the responsibilities. To the extent that heralds drew their power and authority from the Olympian gods, any transgressions committed in the course of their mortal duties had dire consequences. Plato wrote in the fourth century that if a herald on a mission to a friendly or hostile State distorted or fabricated a message it was considered as an offense against the sacred messages and commands of Zeus and Hermes.[42] Aristophanes and Athenaeus alluded to a sacrificial rite in which the tongue of a lying messenger was cut out and dedicated to Hermes.[43] Here, as already discussed,[44] was the coercive element in controlling the conduct of sanctified messengers.

Despite these disincentives, hereditary classes of heralds evolved. We know about two groupings of families – one in Athens, and the other in Sparta. In Lacedaemon it was the *talthybioi* or *talthybiadai*, the descendants of Talthybius, the legendary herald of Agamemnon. Indeed, at Sparta, Talthybius was worshipped as a minor deity.[45] In Athens the heralds belonged to the kin group of Kerykes and Eumolpidae.[46] One writer has suggested that, by the age of Solon, the Athenian law-giver who flourished around 597 BCE, heralds had "been a recognized part of the Athenian constitution, and [were] regarded as a sort of magistracy."[47] Members of all these families enjoyed substantial social and religious prestige.

Even before the time that Greek history was fully recorded, the status and functions of heralds came to be distinguished from those of other, political envoys. "Society and its institutions changed radically after the archaic period and although certain religious and ceremonial tasks were retained by successive generations of particular families[,] diplomatic

---

[40] See 1 Homer, *Odyssey, supra* note 1, at 351–53 (passage x.101). See also M. I. Finley, *The World of Odysseus* 111–12 (1956).   [41] Karavites, *supra* note 4, at 56.

[42] See 10 Plato, *supra* note 9, at 475 (*Laws,* passage xii.1.941A).

[43] See 2 Aristophanes, *Plays* 334 (Patric Dickinson transl. 1970) (*The Ploutos,* line 1110) (written around 388 BCE); 1 Athenaeus, *The Deipnosophists* 71 (C. B. Gulick transl. 1927) (Loeb Classical Library reprint 1969) (passage i.16B).   [44] See *supra* note 9 with text.

[45] See Karavites, *supra* note 4, at 46.

[46] See 4 Plutarch, *supra* note 12, at 97 (*Alcibiades,* passage xxxiii.1–3); 5 Diodorus, *supra* note 14, at 315 (passage xiii.69.2) (both sources describing the incident in which the traitor-general Alcibiades was readmitted to Athens after the Kerykes and Eumolpidae gave their sanction).   [47] Leech, *supra* note 9, at 31.

tasks were more especially political in nature and naturally they were assigned by election in political assemblies as the occasion required."[48] While some classicists have made much of the distinction between the religious formalities conducted by heralds and the political intrigues of diplomats,[49] other scholars have cautioned that the sources are themselves ambivalent in distinguishing between these two classes of officials. Mosley has suggested that Herodotus, Xenophon, and Plato may have confused the respective roles and functions of heralds and diplomats in each of their narratives.[50] This confusion is understandable. To take one example, Thucydides' history of the Athenian expedition in Sicily,[51] the literary role for heralds is almost epiphanic; their appearance in the texts serves as a way to mark the transitions between significant events.[52] So, quite apart from their precisely defined tasks, heralds must have been perceived as essential organizers of historic events.

While political envoys were not granted the same ritual respect as heralds, they were at least accorded the same privileges and immunities as a matter of international custom.[53] This point will be considered further below.[54] Suffice it to note that, in both Greek and Roman practice, some distinctions came to be formed. They were based not only on the generic character of the person performing diplomatic tasks, but also on the actual power and authority wielded by individual envoys in particular situations. The process of sending and receiving ambassadors in antiquity will be considered next.

Instructions, credentials, and receptions

Even in the very early history of the ancient Near East it came to be established that messengers from one sovereign to another carried with them some sort of document revealing their identity and status, and perhaps even the very nature of their mission. Today, in modern diplomatic parlance, we would call these an envoy's instructions and credentials.

---

[48] Adcock and Mosley, *supra* note 26, at 53.

[49] See, e.g., 1 Phillipson, *supra* note 1, at 304–07.

[50] See Mosley, *supra* note 9, at 89 (citing 2 Herodotus, *supra* note 17, at 75 (passage iii.58); 2 Xenophon, *Hellenica and Anabasis* 345 (Carleton L. Brownson transl. 1921) (Loeb Classical Library reprint 1932) (*Anabasis*, passage ii.3.1–3); 10 Plato, *supra* note 9, at 475 (*Laws*, passage xii.1.(941A))).

[51] See 3 Thucydides, *supra* note 14, at 239 (passage vi.32.1); 4 *ibid.* 7, 169 (passages vii.3.1, vii.82.1).   [52] See Lateiner, *supra* note 37, at 103–04.

[53] See *supra* note 48 with text.   [54] See *infra* notes 113–46 and accompanying text.

References to a "commission," or credentialing document, were made in extant cuneiform tablets from ancient Mesopotamia.[55] In one well-documented mission between Assyria and the growing Babylonian empire of Hammurabi, the mention of credentials is significant. The prince of Mari, Zimri-Lim, and Hammurabi were ostensible allies. Indeed, Zimri-Lim had loaned the Babylonians some troops for use in some foreign adventure, but the Assyrian ruler at Mari needed these forces back and sent an envoy (by the name of Yaqqim-Adad) to Babylon, carrying a fairly brusque message asking for the return of his men. The importance of this fragment is that the diplomatic message was distinct from the envoy's credentials – indeed, they must have been on two separate tablets. We know this because, upon arriving in Babylon, Yaqqim-Adad learned that the troops were on their way back home. Upon advice from Mari's resident diplomat in Babylon, it was decided to "suppress" their ruler's somewhat intemperate message as being moot. Nonetheless, the envoy had to present himself to Hammurabi and so presented his credentials. Undoubtedly bewildered as to the nature of Yaqqim-Adad's abortive mission, Hammurabi nonetheless granted the envoy permission to return home, his mission accomplished.[56]

Even this early, an elaborate system of written documents had grown up around the practice of diplomacy. Ambassadors were dispatched not only with the written message to be communicated between sovereigns, but also with some sort of certificate of identity to be presented to the host. In exchange, the visiting envoy would receive a safe conduct, a kind of passport.[57] This seemed to be the practice for Egypt as well as for Mesopotamia.[58] It appeared to be the norm in inter-regional communications between these two clusters of civilization in the ancient Near East. The famous diplomatic negotiation between the Egyptian and Hittite empires in 1280 BCE

[55] See 2 *Archives Royales de Mari: Lettres Diverses* (C. F. Jean transl. 1950) (passage xxxix.5–7) (hereinafter "2 ARMT"); J. M. Munn-Rankin, Diplomacy in Western Asia in the Early Second Millennium BC, 18 *Iraq* 68, 100–01 (1956).

[56] This extract is drawn from Munn-Rankin, *supra* note 55, at 100–01. See also Louis Lawrence Orlin, *Assyrian Colonies in Cappadocia* 114–38 (1970) (for more on Assyrian practice); F. Thureau-Dangin, *Rituels Akkadiens* (1921). For more on Babylonian diplomacy, see 2(1) *Cambridge Ancient History* 180–82 (3rd ed. 1973). For contemporary Egyptian diplomatic practice, see 2(1) *Cambridge Ancient History* 297, 485–86 (3rd ed. 1973); 2(2) *Cambridge Ancient History* 23–26 (3rd ed. 1975).

[57] See Munn-Rankin, *supra* note 55, at 100–01 (citing 5 *ARMT: Correspondence de Iasmah-Addu* (G. Dossin transl. 1950) (passage xi.5–6)).

[58] See 22 K. Sethe and W. Helck, *Urkunden der 18. Dynastie* 13–14 (Leipzig 1906); Karavites, *supra* note 4, at 67–68.

(and the treaty of the same year)[59] began with all of these formalities when a messenger of the Hatti arrived in the capital city of Ramses in the Nile Delta, bearing a missive from his master.[60]

The contours of Greek and Roman diplomatic practice are even better documented. As already implied,[61] Greek missions usually consisted of envoys (with their entourages) accompanied by one or more heralds.[62] Distinctions seem to have been made in the various ranks of envoys on a mission, with one individual being chosen as the head or plenipotentiary.[63] At least in archaic times, embassies were dispatched and entertained like any other traveler. The members of a mission, prior to departure, went through a ritual washing of the hands and observed a brief moment of prayer for the successful completion of their assigned task. In later historical periods, some form of leave-taking ritual was followed.[64] Roman practice, at least as regards the staffing of embassies, was nearly identical to Greek procedures.[65]

Terminology aside (and there is a substantial literature on the subject),[66] general agreement exists among classicists that Greek

---

[59] For more on which see the next chapter.

[60] See *Ancient Near Eastern Texts Relating to the Old Testament* 199 (3rd ed. James B. Pritchard ed. 1969). In Mesopotamian practice, the host state had an obligation to provide for the comfort and safety of the envoys on their return home. See Munn-Rankin, *supra* note 55, at 105. Periodically, disputes arose out of the entitlement of visiting diplomats to certain gifts. One set of Assyrian delegates thought they were being discriminated against when Hammurabi declined to give lavish garments to everyone in their entourage. Hammurabi complied but pungently noted: "You are continually making difficulties for me. Are you now claiming to give orders to my palace about garments? I clothe whom I like and and him I do not like I do not clothe." 2 ARMT (passage 76). See also 2(1) *Cambridge Ancient History* 189–90 (3rd ed. 1973).

[61] See *supra* notes 48–54 and accompanying text.

[62] See 2 Thucydides, *supra* note 14, at 413 (passage iv.118.6). See generally Karavites, *supra* note 4, at 80.

[63] See 1 Phillipson, *supra* note 1, at 306 (citing, among other sources, 5 Diodorus, *supra* note 14, at 33, 267 (passages xii.53.2, xiii.52.2), 6 *ibid.* at 81 (passage xiv.25.1)).

[64] See Karavites, *supra* note 4, at 88–89.

[65] See 1 Phillipson, *supra* note 1, at 306 (suggesting that the role of heralds was filled by the *fetials* or *caduceatores*), 327–28 (describing the suites, or *comites legati*, of missions; Karavites, *supra* note 4, at 80 n.71. See also 1 Livy, *supra* note 2, at 83, 107 (passages i.24 and 30), 7 *ibid.* at 409 (passage xxvii.51), and 12 *ibid.* 345 (passage xlii.19).

[66] Consulting 1 Phillipson, *supra* note 1, at 304–07, will reveal the multiplicity of nuances attached to the use of different terms for different sorts of Greek diplomatic missions. These included special phrases denoting (1) a sacred embassy, (2) a mission to an oracle, (3) an envoy with powers to sign a treaty, (4) an ambassador sent to a congress as a select commissioner, or (5) a diplomat sent to an enemy to demand reparations or some other sort of satisfaction. See *ibid.*

diplomats embarked on missions with precisely delimited powers and clearly drafted instructions. Credentials were in wide use,[67] although there was little consistency in the technical terms employed therein.[68] The instructions given to Greek diplomatists were notoriously vague and, at the same time, severely restricted. Missions were often instructed "to achieve whatever benefits they could,"[69] although such "open" instructions did not provide the envoys the power actually to conclude an agreement with another city-State.[70] The historical record reflects, instead, and as D. J. Mosley has demonstrated,[71] that Greek ambassadors were rarely given more authority than to present a position already espoused by their city's ruling institutions, to negotiate within a narrow range of possibilities, and then to return to their capital for further consultations. Even though some missions were considered *autocratores*,[72] endowed with full powers, in practice these envoys dared not exercise that prestige and bind their city to a solemnized agreement.[73]

All Greek envoys were subject to an audit upon return to their homes, and any misstep (a lavish gift received, the appearance of collusion, or a promise made in excess of instructions) was severely punished.[74] Here we see again a strongly coercive element in diplomacy. A prudent citizen, assigned the honor of a diplomatic mission, would rarely

---

[67] See *ibid.* (citing a number of significant inscriptions, as well as Lysias, *Orations* 43 (W. L. Lamb transl. 1930) (Loeb Classical Library reprint 1988) (*De bonis Aristophanis*, passage 25)). See also Margaret M. Mitchell, New Testament Envoys in the Context of Greco-Roman Diplomatic and Epistolary Conventions: The Example of Timothy and Titus, 111 *Journal of Biblical Literature* 641, 650 (1992).

[68] See Mosley, *supra* note 9, at 21 (citing, *inter alia*, 2 Thucydides, *supra* note 14, at 235 (passage iv.15.2), 3 *ibid.* 87 (passage v.45.1); Xenophon, *supra* note 50, at 363 (*Hellenica*, passage iv.8.12); Aeschines, *Speeches* 357 (Charles Darwin Adams transl. 1919) (Loeb Classical Library reprint 1988) (*Against Ctesiphon*, lines 62–63); as well as inscription materials).   [69] See Mosley, *supra* note 9, at 25–26.

[70] See Aeschines, *supra* note 68, at 237–39, 249–50 (*On the Embassy*, passages 104 and 120) (who noted that an Athenian mission to Philip of Macedon was left to decide whether a possible agreement exceeded their authority and could thus be repudiated).

[71] See Mosley, *supra* note 9, at 35–36.

[72] This term was in common use in ancient Greece. See, e.g., 2 Aristophanes, *Plays* 225 (Kenneth McLeish transl. 1993) (*The Birds*, lines 1587–95) (Poseidon comes to negotiate an end to the war with the Gods, and announces he has full powers).

[73] See Mosley, *supra* note 9, at 30–31. The authorities note but a few exceptions to this trend. In only one recorded instance did envoys make oaths for the conclusion of a treaty without reference home. See *ibid.* at 35 (Olynthians and Sparta in 379 BCE).

[74] See Adcock and Mosley, *supra* note 26, at 165 and nn. 361 and 362 (Timagoras, on a mission from Athens to Persia, accepted lavish gifts and was condemned to death after his return; other embassies were closely questioned on the gifts they received) (citing Plutarch, Demosthenes, and Xenophon).

jeopardize his status by showing much by way of initiative. As Mosley has written:

> The retardment of diplomatic processes consequent upon the lack of powers given to envoys . . . meant that even simple issues could not normally be finally settled by the despatch of only one embassy . . . In the management of the city-state[,] diplomacy was an ancillary of government, the state was not moulded for the convenience of diplomacy. As a general matter it was safer, constitutionally, to impose close control upon servants of state, rather than to give them too much latitude, whether they were financiers, generals or diplomats.[75]

These constraints were significant, and will be considered in fuller detail when Greek treaty-making is discussed.[76]

If the powers of Greek envoys were subject to substantial constitutional restraints, the reception of diplomats was only generally conditioned by the traditional norms of hospitality. Although it was considered an affront to refuse to receive a messenger,[77] visiting officials had no further expectations as to their reception. Ambassadors sometimes had a right of audience with the public assemblies of the city being visited,[78] but this was often viewed as a privilege granted only to "friendly" States.[79] Formal hospitality was often extended to official visitors (typically including a public banquet),[80] but just as often diplomats fended for themselves, staying at an inn or at the home of a *proxenos*, a citizen of their city resident in the foreign capital.[81] Some Greek polities made agreements to respect ritual hospitality when envoys of one visited the other.[82] Tokens were

---

[75] Mosley, *supra* note 9, at 95.   [76] See Chapter 5.

[77] See Adcock and Mosley, *supra* note 26, at 164–65 (citing Herodotus, Xenophon, and Demosthenes). In 480 BCE, the Athenians refused an audience to the envoy of Persia. In 371 BCE, the Athenians again snubbed a messenger from Thebes. See *ibid*.

[78] See, e.g., 2 Polybius, *supra* note 15, at 385 (passage iv.34) (in 220 BCE, the ambassador of the Aetolians personally addressed a public assembly at Sparta). See also 1 Phillipson, *supra* note 1, at 314–15. See also Mitchell, *supra* note 67, at 648 (discussing a number of extracts from Polybius).

[79] See Adcock and Mosley, *supra* note 26, at 165 and n.365 (citing an Athenian–Chalcidian agreement of 446 BCE).

[80] See the inscription erected by Athens in 405 BCE, honoring the Samians, in which traveling expenses were offered to Samian envoys visiting Athens, reprinted in 1 *Translated Documents of Greece and Rome: Archaic Times to the End of the Peloponnesian War* 196–97 (Charles W. Fonora transl. 2nd ed. 1983).

[81] See Adcock and Mosley, *supra* note 26, at 164 and nn. 358–60. For more on the *proxenos* institution, see pp. 130–34 below.

[82] See *ibid*. at 165 and nn. 363 and 364 (discussing an Athens–Sidon treaty of 367 BCE and an agreement between Athens and satrap Orontes in 348 BCE) (citing inscription materials, including 2 *Inscriptiones Graecae* Nos. 141, 207 (2nd ser.) (Berlin 1925) and 2 M. N. Tod, *A Selection of Greek Historical Inscriptions* No. 139 (1948)).

often minted and exchanged, granting "formal recognition of the right to receive, and the obligation to bestow, hospitality."[83] In this fashion, Hellenic notions of ritualized friendship were conformed to the realities of international politics.

Roman practice in the reception of envoys closely tracked that of the Greeks, but with much more regularity. Credentials and instructions, for example, followed definite patterns,[84] while also allocating far greater authority to Roman envoys than their Greek counterparts enjoyed. Although, as already noted,[85] the Romans were nearly fanatic in their limitation of the right to legation to recognized States, they fully accepted that an embassy from a friendly power was not to be turned away without a hearing. Moreover, they believed this duty was imposed by the law of nations. As Livy commented in his narrative of Hannibal's refusal to see emissaries from his putative Spanish allies in his campaign against Rome in 220 BCE, such an action violated the *ius gentium* that all ancient nations acknowledged.[86] Other Roman authorities also believed that a refusal to receive friendly missions violated the law of nations.[87] It was certainly true that refusal to receive a Roman ambassador could be a cause for war, as the Veientians learned in 406 BCE and the Samnites discovered in 300 BCE.[88]

It must be emphasized that the duty to receive foreign ambassadors was limited to those missions from a State with which Rome had amicable relations, or, at least, was not engaged in hostilities.[89] This condition was not peculiar to Rome: it was observed by all of the peoples whom the Romans

---

[83] *Ibid.* See also Mitchell, *supra* note 67, at 658–59 (discussing celebratory decrees of Greek city-States, issued after a successful conclusion of an embassy).

[84] These included the attachment of relevant documents, including decrees, *senatusconsulta*, and letters of credit, indicating the identity, power, and authority of the emissaries. See Tacitus, *Annales* 339 (John Jackson transl. 1931) (Loeb Classical Library reprint 1956) (passage i.57) (special commission to settle affairs with German tribes in 4 CE); 5 Polybius, *supra* note 15, at 183 (passage xviii. 44) (Roman mission to Greece in 196 BCE). The Romans acknowledged a special status for diplomats having full powers, *libera mandata*. See 9 Livy, *supra* note 2, at 343 (passage xxxiii.24), 10 *ibid.* 461 (passage xxxvii.55 and 56) (missions to Asia Minor in 191 BCE). See also Mitchell, *supra* note 67, at 657.

[85] See *supra* notes 21 and 22 and accompanying text.

[86] See 5 Livy, *supra* note 2, at 27 (passage xxi.9).

[87] See 1 Phillipson, *supra* note 1, at 311 n. 2 (citing Donatus, Ad prologum *Hecyrae* Terentii). This may have been the view in ancient Greece as well. The only recorded instance of a city refusing to receive a herald from another state was noted in Pericles' suggestion to the Athenian assembly in 431 BCE. See Adcock and Mosley, *supra* note 26, at 154 and n. 304.   [88] See 2 Livy, *supra* note 2, at 447 (passage iv.58), 4 *ibid.* 399 (passage x.12).

[89] See 12 *ibid.* at 397 (passage xlii.36) (Romans refused to receive ambassador of King Perseus of Macedon, with whom they were at war, in 171 BCE), 8 *ibid.* 449 (passage xxx.23) (Roman refusal to receive Carthaginian mission during Second Punic War in 205 BCE); Servius, *Ad Aeneida Commentarii*, passage vii.168 (same incident in Punic Wars).

encountered in their years of transmarine expansion, including Carthage,[90] Macedon,[91] and Rhodes.[92] When a foreign mission finally arrived at Rome it was obliged to submit its credentials to a *quaestor urbanus* and then to the *praetor peregrinus* (an office established c. 242 BCE). These magistrates carefully reviewed the identifying documents brought by the embassy, and confirmed that Rome was at peace with the sending State. If some defect were found in the credentials, or the officials determined that the embassy would not be received for some other reason, the putative envoys were ordered to leave Roman territory without delay.[93] But when a friendly mission was admitted into the city of Rome, the foreign diplomats were treated with great hospitality. Special houses, *hospitia publica* or *aedes liberae*, were allocated to them. Envoys would be invited to public festivals and special events. Lavish gifts might be bestowed.[94]

Permanent missions and rupture of relations

International relations in antiquity did not utilize diplomats permanently stationed in a foreign capital. Given the long distances that envoys traveled to reach their destinations, however, their stays tended to be lengthy. For this reason, the frequency and intensity of diplomatic contacts came to approximate modern standards, even though the notion of a "permanent" mission to a foreign sovereign was unknown. The exceptions, as is so often the case, proved this general rule. Some of the palace courts in ancient Mesopotamia developed a practice of permanent missions, and such existed between Babylon and Assyria.[95] Dynastic Egypt also

---

[90] See 4 Polybius, *supra* note 15, at 463 (passage xv.1) (Roman mission to Carthage, during truce of 203 BCE).

[91] See 12 Livy, *supra* note 2, at 297 (passage xlii.2) (Roman mission to Perseus in 173 BCE).

[92] See 2 Polybius, *supra* note 15, at 49, 55 (passage iii.20 and 23) (Rhodian delegate at Heraclea in 207 BCE).

[93] See Sallust, *The Jugurthine War* 193 (J. C. Rolfe transl. 1921) (Loeb Classical Library reprint 1985) (passage 28) (Jugurtha's envoys told to leave Italian territory in ten days after being turned away at Rome); Numelin, *supra* note 24, at 302. See also 1 Phillipson, *supra* note 1, at 315–17.

[94] See 5 Livy, *supra* note 2, at 321 (passages xxii.37.1–3) (embassy from Hiero of Syracuse in 216 BCE), 13 *ibid.* 13, 25 (passages xliii. 3.6 and xliii. 6.11) (Massinissa's envoys in 171 and 170 BCE). See also Numelin, *supra* note 24, at 302; Louise E. Matthaei, On the Classification of Roman Allies, 1 CQ 182, 195–96 (1907); *Digest* 1.16.6.3 (Ulpian, *Duties of Proconsul* 1) (urging moderation in the acceptance of gifts).

[95] See *supra* notes 55 and 56 with text. For the inscription materials, see 2 ARMT, at 23, 72–73. See also F. M. Böhl, *Opera Minora* 354 (Groningen 1956); Karavites, *supra* note 4, at 42; J. R. Kupper, 42 *Revue d'Assyriologie et Archéologie orientale* 40 (1942); Munn-Rankin, *supra* note 55, at 101–02.

may have had a network of permanent legations.[96] Likewise in ancient Greece, some international confederations, most notably the Second Athenian Confederacy and the Macedonian-inspired League of Corinth, had ostensibly permanent councils to which envoys would be accredited. They never did operate, however, as continuous diplomatic establishments.[97]

In all of the ancient societies considered here, the rupture of diplomatic relations was tantamount to preliminaries leading to armed conflict.[98] Other reasons, for sure, could lead to the conclusion of a diplomatic mission: the death of the sovereign to which the envoys had been accredited or a fundamental failure to achieve the objective of the mission. It is not surprising that the status of diplomatic relations between two ancient polities was a sure guide to whether they were at peace or at war. Although much will be said later about the formalities leading to the outbreak of hostilities, and the diplomatic institutions which participated in such a declaration,[99] it needs to be noted here that even under these conditions foreign embassies were given a decent interval to withdraw from the territory of the offended State.[100]

Privileges and immunities of diplomats

As with any kind of traveler in antiquity, diplomats were constantly in danger. The hazards were those common to any long journey: treacherous weather, difficult terrain, and thieving brigands. The custom in antiquity,

---

[96] See Aristide Théodoridès, Les relations de l'Egypte pharaonique avec ses voisins, 23 RIDA 87, 110 (1975).

[97] See 7 Diodorus, *supra* note 14, at 23 (passage xv.28.3). See also Mosley, *supra* note 9, at 81–82. See also Chapter 5 for more on the international legal aspects of these confederations and councils.

[98] For Roman practice, see 13 Livy, *supra* note 2, at 311 (passage xlv.20) (Rhodian embassy to Rome in 169 BCE turned away; hostilities ensued); 6 Polybius, *supra* note 15, at 233 (passage xxxii.1) (embassy from Ptolemy of Egypt refused entry into Rome; treaty of alliance with Egypt later cancelled). See also 1 Phillipson, *supra* note 1, at 309–10.

[99] See Chapter 6.

[100] For Greek practice, see Adcock and Mosley, *supra* note 26, at 164 and n. 357 (citing Demosthenes) (Spartan envoys given, in 404 BCE, ultimatum to leave Argos by sundown). See also 1 Thucydides, *supra* note 14, at 281 (passage ii.12.1–2) (Spartan ambassador, Melesippus, ordered to leave Athens in 431 BCE and escorted to the frontier). For Roman practice, see 10 Livy, *supra* note 2, at 293 (passage xxxvii.1) (Aetolian ambassadors given fifteen days to leave Italy), 12 *ibid.* 399 (passage xlii.36) (Macedonian ambassadors told to leave Rome immediately in 171 BCE); 11 Diodorus, *supra* note 14, at 373 (passage xxxi.23) (Egyptian embassy given five days to leave Rome in 161 BCE).

as already suggested, was for a host State to alleviate as many of these risks as feasible for the official representatives of other nations.[101] The physical security of the mission and its entourage was vital. But apart from the perils posed by marauders and the agents of third countries, which will be considered later,[102] there was the fundamental issue of protecting the privileges and immunities of envoys from infringement by the host nation. So it is important, at the outset, to be certain whether a host State was merely under an obligation to respect the freedom and security of a foreign mission, or whether this duty extended so far as to be a guarantor of the safety of the ambassadors within its territory from any offense whatsoever.

In ancient Babylon, there were instances where these two distinct obligations were confounded and frustrated. Hammurabi was angered by the message carried by some envoys from Elam and ordered that an *alik idi*, a court official charged with the safe conduct of visiting emissaries, not escort this mission back to the frontier and thence home.[103] According to Munn-Rankin, Hammurabi's action must have been a violation at least of custom and was "tantamount to breaking off relations" with Elam.[104] The threat to refuse an escort for a mission from Babylon was especially potent since there appeared to be no custom that other polities need respect the inviolability of envoys transiting their territory to and from other countries.[105]

The overall picture from the ancient Near East is that respect for the privileges and immunities of envoys was uncertain. Although court ceremonial in Sumer certainly implied such duties by the host State, there did not appear to be any cogent recognition of immunizing a foreign diplomat from a criminal charge. Consider this fragment, a message from one Mari prince to another, concerning an envoy from another State:

In the matter of the messenger of Telmun you sent word to me to this effect, "He entered the house of a merchant and took a palm trunk and was beaten. For this reason I have for the moment not sent him." Thus you sent word to me. fine! Let

---

[101] In ancient Mesopotamia, escort troops were provided by a host State to foreign envoys traversing its territory. See *supra* note 60. This was a necessity since ancient diplomats – at all places and at all times – often carried lavish gifts and sensitive documents, making them a tempting target for detention, ransom, plunder, or murder. See Munn-Rankin, *supra* note 55, at 105–06.

[102] See *infra* notes 105, 143–46, 177–80 and accompanying text.

[103] See 6 *Archives Royales de Mari: Correspondance de Bahdi-Lim* (J. R. Kupper transl. 1954) (passages 19, 21, 23, 79) (hereinafter "6 ARMT").

[104] Munn-Rankin, *supra* note 55, at 106–07.

[105] See *ibid.*, at 107–08 (citing 6 ARMT, *supra* note 144, passage xix.4–11).

him be beaten! But is he incapable of getting on a donkey? Why have you not sent him before this? You ought to have sent him twenty days ago.[106]

The implication of this passage seems to be that it was permissible to sanction the flogging of an envoy caught committing a criminal offense in the host State. But the senior Mari princeling, by the peremptory tone of his rescript, seems also to say that a prolonged detention was unwarranted, and maybe impermissible. We can gather that the offending messenger was alone on this mission, otherwise he could have been detained and the remainder of the mission sent on to the Mari capital. It is less clear whether the elder prince was acting from political expediency (the need to learn the contents of the message from Telmun) or from a sense of obligation.

By contrast to the studied ambivalence of Babylonian and Assyrian practice, the ancient Israelites and Egyptians represented the polar extremes of the privileges to be accorded emissaries. Dynastic Egypt clearly considered envoys as a kind of hostage.[107] In its most infamous manifestation, reported by Herodotus,[108] this practice resulted in the actual slaughter of Persian messengers sent by Cambyses of Persia to negotiate the terms of the surrender of besieged Memphis. In a retaliation completely characteristic of the Persians,[109] once Memphis fell to their forces, ten Egyptians were sacrificed for every one of the messengers killed.[110] In contrast, the ancient Israelites seemed to realize that the failure to respect the special status of envoys would lead to dire consequences.[111] Certainly in the conduct of their relations with their neighbors, an offense to an Israelite ambassador was a cause for war.[112]

If one is looking for a unifying theme of ancient Near Eastern diplomatic practice, it might be that strong (but not insurmountable)

---

[106] Munn-Rankin, supra note 55, at 108 (citing 1 Archives Royales de Mari: Correspondance de Samsi-Addu (G. Dossin transl. 1950) (passage 21) (hereinafter "1 ARMT")). See also Orlin, supra note 56, at 119 (for an incident involving an Assyrian envoy).

[107] Arthur Nussbaum, A Concise History of the Law of Nations 4–5 (rev. ed. 1954). See also 2(2) Cambridge Ancient History 24 (3rd ed. 1975) (indicating that Egyptians had detained Assyrian envoys as a reprisal for an Egyptian diplomat having been captured by a third party).   [108] 2 Herodotus, supra note 17, at 17 (passage iii.13).

[109] See ibid. at 19 (passage iii.14). See also supra note 18 with text.

[110] See also John Hosack, On the Rise and Growth of the Law of Nations 4–5 (London 1882) (reprinted 1982).

[111] See 2 Samuel 10:1–4 (Hannon, king of Ammon, mistreated David's envoys; offense avenged by Ammon's defeat).

[112] See 8 Josephus, Collected Works 59 (Ralph Marcus transl. 1963) (Loeb Classical Library reprint 1990) (Antiquities, passage xv.5.2) (narrating an incident where envoys from King Herod were murdered; a war against the tribes ensued). See also Shabtai Rosenne, The Influence of Judaism on the Development of International Law, 5 Netherlands ILR 119, 141 (1958).

customary rules barred a host State's actual injury or prolonged detention of an envoy. As just sketched, there were exceptions and qualifications to the general rule. What we do not know (at least with any historical certainty) is the degree to which, in actual State practice, these rules of diplomatic immunity were respected because they were norms deemed binding on all members of the relevant international community.

Greco-Roman diplomatic experience gives us much more historical breadth in perspective, and just enough depth, too, to understand the real normative power of rules of diplomatic conduct and the sanctions for their violation. Some maintain that ancient Greek city-States did not have a cogent "theory of diplomatic immunity . . . until the emergence of Roman power."[113] And, ironically enough, only one ancient writer made such a claim. Cornelius Nepos, writing much later of events occurring in the fourth century BCE,[114] had two Theban envoys subjected to an arbitrary detention by a hostile third State object to their treatment thinking that they were "amply protected by the inviolability of ambassadors, which it had been customary to hold valid amongst all peoples."[115]

For today's international lawyer, the words of the captured envoys are significant. If their declamation was properly recounted – and there is, of course, substantial dissension among classicists whether it was[116] – they were surely appealing to some notion of customary international law. Indeed, they even said that they were relying on the practice of nations as a binding ("valid") norm for all nations. Despite suggestions that the extension of diplomatic immunities had to be agreed upon by treaty in order to be valid,[117] it seems that the preferable understanding of Greek

---

[113] Adcock and Mosley, *supra* note 26, at 122.

[114] For more on the incident giving rise to this passage, see *infra* note 139 with accompanying text.

[115] Cornelius Nepos, *Great Generals of Foreign Nations* 191 (John C. Rolfe transl. 1929) (Loeb Classical Library reprint 1984) (xvi *Pelopidas*, passage v.1–2).

[116] See Mosley, *supra* note 9, at 81; F. Poland, *De Legationibus Graecorum Publicis* 46 (Leipzig 1885). As Professor Mosley points out, other classic sources discussing the incident with the two Theban envoys present disparate accounts. See *ibid.* (citing 7 Diodorus, *supra* note 14, at 149 (passage xv.71.2) and 5 Plutarch, *supra* note 12, at 391 (*Pelop.*, passage xxi.1)).

[117] Professor Mosley refers to that provision of the treaty establishing the Hellenic League which admonishes that envoys between contracting states should not be arrested. Mosley, *supra* note 9, at 81 (citing the inscription of the treaty). From this he apparently infers that diplomatic immunities were not custom but, rather, had to be positively legislated by treaty. This provision has already been considered above. See *supra* note 9. I interpret the clause as a prohibition against a *sending* city sanctioning their envoy for actions taken at a League meeting. It does not, therefore, have any bearing on the law and custom of diplomatic immunity. Mosley also refers, *ibid.* at 82–83, to a resolution of the Athenian assembly which invited King Philip II of Macedon to send an embassy to

diplomatic history is that there existed (at a minimum) an inchoate custom of respecting the fundamental personal integrity of envoys. This obviously begs the question of whether that custom had acquired the force of law by virtue of the sense, shared by all actors in Greek international relations, that the duty to respect diplomatic immunities was a legal obligation, and not merely an expression of courtesy or hospitality. In the same vein, King Philip II of Macedon, father of the famous Alexander, was said to have told the Athenians that a "violation of the rights of heralds and ambassadors is regarded by all men as an act of impiety, and by none more than by you."[118] Even though there is emphasis in this passage on the universal character of diplomatic inviolability, there is also the sense of a purely religious sanction for the violator: the imprecation of being "impious."

This all squares with what has already been suggested for most ancient civilizations. While "[a]mbassadors were not automatically inviolable . . . they rarely came to harm, and when they did it was something rather shocking, whether it was Greek or barbarian that was harmed."[119] One may legitimately make a nuanced distinction between ancient people's respect for the inviolability of an envoy and the extension of immunities to them. A number of current writers have done so.[120] As just noted, the pattern and practice of ancient societies was to respect the essential principle of the inviolability of the diplomat. Beyond that, though, the record is much more mixed about the extent to which emissaries were immunized from the consequences of their conduct.

The idea that diplomatic personnel were inviolable had religious and secular origins. While, as already discussed in some detail,[121] the origins

---

Footnote 117 (*cont.*)

Athens and explicitly stated that it would be given safe conduct. See *ibid.* (citing Aeschines, *supra* note 68, at 241 (*On the Embassy*, line 109)). This action hardly speaks to the positive character of the rule against harming emissaries. Indeed, it seems entirely consistent with it.

[118] 1 Demosthenes, *Collected Works* 335 (A. T. Murray transl. 1930) (Loeb Classical Library reprint 1989) (*Philip's Letter,* passage iii); 3 Euripides, *Collected Plays* 275 (A. S. Way transl. 1912) (Loeb Classical Library reprint 1979) (*Children of Heracles*, line 271).

[119] Mosley, *supra* note 9, at 93.

[120] See *ibid.* at 81; Louise M. Wéry, Le fonctionnement de la diplomatie à l'époque homérique, 14 R.I.D.A 195 (1967).

[121] See *supra* notes 25–47 with text. For more on references to diplomatic immunities in the Homeric epics, see Audinet, *supra* note 4, at 30; Karavites, *supra* note 4, at 73–74. Some relevant passages of the 1 *Iliad*, *supra* note 9, are at 181–83 (passage iv.384–98), 253 (passage v.804–808), 491 (passage xi.130–41), 579 (passage xxiv.234–35), 2 *ibid.* 119 (passage xv.174). As for the *Odyssey*, see *supra* note 1, at 409 (passage ix.371), 2 *ibid.* 305 (passage xxi.21–22).

of the heraldic institution dated back to mythic and epic periods in Greek life, this was no sure guide to explaining historic practice by the Greek city-States. First, while "Homer might be quoted by clever diplomats to support their arguments and propaganda, not everyone took the chivalry of the Heroes for his pattern, and morality had no absolutes."[122] Plutarch[123] and Strabo[124] record instances where an envoy quoted from epic texts to support some claim to immunity and protection. The same Themistocles who perpetrated the fraud on Sparta in 478 BCE,[125] some years earlier on a different mission to the recalcitrant Andrians, had warned his hosts he was escorted by two goddesses, Persuasion and Force. To this the clever Andrians replied indignantly that they already had two goddesses in residence, Poverty and Impotence.[126] By the fourth century BCE, Greek diplomats preferred, when making claims to immunities and privileges, to premise their arguments on expediency, and not the guidance of the epic texts.[127] By this time, at the conclusion of the Persian and Peloponnesian Wars, immunity came to be recognized as a secular, not a religious, notion. As will be seen below,[128] the immunities of all foreigners and visitors (and not just envoys) came to be considered as part of the same idea, but one controlled by reciprocal grants of right and favor.[129]

The second reason for the growing secularization of Greek diplomatic practice, even in the fifth and fourth centuries BCE, was the definitive split between the roles of heralds and envoys. Alluded to already,[130] it came to be that while heralds were unconditionally inviolable, envoys had to employ heralds in order to secure their freedom of movement and integrity in cities they visited and transited.[131] The practice was that one herald would accompany a mission on its journey, or, alternatively, the herald would make arrangements in advance for the safe conduct of the delegation.[132] These preliminaries were probably unnecessary when two cities were on good terms; envoys could move freely without heraldic escort or advance notice. However, when conditions became uncertain, whether because of dangers on the intervening route or by virtue of the

---

[122] Mosley, *supra* note 9, at 89.
[123] See 1 Plutarch, *supra* note 12, at 427 (*Solon*, passage x.1).
[124] 4 Strabo, *The Geography* 255 (H. L. Jones and J. R. Sitlington Sterrett transl. 1927) (Loeb Classical Library reprint 1989) (passage ix.1.10).
[125] See *supra* note 14 with accompanying text.
[126] See 4 Herodotus, *supra* note 17, at 115 (passage viii.111).
[127] See Mosley, *supra* note 9, at 89.   [128] See pp. 120–35 below.
[129] See Mosley, *supra* note 9, at 89 (citing epigraphic record of honors and privileges granted to Thasian ambassadors in Athens).
[130] See *supra* notes 48–54 with text.   [131] See Karavites, *supra* note 4, at 73–74.
[132] See Adcock and Mosley, *supra* note 26, at 54.

unknown reception to be given the envoys at their destination, the use of heralds seemed to be the safe course of action. It was also the legally correct course, the historic record being replete with examples where permission for safe conducts had to be procured in advance of a mission's journey.[133]

Once a mission safely arrived at its destination and was formally received by the host State, the normal rules of hospitality applied. This did not mean, though, that visiting envoys were left to roam free around the city. Although it was regarded as an exceptional measure, restraints could be placed on the liberty of visiting ambassadors.[134] In the story of the Spartan envoys tricked by Themistocles to visit Athens, and then held there as surety for his own safety,[135] the Lacedaemonians were certainly not in a state of open arrest and seemed to have the liberty of the city. There are, however, other notable instances where envoys were subject to actual detention. Spartan envoys were arrested in suspicious circumstances at the house of Callias in Athens in 378 BCE.[136] The Persians were also known for prolongedly detaining embassies if they were concerned they would carry back sensitive intelligence on their plans or military dispositions.[137] One instance, again already recounted here,[138] was the incident that spurred the later Cornelius Nepos to speculate on the legal character of the rule to respect the inviolability of embassies. This was the detention of two Theban ambassadors by the tyrant, Alexander of Pherae in 366 BCE. Although there appeared to be strong evidence that the Thebans were conspiring against Alexander in Thessaly, the Theban government retaliated by threatening war, and the envoys were quickly released.[139]

There appears to be only one recorded instance in which a Greek host city put to death a foreign ambassador, and it was a *cause célèbre*.[140] Already

---

[133] See Mosley, *supra* note 17, at 164–67. For more on this, see *infra* notes 143–46 with text.

[134] See Mosley, *supra* note 9, at 82 (citing Aeneas the Tactician's suggestion that the movements of foreign diplomats be controlled and their contact limited with unauthorized individuals).   [135] See *supra* note 14 with text.

[136] See Adcock and Mosley, *supra* note 26, at 154 and n. 305.

[137] See 1 Xenophon, *supra* note 50, at 29, 33 (*Hellenica*, passages i.3.8–9 and i.4.1–10). See also 8 Strabo, *supra* note 124, at 71 (passage xvii.1.19). See generally Mosley, *supra* note 9, at 82–83; 1 Phillipson, *supra* note 1, at 329.

[138] See *supra* notes 114–15 and accompanying text.

[139] See also Leech, *supra* note 9, at 43; Mosley, *supra* note 9, at 81; 1 Phillipson, *supra* note 1, at 330.

[140] But see the suggestion that the Sybarites massacred thirty envoys from Crotonia – an incident that has been disputed in the literature. See Peter Karavites, *Capitulations and Greek Interstate Relations* 24 n. 10 (1982).

narrated in Chapter 3, the story can be briefly retold. King Darius of Persia sent his heralds to Athens and Sparta in 491 BCE. As was common in Persian diplomatic practice, they came to demand earth and water of the Greek cities as tokens of submission. The Athenians thereupon threw them into prison, and the Spartans dropped them into a well, inviting them to take their earth and water there. Both sets of Persian envoys were subsequently killed. Only later did the Spartans send two nobles to Darius' heir, Xerxes, as expiation for their previous misdeed. It was a sacrifice the Persian king declined, saying that he would not "make havoc of all human law" in harming an envoy.[141] Here, at last, is the needed statement that the custom of host States ensuring the fundamental security of envoys was legal in character, and not merely an expression of comity or courtesy. That this statement is uttered (through Greek narration) by a Persian king is surprising, but not startling given the apparently universal character of many of these rules of diplomatic behavior.[142]

Despite the exceedingly strong consensus on a host city's obligation *vis-à-vis* visiting envoys, Greek diplomatic history is more ambivalent towards the treatment of envoys by third parties. It does not appear that a belligerent was under any real duty to respect the inviolability of an enemy's envoy transiting another territory. In 430 BCE, a delegation of Spartan envoys was traveling to Persia to enlist its King to participate in the Peloponnesian War. The mission was detained in Thrace, and thence turned over to the Athenians who executed them.[143] The Spartans returned the favor in 396 BCE, well after the end of the War, when they captured an Athenian mission returning from Persia. Athens and Sparta were supposed to be allied, so the Athenian mission to enemy Persia was certainly considered a treasonous act by Sparta. The Spartans thus felt at

---

[141] The account comes from 3 Herodotus, *supra* note 17, at 435–39 (passage vii.133–36). Additional accounts are found in 4 Polybius, *supra* note 15, at 89 (passage ix.38). For a sampling of the commentary on this incident, see Hosack, *supra* note 110, at 3; Leech, *supra* note 9, at 46–47; 1 Phillipson, *supra* note 1, at 329–30; Thomas A. Walker, *A History of the Law of Nations* 42 (1899); Franciszek Przetacznik, *Protection of Officials of Foreign States According to International Law* 24, 225 (1983); 1 Robert Ward, *An Enquiry into the Foundation and History of the Law of Nations in Europe* 176 (London 1795); L.-M. Wéry, *Le meurtre de hérauts de Darius en 491 et l'inviolabilité du heraut*, 35 *L'antiquité classique* 468 (1966). See also Barry S. Strauss and Josiah Ober, *The Anatomy of Error: Ancient Military Disasters and their Lessons for Modern Strategists* 26 (1990).

[142] See *supra* notes 15–20 with text.

[143] See 1 Thucydides, *supra* note 14, at 381 (passage ii.67.1); 3 Herodotus, *supra* note 17, at 435–41 (passage vii.133–37). Interestingly enough, the Spartan diplomats killed by the Athenians were the sons of the Spartan emissaries sent to Xerxes of Persia, in expiation of the murder of Darius' envoys. See Chapter 3, at notes 22, 26–27 with text.

liberty to put the Athenian envoys to death.[144] Other instances of transiting envoys being detained occurred in 427 BCE when the Syracusans intercepted an Athenian embassy bound for Rhegium in Sicily,[145] and again in 425 BCE when a Persian messenger was interdicted by Athenians.[146]

So the Greek practice of diplomatic immunities reduced to a fairly simple paradigm. Heralds, by virtue of their quasi-religious office, were inviolable under all conditions. Indeed, as Lateiner has written, heralds' "lives depended on the legal fiction that enemies are inviolable if they come as 'heralds'."[147] Once the position of a political envoy became separate and distinct from the heraldic office, ambassadors were considered immune from threats to their personal safety and integrity only when accompanied by heralds, or by prior arrangement, or upon reception in a host city when the attendant rules of ritual hospitality applied. Compare this legal construct of diplomatic privileges and immunities with the one developed by the Romans. Quite apart from the socio-religious institution of the *fetials*, which has been considered previously[148] and will be discussed further in the following chapters, the rules of inviolability extended to *all* foreign emissaries.

These rules had a definitive religious basis. As already noted,[149] the maltreatment of a visiting envoy was regarded by the Romans as a breach of the *hospitium* extended to all guests and patrons. Moreover, envoys were considered the personification of the sending nation.[150] Later codifications of Roman law make clear that harming a foreign envoy was a violation not only of the Julian law on public violence[151] but also of the law of nations.[152] A Roman citizen who harmed an ambassador was subject to noxal surrender, a ritual by which the person was handed over to the offended nation

---

[144] See 1 Xenophon, *supra* note 50, at 111 (*Hellenica*, passage ii.2.20).
[145] See Mosley, *supra* note 9, at 83 and nn. 35–36.
[146] See 2 Thucydides, *supra* note 14, at 297 (passage iv.50).
[147] Lateiner, *supra* note 37, at 103.
[148] See Chapter 3 at notes 24–25, 140–59 and accompanying text.
[149] See *supra* notes 1–2 and text.
[150] See 1 Livy, *supra* note 2, at 82 (passage i.24) ("Rex, facisne me tu regium nuntium populi Romani Quiritium"). See also Audinet, *supra* note 4, at 30.
[151] See 4 Digest, *supra* note 21, at 817 (48.6.7 (ad legem Julianam de vi publica); Ulpian, *Duties of Proconsul* 8). See also 1 Phillipson, *supra* note 1, at 330–31; Przetacznik, Special Protection of Diplomatic Agents, 50 *Revue de Droit International de Sciences Diplomatiques et Politiques* 273, 280 (1972).
[152] See 4 Digest, *supra* note 21, at 922 (50.7.18[17]; Pomponius, *Quintus Mucius* 37) ("Si quis legatum hostium pulsassit contra ius gentium id commissum esse existimatur, quia sancti habentur legati.").

for punishment, thus absolving the Roman State from the violation of the law of nations.[153] Cicero made clear that the purpose of such a surrender (a kind of extradition) was to free the state from a religious taint.[154] Cato the Younger, denouncing Caesar's victory over the Usipetes and Tencteri in Gaul because it was procured by violating a truce and slaughtering the tribal envoys, called for Caesar's extradition lest "the pollution of his crime fall upon the city."[155] Roman history is replete with the accounts of such noxal surrenders. Postumius Albinus was conveyed to the Samnites in 321 BCE for an offense against their embassy.[156] Fabius Apronius was extradited to the Apolloniates around 266 BCE.[157] In 188 BCE, Lucius Minucius Myrtilus and Lucius Manlius were delivered to the Carthaginian ambassadors whom they had struck, and taken back to Carthage.[158]

Coupled with the expressly religious sanction of noxal surrender were corollary civil sanctions. Even if an offended State refused the "sacrifice" of the individual offender – as Xerxes did with the Spartan envoys in the earlier, Greek tradition – and returned them to Rome, they could be stripped of their citizenship.[159] In any event, these unambiguous rules as to the protection of envoys were deemed by the Romans to derive from the *ius gentium*.[160] Quintus Mucius, speaking indirectly through the post-Classical *Digest* of Justinian,[161] clearly stated that rules of diplomatic immunity were part of the law of nations.[162] In Livy's narration, after

---

[153] See generally, Rich, *supra* note 13, at 109 (discussing Rome's demand to Carthage for the noxal surrender of Hannibal in 218 BCE); T. R. S. Broughton, Mistreatment of Foreign Legates and the Fetial Priests: Three Roman Cases, 41 *Phoenix* 50 (1987). Noxal surrender was also employed when a Roman envoy made, on his own authority, a treaty with a foreign power, and that agreement was later repudiated. For examples of such instances, see Chapter 5. See also *ibid.* at 50–51, 53 n. 9.

[154] See 9 Cicero, *The Speeches* 197 (H. G. Hodge transl. 1927) (Loeb Classical Library reprint 1974) (*Pro Caecina*, passage xxxiv.98) ("Ut religione civitas solvatur civis Romanus deditur . . ."). See also 2 Tacitus, *supra* note 84, at 310 (passage i.39.5) ("ni aquilifer Calpurnius vim extremam arcuisset, rarum etiam inter hostis, legatus populi Romanis in castris sanguine suo altaria deum commaculavisset").

[155] 8 Plutarch, *supra* note 12, at 359 (*Cato Minor*, passage li.1).

[156] 4 Livy, *supra* note 2, at 201 (passage ix.10.10).   [157] See Broughton, *supra* note 153, at 51.

[158] See 11 Livy, *supra* note 2, at 145 (passage xxxviii.42.7). See also 3 S. Gsell, *Histoire ancienne de l'Afrique du Nord* 300 (1920); Broughton, *supra* note 153, at 51–52.

[159] See Broughton, *supra* note 153, at 52–53 (weighing contradictory authority mentioned in 4 *Digest*, *supra* note 21, at 922 (50.7.18[17]; Pomponius, *Quintus Mucius* 37), and from Cicero). See also Alan Watson, *The Law of Persons in the Later Roman Republic* 244–47 (1967); Alan Watson, *International Law in Archaic Rome: War and Religion* 41 (1993).

[160] For more on which see the discussion in Chapter 3, pp. 84–85 above.

[161] 4 *Digest*, *supra* note 21, at 922 (50.7.18[17]).

[162] See Watson, *Law of Persons, supra* note 159, at 165.

Tatius (King of the Sabines and a colleague of Romulus) had committed a gross outrage upon some envoys of the Laurentes, the offended nation commenced proceedings "*iure gentium.*"[163] Tacitus[164] and Seneca[165] made similar remarks. Needless to say, when a Roman legate suffered some injury at the hands of a foreign sovereign, Roman indignation was harsh and their response swift and deadly, as Carthage learned in 202 BCE[166] and Corinth in 146 BCE.[167]

There were, to be sure, noted instances when the Romans did not observe the letter or the spirit of the law of diplomatic inviolability. During the height of the Second Punic War, with Hannibal bearing down on Roman forces in Italy, the city of Tarentum sent an envoy, one Phileas, to Rome. During his stay, he contrived to procure the release of Tarentine hostages kept at Rome for the purpose of ensuring his city's alliance in the war with Carthage. Phileas bribed some guards, and the entire Tarentine entourage contrived to escape, but only to be quickly recaptured. The Romans quickly put them all to death.[168] Livy rationalized this Roman violation of the *ius gentium* by implying that Phileas was not really a properly credentialed emissary.[169]

Of equal interest are those two occasions in Roman history when a citizen was charged with violating some diplomatic immunity or privilege, proceedings were brought against that individual by the College of Fetials before the Roman Senate,[170] and the Senate then refused to

[163] See 1 Livy, *supra* note 2, at 51 (passage i.14). Livy is replete with consistent references to the *ius gentium*. See 1 *ibid.* at 231 (passage ii.4) (envoys of expelled Tarquin allowed to go free despite being involved in a coup attempt), 2 *ibid.* 313, 361 (passages iv.17–19 and 32), 3 *ibid.* 261 (passage vi.19), 4 *ibid.* 16 (passage viii.5) ("Annius, tamquam victor armis Capitolium cepisset, non legatus iure gentium tutus"), 199 (passage ix.10), 5 *ibid.* 71 (passage xxi.25), 11 *ibid.* 295 (passage xxxix.25) ("legatis, qui iure gentium sancti sint").

[164] 1 Tacitus, *The Histories* 469 (Clifford H. Moore transl. 1925) (Loeb Classical Library reprint 1980) (passage iii.80) ("Sacrum etiam in exteras gentes legatorum ius et fas.").

[165] 1 Seneca, *Moral Essays* 257 (John W. Basore transl. 1928) (Loeb Classical Library reprint 1985) (*De ira*, passage iii.2.5) ("Violatae legationes rupto iure gentium").

[166] See 4 Polybius, *supra* note 15, at 467 (passage xv.2) (truce in Second Punic War ended when Carthaginians plotted against Roman envoys who had come to treat with them).

[167] See 9 Cicero, *supra* note 154, at 23 (*Leg. Man.*, passage v.11).

[168] See 6 Livy, *supra* note 2, at 367 (passage xxv.7).

[169] See *ibid.* (Phileas merely sojourned at Rome "diu jam per speciem legationis"). See also Leech, *supra* note 9, at 44–45.

[170] The precise modalities of the *fetials* bringing a formal action against an individual charged with this sort of violation of the law of nations are recounted in Broughton, *supra* note 153, at 56–58. There is substantial division in classicist historiography over the functions and practices of Roman institutions under these circumstances. See also E. S. Gruen, *Roman Politics and Criminal Courts, 149–78 BC*, at 168–69 (1968).

extradite the individual to the tender mercies of the offended State. The first instance has been recounted already.[171] When the Senonian Gauls, led by Brennus, were besieging Clusium in 390 BCE, the Romans sent a delegation led by Fabius Ambustus as an ambassador to their camp with proposals of peace on behalf of the Etruscan tribe, who were Roman allies. But upon receiving a harsh answer, Fabius thought himself released from his character as an ambassador, and other members of his embassy rashly took up arms for the Clusians. The Romans won the combat, but the Gauls called upon the gods to witness Fabius' violation of the common law of all nations, in coming to them as an ambassador and then fighting against them as an enemy. Brennus sent a herald to Rome to accuse Fabius of bearing arms against them, contrary to the treaties and good faith, and without a declaration of war. Upon this the *fetials* ordered the Senate to deliver him up to the Gauls, but Fabius appealed to the people and he was screened from the sentence. Soon after this, the Gauls marched to Rome, and sacked the city.[172] This is one noted occasion where noxal surrender was sought for a Roman envoy who had abused his diplomatic privileges by waging war against an ostensibly friendly power. Apart from the political forces at work in Rome, no explanation is given why Fabius was not extradited to the Gauls. There surely was no doubt that a violation of the ancient law of nations had occurred.[173]

The second occasion when the Romans disclaimed responsibility for their violation of diplomatic law occurred in 101 BCE. The only record of the transaction is from Diodorus Siculus.[174] A mission from King Mithridates of Pontus arrived in Rome that year, bringing with them a large sum of money with which to bribe the Roman Senate to forbear from initiating hostilities against Pontus. One popular leader, L. Appuleius Saturninus, sought deliberately to provoke and offend the Pontan ambassadors and thus expose their design. The envoys lodged a complaint against the insolent Saturninus, and, with the cooperation of some

---

[171] See Chapter 3 at notes 21, 24–25 with text.

[172] See 1 Plutarch, *supra* note 12, at 349–51 (*Numa*, passage xii.7), 2 *ibid.* at 129–37 (*Camillus*, passages 17 and 18); 3 Livy, *supra* note 2, at 123 (passage v.36); 1 Appian, *Roman History* 99 (Horace White transl. 1912) (Loeb Classical Library reprint 1982) (*De rebus Gallicis*, passage 1); 6 Diodorus, *supra* note 14, at 303, 309 (passage xiv.113–15).

[173] See generally 1 Phillipson, *supra* note 1, at 341.

[174] See 12 Diodorus, *supra* note 14, at 178–81 (passage xxxvi.15). For background on this incident, see A. N. Sherwin-White, *Roman Foreign Policy in the East, 168 BC to AD 1*, at 104–05 (1983).

corrupt senators, a public trial for Saturninus was held. When public sentiment turned in favor of Saturninus, he was acquitted of all charges. It is not clear from Diodorus' account exactly what offense Saturninus gave to the ambassadors of Mithridates. The historian implies that he was "great[ly] insolent."[175] Although Saturninus did not appear to have threatened the security of the mission, his conduct was sufficient to implicate the Fetial College, along with the Senate, in punishing these transgressions.[176] In two of these exceptional cases, the historical record remains murky whether the conduct of Roman citizens violated the *ius gentium*. Phileas of Tarentum may not have been properly accredited as an envoy to Rome. Saturninus' offense may not have been grave enough to trigger noxal surrender or capital punishment. As for Fabius, the Romans themselves acknowledged that their failure to extradite him to Brennus was a grievous error for which their city paid dearly.

Despite these aberrations, which the Roman legalistic mind was able to distinguish, the overall picture is of general compliance with established norms of diplomatic conduct. The duty of hosts to protect the inviolability of envoys was taken seriously. The ostensible neutrality that Roman legates had to observe was also considered sacrosanct. The Romans, like the Greeks, did dissemble regarding the status of third-country envoys transiting their territory or otherwise falling under their control. The Republic, to be sure, was easily offended when envoys accredited to it were intercepted by a third country. In 189 BCE, it demanded the return of Aetolian ambassadors held captive by the rival Epirotes.[177] Likewise, among the Thessalians' complaints against Philip of Macedon in 187 BCE was that he had plotted against the safety of other Greek missions bound for Rome.[178]

The Romans did not show such mercy to the envoys of belligerent powers encountered during their travels. Macedon's embassy to Hannibal of Carthage in 215 BCE was intercepted at sea, and they were conveyed as prisoners to Rome.[179] Earlier, in an attempt to ingratiate themselves with the Romans, the Latins in 495 BCE handed over Volscian envoys to their enemies.[180] These incidents were contrary to other indications that the rule of diplomatic inviolability was extended to the ambassadors of bel-

---

[175] See Broughton, *supra* note 153, at 54.
[176] See *ibid.* at 56–62.   [177] See 5 Polybius, *supra* note 15, at 295 (passage xxi.26).
[178] See 11 Livy, *supra* note 2, at 294 (passage xxxix.25.10) ("Iam ne a legatis quidem, qui iure gentium sancti sint, violandis abstinere: insidias positas euntibus ad T. Quinctium.").
[179] See 6 *ibid.* at 115 (passage xxiii.33–34).   [180] See 1 *ibid.* at 289 (passage ii.22).

ligerent powers. Livy,[181] Cicero,[182] and Tacitus[183] said as much; the *Digest* even contains such a provision.[184]

As with the Greeks, the Roman refusal to accord protection to enemy envoys seems only to have occurred at the height of a life-or-death struggle in belligerency. Hence the only real examples of such an infringement are from the critical phases of the Peloponnesian[185] and Second Punic Wars. Yet, even under such conditions the Romans were said to have been remarkably scrupulous. During the War with Hannibal, Scipio's envoys had been maltreated by the Carthaginians. An unlucky Punic mission which later fell into the consul's power did not suffer the same fate. In what contemporary writers no doubt upheld as a superb example of Roman *bona fides*, Scipio (like Xerxes) generously released the emissaries and saw to their safe return to Carthage.[186] In a similar vein, when Jugurtha was in Rome on a peace mission he was protected from interference despite being in a state of war with the Republic. Unfortunately, Jugurtha used his stay in Rome to have one of his Numidian rivals, Massiva, murdered.[187] A member of Jugurtha's entourage was implicated, and, despite claims of immunity from criminal prosecution by virtue of his status, he was punished. Sallust, in narrating these events,[188] seems to imply that the procedure was irregular and that, normally, rules of diplomatic immunity would have protected Jugurtha's minion. But this was not a normal situation; the offender was punished "rather for reason of equity than by the law of nations."[189]

As has already been intimated,[190] there might be a distinction to be drawn between the ancient respect for diplomatic inviolability and the extension of diplomatic immunities. As Coleman Phillipson suggested,

---

[181] See 6 *ibid.* at 280 (passage xxiv.33) ("Legatis in periculum adductis ne belli quidem iura relicta erant.").

[182] See 2 Cicero, *supra* note 154, at 97 (*In Verr.*, passage iii.34) ("Legatorum ius divino humanoque vallatum praesidio, cuius tam sanctum et venerabile nomen esse debet, ut non modo inter sociorum iura, sed et hostium tela incolume versetur.").

[183] See Tacitus, *supra* note 84, at 316 (passage i.42) ("Hostium quoque ius et sacra legationis et fas gentium rupistis.").

[184] See 4 *Digest*, *supra* note 21, at 922 (50.7.17; Pomponius, *Quintus Mucius* 37) ("si cum legati apud nos essent gentis alicuius, bellum cum eis indictum sit? responsum est, liberos eos manere; id enim iuri gentium convenit esse").

[185] See *supra* notes 177–80 with text.

[186] See 11 Diodorus, *supra* note 14, at 217 (passage xxvii.12).

[187] See Strauss and Ober, *supra* note 140, at 182.

[188] Sallust, *supra* note 93, at 211 (passage xxxv).

[189] *Ibid.* at 212 (passage xxxv.7) ("Fit reus magis ex aequo bonoque quam ex iure gentium").

[190] See text with *supra* note 120.

"[t]he principle of extraterritoriality follows naturally from that of inviolability. The latter represents the positive aspect of that protection; the
former, implying judicial independence in regard to the foreign State, represents the negative aspect."[191] The *Digest* seems to record a careful inter-
play of laws respecting the immunities of foreign ambassadors from
various types of proceedings. Reduced to their essence,[192] foreign envoys
were *not* insulated from actions seeking contractual redress for agreements undertaken in Rome,[193] but were otherwise immune from all other
actions, including (presumably) criminal prosecutions.[194]

The status and protection of alien visitors

I have left for the end of this chapter a discussion of how foreigners were
treated in ancient polities. While this topic seems to subsume the narrower issue of diplomatic privileges and immunities, I have reserved
comment on it in order sensibly to develop an understanding of ancient
diplomatic practice and law. The problem of aliens resident in ancient
States had implications for the whole of ancient international relations.
It was certainly so for commerce (surely the principal reason for cultural
interpenetrations), but also for other social and political relations.

The point has already been made about the primary tension within the
ancient State's perception of strangers: religious and ethnic particularism
was balanced against the pragmatic institution of hospitality.[195] What
needs to be borne in mind is that ancient peoples had self-consciously to
elevate a status for strangers. It has been well noted, for example, that in
ancient Greek and Latin, the terms for "barbarian," "stranger," and
"enemy" were originally synonymous.[196] Aristotle quoted earlier poets as
writing that "[i]t is [right] that Hellenes should rule over barbarians," as if,
Aristotle opined, such writers believed "that the barbarian and slave were

[191] 1 Phillipson, *supra* note 1, at 337.   [192] See generally *ibid.*, at 339–41.
[193] See 1 *Digest, supra* note 21, at 164–65 (5.1.2.4–5; Ulpian, *Edict* 3). Under the *lex Gabinia* of
67 BCE, confirming a Senatorial decree of 94 BCE, no one who loaned moneys to foreign
emissaries had a right of action thereon. See 1 Cicero, *Letters* 409–11 (E. O. Winstedt
transl. 1912) (Loeb Classical Library reprint 1980) (*Ad Att.*, passage v.21.12). Some have
speculated that this was an attempt to eliminate abuses of diplomatic immunity by
foreign missions, it being doubtful that any moneylender would loan to a foreign envoy
if there was no right to recover on the sums. See 1 Phillipson, *supra* note 1, at 340–41.
[194] See 1 *Digest, supra* note 21, at 164 (5.1 (de iudiciis).2.3; Ulpian, *Edict* 3) ("Legatis in eo
quod ante legationem contraxerunt . . . revocandi domum suam ius datur.").
[195] See Chapters 2 and 3 as well as the first section of this chapter.
[196] See Ward, *supra* note 141, at 174–76; Henry Wheaton, *History of the Law of Nations in
Europe and America* 1 (New York 1845).

one."[197] Yet, in the same pages of his tract, Aristotle could recite no fewer than three instances in which foreigners were asked to restore law and order to Greek city-States wracked by civil disturbance.[198] It is precisely this ambivalence which marks the ancient record of the legal status and treatment accorded to strangers living in the midst of cognizable political entities. This part will, therefore, consider the legal liabilities that came with that treatment and the ideological transformation of that status.

The bulk of this examination is necessarily confined to Greco-Roman practice. Sources for ancient Middle Eastern customs are surprisingly sketchy on the matter of how aliens were treated in those societies. Indeed, the ideas surrounding the international law of protection of foreigners were peculiarly the preoccupation of ancient Mediterranean cultures.[199] While the historic record for the ancient Israelites reflects the same tensions between tolerance and hostility for strangers,[200] we know little more than what Biblical and Talmudic texts recite.[201] Likewise, all we discern about the ancient Egyptians was that they were surprisingly liberal in according extraterritorial rights to foreign communities living within their midst.[202]

We know much more about the status of aliens in ancient Greek city-States, particularly in Athens. For a foreigner to acquire all of the rights of citizenship in Athens was most difficult.[203] In the rest of Greece it was nearly impossible.[204] In the legislation of Solon, as recounted by Plutarch, foreigners were barred from becoming full citizens of Athens unless they had been exiled for life from their native cities, or had removed

---

[197] Aristotle, *Politics* (H. Rackham transl. 1932) (Loeb Classical Library reprint 1990) (passage i.2.9). For a gloss on this passage, see Vilho Harle, *Ideas of Social Order in the Ancient World* 179–83 (1998).

[198] See Aristotle, *supra* note 197, at 1274, 1285 (passages 23–26, 30–31) (Pittacus as *aisymnetes* at Mytilene; Demonax the Mantinean as lawgiver for Cyrene; Andromadas of Rhegium as lawgiver for Thracian Chalcis).

[199] This preoccupation was partly manifested in practices involving international arbitration. See Chapter 1, at note 14, for sources.

[200] See Chapter 3, notes 73–77 with text.

[201] See Prosper Weil, Le Judaïsme et le Développement du Droit Internationale, 151 RCADI 253, 288–89 (1976–III). See also Dennis J. McCarthy, *Treaty and Covenant* 61 and n. 29 (1963) (discussing ancient Syrian treaties concerning citizens of one country who commit crimes in the territory of the other).

[202] See 1 Phillipson, *supra* note 1, at 193.

[203] See Plutarch, *supra* note 12, at 109 (*Pericles*, passage xxxvii.3–4); Aristotle, *supra* note 197, at 205 (*Politics*, passage iii.5).

[204] For more on Spartan practice, including the Xenelasia prohibiting contact with foreigners, see 1 Plutarch, *supra* note 12, at 227 (*Agesthines*, passage x; *Lycurgus*, passage vii).

voluntarily to Athens (with their entire family) to practice their trade or profession. Plutarch believed that the object of Solon's policy was not so much to deny citizenship to broad classes of peoples, but, rather, to provide a mechanism for asylum, since it was thought that asylees would thereby become good and faithful citizens of their new home.[205]

In Athens, for example, there always subsisted a large class of legally recognized aliens, the *metoikoi*, or metics. *Metoikoi* were permanent residents of Athens, officially registered as such. Their status was strictly defined in exchange for the privilege of permanent domicile.[206] Metics paid an annual tax (the *metoikion*), and they could be enslaved if they failed to tender it to the city.[207] *Metoikoi* had no political rights and could not acquire real estate within Athens. Like citizens, they were subject to military conscription, although they were eligible to serve only in the lower ranks or on the benches of the galleys.[208] They were subject to some of the same liturgies and observances that citizens were required to make.[209] While they enjoyed full judicial protection as residents, their access to justice was circumscribed.[210] *Metics* were particularly numerous in Athens – more than probably any other Greek city – and at their zenith they numbered some tens of thousands souls, constituting between a tenth and an eighth of the population.[211]

More occasional visitors, individuals who were not accorded *metoikoi* status, were subject to additional inconveniences and indignities. Travelers were often searched at city frontiers, their goods subject to customs levies or outright confiscation. Itinerant merchants often were obliged to carry passports or safe-conducts, even in times of relative peace.[212] Clearance passes sometimes permitted dealers to be exempted from customs liabilities.[213]

Foreigners were routinely subject to reprisals. Self-help measures were common to all primitive legal cultures, and they were surely significant in some aspects of ancient international relations. Some have said that

---

[205] 1 Plutarch, *supra* note 12, at 471 (*Solon*, passage xxiv).

[206] See *Translated Documents*, *supra* note 80, at 212.

[207] *Ibid*. It is speculation whether *metics* were actually subject in Athens to enslavement for failure to pay the *metoikion*. See D. Whitehead, *The Ideology of the Athenian Metic*, 4 Cambridge Philological Proceedings Supplement (Cambridge 1977). See also H. Francotte, *De la condition des étrangers dans les Cités grecques* (Louvain-Paris 1903).

[208] See 2 Thucydides, *supra* note 14, at 25 (passage iii.16).

[209] See *Translated Documents*, *supra* note 80, at 212.

[210] See *ibid*. There is substantial debate on this point, which will be considered *infra* at notes 249–58 and accompanying text.   [211] See Nussbaum, *supra* note 107, at 6.

[212] See 1 Phillipson, *supra* note 1, at 132–33.

[213] See V. Thumser, *De civium Atheniensium muneribus* 110 (Vienna 1880).

the practice of reprisal "suggests a crude legal notion of joint responsibility of a community for actions of its members [and is] symptomatic of lawlessness and barbarism."[214] But as Sir Paul Vinogradoff wrote:

[Such measures] were not by any means simple outbursts of unlawful violence. As frequently happens in ancient law, distress was used as a means of obtaining justice by self-help. Another feature of the procedure was that distress or reprisals were not necessarily directed against one's opponent, but might be levelled against relatives of his, or even against his countrymen at large.[215]

The principle of reprisal found its legal vindication in the custom of *androlepsia* – literally "man seizure"[216] – practiced in Athens and elsewhere in Greece. *Androlepsia* was invoked whenever a citizen of a town was murdered by an alien or by a foreign government. Relatives of the deceased[217] could, under the sanction of law, seize three fellow-countrymen of the killer, and then hold them for ransom or for judicial condemnation to pay compensation. If neither was forthcoming, the foreigners could be put to death in satisfaction of the blood debt. According to the law as cited by Demosthenes, it would seem that *androlepsia* could be applied indiscriminately against the nationals of any foreign polity.[218]

It hardly needs comment that if reprisals and *androlepsia* had prevailed as a general feature of international relations in ancient Greece the entire context for the development of international law would have been different. As it turned out, however, the availability and widely sanctioned use of self-help measures, which would be natural with any primitive legal society, conditioned the need for a response. The alternative chosen by the Greeks was premised on the rule of law. This was the development of forms and institutions which could moderate the atavistic and particularistic tendencies of atomized Greek city-States, and elevate the status of foreigners and visitors. Some of these legal responses will be reviewed in fuller detail in the next chapter, but they need to be introduced here in order to give a sense of how at least one ancient State system confronted

---

[214] Nussbaum, *supra* note 107, at 8. See also Michael Gagarin, *Early Greek Law* (1986).

[215] Sir Paul Vinogradoff, Historical Types of International Law, in 1 *Biblioteca Visseriana Dissertationum ius internationale illustrantium* 1, 14 (1923).

[216] See 2 Phillipson, *supra* note 1, at 349.

[217] Relatives eligible to indulge in *androlepsia* were limited to those closest degrees of consanguinity. We have confirmation of this in 5 Demosthenes, *supra* note 118, at 99 (*Macart.*, passage lvii).

[218] See 3 Demosthenes, *supra* note 118, at 273 (passage *Against Aristocrates*, line 84). Furthermore, an aggrieved individual could kidnap any foreigner found in the territory of an opposing city. See *infra* note 237 with text (for an agreement which specifically barred such a practice).

the problem of interpersonal relations amongst citizens of different polities.

Agreements: xenoi, asylia, isopoliteia, and symbola

The Greeks understood the necessity for elevating the status of aliens. Without such an alteration, the presumption was that the normal state of international relations permitted reprisals and self-help to be undertaken against the citizens of foreign city-States. As a consequence of this insight, the Greek city-States fashioned a number of different arrangements that were used to elevate the status of individual foreigners (or groups of residents) living within their precincts. Alternatively, international agreements were concluded that would place the posture of relations between two city-States on an entirely different footing. While that latter category of agreements will be discussed in the next chapter, the multiplicity of such legal classifications for foreigners is what gave Greek international relations its striking character.

The most rudimentary form of international agreement for the bestowal of special grants to a foreigner were those recognizing a *xenos* during time of war or conflict. Accepted as a direct outgrowth of the institution of hospitality and ritual friendship, the *philia* or *xenia* rank was granted as a sign of respect and devotion between the leaders of allied military contingents.[219] In this sense, the *xenoi* custom was confined to the highest levels of individual power and authority. Indeed, this practice seemed nearly universal, as it was observed by the Mauryan Indian[220] and Egyptian[221] dynasties, and by the Carthaginians,[222] as well as by the Greek city-States and their Macedonian conquerors.[223]

While not bearing directly on the issue of the treatment of foreigners living in independent polities, the status granted by a recognition of *xenia*

---

[219] See 3 Herodotus, *supra* note 17, at 341 (passage vii.27–29 and 39); Xenophon, *supra* note 50, at 275 (*Hellenica*, passage iv.1.29). See also Herman, *supra* note 1, at 50–54 (on the strongly related concepts of *pistis* and *dexia*).

[220] See 2 Herodotus, *supra* note 17, at 27–28 (passage iii.21); 2 Xenophon, *Cyropaedia* 149 (W. Miller transl.) (Loeb Classical Library reprint 1914) (passage vi.2.1). References to similar agreements were made in ancient Mesopotamia: see Munn-Rankin, *supra* note 55, at 76.

[221] See 2 Herodotus, *supra* note 17, at 53 (passage iii.39) (for the *xenia* concluded between Polycrates of Samos and Amasis of Egypt).

[222] See 3 Polybius, *supra* note 15, at 421 (passage vii.9) (Hannibal's "covenant" with Philip V of Macedon).

[223] See Gabriel Herman, *Ritualized Friendship and the Greek City* 45–46, 132–39 (Cambridge 1987). Professor Herman has a comprehensive analysis of occasions in which *xenoi* or *philoi* are mentioned in classic Greek literature. See *ibid.* 135 n. 50. These treaties of alliance and friendship will be considered in more detail in Chapter 5.

or *philia* was surely influential in directing the contours of other Hellenic institutional arrangements between city-States. *Xenia* was an affirmative legal status, concluded often by a written agreement solemnized by oath and ritual. The other Greek institutional arrangements considered here were made in a like fashion. They were more than individual grants of favor bestowed by a citizen of a State upon a visitor or foreign friend. They were conscious acts made by a recognized political entity to moderate what would have been an otherwise decidedly unfriendly or hostile attitude towards alien residents.

Consider first the institution of *asylia*, where one city-State extended to a particular foreigner (or his family or extended clan) a promise that he would not be subject to self-help measures by its citizens, including protection from *androlepsia*. A grant of *asylia* meant that "though his fellow-citizens still might be fair game, he personally was exempt"[224] from the liabilities of being a stranger. Many inscriptions of *asylia* proclamations from ancient Greece are still extant; they indicate that such grants were quite common.[225] Aside from making grants of *asylia* to named individuals, there is evidence that they were also made to classes of foreigners engaged in important work or activities, including athletes[226] and artisans for public works.[227] Just as significantly, *asylia* was important for immunizing the vessels and cargoes of merchants from maritime reprisals, including State-sponsored piracy and depredation on the high seas.[228] Although privateering was usually confined to wartime, it was always regarded as a menace by merchants of all nationalities.[229] Once given an *asylia*, an individual was immune from seizures of property or from *androlepsia*, unless

---

[224] J. A. O. Larsen, *Greek Federal States: Their Institutions and History* 212 (1968).

[225] See *ibid.* at 207.

[226] See P. Haussoullier, Comment, 5 *Bulletin de correspondance hellénique* 372 (1881) (cited in 2 Phillipson, *supra* note 1, at 362–63) (quoting an inscription from Aetolia granting *asylia* for those participating in games sponsored by King Eumenes).

[227] See Dareste, Haussoullier and Reinach, *Recueil des inscriptions juridiques grecques* 143 (Paris 1891) (the town of Eretria in Euboea granted *asylia* to a contractor for draining a marsh). See also Andocides, *Minor Attic Orators* 557 (K. J. Maidment transl. 1941) (Loeb Classical Library reprint 1980) (*Alcibiades*, passage xviii) (Alcibiades violated a treaty by imprisoning a worker from another city in order to compel him to execute certain work. Andocides concluded: "In our treaties with other states we make it a condition that no free man shall be imprisoned or placed in durance, and a heavy fine is prescribed as the penalty for so doing.").

[228] For different terms describing this practice, see 5 Polybius, *supra* note 15, at 93 (passages xviii.4.8 and xviii.5.1–3). See also Adcock and Mosley, *supra* note 26, at 188–89.

[229] See 2 Polybius, *supra* note 15, at 367 (passage iv.26.7), 427 (passage iv.53.2), 5 *ibid.* 351 (passage xxii.4.13) (reprisal made by Cretan city of Eleutheria against Rhodes in 220 BCE; Achaeans sanction privateering against Aetolians in the same year; Achaean privateering against Boeotians in 187–86 BCE). See also Larsen, *supra* note 224, at 211–12.

they had been publicly adjudged a debtor, or unless that individual's city of origin agreed to the intended sanction.[230] A number of *asylia* proclamations provided penalties for anyone who did derogate from the rights of a protected foreigner, including civil penalties or criminal prosecution.[231]

The custom of *asylia* was analytically different from the practice of granting protection to refugees – what we would today call political asylum. As will be considered subsequently,[232] asylum had a spatial context as well: certain towns and sites were considered sanctuaries.[233] In its status context, asylum could be by treaty between two or more city-States, guaranteeing the right of citizens of one town to seek and receive refuge in another.[234] Violations of the duty to provide refuge to individuals were sharply criticized by ancient Greek writers, Herodotus especially.[235] The Greeks also confronted the problem of according asylum to individuals who were wanted by their home States for criminal punishment. A too-generous system for according refuge had the potential thereby to strain relations between city-States. Indeed, the failure to extradite a criminal responsible for murder could result in the perpetuation of a blood-feud, and its international manifestation in the custom of *androlepsia*.[236]

The Greeks resolved this paradox – respecting hospitality and granting asylum or delivering up criminals and averting conflict – by negotiating a system of agreements known as *isopoliteiai*. In its most basic form, an *isopoliteia* was an agreement made between two cities mutually relieving their respective citizens of the risk of *androlepsia*. Self-help and reprisal

[230] See 2 Phillipson, *supra* note 1, at 362 and n. 5.

[231] See the Aetolian decree reprinted in Haussollier, *supra* note 227, at 372–83. See also 2 Phillipson, *supra* note 1, at 363; Adcock and Mosley, *supra* note 26, at 188 (describing the fifth-century BCE agreement between Oeantheia and Chaleion). For further material on *asylia*, see M. Holleaux, Études d'historique hellénistique: Remarques sur les décrets des villes de Crète relatifs à l'*asylia* de Téos, 13 *Beiträge zur alten Geschichte* (1913); Charles Lécrivain, Le droit sur se faire justice soi-même et les représailles dans les relations internationales de la Grèce, 9 *Mémoires de l'Académie de Toulouse* 277 (1897); E. Schlesinger, *Die griechische Asylie* (Giessen 1913).   [232] See Chapter 6.

[233] Aside from asylum granted by temples and religious sanctuaries, the Greeks had one secular equivalent offered by the town of Teos, which, by a treaty ratified by more than twenty-five polities (including Rome in 193 BCE), was recognized as a safe haven for refugees fleeing persecution. See 1 Phillipson, *supra* note 1, at 354. The isle of Samothrace was also considered a reliable place for refuge. See 13 Livy, *supra* note 2, at 263 (passage xlv.6) (Perseus, last king of Macedon, sought refuge on Samothrace from the Romans).

[234] An inscription survives with a note exchanged between the Ionians of Paros and the Allarians of Crete on the subject of mutual asylum. See 2 J. Barbeyrac, *Histoire des anciens traités*, at No. 338 (Amsterdam 1739).

[235] See, e.g., 1 Herodotus, *supra* note 17, at 201–03 (passage i.160) (describing the woes that befell the Chians who betrayed Pactyas to his Persian pursuers).

[236] See *supra* notes 216–18 and accompanying text.

was thus replaced with a reciprocal promise to "grant justice" to the citizens of the other city. As a starting point, consider the fifth-century BCE agreement between Chaleion and Oiantheia, which provided that:

> it is forbidden to any man of Oiantheia to carry off a foreigner on the territory of Chaleion, and to any man of Chaleion to carry off a foreigner on the territory of Oiantheia, or to seize property by way of distress. Whoever distrains property belonging to a foreigner ... without right, the fine shall be four drachmae ... If a man of Chaleion is a resident established more than a month at Oiantheia, and *vice versa*, he shall have recourse to the justice of the city.[237]

Substantial debate has transpired concerning the real effect of these *isopoliteiai*. E. W. Weber suggested that they were merely a variant of political alliances, and so quite unexceptional in the course of Greek international relations.[238] The better view seems to be that *isopoliteiai* were concluded in real indifference of the state of relations between Greek city-States.[239] Their purpose was to relieve the friction caused by occurrences of *androlepsia* and by conflicts over grants of asylum for criminals. Having in force an *isopoliteia* provided a recourse for the family of an individual murdered by a foreigner in another city: they could seek "the justice of the city" and forego the need for self-help. If that justice were denied, which usually meant that if the culprit was not punished or not extradited to the aggrieved city's jurisdiction, then the right of *androlepsia* could be invoked.[240]

Now, it is true that some *isopoliteiai* did make provision for a mutual exchange of privileges of citizenship between two independent cities. That is why they have been thought to be precursors to formal alliances in ancient Greek diplomatic practice.[241] Some provisions of these treaties waived the formality of one city granting permission to the citizens of the other to settle upon its territory and own houses or property.[242] Other clauses could grant the right of intermarriage,[243] or unrestricted

---

[237] The translation is from Vinogradoff, *supra* note 215, at 15. See also Adcock and Mosley, *supra* note 26, at 188 (for more on this agreement).

[238] See E. W. Weber, *Demosthenis oratio in Aristocratem* 298 (Jena 1845).

[239] See, e.g., 2 M. H. E. Meier, *Opuscula academica* 189 (Halle 1863). See also Adcock and Mosley, *supra* note 26, at 187; J. A. O. Larsen, Isopoliteia, in *The Oxford Classical Dictionary* 461 (1953).   [240] See 2 Phillipson, *supra* note 1, at 351.

[241] See, e.g., 5 Polybius, *supra* note 15, at 57 (passage xvi.26); 9 Livy, *supra* note 2, at 47 (passage xxxi.15) (both concerning later alliance between Athens and Rhodes, characterized as a form of *isopoliteia*). See also 1 Phillipson, *supra* note 1, at 141–42.

[242] See 1 Phillipson, *supra* note 1, at 161 (discussing Hierapytna–Priasnos and Latiani–Olontani treaties). See also 7 Xenophon, *Scripta Minora* 197 (E. Marchant transl. 1925) (Loeb Classical Library reprint 1984) (*De vectig.*, passage ii.6).

[243] See 1 Phillipson, *supra* note 1, at 141.

trade.[244] Still others made standing invitations to participate in games or religious observances.[245] Although there is dispute on this issue,[246] some isopolitic conventions – to the extent they extended to participation in "all things divine and human"[247] – may even have granted political rights to foreigners. A handful of these reciprocal treaties may have even provided for a *sympoliteia*, practically a federal union of States with interchange of full civic and political rights. These were quite rare, and, in effect, created a double or treble citizenship for the individuals living in the cities involved, though such a *sympoliteia* or *to plethos* was susceptible to dissolution at the pleasure of any of the allied communities.[248]

Short of entering into a *sympoliteia*, Greek city-States were confronted with the problem of how to resolve private conflicts between individuals owing allegiance to different cities and thereby reduce the need for recourse to self-help measures. As already noted, a common feature of *isopoliteia* was a promise to "grant justice" to foreigners. This commitment, in turn, spawned a diverse complex of additional agreements and institutions. At its most basic, an assurance to "grant justice" (known generically as a *symbolon* when it appeared in a written text concluded between two independent[249] States) was that "justice shall be administered to individual citizens of each State according to their ancestral customs."[250] In the

---

[244] Commercial treaties, as such, seem to have been unknown in ancient Greece. While an *isopoliteia* could grant special commercial rights to citizens of one city sojourning in another, this seemed to be exceptional. See A. B. Büchsenschütz, *Besitz und Erwerb im griechischen Altertume* 516 (Halle 1869). See also 3 Plutarch, *supra* note 12, at 85 (*Pericles*, passage xxix.4) (Megarian merchants' complaint that they had been excluded from the market at Athens).

[245] See Leech, *supra* note 9, at 35. See also the stipulations of an inscription quoted by 2 Demosthenes, *supra* note 118, at 77 (*De corona*, line 91) (towns of Byzantium and Perinthus granting rights to Athenians).

[246] See 2 B. G. Niebuhr, *Römische Geschichte* (Berlin 1873); de Taube, *supra* note 1, at 36–37.

[247] See 1 Phillipson, *supra* note 1, at 143 (quoting an agreement between Hierapytna of Crete and Magnesia) (translated from P. Cauer, *Delectus inscriptionum Graecarum* No. 118 (Leipzig 1883)).

[248] See 1 Phillipson, *supra* note 1, at 144. See also E. L. Hicks and G. F. Hill, *A Manual of Greek Historical Inscriptions*, at No. 176 (1901) (inscription of *sympoliteia* between Magnesia and Smyrna); William P. Merrill, To PLETHOS in a Treaty Concerning the Affairs of Argos, Knossos and Tylissos, 41 CQ 16 (1991).

[249] A substantial body of modern historiography has closely examined the use of *symbola* in dependent relations between Greek city-States. Compare Adcock and Mosley, *supra* note 26, at 186–87 ("The existence of such *symbolai* in no way implied the subordination of interests of one state to those of another.") with R. J. Hopper, Interstate Juridical Agreements in the Athenian Empire, 63 JHS 35 (1943) (who persuasively argues that such was, indeed, the case for Athenian dependants).

[250] The quote is from the sixth clause of the treaty between Sparta and Argos of 418 BCE, as translated in Vinogradoff, *supra* note 215, at 16.

practice of some communities, the promise to "grant justice" was merely an agreement to accord a resident foreigner the process due to a citizen.[251] Similarly, a *symbolon* could be an invitation for an alien to apply his own city's law in a dispute with a resident of another city. This apparent choice of law dilemma has been noted by several authorities,[252] and whether Greek city-States applied their own law to disputes with resident aliens,[253] or, instead, adopted a different rule depending on the identity of the parties in a civil action,[254] has never really been satisfactorily resolved.

Putting aside those *symbola* that referred disputes to neutral, third-party arbitration,[255] it was clearly intended that instead of resorting to self-help or *androlepsia*, disputes between citizens of two cities would be resolved in the courts of one. Some *symbola* reposed confidence in the regular judicial institutions of the participating cities.[256] Others granted jurisdiction to *xenodikai*, special tribunals charged with handling disputes between foreigners or between aliens and citizens.[257] In Athens, generic *xenodikai* were replaced by the permanent office of the *polemarchos*.[258]

---

[251] See, e.g., the surviving inscription of fourth-century *symbola* between Athens and Siphnos. See 2 H. Bengtson, *Die Staatsverträge des Altertums* No. 294 (Berlin and Munich 1962).

[252] See de Taube, *supra* note 1, at 35; Georges Ténékidès, Droit International et Communautés Fédérales dans la Grèce des Cités, 90 RCADI 469, 540–41 (1956–II). See also *infra* note 289 with text.

[253] This is strongly suggested in Demosthenes' narration of juridical relations between Athens and Macedon on the eve of the Macedonian invasion. See 1 Demosthenes, *supra* note 118, at 157 (*De Halonneso*, passages xi–xiii) ("[I]t would not have paid to make [a compact] which would entail a voyage from Macedonia to Athens or from Athens to Macedonia in order to obtain satisfaction. Instead, we sought redress in Macedonia under their laws and they at Athens under ours.").

[254] See Vinogradoff, *supra* note 215, at 16 (citing 1 G. Gilbert, *Handbuch der griechischen Staatsalterthümer* 487 (Leipzig 1881) (English transl. 1895)).

[255] For sources on which, see Chapter 1, at note 14.

[256] The *symbola* between Hierapytna and Priasnos provided recourse for most disputes to the "common courts" of the other. See Leech, *supra* note 9, at 34–36.

[257] The 450 BCE *symbola* between Athens and the Phaselites, whereby civil actions between Phaselites were excluded from the jurisdiction of any magistrate other than the *polemarch*. See Hopper, *supra* note 249, at 43, 50–51. See also 1 Phillipson, *supra* note 1, at 193–97. A modified procedure was provided for in the treaty between Oianthea and Chaleion, quoted *supra* at note 237. See also Aristotle, *supra* note 197, at 367 (*Politics*, passage iv.13.2).

[258] There is a vast literature on proceedings before the *polemarchos* and related tribunals. For a sampling, see Edward E. Cohen, *Ancient Athenian Maritime Courts* (1973); 1 Phillipson, *supra* note 1, at 197–200; Hopper, *supra* note 249, at 39–40. See also *Translated Documents*, *supra* note 80, at 68 (Athenian decree from c. 450 BCE benefiting Phaselis and granting access to justice).

The proxenia institution

The proxeny is undoubtedly the most copiously documented political institution of antiquity. It is attested to by thousands of inscriptions[259] from the entire Greek world, covering the period from the seventh century BCE[260] to 200 CE.[261] While one recent scholar has noted that "[p]roxeny decrees are remarkable documents, for which it is hard to find parallels in other cultures,"[262] evidence suggests that the *proxenia* institution was by no means peculiar to Hellenic nations.[263] Yet, it is only in its

---

[259] As Herman has described, *supra* note 223, at 131, some proxeny decrees are short and uninformative, others are long and minutely detailed. Whatever their length, they all follow a rigid stylistic pattern. The decrees typically feature an introduction giving the details of the issuing community or agency, followed by a citation of the individual receiving the proxeny honor and his good deeds, followed by the honors and privileges that would be accorded to the grantee. See also Michael B. Walbank, *Athenian Proxenies of the Fifth Century BC* 5–6 (1978). Professor Herman translates an Athenian decree from 408/07 BCE, which he considers paradigmatic of the form:

> Gods, Resolved by the Boule and the People . . . Since he is a good man, Oiniades of Palaiskiathos, to the city of the Athenians, and zealous to do whatever good he can, and is of benefit to [any] Athenian who comes to Skiathos, commendation shall be given him and he shall be recorded as *proxenos* and *euergetes* of the Athenians, and his descendants [as well]; and that he be not harmed shall be the responsibility both of the Boule, whichever is in office, and of the generals and the Athenian governor in Skiathos, whoever he may be on each occasion. This decree shall be inscribed by the Secretary of the Boule on a stele.

> *Ibid.* (interpolations in the original translation). For further examples, see *Translated Documents, supra* note 80, at 18 (Locria–Corcyra, c. 600 BCE), 159–60 (Athens–Persia, 389 BCE). *Euergetes* meant "benefactor" in ancient Greek, a term closely related to the *proxenia* institution. See *ibid.* at 135 and n. 53. See also P. Monceaux, *Les Proxénies grecques* (Paris 1885).

[260] It may be extravagant to claim that the proxeny institution was known in the epic Greek period, as suggested by some ancient sources. See Eustathius, *Ad Iliad.*, passages iii.204 and iv.377; 1 Livy, *supra* note 2, at 9 (passage i.1). Nonetheless, proxeny decrees have been definitively dated to the early 600s BCE. See 1 Phillipson, *supra* note 1, at 147 (collecting citations to inscriptions from Olympia, Locris, Corcyra, and Petilia) (citing H. Roehl, *Inscriptiones Graecae antiquissimae* 113, 117–18, 322, 342, 544 (Berlin 1882)).

[261] The proxeny institution fell into disuse as "Greek cities ceased to be autonomous, and their relations were regulated by the imperial power," whether Macedonian or Roman. See Vincent A. Smith, Asoka Notes (IV): Consular Officers in India and Greece, *India Antiquary* 200, 201 (September 1905) (also noting that the major period from which proxeny inscriptions originated was between 336 BCE and 14 CE).

[262] Herman, *supra* note 223, at 130.

[263] See 3 Xenophon, *supra* note 50, at 119, 145 (*Anabasis*, passage v.4.2 and v.6.11) (describing the prevalence of the institution even among barbarous Black Sea nomads). See also Leech, *supra* note 9, at 56; 1 Phillipson, *supra* note 1, at 147, 150–51 (discussing the use of *proxenia* by Carthaginians and Egyptians).

Greek context that our knowledge is sure and certain as to the character of this most formalized aspect of ritualized hospitality between ancient States.

Almost invariably, the grantor of a proxeny decree was a city or other polity. The grantee, the recipient of the title of *proxenos*, was always a stranger, usually resident elsewhere. Whereas an *asylia* was a grant of protection to a resident alien, a proxeny was a grant of favor to an alien living abroad. Those who held the title of *proxenos* were thus expected to further the interests of the granting community in their native cities. As Aeschines noted, "*Proxenoi* are those who in their own fatherlands look after [the affairs of] other cities."[264] The *proxenos* was thus "a prominent citizen to whom a foreign state officially entrusted the protection of its citizens and various diplomatic functions within his own state."[265]

The overall significance of the *proxenia* institution to ancient Greek thinking about ordered international relations was apparently immense. As with the possibility of individuals acquiring dual nationality through the mechanism of a *sympoliteia*, a grant of a proxeny was a recognition of the possibility of multiple political loyalties, and thus a repudiation of Greek civic exclusiveness within the *polis*.[266] Recent scholarship has suggested that *proxenia* was the ultimate institutional expression of the "guest-friend" status in ancient Greece. Like *xenia*, probably the most rudimentary of these relationships,[267] *proxenoi* were given an elevated status acknowledged by solemn inscriptions. Likewise, the grant of a proxeny was hereditary, implicating a quasi-kinship relationship that devolved

---

[264] Aeschines, *supra* note 68, at 357 (*Against Ctesiphon*, passage iii.138).

[265] Nussbaum, *supra* note 107, at 6. While parallels between *proxenia* and the modern consular institution have been consistently made, there are notable distinctions. See *ibid.* at 6–7; 1 Phillipson, *supra* note 1, at 149; Smith, *supra* note 261, at 201; C. Tissot, *Des proxénies grecques et de leur analogie avec les institutions consulaires modernes* (Dijon 1836). First, the modern consul is usually a native of the country which appoints him, whereas just the opposite held for proxeny. Secondly, appointment as a *proxenos* did not usually confer on an individual any rights or privileges in his own country, just in that of the granting city, again in distinction to modern practice. Thirdly, modern consuls have no truly diplomatic functions, whereas *proxenoi* appear to have had such responsibilities. For more on modern consular practice, see generally the Vienna Convention on Consular Relations, done 24 April 1963, 596 UNTS 262; Luke T. Lee, *Consular Law and Practice* (2nd ed. 1990).

[266] See 2 F. Laurent, *Histoire du droit des gens et des relations internationales* 113 (2nd ed. 1880) ("La proxénie est un grand pas fait par la Grèce hors d'isolement oriental"); Nussbaum, *supra* note 107, at 6; 1 Phillipson, *supra* note 1, at 148. See also Herman, *supra* note 223, at 131 ("The proxeny [was] an agreement between a community of people personified as a single individual, and a 'real' individual outsider"). See also Chapter 2, pp. 31–41 above.   [267] See *supra* notes 219–23 and accompanying text.

automatically upon the descendants of the grantee and was theoretically unbreakable.[268] Of course, both titles – *xenoi* and *proxenoi* – shared the same, essential root idea in ancient Greek: the guest-friend meal or banquet, known simply as *xenia*.[269]

Despite the formal aspects of the *proxenia* institution, it retained a supple, and actually very personal, character. Since the fundamental duty of the *proxenos* was to protect the interests of the granting State in his homeland, the success or failure of that mission was ultimately dependent on the mutual levels of trust reposed by the granting and host States in the person of the *proxenos*. If "Greek states displayed a basic mistrust of ties which were formal, temporary, and official,"[270] proxeny had to represent a sort of compromise. For example, it seems clear that a granting State could have a number of *proxenoi* in another polity.[271] This suggests that a grant of proxeny was not a purely State function, but may have also corresponded to private networks of *xenia* relationships between different sets of individuals in the respective towns.[272]

The duties of a *proxenos* could well be onerous, as might be expected for any formal manifestation of a ritual friendship relation. Citizens of the State which appointed him could claim his hospitality, including meals and lodging.[273] He often functioned as a commercial facilitator between merchants of the two cities.[274] He had the special duty to entertain emissaries from his adopted city and to formally introduce them to the authorities of his resident town.[275] In case of a legal dispute arising between a

---

[268] See Herman, *supra* note 223, at 135. Even though the grant of *proxenia* was hereditary, every new incumbent needed to be confirmed by the granting state. See *ibid.* at 138 and n. 56; Leech, *supra* note 9, at 49–50 (glossing 2 Xenophon, *supra* note 50, at 37 (*Hellenica*, passage vi.3)).

[269] See Herman, *supra* note 223, at 136. See also Ténékidès, *supra* note 251, at 535–38; Walbank, *supra* note 259, at 5–6; Clayton Miles Lehmann, Xenoi, Proxenoi, and Early Greek Treaties, 21 *Helios* 9, 9–10 (1994).   [270] See Herman, *supra* note 223, at 139.

[271] See Aristophanes, *supra* note 72, at 199 (*Birds*, line 1021); 4 Euripides, *Collected Plays* 59, 103 (Arthur S. Way transl. 1912) (Loeb Classical Library reprint 1971) (*Ion*, lines 551 and 1039); 2 *ibid.* 499 (*Andromache*, line 1103); 2 Thucydides, *supra* note 14, at 5, 127 (passages iii.2.3 and iii.70.1) (Athenian proxeny in Mytilene and Corcyran proxeny in Corinth).

[272] See Herman, *supra* note 223, at 139; Lehmann, *supra* note 269, at 10–17.

[273] See Leech, *supra* note 9, at 51–52 (noting also, according to Pollux, *Onomasticon*, passage iii.59, that a *proxenos* also was obliged to procure seats at games and festivals for travelers); Smith, *supra* note 261, at 201.

[274] See 1 Phillipson, *supra* note 1, at 152–53 (citing Pollux iii.59 and vii.4 for occasions where a *proxenos* provided security for a loan or acted as a broker). See also Ténékidès, *supra* note 252, at 537.

[275] See Leech, *supra* note 9, at 51–52; Smith, *supra* note 261, at 201; Ténékidès, *supra* note 252, at 536 and n. 2.

citizen under his protection and one of his own countrymen, the *proxenos* was obliged to represent the foreigner before the tribunals of his city.[276] If war broke out between his two cities, he was responsible for arranging the ransom of prisoners, the proper burial of the slain, and the disposition of their effects.[277] *Proxenoi* were used as mediators to resolve disputes,[278] and were often appointed by their native cities to serve as ambassadors to their adopted city.[279] More exceptionally, they were appointed as arbitrators to settle affirmatively individual or inter-city disagreements.[280]

The privileges and immunities accorded to *proxenoi* varied widely according to the constituent decrees, but usually were more than mere *asylia* and *isopoliteia* grants and usually less than an outright extension of citizenship.[281] A *proxenos* visiting his granting city would usually be provided with a right of (at least temporary) residence, freedom from liturgies, the right to seek speedy justice without the need of a patron (*prostates*), and a guarantee not to be encumbered with any obligations in excess of those that citizens were burdened with.[282] In the event of an outbreak of hostilities between a *proxenos*'s city and his adopted polity, his life and property were to be spared.[283] It is important to note, though, that appointment did not confer on the *proxenos* any official status in his

---

[276] See Leech, *supra* note 9, at 53; 1 Phillipson, *supra* note 1, at 157. This sometimes involved certifying documents. See *ibid.* at 54.

[277] See Leech, *supra* note 9, at 50–51; Smith, *supra* note 261, at 201.

[278] See 3 Thucydides, *supra* note 14, at 115 (passage v.59) (instance of a *proxenos* suggesting the conclusion of a treaty). See also Ténékidès, *supra* note 252, at 537 (glossing this passage from Thucydides). See also *Translated Documents, supra* note 80, at 159–60 (Athens honors Herakleides of Klazomenai in helping to conclude treaty with Persia, probably in 389 BCE).

[279] See 2 Plutarch, *supra* note 12, at 455 (*Cimon*, passage xvi) (Cimon of Athens, Sparta's *proxenos*, recalled from exile to negotiate a truce with Sparta); 2 Thucydides, *supra* note 14, at 91 (passage iii.52) (Lacon, a Plataean *proxenos* of Sparta, asked to plead their cause before Spartan judges, in the incident narrated in Chapter 3, at note 30), 3 *ibid.* 143 (passage v.76) (Lichas, *proxenos* of Argos at Sparta); 1 Xenophon, *supra* note 50, at 17 (*Hellenica*, passage i.1.35), 2 *ibid.* 3, 39 (passages vi.1 and vi.3.3) (Clearchus, Polydamas, and Callias).

[280] See 1 Phillipson, *supra* note 1, at 154. See also 2 Plutarch, *supra* note 12, at 449 (*Cimon*, passage xiv) (Cimon of Athens, the *proxenos* of Sparta, named as an arbitrator between Athens and Sparta).

[281] See Ténékidès, *supra* note 252, at 537; Walbank, *supra* note 259, at 5–6.

[282] See generally *Translated Documents, supra* note 80, at 214; 1 Phillipson, *supra* note 1, at 154–56.

[283] See 3 Polybius, *supra* note 15, at 231 (passage v.95) (Achaean admiral making a raid into Naupaktus accidentally took captive Achaean *proxenos* in the town; he was released without ransom); 1 Demosthenes, *supra* note 118, at 169 (*Halonnesus*, line 38), 3 *ibid.* 277 (*Against Aristocrates*, line 89). *Proxenoi* were sometimes appointed from among the ranks of former hostages. See 1 Phillipson, *supra* note 1, at 151.

own country, although the custom seemed to be that the host State was under an obligation not affirmatively to hinder the activities of a citizen acting as *proxenos* to another power. In undertaking certain official duties, such as certifying the official character and good faith of a mission from his adopted State,[284] he was cloaked with nearly the character of a herald.[285]

Western Mediterranean analogues

The Romans confronted the same problems as the Greeks in ordering their relations with neighboring city-States on the Italian peninsula. Although the practice of *androlepsia* was not as common in early Latin relations with their neighbors, there was still substantial concern about self-help measures being adopted to resolve personal feuds or commercial disputes.[286] We do have strong evidence about how private commercial relationships were structured between Roman citizens and Carthaginian subjects, at least based on the c. 500 BCE peace treaty concluded between the two nations, as reported by Polybius.[287] According to this treaty, commerce was facilitated by functionaries variously called "clerks," "scribes," or "heralds,"[288] and was apparently governed by some choice-of-law mechanism similar (although not precisely attuned) to Greek practice under *symbola*.[289] A generalized right to trade and do business in the territory of another State, what was known in Roman practice as *commercium*, was apparently[290] evidenced by the 348 BCE treaty between Rome and Carthage.[291] Likewise,

---

[284] See *supra* note 275 and text.   [285] See Leech, *supra* note 9, at 55.

[286] See Stephen Verosta, *International Law in Europe and Western Asia Between 100 and 650 AD*, 113 RCADI 484, 521–22 (1964–III).

[287] See 2 Polybius, *supra* note 15, at 55 (passage iii.22.8). Similar treaties may have been entered into by the Romans with the Etruscans. See Aristotle, *supra* note 197, at 215 (*Politics*, passage iii.5.10 (1280a)).

[288] See M. David, The Treaties Between Rome and Carthage and Their Significance for Our Knowledge of Roman International Law, in *Symbolae ad Jus et Historiam pertinentes Juliano Christiano Van Owen dedicatae* 231, 235–37 (M. David, B. A. van Groningen, E. M. Meijers eds. 1946).

[289] See David, *supra* note 288, at 237, 240. See also *supra* notes 252–54 and accompanying text.

[290] Whether the right of *commercium* was, in fact, reciprocal and freely granted has been hotly debated. Compare Huvelin, *Etudes d'histoire du droit commercial romain* 20 (1929) with David, *supra* note 288, at 239–40.

[291] See 2 Polybius, *supra* note 15, at 59 (passage iii.24.12–13) ("In the Carthaginian province of Sicily and at Carthage [a Roman citizen] may do and sell anything that is permitted to a citizen. A Carthaginian in Rome may do likewise."). For the dating of this treaty, see David, *supra* note 288, at 231 n. 1.

that same agreement seemed to provide for a mutual release of individuals captured by the allies of the other.[292]

Early Roman practice also had an analogous institution to the proxeny of the Greek city-States: the *recuperatores*.[293] These seem to have been the representatives of foreigners within Roman communities. They were asked periodically to defend and look after the interests of their fellow countrymen. The *recuperatores* could also act as arbitrators, deciding a class of disputes referred to them by treaty.[294] Livy reported that in 171 BCE the inhabitants of Spain, who had been cruelly oppressed by Roman officials stationed there, sought redress from the Senate.[295] A panel of *recuperatores* was appointed to redress their grievances.[296]

Ritualized friendship in an ancient law of nations

If the primary impediment to ancient State relations was cultural and religious particularism, then friendship and diplomacy was its logical antidote. It seems plain that the ancient State was able to conceive not only of different kinds of status being extended to aliens living in their midst, but also of rituals and customs having the effect of legitimizing individual and communal friendship. Without this ability to understand the essential nature of comity, international law would have been an impossibility in ancient international relations. Not only would it have been impossible for ancient States to pledge their faith with one another in a positive law-making act (which is considered in the next chapter), but no other rule of State conduct could have had any force and effect.

What I think is important to realize is that the process of making foreign friends in antiquity was largely one of legal process. The highly

[292] See 2 Polybius, *supra* note 15, at 59 (passage iii.24.6): "If any Carthaginians take captive any of a people with whom the Romans have a treaty of peace, but who are not subject to Rome, they shall not bring them into Roman harbors; but if one be brought in and a Roman lay hold of him, he shall be set free." For more on Roman understandings of bond-friendship and ritual embraces, see Herman, *supra* note 1, at 50–54.

[293] See Wenger, Recuperatio, in 1 A. A. Pauly and G. Wissowa, *Real-Encyclopädie der classischen Alterthums-Wissenschaft* 405 (Stuttgart 1894–1905). Compare also Bruno Schmindlin, *Das Rekuperatorenverfahren* (1963) (who supports the view that *recuperatores* were originally an international dispute settlement mechanism) with J. M. Kelly, *Studies in the Civil Judicature of the Roman Republic* 40–47 (1976) (who strongly opposes this position).

[294] See J. H. Ralston, *International Arbitration from Athens to Locarno* 169 (1929) (quoting Mougins de Roquefort, *De la solution juridique* 102 (1889)).

[295] See 13 Livy, *supra* note 2, at 7 (passage xliii.2).

[296] See also Louise E. Matthaei, The Place of Arbitration and Mediation in Ancient Systems of International Ethics, 2 *Classical Quarterly* 241, 243 (1908). It is possible that all of the recuperators for the case were Roman senators. See *ibid.*

refined forms of friendship statuses observed within Greek city-States, and the elaborately articulated vassalage relationships practiced by the cultures of the ancient Near East and by the Romans, were all conceived as *legal* relationships, governed by pre-conceived notions of rights and responsibilities. The actors, whether they were the alien resident in a foreign city or a polity in political association with another, were controlled by a rule of law.

These norms of State conduct were drawn and enforced from sources of obligation rooted (as already suggested in the previous chapter) in religion, in ritual and custom, and in reason. Legal doctrine, as we would probably recognize it today, did intrude in the process to the extent that different States could adopt different attitudes on finer points of practice involving diplomats and their prerogatives. As suggested in this chapter, disputes concerning the distinction between privileges and immunities were a common staple of ancient State relations. Vexatious questions these were, typically involving the host State's obligation to be the ultimate guarantor against any misfortune which befell a foreign diplomat, or the rights of third parties to take sanctions against envoys of belligerent nations. Some consistency was achieved in an ancient law of nations in developing answers to these questions, but by no means were universal rules of diplomatic intercourse absolutely enforced at all times in antiquity.

The critical point to be made here is in seeing how the ancient mind was able to overcome particularism, whether expressed as *androlepsia* in Greek State relations or sanctioned murders of hostile envoys in other cultures. In the process of making friends, ancient polities achieved critical insights into the nature of State relations. The positive act of the ancient State making faith with its neighbors will be considered next.

5   Making faith: treaty practices amongst ancient peoples

This chapter continues the previous discussion of the ancient world's engagement with the ideas of community, tolerance, and trust, the basic prerequisites for the development of international law. The focus shifts away from ancient civilizations' treatment of individual foreigners, whether they be visiting merchants, resident aliens, or honored guests and emissaries. Instead, the goal now is to explore the ways that ancient peoples pledged their troth in international relations. The emphasis here must be on the formal methods and structures of ancient treaty-making, the nature and sources of international legal obligation (partly manifested in international agreements) having already been considered earlier in this study.[1] This chapter will examine the forms of treaties in antiquity, their substantive terms and conditions, as well as consider the procedures by which they were concluded, altered, and terminated.

Beginnings of the ancient treaty tradition in the Near East

General suppositions and the earliest texts

Much historiographic attention has been directed to examining the structure and forms of ancient Near Eastern international agreements.[2] The bulk of this literature was inspired by parallels between biblical texts and the extant records of Egyptian and Hittite international transactions. As

---

[1] See Chapter 3.
[2] For a sampling, see F. Charles Fensham, Common Trends in Curses of the Near Eastern Treaties and *Kudurru*-Inscriptions Compared with Maledictions of Amos and Isaiah, 75 *Zeitschrift für die Alttestamentliche Wissenschaft* 155 (1963); Delbert R. Hillers, *Treaty Curses and the Old Testament Prophets* (Rome 1964); Dennis J. McCarthy, *Treaty and Covenant* (1963); George Mendenhall, *Law and Covenant in Israel and the Ancient Near East* (1955).

a result of this investigation, the contours of which will be reviewed here,[3] some scholars have suggested that there is an essential unity in "the ancient oriental treaty pattern."[4] Although the order and appearance of parts of treaty texts can vary, the "basic unity of conception"[5] remains the same for international agreements concluded by States within the Sumerian, Egyptian, Hittite, Assyrian, and Israelite cultures.

Ancient Near Eastern treaties followed a definitive form, and that construct was consistently repeated in not only Mesopotamian and Eastern Mediterranean cultures, but also, I suggest in this chapter, throughout the entire ancient world for the entire breadth of time scrutinized here. As Dennis J. McCarthy noted in 1963:

> Everywhere the basic elements are the same: the provisions are imposed under oath and placed under the sanction of the divine witnesses invoked. And this divine guardianship is invariably made more vivid through the curses which represent (and effect) the dreadful fate of an eventual transgressor. Hence the essential elements of the form: stipulations, the god lists or invocations, and the curse formulae.[6]

Beyond this typical construct for an ancient Near Eastern treaty, the critical distinction appeared to be whether the international agreement was concluded between co-equal sovereigns. If so, it could be characterized as a full international agreement. If not, the text took on much the tone of a master dictating terms of protection and fealty to a vassal. The vast body of surviving inscriptions of ancient Near Eastern treaties fall into the latter category of vassalage agreements. They are significant for a complete understanding of the forms and functions of true international agreements, but the primary thrust of this chapter will be to consider this class of texts as an adjunct only to a specific inquiry into the nature of ancient treaty-making.

Another feature that is marked for ancient Near Eastern treaties is their strongly contractual flavor. In part this is attributable to a sensibility that saw a secular contract being formed out of the exchange of solemnized oaths and promises. An individual bond of friendship between two co-equal rulers was elevated to an international undertaking.[7] In this respect, the international agreements concluded by the Egyptian, Semitic, and Mesopotamian peoples were distinctive. One can test this hypothesis by checking the forms of the international agreements, specifically the

---

[3] See *infra* notes 93–105 and accompanying text.   [4] McCarthy, *supra* note 2, at 80.
[5] *Ibid.* at 80 n. 1.   [6] *Ibid.* at 80.
[7] See Le Baron Michel de Taube, L'inviolabilité des Traités, 32 RCADI 291, 306–07 (1930–II).

extent to which they adopted first-person grammars, specific personal allusions, and affinities toward epistolary forms.[8]

Lastly, one must try to place the conclusion of treaties in a larger context. As Dennis McCarthy also wrote, these treaty texts "are not merely documents: they reflect ceremonies," as well as "the background of society and ideas which governed [the] formation" of these agreements.[9] It is not enough to understand what ancient peoples wrote into their treaties, although that is certainly hard enough. What remains to comprehend is the ends they legitimately believed were being served by the exercise of making faith with another sovereign.

Consider the very earliest Sumer treaty texts, of which we have very few exemplars from the third millennium. The first of these is an agreement made between Eannatum of Lagash and the nearby city-State of Umma, dated at approximately 2500 BCE, and recorded on the so-called Stele of Vultures.[10] This treaty was made under oath to six or seven of the most powerful Sumerian gods who served as guarantors of the boundary delimited by the agreement. Yet, the fact that only one set of gods was sworn to has been suggestive of a dependent status for Umma, which had been defeated in a conflict with Lagash.[11] The men of Umma had repetitively to swear by their gods that they would observe the terms of the peace treaty.[12] If they did not, "the great net" – the favored instrument of mayhem and destruction of at least one of the named gods – "would destroy them."[13] For good measure, a neighboring princeling, Mesilim of Kish, was apparently charged with the task of actually marking the boundary by digging a ditch and filling it with stones, although some have surmised that he may have also served as a secular arbitrator in case of a dispute arising between the parties.[14]

From early Mesopotamia, prior to the period of intense treaty-making

---

[8] See S. Langdon and Alan H. Gardiner, The Treaty of Alliance Between Hattusili, King of the Hittites, and the Pharaoh Ramesses II of Egypt, 6 *Journal of Egyptian Archaeology* 179, 199–200 (1920).   [9] See McCarthy, *supra* note 2, at 80–81.

[10] See F. Thureau-Dangin, *Die Sumerischen und Akkadischen Königsinschriften* 10–21 (1907). See also 1(2) *Cambridge Ancient History* 119–19 (3rd ed. 1971); A. Parrot, *Tello; synthèse de vingt campagnes* 95–98 (1948); E. Solberger, *Corpus des inscriptions "royales" présargoniques de Lagas* 9 (1956).

[11] See McCarthy, *supra* note 2, at 15–16; Arthur Nussbaum, *A Concise History of the Law of Nations* 1–2 (rev. ed. 1954).

[12] It has been noted that this type of repetition was consonant with Sumerian literary technique. See A. Falkenstein- W. von Soden, *Sumerische und Akkadische Hymnen* 30–31 (1953).   [13] See McCarthy, *supra* note 2, at 16 and n. 3.

[14] See Rostovtseff, International Relations in the Ancient World, in *The History and Nature of International Relations* 40 (E. Walsh ed. 1922). See also T. Jacobsen, *The Sumerian King-List* 181 n. 29 (Assyriological Studies No. 11) (1930); W. W. Hallo, *Early Mesopotamian Royalty* 25–30 (1957).

by the Hittites and Assyrians,[15] we have only a few other examples. There is a treaty of friendship between Lagash and Uruk of a somewhat later date than the one between Lagash and Umma.[16] A vassal treaty between Sargon and another prince, written in Akkadian, does survive although it is possible to date it only approximately around 2500 BCE.[17] Lastly, there is a treaty of alliance between Naram-Sin, fourth king of the Akkad dynasty, and the ruler of Elam. One editor and translator of that text notes that:

[t]he names of the great gods of Elam and Accad are invoked, the conquered are made vassals and swear their fidelity, curse the enemies of Naram-Sin who have now become their enemies, and bless his friends who are now their friends . . . The oath is repeated several times, with different curses and blessings at the end of each paragraph.[18]

Without further historical information, it is difficult to know whether the king of Elam was a vassal of the Akkadian emperor. Nonetheless, the treaty text with its formulary of having the Elamite ruler say that "Naram-Sin's enemy is my enemy; Naram-Sin's friend is my friend," is strongly suggestive that he was.[19]

The early Sumerian agreements are thus ambivalent on at least one significant point of ancient treaty practices: it is hard to know whether a particular instrument is being concluded with a co-equal sovereign or with a vassal. Each of the four texts just mentioned here has strong tendencies to follow patterns that later Hittite and Assyrian practice would regard as being typical for unequal treaties made between a master and inferior, conqueror and vanquished.[20] We need to determine if it is only the "defeated people or the subordinate prince who is subject to the stipulations [of the treaty] and who takes the oath."[21] If the stronger party does not bind himself to anything, then quite clearly one has found a vassal treaty. Otherwise, the treaty obligations should be reciprocal. Or, as Korosec wrote, an equal treaty should have two symmetrical moments: one in which both parties accept reciprocal (or nearly reciprocal) obligations, and the other in which they each ratify their obligations by binding themselves under oath to observe them.[22]

---

[15] See McCarthy, *supra* note 2, at 15.
[16] See J. A. Thompson, *The Ancient Near Eastern Treaties and the Old Testament* 9 and n. 8 (1964). See also Thureau-Dangin, *supra* note 10, at 36.
[17] See Ragnar Numelin, *The Beginnings of Diplomacy* 291–92 (1950).
[18] 11 V. Scheil, *Mémoires de la délégation en Perse* 1–11 (Paris 1912).
[19] See Thompson, *supra* note 16, at 9 and n. 9.   [20] See *ibid.*
[21] McCarthy, *supra* note 2, at 18.
[22] H. Korosec, *Hethitische Staatsverträge: Ein Beitrag zu ihrer juristichen Wertung*, 60 *Leipziger Rechtswissenschaftliche Studien* 35 (Leipzig 1931).

The Babylonians, Hittites, and Assyrians

In the 1,200 years between 1800 and 600 BCE, four great empires flourished in the Fertile Crescent, all of which were regarded as co-equal sovereigns.[23] Of Mitanni treaty practice we know virtually nothing. From the earliest periods documented here, from approximately 1750 to 1530 BCE, when Mesopotamia was under the domination of the first Babylonian state led by Hammurabi, we have some scant evidence of treaty rescripts and ratifications. From the Mari archive we have a document denominated as a "tablet of the life of the gods," a phrase that refers to the central act of oath-taking in the ratification ceremony.[24] There is another tablet documenting a treaty made between Yarîm-Lim of Yamhad and Amût-pî-il of Qatanum, where it was said that "We shall set down good words between myself and him by the life of the gods and mighty bonds."[25]

As far as we can tell, the major subject-matter of early Babylonian parity treaties was to arrange for alliances. A defensive alliance could be phrased simply: "If the enemy turns back against you, my troops will come to your aid, but if the enemy turns back against me, let your troops come to my aid," a promise that was exchanged between Hammurabi and Rîm-Sin of Larsa.[26] Likewise, an offensive alliance could be couched in an even more simple formula: "We will seize" some stated enemy city.[27] By similar formularies, neutrality pacts were entered into by Babylon and its neighbors.[28] Apart from treaties concerned with matters of war and peace, the early Babylonian archives are also replete with examples of parity agreements in which provisions were made for the return of fugitives[29] or of individuals unlawfully taken from the territory of the other party.[30]

[23] See Hans-Ulrich Scupin, History of the Law of Nations: Ancient Times to 1648, in 7 *Encyclopedia of Public International Law* 132, 134 (Rudolph Bernhardt ed. 1984).

[24] 1 *Archives Royales de Mari: Correspondance de Samsi-Addu* (G. Dossin transl. 1950) (document xxxvii.24) (hereinafter "1 ARMT").

[25] J. M. Munn-Rankin, Diplomacy in Western Asia in the Early Second Millennium BC, 18 *Iraq* 68, 84 (1956).

[26] 2 *Archives Royales de Mari: Lettres Diverses* (C. F. Jean transl. 1950) (document lxxii.13–16) (hereinafter "2 ARMT").

[27] See Munn-Rankin, *supra* note 25, at 92 and n. 1 (quoting agreement between Zalmâqum and Bîn-Yamîn).

[28] See *ibid.* at 92–93 (describing a pact between Bunu-Istar and Qarni-Lim to not intervene in a dispute between Zimri-Lim and Bîn-Yamîn).

[29] See 2 ARMT, *supra* note 25 (document lxxii.19–27); 4 *Archives Royales de Mari: Correspondance de Samsi-Addu* (G. Dossin transl. 1950) (document v) (hereinafter "4 ARMT"); 5 *Archives Royales de Mari: Correspondance de Iasmah-Addu* (G. Dossin transl. 1950) (document xliv) (hereinafter "5 ARMT"); 6 *Archives Royales de Mari: Correspondance de Bahdi-Lim* (J. R. Kupper transl. 1954) (document xxxv) (hereinafter "6 ARMT").

[30] See 5 ARMT, *supra* note 29 (documents vii and viii).

The process of treaty negotiation and ratification has been extensively documented for the early Babylonian period. It appears that agreements were typically drafted with the use of envoys and intermediaries; the principals rarely met in person to negotiate. As a consequence, the Mari archives hold a number of examples where treaty terms were altered or otherwise bickered over until all the parties were satisfied and the ceremony of ratification could proceed.[31] This ceremonial has been previously discussed,[32] and took the form of the prince or sovereign swearing an oath by the enumerated gods to observe the terms of the treaty. In the parlance of Hammurabi's time, this act was known as "touching the throat," certainly evocative of the mortal consequences for failing to keep faith after concluding a treaty.[33] Quite understandably, Babylonian kings and their treaty partners were reluctant to ratify an agreement until its terms were totally satisfactory and they had complete assurances that the other party was likewise prepared to ratify. Indeed, it appears that there was substantial concern that a treaty ratification could be unilateral. In other words, one party would still be bound to observe a treaty, assuming the proper oath had been sworn, even though the other party had not yet ratified it.[34] This sense of formal obligation in treaty observance may have caused Hammurabi to have attempted to trick Zimri-Lim to alone ratify a treaty by using as an excuse that the day selected for him to "touch his throat" was inauspicious.[35]

Of Hittite and Assyrian international agreements substantially more knowledge is available. Hittite treaties, mostly vassalage agreements, are particularly well documented with twenty-four extant documents being available from the period between 1500 and 1300 BCE.[36] Of Assyrian treaties four examples exist from the narrower time-frame of 850 to 700 BCE, reflecting the height of the New Assyrian Empire.[37] We also have a smat-

---

[31] See 1 ARMT, *supra* note 24 (document xxxvii. 19–29); 4 ARMT, *supra* note 29 (document xx).   [32] See Chapter 3.   [33] See Munn-Rankin, *supra* note 25, at 84–85.

[34] See *ibid.* at 87–88.

[35] See *ibid.* (citing 2 ARMT, *supra* note 25 (document lxxviii)). See also R. F. Harper, *Assyrian and Babylonian Letters* No. 354 (1902) (later Assyrian ruler advised that the twentieth, twenty-second, and twenty-fifth days of the lunar cycle were the most auspicious for taking oaths).

[36] See McCarthy, *supra* note 2, at 12. See also Guy Kastemont, *Diplomatique en droit international en Asie Occidentale (1600–1200 av. JC)* 91–114, 291–334 (1974) (for tables and concordances of Hittite treaties). See also 2(1) *Cambridge Ancient History* 672, 679 (3rd ed. 1973); 2(2) *Cambridge Ancient History* 6 (3rd ed. 1975).

[37] See *ibid.* See also Louis Lawrence Orlin, *Assyrian Colonies in Cappadocia* 114–38 (1970); Thompson, *supra* note 16, at 10.

tering of agreements made by lesser powers in the Syrian hinterland.[38] What must be regarded as significant is the extent to which a near millennium of regional treaty practice was almost entirely consistent. As just one example, consider the means by which ancient Near Eastern treaty texts were preserved, thus at least partially accounting for why so many remain extant today. Delbert Hillers explained that, because "the ancient treaty was a *public* document . . . [c]opies . . . were distributed, preserved, and published."[39] It was obligatory on the parties to keep copies of the treaty, to have copies deposited in the temples of the gods who served as guarantors for the agreements, and to read publicly the treaty text at least twice or thrice a year.[40] The common language of treaties between 1500 and 500 BCE was Akkadian or Hittite, later giving way to Aramaic.[41]

In addition, there were close structural and stylistic parallels between Assyrian and Hittite treaties. The same methods of sealing and physical preparation of the *stelae* or treaty tablets was widely observed.[42] The use and etymology of certain technical terms, including that for "oath" (*adē*), was consistent.[43] The use of second-person imperatives – the "thou shalt" or "thou shalt not" forms – has been particularly noted by modern philologists, particularly for its biblical relevance.[44] The presence of such language in treaty texts implied strong personal bonds between the parties, sometimes of genuine friendship, more often of fealty and dependent status. McCarthy has speculated that:

the familiar imperative form arose at least in part from the fact that the business was really all in the family, so to speak. It is a natural mode of expression in the circumstances. Moreover, it was not only used by [a] king . . . speaking to his vassal, but is used by the vassal speaking to the king![45]

As already mentioned, treaties containing such language were strongly familiar and contractual in tone. While such did not invariably disqualify them from being parity treaties, they were typical of unequal agreements.

---

[38] For one example, a treaty concluded between the towns of Idrimi and Pillya, see McCarthy, *supra* note 2, at 61. For more analysis on these Syrian treaties, see *ibid.* at 66–67. See also Korosec, *supra* note 22, at 175–76 (for a translation of an agreement between Niqmepa of Alalakh and Ir-Im of Tunip).   [39] Hillers, *supra* note 2, at 80.

[40] See Korosec, *supra* note 22, at 100–02; McCarthy, *supra* note 2, at 37–38, 76; D. J. Wiseman, *The Vassal Treaties of Esarhaddon* (1958); Peter Karavites, *Promise-Giving and Treaty-Making: Homer and the Near East* 188–89 (1992).

[41] See Hillers, *supra* note 2, at 81; André Dupont-Sommer, *Les Araméens* 84–98 (Paris 1949).

[42] See McCarthy, *supra* note 2, at 81 and n. 6.   [43] See *ibid.* at 98.

[44] See the sources mentioned at *supra* note 2. See particularly, McCarthy, *supra* note 2, at 37–38.   [45] McCarthy, *supra* note 2, at 37.

More significant, the very structure of international agreements (whether made between equal partners or between master and vassal) was remarkably constant. The essential elements of the form were some sort of preamble, the actual treaty stipulations, the god lists or invocations, and the curse formulae. While only Hittite treaties characteristically included long preambular passages reciting the history of relations between the two parties,[46] such clauses were still to be found in Assyrian and other cultures. Apparently, the purpose of these historical provisions was to enlighten and caution the parties – and their descendants. Concerning this, Dennis McCarthy wrote:

The Hittite sought wisdom in history, and characteristically he added a historical prologue to his document, whether royal constitution or treaty, that the reader might learn from it . . . [I]n the case of the treaty he took a basic conception from the older culture of Mesopotamia and added a touch responding to his own interest and insight.[47]

The other distinctive feature of Hittite and Assyrian treaties – and, indeed, of all ancient Near Eastern instruments – were the curse invocations. In some documents, the curses were accompanied by reciprocal blessings to be bestowed upon the party that observed the conditions of the treaty in good faith. But most treaties featured relatively simple curses standing alone. The formula, "May the gods destroy you, your family and country," occurs in many inscriptions.[48] In others, "the evils wished are varied, specific and formidable."[49] The curses are recounted with extraordinary and creative detail, a whole parade of deities summoned to produce some catastrophe or another.

The only distinction to be made in the curse formulas used by ancient Near Eastern cultures was that the Hittites preferred generic curses, while earlier Mesopotamian cultures structured their treaties so that one specific malediction followed another.[50] Hittite treaty practice saw the compact instrument as an organic whole; the Babylonians tended to tie particular curses to the failure to observe particular duties. For the Assyrians, the utterances of these curses were accompanied by formal rites, usually the invocation of objects which symbolized the fate to befall

---

[46] See *ibid.* at 99. See also *Ancient Near Eastern Texts Relating to the Old Testament* 203–05 (3rd ed. James B. Pritchard ed. 1969).

[47] See *ibid.* at 102. See also *ibid.* at 99 and n. 12. See also Gurney, *Hittites* 171–73 (1954).

[48] See McCarthy, *supra* note 2, at 102.

[49] *Ibid.* See also Pritchard, *supra* note 46, at 531–41 (for a catalogue of Assyrian curses used in their vassal treaties).   [50] See McCarthy, *supra* note 2, at 103 n. 24.

a party which broke the compact.[51] The idea underlying this ritual was that the oath-takers were transmuted into the things broken, burned or destroyed upon treaty breach. This ceremony of substitution was "deadly serious to the people concerned," and so "the observance of the treaty [was secured] by multiplying . . . the religious sanction and by the use of rites which were thought infallible to bring about the ruin of the transgressor."[52]

Assyrian and Hittite treaties show a wide range of substantive provisions. Most covenants, particularly the vassalage agreements, covered questions of fealty and provisions for military support.[53] Extradition of fugitives was also another popular topic.[54] One treaty, that between the Hittites and Amurru of c. 1250 BCE, called for a mutual trade embargo against the Assyrians.[55] Even those instruments which were unquestionably vassalage treaties contained provisions that were reciprocal in nature. Such clauses granted to the subordinate party the right to have its political fugitives returned from the Hittites.[56] Likewise, the vassal might be permitted to regulate its own internal succession.[57] Indeed, with some

---

[51] See *ibid.* See also Orlin, *supra* note 37, at 114–38.

[52] McCarthy, *supra* note 2, at 104. For more on the sense of legal obligation raised by this ceremonial, see Chapter 3.

[53] See Mendenhall, *supra* note 2, at 30–31. See also Orlin, *supra* note 37, at 115, 124.

[54] See Nussbaum, *supra* note 11, at 2 n. 4; McCarthy, *supra* note 2, at 33. See also O. R. Gurney, The Treaty with Ulmi-Tesub, 43 *Anatolian Studies* 13 (1993) (discussing boundary and levy provisions in a Hittite vassalage treaty).

[55] See 2(2) *Cambridge Ancient History* 262, 292 (3rd ed. 1975); 23 *Keilschrifturkunden aus Boghazköi* 1 (1956); E. Farrer, Assyrien, 1 *Reallexikon der Assyriologie* 228, 272 (1932).

[56] For more on fugitives in ancient Near Eastern treaties, see Karavites, *supra* note 40, at 148–50.

[57] See McCarthy, *supra* note 2, at 33–34. The treaty offering the greatest detail on the subject of succession disputes is the Assyrian decree of Esarhaddon in 679 BCE, assuring the recognition of his son, Assurbanipal, as heir to the throne. See *ibid.* at 73–78; Wiseman, *supra* note 40. For a summary of the extensive obligations undertaken by Esarhaddon's vassals to ensure Assurbanipal's succession, see Wiseman, *supra* note 40, at 23–24. See also 3(2) *Cambridge Ancient History* 125–26 (3rd ed. 1970). See also Fensham, *supra* note 2, at 133–41, who discusses the obligations of the senior party in Hittite vassal treaties. One such clause, found in the vassal treaty between Muwattalis of Hatti and Alaksandus, was:.

The one who is your enemy,
is also the enemy of the Sun.
The one who is the enemy of the Sun,
should also be your enemy.

Ibid. at 141. This was simply a literary reformulation of the phrase: "He that is your enemy is my enemy; He that is my enemy is your enemy."

texts, including the treaties made by the Hittites with Shattiwaza of Mitanni and with Sunassura of Kizzuwatna, there are real doubts whether the compact is made between equivalent powers or with vassals.[58]

While much more remains to be written about the typology and structural analogues of ancient Near Eastern treaties,[59] one should not lose sight of the point that the vocabulary of those treaties did evolve with time. Within each political culture, treaty terminology and ceremony began in a rudimentary condition and quickly became more systematized and predictable. For the entire region, whether seen in Babylonian, Hittite or Assyrian inscriptions, there was "a divergence [in treaty forms and practices] but not a significant difference. It is an evolution, a developing expression of the fundamental idea."[60]

The Egyptians and the treaty with the Hittites of 1280 BCE

Ample evidence exists that dynastic Egypt had a system of tributary relations with its smaller neighbors, and that these arrangements were regulated by treaty. A cache of documents, known as the Amarna letters, recount in some detail the existence of a system of feudal treaties, prevalent during the period when Egypt dominated Syria between the Battles of Megiddo (1480 BCE) and Kadesh (1299 BCE).[61] Another set of inscriptions reveals feudal covenants with nomadic, Libyan tribes on Egypt's western periphery.[62] On a somewhat different footing, the Egyptians appear to have had a set of commercial treaties with major trading States in the eastern Mediterranean, regulating such issues as extraterritorial privileges and the protection of assets of deceased traders.[63]

[58] See Johannes Friedrich, *Hethitisches Wörterbuch* (1952); Paul Koschaker, *Babylonische-Assyriches Bürgschaftsrecht* (1911); Fritz Schachermeyr, Zur staatsrechtlichen Wertung der hethitischen Verträge, in *Meissner Festschrift II* 180–86 (1926) (1985 reprint). See also McCarthy, *supra* note 2, at 47–48. For the doubts expressed as to Esarhaddon's treaties, mentioned in *supra* note 57, see *ibid.* at 77–78; Mendenhall, *supra* note 2, at 30 and n. 15; Wiseman, *supra* note 2, at 28.   [59] See the sources cited in note 2.
[60] McCarthy, *supra* note 2, at 98. See also Karavites, *supra* note 40, at 119–24 (on suzerainty treaties in ancient Near East and Homeric periods).
[61] See David Lorton, *The Juridical Terminology of International Relations in Egyptian Texts Through Dyn. XVIII*, at 177–79 (1974).
[62] See McCarthy, *supra* note 2, at 105. See also 2(1) *Cambridge Ancient History* 471–75, 484 (3rd ed. 1973); Cord Kühne, *Zum status der Syro-Palästinischen Vassalen des Neuen Reiches* 71–75 (Andrews University Seminary Studies No. 1) (1963); M. Abdul-Kader Muhammad, The Administration of Syro-Palestine During the New Kingdom, 56 *Annales du Service des Antiquités de l'Égypte* 105 (1959).
[63] See, e.g., Numelin, *supra* note 17, at 293. See also Chapter 4 at note 262. For the treaty concluded between the Cretans and Egyptians, see Lorton, *supra* note 59, at 88.

Some Egyptian treaties are extant. The language used in these treaties is sometimes opaque, but some instances of treaty terminology are revealing. A few inscriptions feature the phrase "to make peace," which was usually associated with a military conquest and a subsequent fealty status for the subjugated territory. The Syrian princes who rebelled against Egyptian authority, and who were defeated at the Battle of Megiddo in 1480 BCE, were said (at least by Egyptian sources) to "have made peace" with their Egyptian overlords.[64] In one version they sought the "breath of life" from the victorious Egyptians.[65] The juridical construction "to make peace" was combined with the dynastic Egyptian obligation to "be generous to" or "do good to" the new vassals.[66] Subsequent instruments with the Syrian vassals regulated such matters as payment of tribute, pronouncements of homage to the Pharaoh, and the settlement of disputes among the Syrian polities.[67] These fealty treaties were thus quite similar to those concluded by the Assyrians and Hittites.

Of all of the treaties dynastic Egypt concluded, none is as famous (and justifiably so) than the agreement of 1280 BCE between Pharaoh Rameses II and King Hattusili III of the Hittite Empire. Alone among ancient Near Eastern treaties, it is the only instrument for which we have reciprocal versions[68] – one in Egyptian hieroglyphs and the other in Akkadian.[69] One version was found at the temple of Amon at the Egyptian dynastic capital of Karnak; the other at Ramesseum, in Asia Minor.[70] We thus have two official texts of the treaty: one recorded by Egyptian scribes, the other by Hittite officials.[71]

There is no doubt that this is the best example of a parity treaty made in the ancient Near East. The two parties were the greatest powers in the

[64] See Lorton, *supra* note 59, at 77–78.   [65] See *ibid.*   [66] See *ibid.* at 88.
[67] See Aristide Théodoridès, Les relations de l'Egypte pharaonique avec ses voisins, 23 RIDA 87, 105–07 (1975). Substantial literature has been devoted to the decrees of Pharaoh Thoutmosis III to the Syrian princes. See, e.g., Wilson, 7 JNES 130 (1948); Goedicke, 49 *Journal of Egyptian Archeology* 79 (1963).
[68] See Nussbaum, *supra* note 11, at 203; Théodoridès, *supra* note 65, at 112. There was an earlier treaty concluded between the two countries in c. 1470 BCE, concerning mutual security in northern Syria.
[69] See 2(1) *Cambridge Ancient History* 462–63, 671 (3rd ed. 1973); 2(2) *Cambridge Ancient History* 9, 81 (3rd ed. 1975); J. B. Pritchard, *Ancient Near Eastern Texts Relating to the Old Testament* 395 (2nd ed. 1955).
[70] See R. von Scala, *Die Staatsverträge des Altertums* 6 (1898). See also Paul Guggenheim, Contribution à l'Histoire des Sources du Droit des Gens, 94 RCADI 1, 55 (1958–II).
[71] There are slight differences between the two versions. Professor Gardiner has speculated that the Egyptian version was a translation from the Akkadian (Hittite) text, edited to give greater prominence to the Egyptian role. A. Gardiner, 6 *Journal of Egyptian Archeology* 180, 185, 200 (1920).

region at that time. They had fought a long-simmering war for control of Palestine and the Syrian hinterland. The conflict had lasted over two centuries, culminating in the Battle of Kadesh in 1299 BCE, when a northward thrust of the Egyptian empire was defeated by Hittite forces. The treaty of 1280 BCE was intended to be a "perpetual peace" between the two great kingdoms,[72] marking off their respective spheres of influence in the region.[73] The treaty had been the subject of years of delicate negotiations between the two kings, carried on through the medium of diplomatic interchange. The principals are not thought to have ever met in person.[74]

With just a few exceptions, the terms of the treaty are perfectly symmetrical. Indeed, the structure of the mutual oaths undertaken by the parties, and as reflected in their respective versions of the text, are illustrative of a "perfect" parity treaty.[75] In most other respects, though, both versions of the treaty follow the form already described for Hittite and Assyrian feudatory instruments.[76] There is a historical prologue, much utilized in Hittite treaty practice, although (as Dennis McCarthy has noted) "the history [of the past relations between the Hittite and Egyptian empires] was embarrassing and had to be drastically edited."[77] The Hittite text says that "as for the relationship between the land of Egypt and the Hatti land, since eternity the god does not permit the making of hostility between them because of a treaty valid forever."[78] The Egyptian version of the prologue is more honest, acknowledging that the two countries had recently been at war.[79]

After the historical sketch, the substantive terms of the treaty follow, including clauses proclaiming a perpetual peace between the two States, a defensive alliance, and provisions for the extradition of political refugees.[80] In the Hittite version the declaration of perpetual peace is along

---

[72] See *ibid.* See also 2(1) *Cambridge Ancient History* 229, 258–59 (3rd ed. 1973) ("The peace of the world seemed assured for a long time to come."); Nussbaum, *supra* note 11, at 2–3; Théodoridès, *supra* note 65, at 112–13.

[73] See Kastemont, *supra* note 36, at 438–39. For more on the political situation between the two countries, see Langdon and Gardiner, *supra* note 8, at 201–05.

[74] See Evan Luard, *Conflict and Peace in the International System* 15 (1968). The explanatory introduction of the treaty in the Egyptian text recounts that a Hittite messenger brought the final text of the agreement on a "tablet of silver." See Langdon and Gardiner, *supra* note 8, at 185.

[75] See Kastemont, *supra* note 36, at 47; 2 Jacques Pirenne, *Histoire de la Civilisation* 361 (1961).

[76] See *supra* notes 46–52 and accompanying text.   [77] See McCarthy, *supra* note 2, at 99.

[78] *Ibid.* at 23. See also Munn-Rankin, *supra* note 25, at 72.

[79] See McCarthy, *supra* note 2, at 23; see also Langdon and Gardiner, *supra* note 8, at 187 (Egyptian parallel text). Readings of the treaty suggest that it may have been drafted to reinstate an earlier peace agreement, one broken by the outbreak of hostilities in the reign of earlier rulers. See *ibid.* See *supra* note 68.

[80] See Rostovtseff, *supra* note 14, at 41–43.

these lines: "[Rameses II of Egypt has agreed] from this day to give good peace and good brotherhood between us forever; and he is a brother to me [the king of Hatti] and at peace with me, and I am a brother to him and at peace with him forever."[81] The clause goes on to bind the children and grandchildren of the parties, concluding in grandiloquent terms: "And Egypt with the land of Hatti – they are at peace, they are brothers like us forever."[82] The next clause stipulates that neither country will invade the other.[83]

The two rulers then undertook a defensive alliance, in language typical of such provisions for Hittite feudal treaties: "And if another enemy come [against] the land of Hatti . . . the great king of Egypt shall send his troops and his chariots and shall slay his enemy and he shall restore confidence to the land of Hatti."[84] The Egyptian text appears reciprocal.[85] Then follow provisions for aiding each other in suppressing rebellions.[86]

The remaining substantive provisions of the treaty concern the extradition of fugitives, both "great" and "unknown." For both important political refugees and for common criminals, each sovereign promised to return them to the country from which they had fled. But both sovereigns deigned to show clemency to those who had been returned: "But as for the man who shall be brought [back] . . . let not his crime be charged against him, let not his house or wives or his children be destroyed, let him not be killed, let no injury be done to his eyes, to his ears, to his mouth or to his legs."[87] This provision appears to have been added as an afterthought; it appears in the Egyptian text to have been tacked-on at the end, after the curse and closing formulae.[88]

At the conclusion of the entire instrument was a truncated form of an oath before the deities of both nations. Only the Egyptian text is extant for this provision of the treaty, but in its style one can tell that it was

---

[81] Langdon and Gardiner, *supra* note 8, at 188 (Hittite parallel text). For more on "brotherhood" expressed in ancient Near Eastern treaties, see Karavites, *supra* note 40, at 48–52.   [82] *Ibid.* For a simplified version, see Pritchard, *supra* note 46, at 199–200.

[83] See Langdon and Gardiner, *supra* note 8, at 189 ("[T]he great king of Egypt will not trespass into the land of Hatti to take aught from therein; . . . and the great king of Hatti shall not trespass into Egypt to take aught from therein.") (Hittite parallel text).

[84] See *ibid.* at 190 (Hittite text).   [85] See *ibid.*

[86] See *ibid.* at 190–91. For simplified versions, see Rostovtseff, *supra* note 14, at 42.

[87] Langdon and Gardiner, *supra* note 8, at 197–98. See also Théodoridès, *supra* note 65, at 134–35 (speculating that such a humane provision may have been dictated by economic factors in order to discourage mass movements of populations).

[88] See *ibid.* at 192. The Hittite text breaks off just before these passages, so no parallel reading is possible. See *ibid.* See also Adolf Erman-Ranke, *Aegypten und ägyptisches Leben* 721 (Charles Mathien transl. 1952).

drawn from Hittite forms. The key provision is: "As for these words of the treaty [written] upon this tablet of silver, a thousand gods, male gods and female gods of those of the land of Hatti, together with a thousand gods, male gods and female gods of those of the land of Egypt – they are with me as witnesses."[89] At the end of the passage, further witnesses are acknowledged, including "the mountains and rivers of the land of Egypt; the sky; the earth; the great sea; the wind; the clouds."[90] The ultimate provision of the treaty, as per Hittite form, was the curse clause, which said:

As to these words which are upon this tablet of silver . . . as to him who shall not keep them, a thousand gods of the land of Hatti and a thousand gods of the land of Egypt shall destroy his house, his land and his servants. But he who shall keep these words . . . be they Hatti or be they Egyptians, and who do not neglect them, a thousand gods of the land of Hatti and a thousand gods of the land of Egypt will cause him to be healthy and to live, together with his houses and his land and his servants.[91]

Scholars have acknowledged that this curse and blessing clause must have been modified to suit Egyptian sensibilities, otherwise it would have been much more elaborate in keeping with Hittite practice.[92]

The 1280 BCE agreement between the Hittites and Egyptians stands as the epitome of parity treaties in the ancient Near East. The structure of the clauses, the phrasing of the language, and the relatively modest scope of the provisions indicate a desire for two great powers to regulate the most basic elements of their political relationship. As a paradigm of the ancient Near Eastern treaty, this instrument would have an enduring influence on later traditions of treaty-making in the ancient world. Its inspiration would first be felt in Israelite practice, and then in Greek and western Mediterranean treaty models.

Ancient Israelite practice

The entire thrust of what has come to be called covenant historiography has been to trace the parallels between ancient Near Eastern treaty forms and the biblical covenants of Yahweh and the Israelites. Beginning with George Mendenhall's ground-breaking 1955 study,[93] the covenant thesis can be simply stated: the Israelite covenant is similar to early Near Eastern treaties in major emphases and intent.

---

[89] See Langdon and Gardiner, *supra* note 8, at 194 (Egyptian text only). For another translation, see Pritchard, *supra* note 46, at 200–01.

[90] Langdon and Gardiner, *supra* note 8, at 194.   [91] *Ibid.* at 197.   [92] See *ibid.*

[93] See *supra* note 2. For a brief historiography, see McCarthy, *supra* note 2, at 3–6.

God gives the covenant – as at Sinai (*Ex.* 20) or Schechem (*Jos.* 24) – based on his past gracious actions, but without himself swearing to any performance. The human partners are bound to specific obligations toward him and one another (the Decalogue), transgression of which will bring awful retribution.[94]

In short, the theory proposes that the biblical covenants were modeled on the vassal treaties made by the Hittites. Structural surveys of biblical texts have thus been made to draw the similarities between them and Hittite feudal treaties.[95] Apart from technical distinctions made between earlier Hittite forms and later Assyrian texts,[96] which are of little consequence here, the covenant thesis has been largely vindicated.

While a full exploration of the covenant thesis and its historiography is beyond the scope of this study, some essential points need to be made before closely looking at Israelite treaty practice. The first, eloquently made by George Mendenhall, is that "innumerable incidents and ideas in the entire history of Israel can be adequately understood only from this complex of covenant patterns of thought."[97] The covenant form was an essential idea of Israelite culture. It conditioned man's relation with his God. It was integral with God's law. It was the basis of the Israelite State.

[94] Hillers, *supra* note 2, at 135.

[95] See McCarthy, *supra* note 2, at 102. See *ibid.* 2–3 for parallel readings of Hittite treaties and biblical texts. For some examples, consider the following:.

a. Introduction of the speaker.

| These are the words of the Sun, Muwatilis, the Great King, king of the Land of Hatti. | These are the words which Moses spoke to Israel. (Deuteronomy 1:1). |

b. Stipulations.

| Thou, Alaksandus, shall protect the Sun as a friend. | Thou shalt offer the Passover sacrifice to Yahwe thy God! (Deuteronomy 16:2) |

c. Curse and blessing.

| If thou, Alaksandus, break the words of this document, then may these oaths wipe thee out . . . and wipe thy seed from the face of the earth. But if thou keepest these words, then may the thousand gods . . . keep thee, thy wife, thy sons with friendly hand. | If thou dost not obey the voice of Yahwe thy God by keeping his Commandments . . . then all these curses shall come upon thee. If thou obeyest the voice . . . by keeping his Commandments . . . then all these blessings shall come upon thee. (Deuteronomy 28:15) |

Ibid. at 2–3. See also McCarthy's reading of Deuteronomy, *supra* note 2, at 109–10.

[96] See McCarthy, *supra* note 2, at 37; Mendenhall, *supra* note 2, at 30 n. 19.

[97] Mendenhall, *supra* note 2, at 30. See also 1 I. Herzog, *The Main Institutions of Jewish Law* 20 (London 2nd ed. 1965); John T. Greene, *The Role of the Messenger and the Message in the Ancient Near East* 167 (1989); J. Harvey, Le "Rib-Pattern" Requisitoire prophetique sur la rupture de l'alliance, 43 *Biblica* 172 (1962); Herbert B. Huffman, The Covenant Lawsuit in the Prophets, 78 *Journal of Biblical Literature* 351 (1966).

It must have been essential to any legal relations made between the Israelites and other polities.

The second point, subsumed in the entire covenant thesis, is that the Israelites borrowed from the Hittites, who, in turn, borrowed their treaty forms from the Babylonians and earlier Mesopotamian cultures.[98] This implication has already been made above. The ancient Israelites were part of a larger tradition of ancient Near Eastern treaty-making,[99] a tradition that perpetuated itself even in Greek and Roman times. Nonetheless, our knowledge of Israelite treaties is premised solely on biblical texts and inferences. Because references to these treaties occur in different books in the Bible, it is difficult to place them in a true chronology.

Take, for example, the treaty between Judah and Edom, dated to a time before the Syro-Ephraimite War of 735 BCE.[100] Edom's treachery in breaching this treaty was mentioned with particular vehemence in the Bible.[101] Isaiah is said to have remonstrated with the Edomites, telling them to remember their treaty obligations by "look[ing] it up in the covenant-inscription of Yahweh, which is deposited in the temple of Yahweh as a sign that he guarantees the oaths taken in his name."[102] This is a significant extract, one that resonates with other biblical passages where the connection between treaty and covenant is confirmed. Yahweh said through Jeremiah that the men who broke the covenant between king and people to free the Hebrew slaves had broken "my covenant."[103] Likewise, Yahweh was said to have referred to the treaty between Babylon and Judah as "my oath [or curse]" and "my covenant."[104] We also know something of Israelite treaty formalities, by references to religious symbology used in ratification ceremonies, such as uttering the holy number seven and sacrificing animals.[105]

---

[98] See *ibid.* at 27–28.

[99] See McCarthy, *supra* note 2, at 8–9; see also Speiser, 95 *Proceedings of the American Philosophical Society* 587 (1932) (who suggests treating the entire ancient Near East as a cultural-geographical unity).

[100] See Hillers, *supra* note 2, at 49–50 (glossing the biblical passages from 2 Samuel 8:13–14 and Kings).

[101] See Isaiah 34:16. Edom apparently had another chance to breach a treaty with Israel, some years later in 710 BCE, when there was an abortive alliance to overthrow Assyrian domination in Palestine. The conspiracy was apparently discovered, and the Edomites hastened to betray their oath to Judah and submitted to Assyrian rule. See Martin Noth, *Geschichte Israels* 239 (Göttingen 2nd ed. 1954).   [102] Hillers, *supra* note 2, at 52.

[103] Jeremiah 34:18.   [104] Ezekiel 17:19.

[105] See Nussbaum, *supra* note 11, at 3. See also Shabtai Rosenne, The Influence of Judaism on the Development of International Law, 5 Netherlands ILR 119, 141 (1958) (citing Genesis 21:22–32).

We have a sense that the ancient Israelites understood different classifi-cations of treaties. Patriarchal records refer to several intertribal cove-nants.[106] There were also a number of instances of feudatory treaties where tribes agreed to perform services or pay tribute to Judah. The inci-dent with the Gibeonites, discussed in Chapter 3,[107] may have been part of a formal process whereby that tribe sought protection from Israel. After all, in the biblical text the men of Gibeon agreed to be the "servants" of Joshua and Judah.[108] As we know from that parable, the Israelites ruth-lessly enforced the vassal agreements in which they were the superior party. In the time of King David, a vassal treaty was made with Moab (as well as with Ammon and Edom).[109] When Mesha, king of Moab, rebelled, the Israelites, under King Jehoram, invaded and laid waste to the country, self-consciously visiting on the land the specified curses enumerated in the broken treaty.[110]

Israel also entered into true parity treaties. We have mentions of agree-ments made with the ruler of Damascus.[111] We also know of a treaty between Solomon and Hiram of Tyre which not only provided for the exchange of some disputed border villages, but also governed trade between the two countries.[112] Treaties entered into by Israel with the Romans will be considered later in this chapter.[113] In any event, the Israelites were sticklers for observing the terms of parity treaties. For example, the High Priest of Israel was said to have declined the overtures of Alexander the Great because of his oath to Darius of Persia.[114] Likewise, at a much later date, Judas Maccabeus adhered to his oath with Antiochus Eupator concerning the end of the siege of the Temple.[115] Israel did later denounce each of those oaths, declaring them to be personal with the other sovereign, who had subsequently died.[116]

---

[106] See Genesis 14:13 (Abraham and confederate chiefs in Dead Sea area); 21:22–34 (Abraham and Abimelech, the Philistine governor); 26:26–32 (Isaac and Abimelech); 31:44–45 (Laban with Jacob). See also Prosper Weil, Le Judaïsme et le Développement du Droit Internationale, 151 RCADI 253, 278–79 (1976–III).   [107] See text at notes 73–77.

[108] Joshua 9:8, 11, 23–27. See also fealty treaty between David and Achish, king of Gath. 1 Samuel 27. See also Weil, *supra* note 106, at 279–80.

[109] See 2 Samuel 8:6, 14; 2 Samuel 10:19.   [110] See 2 Kings 3:4.

[111] See 1 Kings 15:19 (Baasha and Ben-hadad of Damascus), 20:34 (Ahab and Ben-hadad). One writer has suggested that this may have been a suzerainty treaty since Ben-hadad had been defeated by the Israelites. See Thompson, *supra* note 16, at 18 n. 8.

[112] See 1 Kings 5 and Hebrews 5:24. See also Weil, *supra* note 106, at 280–81.

[113] *Ibid.* See *infra* notes 349–352 and accompanying text.

[114] See 7 Josephus, *Collected Works* 5 (Ralph Marcus transl. 1963) (Loeb Classical Library reprint) (*Antiquities*, passage xii.8.3–4).   [115] See 7 *ibid.* 7 (passage xii.10.7).

[116] See Rosenne, *supra* note 105, at 141–42.

Quite apart from the sense of legal obligation that the ancient Jews considered was a part of their treaties, a question explored in Chapter 3, the
scant historical evidence of Israelite treaty practice does seem to confirm
the central precept of the covenant thesis. Ancient Near Eastern polities
had a unified conception for making agreements with their neighbors.
The emphasis on oaths and curses was a singular aspect of that understanding. By the same token, so also was the sense that treaties were a part
of international history, of the life of nations. And, even more pertinently,
treaty instruments were employed for a wide variety of purposes, regulating matters as diverse as frontiers, trade, extradition, and military alliances. We now turn to the question of how this tradition of treaty-making
continued in ancient Mediterranean cultures.

The Greek city-States

Terminology and types of treaties

The extent of treaty-making by Greek city-States was remarkable. By one
count,[117] nearly 400 treaties are extant (through inscription evidence or
literary allusions) from the period before 338 BCE, when Greece came
under Macedonian domination. To match this diplomatic activity, the
ancient Greeks had an equally extensive lexicon for treaty instruments.
These included generic terms to cover the simple act of covenant, which
was similar to the Greek word for contract.[118] The Greeks also made distinctions as to kinds of treaties made upon the termination of hostilities.
These could properly be considered as peace treaties, or as declarations of
neutrality, or as amnesties ending periods of internal disorder.[119] Likewise,
the Greeks developed terminology to cover different sorts of alliances,
whether purely defensive or offensive.[120] And, as already discussed in the
previous chapter, there were a whole host of agreements establishing

---

[117] See Everett L. Wheeler, Sophistic Interpretations and Greek Treaties, 25 GRBS 253,
255–56 (1984). See also 2 Coleman Phillipson, *The International Law and Custom of Ancient
Greece and Rome* 73 (1911) (who pegs the number at over 200).

[118] See 3 Thucydides, *History of the Peloponnesian War* 59 (C. F. Smith transl. 1919) (Loeb
Classical Library reprint 1980) (passage v.31). See also Aristotle, *Rhetoric* 151 (H. Rackham
transl. 1932) (passage i.15) (equating law with contract).

[119] See 2 Phillipson, *supra* note 117, at 375–76 (citing 1 Herodotus, *Histories* 25 (A. D. Godley
transl. 1920) (Loeb Classical Library reprint 1969) (passage i.22); and 2 Thucydides, *supra*
note 118, at 309, 409 (passages iv.58 and 117), and 3 *ibid.* at 49, 61 (passages v.26 and 32);
and 1 Xenophon, *Hellenica and Anabasis* 265, 271 (Carleton L. Brownson transl. 1921)
(Loeb Classical Library reprint 1932) (*Hellenica*, passage iv.2 and 16)).

[120] See 1 Phillipson, *supra* note 117, at 376–77 (citing 3 Herodotus, *supra* note 119, at 67, 81
(passage v.63 and 73); and 1 Thucydides, *supra* note 118, at 79 (passage i.44)).

special individual or commercial relationships between two cities.[121] Recognition was even given to technical instruments, treaty amendments and protocols.[122]

This diversity of names for international agreements indicated an articulated international legal culture, unrivaled by ancient Near Eastern practice, and probably superior even to Roman understanding. After first examining the content of different sorts of Greek treaties, peace agreements and alliances, this analysis will turn to the nature of Greek treaty-making: how these instruments were made and enforced.

Peace treaties

Up to the fourth century BCE, the Greek city-States concluded peace treaties for a limited time only; because of this there has been the suggestion that war and conflict was "the common condition" of Greek international life.[123] Negotiation of peace treaties typically was initiated in the last stages of conflict, "for it was not normal procedure to indulge in total destruction of a state."[124] Typical provisions of peace treaties of this sort, where one city had vanquished another, was that the defeated city would dismantle its walls and hand over its war materiel,[125] and perhaps also pay an indemnity as war reparations.[126]

[121] See Chapter 4, at notes 237–58 and accompanying text.
[122] See 1 Phillipson, *supra* note 117, at 376.   [123] See Nussbaum, *supra* note 11, at 6.
[124] Sir Frank Adcock and D. J. Mosley, *Diplomacy in Ancient Greece* 196 (1975). For examples of peace treaties which created a subjugated, dependent status for the defeated party, see 1 *Translated Documents of Greece and Rome: Archaic Times to the End of the Peloponnesian War* 109–10, 144–46, 193–94 (Charles W. Fonora transl. 2nd ed. 1983) (for texts of treaties between Athens and Macedon (430 BCE), Athens and Colophon (427 BCE), and Athens and Selymbria (407 BCE)). These tributary agreements, all following an outbreak of hostilities with Athens, involved the payment of tribute (see *ibid.* at 144–45), the return of hostages (*ibid.* at 193–94), and special economic provisions (including the right of free transit of grain across the Hellespont, *ibid.* at 145–46, and the cancellation of pre-existing contracts, *ibid.* at 193).
[125] See Adcock and Mosley, *supra* note 124, at 196–97. The Spartans in 404 BCE systematically destroyed the walls at Athens, which had rendered that city impregnable by land. Likewise, the Athenians destroyed the walls of Thasos (463 BCE), Samos (439 BCE), and Nisaea (424 BCE), upon its defeat of those cities. See 1 Thucydides, *supra* note 118, at 171, 195 (passages i.101.3, 1.117.3).
[126] See *ibid.* Guarantees were sometimes provided by the victor that the existing owners of property could continue to exercise their rights. See 2 Thucydides, *supra* note 118, at 303, 393 (passages iv.54.3, iv.105.2). See also Diodorus Siculus, *History* 229–40 (C. H. Oldfather, C. L. Sherman, C. Bradford Welles and F. R. Walton transl.) (Loeb Classical Library reprint 1946) (passage xvi.59.3). In another, earlier example, after a desultory conflict between Greek and Carthaginian colonies in North Africa, a peace treaty was concluded to demarcate the respective spheres of influence of the two sets of colonies. See E. W. Bovill, *Golden Trade of the Moors* 20–21 (1958).

A "general" peace could end a conflict, which would be signed by a number of cities, some of which may not have been involved in the hostilities.[127] Perhaps the most famous of these was the Peace of Nicias of 421 BCE, ending a phase of the Peloponnesian War between Athens and Sparta.[128] As a prelude to this general peace, it is useful to recall that there was a one-year truce arranged in 423 BCE. The terms of this armistice presaged many of the provisions of the subsequent peace. For example, the truce (as recounted by Thucydides)[129] provided for free access to the oracle at Delphi and the protection of its treasures, renewed safe conducts for heralds and envoys, demarcated a "cease-fire" line and limitations on the projection of Lacedaemonian naval power, renounced the reception of deserters, and allowed for arbitration of disputes arising under the truce.[130]

The Peace of Nicias was a strategic gambit by Sparta, one that would later pay great dividends. In deciding to put a temporary halt to hostilities with Athens, the Spartans were able to consolidate some gains, and prepare for what they believed was an imminent attack by Argos, which they could not have hoped to repel if they had also been fighting Athens. The Peace of Nicias did sacrifice the interests of a number of Spartan allies – the Boeotians, Corinthians, Elians, and Megarans – and those cities did, indeed, refuse to ratify this general peace. The Nician Peace was best known for its offensive and defensive alliance between Athens and Sparta, an issue that will be considered later in this section,[131] but its general clauses showed some concern for the rights of other Greek city-States. One provision stated:

As regards the temples shared by the Greeks[,] whoever wishes shall offer sacrifice and have access to them and consult their oracles and send deputies to them according to their ancestral customs by land and sea without fear. The sacred area and temple of Apollo at Delphi and the Delphians shall be governed by their own laws, and be subject to their own dues and shall have jurisdiction in their own courts both of themselves and of their territory according to ancestral custom.[132]

---

[127] See Scupin, *supra* note 23, at 136.

[128] See N. G. L. Hammond, *A History of Greece to 322 BC* 370–76 (2nd ed. 1967); Barry S. Strauss and Josiah Ober, *The Anatomy of Error: Ancient Military Disasters and their Lessons for Modern Strategists* 58 (1990).   [129] See 2 Thucydides, *supra* note 118, at 411 (passage iv.118).

[130] See 2 Phillipson, *supra* note 117, at 281–84 (for a gloss on the truce of 423 BCE).

[131] See *infra* notes 165–67 and accompanying text.

[132] The inscription text was taken from 2 H. Bengtson, *Die Staatsverträge des Altertums* 188 (1962). It was also reported in 3 Thucydides, *supra* note 118, at 35 (passage v.18). This was translated in Adcock and Mosley, *supra* note 124, at 257–58. See also Rostovtseff, *supra* note 14, at 48.

Even more startling in context were the peace treaties concluded between Athens and Persia. While there is substantial dispute as to the dating and authenticity of some of these instruments,[133] there is no doubt that Athens ratified at least two or three agreements with Persia, beginning with the (dubious) Peace of Kallias and ending with the Peace of Antalkidas (the "King's Peace" of 386 BCE). This record of treaty-making and diplomacy was surprising in view of the oath of everlasting enmity that the Athenians swore against the Persians on the battlefield of Plataea in 479 BCE.[134] In truth, the Athenians were willing and eager to conclude agreements with the Persians if they believed that such would help with their ongoing rivalry with Sparta. Athens was constantly being drawn into domestic Persian disputes. This sometimes meant supporting a struggling Athenian colony in Asia Minor, or siding with a rebellious satrap against the Persian king.[135]

The Peace of Kallias was just that – a termination of hostilities and a promise not to attack one another. The later Peace of Epilykos (in 424 BCE) was far more ambitious, having been concluded by Athens after its abortive Sicilian expedition and when the tide of the Peloponnesian War had definitively turned against it. It has been properly characterized as a *philia*, a treaty of friendship,[136] the generalized terms of which will be considered presently. After Sparta had defeated Athens, and all Greek city-States were under threat from Macedon, the Athenians were compelled to conclude the "humiliating" Peace of Antalkidas with Persia in 386 BCE. As N. G. L. Hammond has suggested, the King's Peace really marked an implied

---

[133] For a summary of the scholarly controversy, see Anthony E. Raubitschek, The Treaties Between Persia and Athens, 5 GRBS 151 (1964). See also H. T. Wade-Gery, *Essays in Greek History* 207–11 (1958); A. Blamire, Epilycus' Negotiations with Persia, 29 *Phoenix* 24 (1975); Gomme, The Treaty of Callias, 65 AJP 332 (1945). Plutarch intimated that the treaty negotiated by Kallias was nearly repudiated upon his return to Athens, when he was accused of bribery, condemned, almost executed, and fined fifty talents. Nonetheless, the Athenians did decide to keep the treaty. See generally, 2 Plutarch, *Lives* 445 (B. Perrin transl. 1917) (Loeb Classical Library reprint 1968) (*Cimon*, passage xiii.5–6).

[134] See 4 Diodorus, *supra* note 126, at 17 (passage ix.10.5).

[135] For the general tenor of Athenian–Persian relations, see Raubitschek, *supra* note 133, at 151–59. See also 1 Demosthenes, *Collected Works* 429 (A. T. Murray transl. 1939) (Loeb Classical Library reprint) (passage xv.28); 1 Thucydides, *supra* note 118, at 191, 193 (passages i.115.4–5 and i.116.1–3), 3 *ibid.* at 159, 167 (passages v.89 and v.105.2). See also J. H. Oliver, The Peace of Callias and the Pontic Expedition of Pericles, 6 *Historia* 254 (1957).

[136] See 1 Andocides, *Minor Attic Orators* (K. J. Maidment transl. 1941) (Loeb Classical Library reprint 1982) (*On the Peace*, passage xxix). See also Robert A. Bauslaugh, *The Concept of Neutrality in Classical Greece* 126–27 (1991).

Persian protectorate over Spartan-dominated Greece.[137] The King's Peace would have been the basis of a united Greek defense against Philip II of Macedon, but this was to no avail.

There were several tensions in the Greek practice surrounding peace treaties. The most obvious of these was how Hellenic city-States regarded the possibility of treaties prescribing the conditions for "perfect and perpetual" peace. On the one hand, the general peaces concluded after rounds of pan-Hellenic conflict, including the Peloponnesian War, were certainly conceived as universal settlements, prescribing rules for such general concerns as access to the Delphic sanctuary and its particular services. As will be discussed below (in reference to the creation of Greek *amphictyones*), there was a strong impulse towards Hellenic unity, of which the general peaces were part. By the same token, the Greeks were clearly able to overcome their notorious disdain for "barbarians," and to treat with their outside enemies, Persia and (later) Macedon, on terms of equality. The Athenian and Spartan treaties with Persia were obviously motivated by strong balance-of-power concerns, which were sufficient to overcome Greek particularism in the recognition and treatment of foreign potentates.

In spite of these suggestions that the Greeks saw the treaty as an instrument to obtain universal peace and order, the evidence strongly contradicts that conclusion. To the extent that peace treaties were imposed upon a vanquished polity, they inevitably recognized the political hegemony and supremacy of the victor. When a peace treaty was made between two equal powers, in circumstances indicating that neither had defeated the other, then they were always for a limited period, usually for never more than fifty years.[138] Indeed, the ancient Greek assumption was that, even if the treaty provisions *were* observed by both parties for the full treaty period, a state of war would resume upon the lapse of the agreement. Sparta's conduct in 421 BCE, seeking a pause in the Peloponnesian War with Athens, was decisively driven by fears that Argos would resume the war ended by a peace made years before.[139] The Argives' scrupulous

---

[137] See Hammond, *supra* note 128, at 465.

[138] See G. E. M. de Ste Croix, *The Origins of the Peloponnesian War* (1972), for a searching (and controversial) view of its subject. The author also suggests that any earlier peace between Athens and Sparta may have been totally illusory. See *ibid.* at 3.

[139] As it turned out, hostilities did not commence between Argos and Sparta, and another peace treaty was made in 418 BCE, this time including an offensive alliance against Athens. See 3 Thucydides, *supra* note 118, at 143, 147 (passage v.77, 79). For a translation, see Adcock and Mosley, *supra* note 124, at 258–59. See also Hammond, *supra* note 128, at 376, 379–82; Peter Karavites, *Capitulations and Greek Interstate Relations* 91–99 (1982) (on the perpetual duration of certain Greek alliances and peace treaties).

conduct in the Peloponnesian War was probably the exception; many Greek city-States seemed untroubled about breaking the terms of a truce or peace.

Alliances and *philiai*

Historians of ancient Greece have identified a number of impulses for Hellenic city-States to conclude alliances with one another. As already suggested, maintenance of a perceived balance of power was assuredly the most significant of these motives. In addition, there were economic considerations which impelled the formation of different sorts of alliances of convenience, as well as the development of federal relationships. It has even been suggested that Greek alliance-making was really driven by the demands of powerful agricultural[140] or mercantile[141] interests. Aside from these perspectives, it remains to look at the different forms that Greek alliances took. While substantial attention is given here to the more complex models of Greek alliance-making, the question of whether the ancient Greeks had a constitutional conception of a federal state is beyond the scope of this study.[142] In short, Greek alliance-making is considered here as an attribute of relationships between separate, independent sovereignties.

The most elemental form of a Greek alliance was a *philia*, or treaty of friendship. The earliest such treaty is extant from between 550 and 525 BCE. It was concluded between the Greek colony of Sybaris in southern Italy and an otherwise unknown neighbor, the Serdaioi. The text of the fragment is short and direct: "The Sybarites and their allies and the Serdaioi united in friendship, faithful and without guile forever. Guarantors: Zeus and Apollo and the other gods and the city of Poseidonia."[143] As modern commentators have noted,[144] the Greek text clearly distinguishes between the status of friendship that was created between Sybaris and the Serdaioi by this agreement, and the alliance that had (apparently) earlier existed between Sybaris and other (unnamed) towns or villages. Friendship (*philia*) was manifestly distinct from alliance (*symmachia*). In short, two polities could be friends, and yet not be allies.

---

[140] See P. Giraud, *La propriété foncière en Grèce jusqu'à la conquête romaine* 615 (Paris 1893).

[141] This is the implicit thrust of G. E. M. de Ste Croix's volume, *supra* note 138.

[142] For more on this subject, see the definitive work by J. A. O. Larsen, *Greek Federal States: Their Institutions and History* (1968).

[143] See *Translated Documents*, *supra* note 124, at 31–32. For more on the possible nature of the relationship between these two colonies, see T. J. Dunbabin, *The Western Greeks: The History of Sicily and South Italy from the Foundation of the Greek Colonies to 480 BC*, at 364–65 (1948); Karavites, *supra* note 40, at 48–58.   [144] See Bauslaugh, *supra* note 136, at 56–57.

This formal distinction appears in other early inscriptions, including the sixth-century treaty between Rome and Carthage, the Greek translation of which by Polybius makes an identical contrast.[145]

This perceived distinction between friendship and alliance has proven to be fertile ground for modern considerations of ancient Greek international relations. Adcock and Mosley suggested that a *philia* was usually a formality. Often a clause announcing a state of friendship between two states was coupled, in the same instrument, with the terms and conditions of an alliance.[146] On other occasions, a declaration of friendship was used as an opening in relations between two distant states which had previously had no occasion for relations.[147] The King's Peace of 387 BCE may be considered a form of *philia*, at least in this sense.[148] Lastly, a declaration of amity may have been nothing more than a reinforcement of an earlier peace treaty and a renewed promise not to initiate hostilities.[149]

The evidence bears out the thesis of Adcock and Mosley that, as a symbol of a rudimentary relationship, a *philia* status could mean different things at different times. They concluded:

The word "friendship" was one which could easily be overworked and devalued in diplomatic exchanges. At best it could signify a positive relationship and at the least it meant little, if anything, more than non-aggression or non-belligerency between powers which might or might not have contracted any formal relationship by treaty . . . Such guarantees were, of course, not worth much more than most promises made in Greek diplomacy, but they by no means constituted mere empty verbiage.[150]

This judgment seems to run counter to the recently advanced theory of Robert Bauslaugh that "*philia* was an official relationship, not a state of mind."[151] As part of his general thesis about the use of neutrality in ancient Greece, Bauslaugh believes that a *philia* status was often invoked

---

[145] See 2 Polybius, *The Histories* 55 (W. R. Paton transl. 1922) (Loeb Classical Library reprint 1975) (passage iii.22.4). For a copy of the inscription, see Bengtson, *supra* note 132 (number 121). See also 1 F. Walbank, *Historical Commentary on Polybius* 339–45 (1957). For more on Roman treaties with Carthage, see *infra* notes 358–64 and accompanying text. Strabo, in narrating the Lelantine War of the late eighth century BCE, suggests that two cities (Chalcis and Eritria) were in "amity." See 5 Strabo, *The Geography* 19 (H. L. Jones transl. 1927) (passage x.1.12); *Translated Documents, supra* note 124, at 9–10.

[146] See Adcock and Mosley, *supra* note 124, at 206 (discussing treaty between Anaitoi and Metapioi of c. 550 BCE and 393 BCE treaty between the Chalcidians and Amyntas III of Macedon; for the texts of which see Bengtson, *supra* note 132, at Nos. 110 and 231).

[147] See *ibid.* (Athenian treaties with Carthage (406 BCE) and Egypt (390 BCE); for the texts of which see Bengtson, *supra* note 132, at Nos. 208 and 236).   [148] See *ibid.*

[149] See *ibid.* at 208–09 (Athens–Chios of 384 BCE and Athens–Syracuse of 367 BCE; for the texts of which see Bengtson, *supra* note 132, Nos. 167 and 280).

[150] *Ibid.* at 208 and 209.   [151] Bauslaugh, *supra* note 136, at 62.

by states wishing to abstain from a general conflict. In the Peloponnesian War, for example, a majority of the Achaean cities refused to join either Athens or Sparta because of amity agreements in force with both sides.[152] As further evidence of the real, binding effect of *philia*, Bauslaugh points to the agreement between Amyntas and the Chalcidians which expressly prohibited either party from concluding agreements with any of a number of other listed cities, absent consent of the other.[153] Likewise, the Spartans' offer for an early end of the Peloponnesian War (rejected by Athens) said merely that a state of "peace and friendship" would be restored, certainly nothing about alliance.

Neutrality, by virtue of contrary sets of *philiai*, came with a price. A friend to all was a friend to none. The Plataeans – whose sad tale was recounted earlier in this study[154] – sought peace by concluding *philai* with both the Athenian and Spartan coalitions.[155] However, Spartan judges condemned the Plataean garrison, despite that supposed protection. Nevertheless, Bruno Paradisi has noted that "the juridical institution of amity [or *philia*] was a signal for a critical moment in the development of ancient international relations."[156] As has been suggested here, it was a vindication of universality in State relations; countries of different religio-ethnic backgrounds and of unequal strength could treat with each other as peers.[157] It surely meant, again as Bauslaugh has written, that Greek states recognized that "[t]he language of diplomacy must be explicit enough to be understood but flexible enough to encompass the broadest possible range of different circumstances and requirements."[158]

Alliances: *symmachia* versus *epimachia*

The prominent model of a treaty of alliance in ancient Greece was a *symmachia* and its related form, *epimachia*. By definition, these were both

---

[152] See 1 Thucydides, *supra* note 118, at 275 (passage ii.9.2).
[153] See Bengtson, *supra* note 132, No. 231 (lines 18–23) ("Neither Amyntas nor the Chalcidians may without the other enter into *philiai* with the Amphipolitans, Bottiaeans, Acanthians, or Mendaeans, but if they agree and deem it beneficial, they may make an agreement with them in common."). As Bauslaugh points out, *supra* note 136, at 62 n. 58, another translation, by J. Wickersham and G. Verbrugghe, *The Fourth Century BC: Greek Historical Documents* (1973), mistranslates *philia* as "alliance."
[154] See Chapter 3 at notes 23, 28 and accompanying text.
[155] See 2 Thucydides, *supra* note 118, at 107 (passage iii.58.4).
[156] See Bruno Paradisi, L'amitié internationale: les phases critiques de son ancienne histoire, 78 RCADI 325, 349–50 (1951–I) (author's translation).
[157] See *ibid.* Interestingly enough, Demosthenes contrasted how easily two democracies may make peace, while a democracy and an oligarchy cannot even safely maintain friendly relations with one another. See 1 Demosthenes, *supra* note 135, at 411 (*For the Liberty of the Rhodians*, passage xv).   [158] Bauslaugh, *supra* note 136, at 63.

"military alliance[s] which acquired at an early stage [in Greek history] the character of a comprehensive alliance going beyond the joint waging of war, but in principle left the legal capacity of the allied City-States untouched."[159] In this way, *symmachiai* were distinct from advanced forms of alliance which resulted in federal unions of cities (*sympoliteiai*) or in international leagues or organizations (*amphictyoneiai*).

As a further distinction, *symmachiai* were considered to be alliances which committed States to support each other in battle, while an *epimachia* required only that the parties render assistance if one suffered an invasion.[160] In short, *symmachiai* were offensive alliances while *epimachiai* were defensive in nature. This distinction seems to have developed a full articulation only in the fifth century BCE.[161] Before that, inscriptions of Greek city-States were ambiguous as to the obligations undertaken in the alliance. Consider, for example, the agreement made between Elea and Heraea c. 500 BCE.[162] It said simply that "[t]his is the covenant between the Eleans and the Heraeans. There shall be an alliance for one hundred years and this year shall be the first; and if anything is needed, either word or deed, they shall stand by each other in all matters and especially in war . . ."[163] By any reckoning, this should be an offensive alliance, but some scholars have suggested otherwise. In the same vein, some Athenian treaties simply provided that "as allies we shall be trustworthy, steadfast, and reliable and we shall provide them with aid . . ."[164]

By the mid-fifth century, Athenian practice was becoming more predictable in the denomination of offensive alliances. The Nician Peace, already referred to,[165] contained provisions establishing a perfectly symmetrical offensive and defensive alliance. The article concerning Athenian obligations to Sparta ran as follows:

If any enemy invade Lacedaemonian territory and harm the Lacedaemonians, the Athenians shall assist the Lacedaemonians in any way in which they can, and to the utmost of their power; and if the enemy ravage their territory and depart, the offending city shall be the enemy of the Lacedaemonians and Athenians, and shall

---

[159] Scupin, *supra* note 23, at 135.

[160] See Adcock and Mosley, *supra* note 124, at 191; Karavites, *supra* note 139, at 30–32.

[161] See Adcock and Mosley, *supra* note 124, at 192–93.

[162] Coleman Phillipson mistakenly dates the treaty to between 588 and 572 BCE. See 2 Phillipson, *supra* note 117, at 54–55. Phillipson posits that the two cities were in the Peloponnese. For a better dating, see *Translated Documents, supra* note 124, at 29.

[163] The translation is from *Translated Documents, supra* note 124, at 29. The editors render the word "covenant" from the Greek word *rhetra*. See *ibid.*

[164] *Translated Documents, supra* note 124, at 142–43 (quoting 433 BCE treaties with Rhegium and Leontini).   [165] See *supra* notes 128–32 and accompanying text.

suffer at the hands of both of them, and neither shall cease from war before the other. These things shall be performed honestly, and zealously, and sincerely.[166]

The obligations of Sparta to Athens were identical. When offensive alliances were concluded, they were invariably joined with specific agreements for supplying forces and allocating command responsibilities for a joint expedition. Although no such protocol was agreed to by Sparta and Athens after the Nician Peace, inscriptions of *symmachiai* are extant between Athens and Sparta and their partners (among them Arcadia, Achaea, Argos, Elis, and Mantinea), providing details of how military campaigns were to be jointly conducted.[167]

In contrast, the agreement that Sparta concluded with Argos just after the Nician Peace[168] was more circumspect in its terms. One provision clearly spoke of a defensive alliance, where the cities promised that "[i]f any party from outside the Peloponnese proceeds by land with hostile intent against the Peloponnese the contracting parties are to take counsel and repel him in concert in such a way as seems most just to the Peloponnesians."[169] Even here, there is a measure of discretion granted in the *epimachia* to the individual parties; one may have (presumably) decided that to repel an invader (likely, the Athenians) would not be the "way as seems most just." In the same fashion, another provision of the treaty between Sparta and Argos from 418 BCE said only that "[i]f there shall be needed a common expedition anywhere the Spartans and the Argives are to take counsel in what way they decide most just for [them and their] allies."[170]

By the late fourth century BCE, Greek practice had refined the defensive alliance to a simple formula, one repeated in Athenian bilateral treaties from 400 to 357 BCE, as well as in the Second Athenian Confederacy of 377 BCE.[171] For example, the treaty between Athens and Boeotia said:

---

[166] This translation is from 3 Thucydides, *supra* note 118, at 45 (passage v.23), as rendered in 2 Phillipson, *supra* note 117, at 55–57.

[167] For the terms of Athens' 362 BCE alliance with Arcadia, Achaea, Elis, and Pylos, see Bengtson, *supra* note 132, at No. 290. For the clauses of Sparta's alliance with Mantinea of the same year, see *ibid.* at No. 291, and 2 Xenophon, *supra* note 119, at 321 (*Hellenica*, passage vii.5.3). For more on these treaties, see Adcock and Mosley, *supra* note 124, at 192.   [168] For more on which see *supra* note 139 and text.

[169] Bengtson, *supra* note 132, at No. 194; see also 3 Thucydides, *supra* note 118, at 145, 147 (passages v.77 and 79).   [170] *Ibid.*

[171] See Adcock and Mosley, *supra* note 124, at 192 (collecting citations to Athenian treaties with Locris (395 BCE), Chios (384), Byzantium (378), Corcyra (375), Syracuse (367), Thessaly (361), and Eretria (341)). See also B. D. Merritt, 15 AJP 69 (1946) (for a review of the Athens–Halieis treaty of 424 BCE).

If anyone proceeds to war against the Athenians either by land or by sea, the Boeotians are to render assistance with all their strength to the utmost of their ability as the Athenians may request. And if anyone proceeds to war against the Boeotians either by land or by sea, the Athenians are to render assistance with all their strength to the utmost of their ability as the Boeotians may request.[172]

The virtue of this clause, as modern writers have indicated,[173] is that it would not obligate a reluctant city to embark on an expedition launched by its alliance partner.

A number of alliances were concluded by Greek cities on less than equal terms. The Athenians and Lacedaemonians recognized the subservient status of their dependencies, and treaty clauses were fashioned to reflect that status. Athens' *symmachia* with Egesta of c. 453 BCE,[174] and her treaty with Chalcis in 446 BCE,[175] both contain provisions suggestive of a vulnerable position for the other treaty partner. Many capitulations, such as when Chios surrendered to the Athenian general, Chabrias, in 363 BCE, were patterned on this form of unequal treaty of alliance.[176] The entire affair surrounding the Athenian imposition (in 426 BCE) of harsh terms on the people of Melos, which led to the famous Melian Dialogue,[177] can be seen as an example of an unequal treaty of alliance. Xenophon[178] and Isocrates[179] both noted that unequal *symmachiai* were a consistent feature of Greek power relations.

The Greek practice of concluding military alliances thus involved sophisticated notions of treaty drafting. Provisions had to be made for whether an alliance would be strictly defensive in character, and, if so,

---

[172] Adcock and Mosley, *supra* note 124, at 192.

[173] See *ibid.* But see Victor Martin, *La Vie Internationale dans la Grèce des Cités* 371–72 (Paris 1940) (reprinted 1979), who saw this as an example of an unreciprocal treaty. Exception to this view was taken by Elie Bikerman, Remarques sur le droit des gens dans la Grèce classique, 4 RIDA (ser. 1) 99, 106–07 (1950).

[174] See *Translated Documents, supra* note 124, at 81.

[175] See Bengtson, *supra* note 132, at No. 155. For an English translation, see Adcock and Mosley, *supra* note 124, at 256–57 (where the Chalcidians swore "I shall be as good and just an ally as I can, and I shall come to the assistance and defence of the people of Athens if anyone wrongs the people of Athens, and I shall obey the people of Athens.").

[176] See Bikerman, *supra* note 173, at 110.

[177] See in 2 Thucydides, *supra* note 118, at 161 (passage iii.91.2), 3 *ibid.* at 155 (passage v.84.1). See also Martin, *supra* note 173, at 355–56.

[178] See 2 Xenophon, *supra* note 119, at 235 (*Hellenica*, passage vii.1.13). See also Bikerman, *supra* note 173, at 108 and n. 37.

[179] See 1 Isocrates, Collected Works 377 (George Narlin transl. 1928) (Loeb Classical Library reprint 1980) (*Archidamus*, passage 51); see also *ibid.* at 233 (*Panegyricus*, passage 176). For a gloss on these texts, see Georges Ténékidès, Droit International et Communautés Fédérales dans la Grèce des Cités, 90 RCADI 469, 519–20 (1956–II).

what conditions would trigger a duty of assistance by the alliance partner. Likewise, an offensive alliance in ancient Greece was useless unless accompanied by a parallel agreement deciding on military objectives, allocating force contributions, and deciding command responsibilities. Underlying Greek military alliances was a profound appreciation of power relationships, causing one party or the other to dictate terms making the treaty instrument fundamentally unreciprocal or unequal in the obligations it imposed.

Leagues and federations

There was a subtle distinction observed in ancient Greece between federal states and looser organizations of cities. Both were known by the generic term of *koinon*, which could have been used to describe virtually any sort of association. Likewise, the phrase *ethnos*, which literally meant tribe, could be used as a synonym for "nation" particularly when referring to aggregates of city-States.[180] J. A. O. Larsen says that the two most technical political terms in classical Greek, and the ones which convey definite international legal meanings, were *hegemonika symmachia*[181] and *sympoliteia*.[182]

A hegemonic *symmachia* was a league of states formed by a dominant city-State.[183] In such a Greek league, the official leadership and decision-making mechanisms were in the hands of the *hegemon*. The Delian[184] and Second Athenian[185] Leagues, both established under Athens' dominance, had officials provided by that city. The Hellenic League, established by

[180] See A. E. R. Boak, Greek Interstate Associations and the League of Nations, 15 AJIL 375, 382 (1921).

[181] See Scupin, *supra* note 23, at 135. See also Bikerman, *supra* note 173, at 99–106; Victor Martin, *supra* note 173, at 138–41, 176–78; Ténékidès, *supra* note 179, at 549 (who considers some hegemonic *symmachiai* to be termed *synedria*, or "congresses").

[182] See Larsen, *supra* note 142, at xiv–xv. See also J. A. O. Larsen, *Representative Government in Greek and Roman History* (1955); William P. Merrill, To Plethos in a Treaty Concerning the Affairs of Argos, Knossos and Tylissos, 41 CQ 16 (1991).

[183] See Chapter 4, at notes 237–48 and accompanying text.

[184] Little is actually known about the Delian League, formed by Athens after the pan-Hellenic coalition against Persia began to disintegrate in the 470s BCE. See Adcock and Mosley, *supra* note 124, at 189; Bauslaugh, *supra* note 136, at 99; de Ste Croix, *supra* note 138, at 298–307; D. Kagan, *The Outbreak of the Peloponnesian War* 40–44 (1969); E. M. Walker, The Confederacy of Delos, 478–463 BC, 5 *Cambridge Ancient History* 40–41 (1970).

[185] See generally, Adcock and Mosley, *supra* note 124, at 244–46 (comparing Second Athenian League with Macedon's League of Corinth). See also John Buckler, Theban Treaty Obligations in IG II² 40: A Postscript, 20 *Historia* 506 (1971).

Philip II of Macedon as *hegemon*, had a facially more egalitarian form of government, led by five officers called *proëdroi*, who served not only as chairmen of the league assemblies but also as a permanent secretariat for the league administration between meetings. There was no doubt that these league officials were answerable to the King of Macedon and had very limited powers.[186]

Treaties constituting hegemonic *symmachiai* were carefully crafted both to ensure the dominant role of the league leader as well as to provide notional assurances of the autonomy of other parties. We have, for example, a copy of the decree establishing the Second Athenian Naval League in 378 BCE, intended to protect against Spartan aggression. It provided that:

> If anyone of the Greeks or of the barbarians dwelling upon the mainland or the islands, provided they are not subjects of the king [of Persia], wishes to become an ally of the Athenians and their allies, he may do so, preserving his freedom and autonomy, in the enjoyment of the constitution he may prefer, without receiving a garrison or governor [from Athens], and without paying tribute, upon the same conditions as the Chians, Thebans, and the other allies . . . And if anyone shall make an attack upon those who have made the alliance either by land or by sea, the Athenians and the allies are to come to their rescue by land and by sea with their full strength in so far as they can.[187]

What is also significant is that, in addition to the instrument creating the Naval League, the members each concluded alliances with one another.[188] So there was an interlocking set of obligations by treaty. And, again, make no mistake: the final say of alliance policy rested with the Athenian assembly.[189]

Philip II of Macedon's structuring of the League of Corinth (the Hellenic League) in 338 BCE was likewise intended to further his ends of dominance over the fractious Greek city-States. The structure he chose for organizing pan-Hellenic unity had already been developed by Isocrates, an Athenian orator, a few years earlier.[190] While Philip did not

---

[186] See Larsen, *supra* note 142, at xvii–xix. See also the scholarship on an Athenian inscription honoring one of the *proëdroi*. L. Robert, Adeimantos et la Ligue de Corinthe, 2 *Hellenica* 15 (1946). For a general treatment on the League of Corinth (or Hellenic League), see Adcock and Mosley, *supra* note 124, at 244–46, 261–62 (for a translation of the oath taken by members of the league).

[187] The translation of the inscription can be found in Boak, *supra* note 180, at 379.

[188] See Martin, *supra* note 173, at 186–89, 242–44, 253–54 (on the operation of the league council), 262–65 (on admission of new members).   [189] See *ibid.*

[190] See J. Kessler, *Isokrates und die panhellenische Idee* (1911). See also Boak, *supra* note 180, at 379–80.

insist that the Greek cities conclude separate bilateral *symmachiai* with Macedon, the unilateral character of the oath sworn by the members of the League was enough (apparently) to ensure compliance. The members swore that:

> I shall abide in peace and shall not infringe the treaty with Philip of Macedon. Neither by land or by sea shall I bear arms with injurious intent against any party which abides by the oath . . . I shall make war upon him who contravenes the Common Peace accordingly as the Allied Council may resolve and as the hegemon may command . . .[191]

In a similar fashion, the League council (*synedrion*) was composed on a proportional basis, giving greater representation to major Greek cities like Athens and Thebes.[192] The *synedrion* of the Corinth League had some limited competence to resolve inter-city disputes without reference to the Macedonian hegemon, but this was sparingly exercised. The League council did, for example, assist in resolving a territorial dispute between Melos and Cimolus by referring it to arbitration by Argos.[193] Likewise, when Thebes intended to defect from the League in 335 BCE and support Persia at the time of Alexander's invasion, the League *synedrion* was called and decided to take action against their feckless partner.[194] The League council even served as a sort of international criminal court, trying the oligarchs of Chios who had attempted to overthrow the democracy there and throw the cities' support over to Persia.[195]

In contrast to these *symmachiai*, Greek federal states operated on a basis of notional sovereign equality tempered by the need of creating a unitary state. As has been previously considered in this study,[196] the culmination of a political union was a *sympoliteia*, in which each city granted the full rights of citizenship to the residents of every other participating city.[197] *Sympoliteia* as a federal union of Greek city-states conveyed not only a permanent military alliance effectuated on a basis of equality, but also a whole host of shared economic rights, which otherwise could only be conveyed by specific sorts of agreements, known generically as *enktesis* (including *isopoliteia* and *symbola*).[198] Examples of true federal arrangements in

---

[191] The translation is from Adcock and Mosley, *supra* note 124, at 261–62 (citing 3 H. H. Schmitt, *Die Staatsverträge des Altertums* No. 403 (Munich 1969)).

[192] See *ibid.* at 244–45.   [193] See *ibid.* at 245.   [194] See *ibid.*   [195] See *ibid.*

[196] See Chapter 4, at note 248 and accompanying text.

[197] See also H. Francotte, *La polis grecque* 151 (1907); E. Szanto, *Das griechische Bürgerrecht* 150 (1892). For a brief historiography of scholarship on questions of Greek citizenship, see Larsen, *supra* note 142, at xxviii n. 2.

[198] See Chapter 4, at notes 237–58 and accompanying text.

168   TREATY PRACTICES AMONGST ANCIENT PEOPLES

classical Greece would include the Boeotian confederation which lasted from 447 to 386 BCE, and the Achaean and Aetolian confederations.[199]

Hegemonic *symmachiai* represented the epitome of Greek power alliances, while *sympoliteiai* effectuated the unifying (almost republican) spirit of Greek inter-city politics. Neither was very successful. The great hegemonic powers – Athens, Sparta, and Thebes – were never able for long to exert commanding influence over their erstwhile allies. Balance-of-power dynamics and localized tensions all but prevented this. Likewise, unifying and federalist tendencies in parts of Greece, as well as pan-Hellenic aspirations, were met with opposition by the constituent cities, jealous of their ancestral customs and prerogatives. *Symmachiai* and *sympoliteiai* were the unfulfilled dreams of two different conceptions of Greek unity.

Amphictyonies

Amphictyonies were local religious leagues based on a common cult. As Adcock and Mosley have pointed out, "they were local or regional associations with a communal religious center."[200] The center might be a common altar, such as the one where the sea-god Poseidon was worshipped at Panionium in Priene. It also might be the site of a religious festival or games.[201] The maintenance of religious institutions led to the development of political and economic ties between the members of these religious leagues. Such ties might have meant the conclusion of generic treaties in which members swore perpetual peace and protection of the common sites of the league.[202] The site of one Peloponnesian *amphictyony*, Caluria, had an alternate name, *Eirene*, meaning peace.[203] In addition to

[199] See generally Larsen, *supra* note 142; Boak, *supra* note 180, at 382. See also 2 Phillipson, *supra* note 117, at 63–64 (describing a "complete" alliance between Hierapythna and Priansus in the third century BCE).

[200] See Adcock and Mosley, *supra* note 124, at 229. For the origins of the Greek word *amphictyon*, as a derivation of the word for "neighbor," see 2 Phillipson, *supra* note 117, at 3 (glossing 1 Homer, *The Odyssey* 41 (A. T. Murray transl. 1919) (Loeb Classical Library reprint 1919) (passage ii.65) and 1 Homer, *The Iliad* 354, 391 (A. T. Murray transl. 1921) (Loeb Classical Library reprint 1929) (passages xviii.212, xix.104 and 109). See also Lord Arundell of Wardover, *Tradition Principally with Reference to the Mythology of the Law of Nations* 361–63 (1872); Karavites, *supra* note 139, at 22.

[201] See Adcock and Mosley, *supra* note 124, at 185–86, 229–31. See also 2 Phillipson, *supra* note 117, at 2–3. See generally, H. Bürgel, *Die Pylaeische-Delphische Amphiktyonie* (Munich 1877); E. A. Freeman, *History of Federal Government in Greece and Italy* 95–111 (London 1893); 2 George Grote, *History of Greece* 169 (London 1872).

[202] See Nussbaum, *supra* note 11, at 7; Thomas A. Walker, *A History of the Law of Nations* 39–40 (1899). [203] See Adcock and Mosley, *supra* note 124, at 185–86.

Panionium and Caluria,[204] Greek *amphictyonies* were established at Thermopylae,[205] Triopium,[206] Itonia,[207] Aegium,[208] Samos,[209] and Delos,[210] sites variously associated with the gods Apollo, Demeter, Poseidon, and Athena.

Of these institutions, the *amphictyony* established to maintain the Oracle at Delphi was the most prominent. The twelve tribes of the Delphic Amphictyony appointed officials to take charge of the care and maintenance of the center, but twice a year a formal meeting of the representatives (*hieromnemones* and *pylagoroi*) was summoned.[211] These meetings observed a rule of strict sovereign equality: each tribe had equal voting power. Athens and Sparta were thus placed on a par with tribes represented by the Dorians and Ionians.[212] On occasion these meetings had a decidedly political overtone, so the delegates were formally accredited by the city-State members of the amphictyony.[213] This was especially so when the amphictyonic council was called to vote sanctions (usually in the form of a punitive military expedition) against a transgressing member.[214]

A number of instances have been recorded of hostilities being launched under the authority of the Delphic Amphictyony. In the first Sacred War of 596–586 BCE, action was taken against the coastal village of Cirrha, which, by virtue of its strategic position, charged exorbitant tolls for visitors to the oracle. The Council of the Amphictyons made war against the offenders, razed Cirrha to the ground, consecrated its territory to Apollo,

---

[204] See *ibid.* at 229–31; 2 Phillipson, *supra* note 117, at 2–3. See also 1 Herodotus, *supra* note 119, at 181–85 (passages i.141–43); Arundell, *supra* note 200, at 264 n. 24.

[205] See 4 Strabo, *supra* note 145, at 429 (passage ix.5.17).

[206] See 1 Herodotus, *supra* note 119, at 185 (passage i.144).

[207] See 4 Pausanias, *Description of Greece* 323 (W. H. S. Jones transl. 1935) (Loeb Classical Library reprint 1979) (Boeotia ix, passage 34.1).

[208] See 3 *ibid.* at 311 (Achaia vii, passage 24.1).

[209] See 4 Strabo, *supra* note 119, at 49 (passage viii.3).

[210] See 2 Phillipson, *supra* note 117, at 4 (considering 2 Thucydides, *supra* note 118, at 181 (passage iii.104)).

[211] See Aeschines, *The Speeches of Aeschines* 357 (Charles Darwin Adams transl.) (Loeb Classical Library reprint 1919) (*Against Ctesiphon*, line 124). There is some authority for suggesting that there may have been a distinction between these two types of delegates to the Amphictyonic Council. See 2 Phillipson, *supra* note 117, at 6. The Council may have also had a permanent secretary and herald. See *ibid.* See also Georges Roux, *L'Amphictionie, Delphes et le temple d'Apollon au IVᵉ siècle* (1979).

[212] See Aeschines, *supra* note 211, at 399 (*Against Ctesiphon*, line 116).

[213] See Adcock and Mosley, *supra* note 124, at 230 (discussing the appointment of the Athenian orator, Aeschines, to plead causes before the Council; see 2 Demosthenes, *supra* note 135, at 107 (passage xviii.134)).

[214] See Bengtson, *supra* note 132, No. 104; Aeschines, *supra* note 211, at 245, 393 (passages ii.115, iii.109–10).

and ordered that it henceforth be laid to waste.[215] The Second Sacred War of 357–346 BCE was overtly political in character. Beginning as a local dispute between Phocis and Thebes, it quickly escalated into nearly pan-Hellenic conflict, with Athens and Sparta allied with Phocis against Theban hegemony. In a rare act of retaliation, the Phocians occupied the Delphic sanctuary and destroyed part of it. This act led to the intervention of Philip II of Macedon into Greek affairs. He expelled the Phocians from Delphi, razed their city, and (as symbolic of his growing power over Greece) replaced them on the Delphic Amphictyonic Council in his new status as "protector" of Greece.[216]

The Delphic Amphictyony periodically served as a consultative organization for resolving inter-Hellenic disputes. Sometimes this was undertaken as part of the religious functions of the League, as when inhabitants of Megara interfered with a sacred delegation (*theoroi*) from the Peloponnesus; the Council condemned the guilty individuals of sacrilege and ordered some executed and others banished.[217] A similar incident occurred in 470 BCE when some Thessalian traders had been plundered and imprisoned by the piratical inhabitants of Scyros.[218] Likewise, Sparta brought a complaint against Thebes before the Council, arguing that the Thebans had erected an improper trophy at the site of a military victory.[219] This dispute was part of a long-running litigation between the two implacably hostile city-States, the forum for which was the Amphictyonic Council.[220]

Greek amphictyonies have been considered last in this survey of Hellenic treaty forms because some have suggested[221] that they represented the most sophisticated complex of treaty relations, approaching even a level of real international organization. This is unquestionably an extravagant claim. It is true that the functions of the Delphic amphictyony had far-ranging effects, including the amelioration of the condi-

---

[215] See 2 Phillipson, *supra* note 68, at 9.

[216] See *ibid.* at 9–10; John Hosack, *On the Rise and Growth of the Law of Nations* 11–12 (London 1882) (reprinted 1982). For original source materials of this incident, see 4 Pausanius, *supra* note 207, at 375–81 (Phocis x, passage 2); *Translated Documents, supra* note 124, at 82. For a vigorous debate on these events, compare N. G. L. Hammond, Philip's Actions in 347 and Early 346 BC, 44 CQ 367 (1994), with John Buckler, Reply, 46 CQ 380 (1996). For more on the Third Sacred War, see John Buckler, Thebes, Delphoi, and the Outbreak of the Third Sacred War, in *La Béotie Antique* 237 (P. Roesch and G. Argord eds. 1985).

[217] See 4 Plutarch, *Moralia* (Frank Cole Babbitt transl. 1936) (Loeb Classical Library reprint 1972) (*Quaest. Graec.*, passage 59).   [218] See 2 Phillipson, *supra* note 117, at 10.

[219] See 2 Cicero, *The Speeches* 235 (H. G. Hodge transl. 1927) (Loeb Classical Library reprint) (*De inventione*, passage ii.23).   [220] See Hosack, *supra* note 216, at 11–12.

[221] See Adcock and Mosley, *supra* note 124, at 186; 2 Phillipson, *supra* note 117, at 11; Sir Paul Vinogradoff, Historical Types of International Law, in 1 *Biblioteca Visseriana Dissertationum ius internationale illustrantium* 1, 21–22 (1923).

tions of conflict, which will be considered later in this study.[222] Even though there was a notional sense of sovereign equality in the operations of amphictyonic institutions, it would be misleading to consider them much more than a "primitive habit of religious fraternisation."[223] Having a restricted membership and rudimentary methods, it is difficult to consider *amphictyonies* as an "attempt to embody the notion of international justice in an organized institution."[224]

It makes more sense to view *amphictyonies* as part of a larger pattern of Greek treaty-making. They were arrangements in which members undertook to cooperate with each other by virtue of membership in the organization, and not necessarily because of independent treaty obligations. The operation of *amphictyonies* thus reflected a further Greek refinement on the question of whether perpetual peace was possible in inter-Hellenic relations. They were, in essence, ritualized and institutional *philai*. The contradictions inherent in this observation will be considered next in the context of actual Greek treaty practices.

The nature of Greek treaty-making

Negotiation, ratification, and publication

As has already been considered in Chapter 4,[225] treaties between Greek city-States were the product of elaborate and often drawn-out negotiations. Heralds would proceed with envoys to open treaty talks.[226] Envoys would shuttle back and forth between the cities, seeking advice from their home government concerning the treaty terms. Public deliberations in the representative assemblies of the affected cities would occur during the negotiations, resulting in refined instructions for the cities' diplomatists and also in the publication of letters (*epistolai*) or decrees, outlining the parties' position to the other cities.[227]

Mosley argues that, taken as a whole, Greek treaties were "simple

---

[222] See Chapter 6, pp. 249–52 below.   [223] 2 Grote, *supra* note 201, at 176.

[224] Vinogradoff, *supra* note 221, at 22.   [225] See notes 71–76 and accompanying text.

[226] See, e.g., 3 Thucydides, *supra* note 118, at 143 (passage v.76) (where heralds make an overture for the negotiation of a treaty).

[227] See 2 R. Genet, *Traité et Diplomatie* § 757 (1933); 1 Phillipson, *supra* note 117, at 413–14; Elie Bikerman, La trêve de 423 av. J.-C. entre Athènes et Sparte, RIDA 199, 206–07 (1952). See also the 430 BCE decree by Athens concerning relations with Methone and Macedon. *Translated Documents*, *supra* note 124, at 144–45. For a further example see 1 Xenophon, *supra* note 119, at 107 (*Hellenica*, passage ii.2.13). For literary allusions to the process of Greek treaty negotiation, see 1 Aristophanes, *Plays* 331, 529, 2 *ibid.* at 51, 231, 273–75 (Patric Dickinson transl. 1970) (*Wasps*, line 1268; *Clouds*, line 691; *Peace*, line 454; *Birds*, lines 1031, 1550, 1582).

documents in essence and couched in general terms rather than enlarging on specific points."[228] Because of this, some types of Greek treaties, including most alliances and some commercial agreements, were susceptible to easy negotiation through the use of formulaic terms and provisions.[229] But difficulties could arise as to the text of treaties and Mosley's supposition probably minimizes the sophistication in language and difficulty in negotiations of some pacts. Even a relatively "simple" defensive alliance, an *epimachia*,[230] had to be carefully constructed in order to evade later subversion. The correct language of obligation had to be chosen. Specific provisions demanding future duties had to be crafted. The reciprocity (or lack thereof) between the parties had to be established, as did any recognitions of equality or subordinance. These objectives of treaty-making, even in the "simple" context of certain kinds of alliances, could not have been achieved easily.

Mosley also probably underestimates the measure of political control exercised over treaty negotiators, even in cases of talks with "simple" objectives to be achieved. It seems undoubted that the political assemblies of the compacting city-States had the final say as to the conclusion of an agreement.[231] In effect, then, an agreement went through a two-step process of affirmance: an act of signing by a responsible official of the city, followed by an act of ratification by the constituent political body of the State.[232] The act of ratification, to be considered presently, was the ritual swearing of an oath to uphold the treaty.

Upon ratification, notices were sent to the other cities parties to the treaty, and perhaps to other States as well.[233] In addition, the consistent practice of most Greek city-States was to erect permanent records of the treaty instrument along with details of its negotiation. In Athens, bronze tablets or marble *steles* with the treaty texts were kept at the Metroon,

---

[228] See D. J. Mosley, *Envoys and Diplomacy in Ancient Greece* 70 (1973).

[229] See *ibid.* (collecting instances where treaty negotiations were accelerated, probably by the use of stock treaty terms).   [230] See *supra* notes 160–64 and accompanying text.

[231] See 1 Phillipson, *supra* note 117, at 383, 413–14; Bikerman, *supra* note 227, at 206–07. See also the Treaty of Peace between Sparta and Argos, already alluded to in this chapter, *supra* note 139, at 258–59, which expressly calls for ratification by both parties.

[232] See Bikerman, *supra* note 227, at 206–07 (glossing 1 Andocides, *supra* note 136 (*On the Peace*, passage iii.35)); Mosley, *supra* note 228, at 11, 26 (noting instances when one party sought to re-open negotiations at the time of ratification); 1 Phillipson, *supra* note 117, at 397–98 (citing inscription evidence). Professor Mosley, in another article, Who "Signed" Treaties in Ancient Greece?, 7 *Proceedings of the Cambridge Philological Society* (ns) 59 (1961), has suggested that signing and ratification were, in some instances, collapsed into a single event. See *ibid.* at 59. This apparently occurred in certain treaties entered into by Athens which actually specified the authorities who were to swear the ratification oaths for each side. See also Andrewes and Lewis, The Peace of Nicias, 77 JHS 177 (1957).   [233] See 1 Phillipson, *supra* note 117, at 414.

under the guardianship of the president of the Senate of the Five Hundred.[234] A treaty placed in depository might be updated by a subsequent, amendatory protocol or by the adherence of a new city.[235] Many treaties called for a fine to be imposed if the record of the treaty text was defaced, damaged or lost.[236] Treaties could also be deposited other than at the capitols of the signatories. Some bronze treaty tablets have been found at Olympia.[237] Moreover, it seemed customary in the period around 420 BCE for both Sparta and Athens to deposit their treaties at religious centers, as at Delphi and at the Isthmus.[238] Finally, special coins might be struck in order to commemorate a treaty's conclusion,[239] and (for some particularly significant agreements) periodic games or festivals would be held to remember the event and to affirm peace.[240]

Treaty oaths, deceit, and hostage-taking

Perhaps the greatest tribute to the Greek practice of memorializing treaty obligations was made by a later orator, Lycortas, appearing before a

[234] See Adcock and Mosley, *supra* note 124, at 177–78; 1 Phillipson, *supra* note 117, at 398. Typically, the Athenian government bore the cost of erecting the record of the treaty, although with certain instruments in which Athens was the dominant party and was extending its protection to a weaker city, that other State was obliged to bear the cost of erection. See Bengtson, *supra* note 132, at No. 155 (446 BCE treaty between Athens and Chalcis).

[235] See 5 Polybius, *supra* note 145, at 435 (passage xxiii.18) (Spartan adherence to the Achaean League). See also the provision of the Second Athenian Naval League of 378 BCE, reprinted in Adcock and Mosley, *supra* note 124, at 259–60 ("On the stone shall be inscribed the names of the cities which are allies and any other city which becomes an ally. That shall be inscribed.").

[236] See Ténékidès, *supra* note 179, at 528. See also the c. 500 BCE treaty between Elis and Heraia, reprinted in *Translated Documents, supra* note 189, at 29 ("And if anyone injures this writing, whether private man or magistrate or community, he shall be liable to the sacred fine herein written."). See also Karavites, *supra* note 40, at 189–91, 192–94.

[237] The treaty between Elis and Heraea, c. 500 BCE, was recorded at Olympia, as was the sixth-century treaty between the Metapians and Anaitoi. See Bengtson, *supra* note 132, at Nos. 110 and 111.

[238] See Adcock and Mosley, *supra* note 124, at 178. See also the terms of the Peace of Nicias, reprinted at *ibid.* at 257–58 ("[The parties] shall set up inscribed pillars at Olympia, in Pythia and at the Isthmus, and at Athens on the Acropolis and at Lacedaemon in the temple of Amyclae.").

[239] See 2 A. Maury, *Histoire des religions de la Grèce antique* 11 n. 1 (Paris 1856–59).

[240] The Nician Peace between Sparta and Athens was supposed to be so commemorated. See 2 Isocrates 247 (George Norlin transl. 1929) (Loeb Classical Library reprint 1982) (*Antidosis*, passage 110). That same orator was also quoted as saying that "[Th]ose who established the great festivals are justly praised for handing down to us a custom which induces us to enter into treaties with one another, to reconcile the hostile feelings that may exist amongst us, and to assemble in one place ..." 1 *ibid.* at 145 (*Panegyricus*, passage 43) (writing c. 380 BCE).

Roman commission at Clitor in 184 BCE. Speaking in defense of the Greek custom to abide by treaty obligation, he said:

What we have ratified by our oaths, what we have consecrated as inviolable to eternal remembrance, by records engraved in stone, they want to abolish, and load us with perjury. Romans, for you we have high respect; and, if such is your wish, dread also; but we respect and dread more the immortal gods.[241]

The irony of this statement could not have been lost on the Romans. Many Greek city-States had notorious reputations for repudiating treaty obligations,[242] and these acts of perfidy tended to reflect badly on the faithfulness of all Greeks.

Greek practice attempted to develop ways to counteract the possibility of deceit or fecklessness in the subsequent observance of the treaty provisions. The first method, considered earlier in this study,[243] was to insist that the parties to an agreement exchange mighty oaths as part of the process of ratification. The typical formality of ratification was performed by delegations sent between the two compacting city-States. These individuals were charged with the responsibility of taking the sacred oaths on behalf of their polity. Although ratification oaths took on many forms they all had the same basic structure: a recitation of the terms of the agreement, "a general imprecation for those who kept or broke the oaths, and the invocation of deities."[244]

The purpose of this discussion here is not so much to review the ways in which divine sanction may or may not have had a role in Greek treaty observance, but, rather, to see how treaty oaths were structured in order to promote compliance. One way was to ensure that the recitation of the treaty terms was complete and symmetrical,[245] leaving no room for a later claim that the ratification oaths did not command obedience to certain treaty stipulations. The early *symmachia* between the Eleans and Heraeans[246] was simple in its obligations (requiring the two cities to

---

[241] See 11 Livy, *History of Rome* 339 (Frank G. Moore, Evan T. Sage and Alfred C. Schlesinger transl. 1922) (Loeb Classical Library reprint 1967) (passage xxxix.37).

[242] The Thessalians, Parians, and Cretans were particularly targeted for their bad faith. See 4 Plutarch, *supra* note 133, at 287 (*Lysander*, passage xx); 1 Phillipson, *supra* note 117, at 118–19.

[243] See Chapter 3. See also Robert Redslob, *Histoire des Grands Principes du droit des gens: Depuis l'antiquité jusqu'à la veille de la grand guerre* 51–53 (1923). See also P. Catalano, *Linee del sistema sovrannazionale romano* 248–70 (1965).

[244] Adcock and Mosley, *supra* note 124, at 216.

[245] Obviously, in cases of unequal or hegemonic *symmachiai*, the ratification oaths were not symmetrical. For one example, the 422 BCE treaty between Athens and the Bottiaean cities, see Bengtson, *supra* note 132, No. 187.

[246] See *supra* notes 162 and 163 and accompanying text.

unite, "should there be need of words or action"), but more naive as to its enforcement (saying only that a party refusing to give aid would pay a fine of a silver talent to the Olympian Zeus).[247]

Other oaths sealing alliances, as between Athens and the Argive Confederacy in 420 BCE,[248] were more complex in character. The operative language of the pledge had the individuals swearing it affirm simply "I will be true to the alliance, and will observe the agreement in all honesty and without fraud or hurt; I will not transgress it in any way or manner."[249] Yet, this treaty was concluded between two sets of alliances, which required the Athenians to swear the oath on behalf of their allies, and for the Argives to do the same.[250] Intriguingly, the treaty required that "the oath shall be taken over full-grown victims and shall be that oath which in the countries of the several contracting parties is deemed the most binding."[251] This was a clear recognition that different Greek polities had divergent ratification formalities, often with different forms and solemnities.[252] Yet, all that mattered to the Argive and Athenian Alliances was that the most binding ratification oath was used.

Some Greek international agreements contained self-consciously styled anti-deceit clauses. Writing in 1984, philologist Everett Wheeler concluded that nearly 15 percent (some 23 of 166) of all inscribed Greek trea-

---

[247] See H. B. Leech, *An Essay on International Law* 27 (1877). On the other hand, this may have been a reference to the custom of a "wager" made in contemplation of prospective litigation between the two cities in case of a dispute arising under the treaty. See Vinogradoff, *supra* note 221, at 20–21. In short, this provision may have been an advance agreement to arbitrate a dispute.

[248] See Leech, *supra* note 247, at 32–33 (for background on this treaty).

[249] The translation is from 3 Thucydides, *supra* note 118, at 91–97 (passage v.47). The treaty between Athens and Corcyra in 375 BCE is substantially similar in language. See Adcock and Mosley, *supra* note 124, at 216–17, 261.

[250] For background on the political problems attendant on the constituent members of an alliance swearing an oath, see Adcock and Mosley, *supra* note 124, at 220–21. In view of the Athenian practice to swear to treaties even on behalf of their co-equal *symmachia* partners, Adcock and Mosley properly conclude that "[i]t cannot be argued that a necessary attribute of independent sovereignty was the power of a state to swear individually to any treaty which committed it." *Ibid.* at 220.

[251] 2 Phillipson, *supra* note 117, at 59. The reference to "full-grown victims" has, by scholarly consensus, been deemed to concern only the slaughter of sacrificial animals, which was a usual requisite of the ratification ceremony. See Chapter 3 at notes 104–08. Human sacrifice was not, of course, practiced by the ancient Greeks.

[252] A surprising number of treaties stipulated in great detail the ratification procedures for the instrument. For one example, see Bikerman, *supra* note 227, at 200–02 (Athens–Sparta truce in 423 BCE). To similar effect were the treaties between Athens and Syracuse (367 BCE), Thessaly (361 BCE), and Eretria (341 BCE), in which provision was made for the "customary invocation" to be made by each party. See Adcock and Mosley, *supra* note 124, at 218.

ties from the period 700 to 300 BCE contained some kind of provision to avoid later fraud or trickery.[253] Most of these anti-deceit provisions were found in *epimachiai, symmachiai,* or peace treaties. Typical of these generic clauses were commands that the parties observe the terms of the treaty "without trick,"[254] and "not with craft nor with stratagem." One proclaimed that the cities "shall devise nothing about this oath, neither by craft nor by any false pretext."[255]

As has been suggested,[256] *epimachiai* were particularly troublesome when it came to their subsequent enforcement. After all, they were entirely open-ended in character, with one city promising to come to the aid of another in the event of an attack by a third city or in the event of internal unrest. One way to have drafted such a clause was to have been particularly exacting about the nature of the defensive assistance to be offered and what conditions triggered the duty to provide aid. Another was to make a more general promise, such as that by the Thessalians to the Athenians in 361 BCE: "I shall render assistance with all my strength to the utmost of my ability if anyone goes to war against the city of Athens or subverts the democracy of the Athenians."[257]

Everett Wheeler also has concluded that the use of anti-deceit provisions of ancient Greek treaties was suggestive of a concern against sophistic interpretations of these pacts. The exceptional presence of these clauses in the ratification oaths, rather than in the main texts of the treaty stipulations, raises concerns about the usually routine recitation of formulae concerning the good will of the parties to observe the treaty. Wheeler sees these provisions as part of a larger context of the specialized Greek vocabulary concerning stratagems and deceit in war and statecraft.[258] In short, anti-deceit clauses were intended to hold the parties to the principle of good faith in the subsequent interpretation of the treaty. It would prevent one party from employing an overly literal interpretation of a disputed clause or to play "on some ambiguity of meaning to produce an interpretation contrary to that intended and obvious."[259] A sophistic interpreter could, if unchallenged, claim fidelity to the treaty, avoid a

---

[253] See Wheeler, *supra* note 117, at 255–56 and n. 12. The total number of Greek treaties during this period, known from both inscriptions and literary sources, is 388. See *ibid.* See also note 117. See also Karavites, *supra* note 139, at 111–14.

[254] See *ibid.* at 256 n. 15 (collecting citations to Bengtson, *supra* note 132 (Nos. 120, 162, 163, 184, 186, 187, 260, 308, 309, 463, 551, 578 and 581)).

[255] See *ibid.* at 256 n. 18 (collecting citations to Bengtson, *supra* note 132 (Nos. 297, 308, 481 and 551)).   [256] See *supra* notes 159–73 and accompanying text.

[257] See Bengtson, *supra* note 132, No. 293.

[258] See Wheeler, *supra* note 117, at 253–54 and n. 7.   [259] *Ibid.* at 254.

charge of perjury and false swearing, but still have the freedom of action under the agreement to achieve its own political ends.

One of the most famous interchanges in ancient Greek diplomacy concerning sophistic interpretations of treaties was the Athenian defensive alliance of 433 BCE with Corcyra against her former parent city, Corinth. This *epimachia* was in arguable violation of the Thirty Years Peace signed in 445 BCE between Athens and her allies and the Spartans.[260] After all, Athens had covenanted not to make any hostile move against Corinth. The Corcyrans and the Corinthians both made petitions to the Athenian assembly. The Corcyrans urged the conclusion of the alliance and advanced a literal reading of the treaty with Sparta.[261] The Corinthians argued that, irrespective of a technical reading of the Peace, an alliance with Corcyra (even one defensive in character) would violate the manifest object and purpose of the Thirty Years Peace. The Athenians decided that the terms of the Thirty Years Peace were ambiguous as to the conclusion of an *epimachia* with a city at virtual war with an ally of Sparta. They decided to proceed with the agreement,[262] which, with later stratagems, was upgraded to an offensive alliance against Corinth and which then resulted in the resumption of hostilities against Sparta and her allies.

The Greeks were the first ancient people to develop rules of interpretation for treaties, in recognition of the fact that any written text was capable of ambiguity and disputed meaning. The nature of ratification oaths and the development of anti-deceit clauses was illustrative of this process. Yet, the results were ambivalent. Greek treaties were not appreciably made more certain in application, nor more binding in character, because of the additions of these features. What made the ancient Greek preoccupation with trust relatively novel in ancient international relations is that they chose to achieve it by largely secular, and humane, means.

When delegates from a compacting city swore a ratification oath it was on behalf of their polity. While the imprecations for violating the oath might have been construed to visit the individuals in their private capacity, it was usually expected that such curses were to be manifested as affecting the fortunes of the city-State as a corporate personality. Other than in this respect, individuals were rarely used as guarantors of treaty obligations. Some peace treaties did stipulate the removal or exile

---

[260] See Adcock and Mosley, *supra* note 124, at 191.

[261] See 1 Thucydides, *supra* note 118, at 73 (passage i.40.2).

[262] See *ibid.* at 79 (passage i.44). See also Ténékidès, *supra* note 179, at 524–26 (glossing 1 Thucydides, *supra* note 118, at 78–79, 91 (passages i.44.1 and i.53)).

of undesirables from the territory of one of the contracting States, or compelled the reception of political refugees.[263] This was, nonetheless, considered exceptional.

Instances of the outright use of hostages in the enforcement of treaty terms were thus scarce in ancient Greece. The only arguable occurrences were with the conclusion of a few peace treaties. Amit has suggested that hostages were used for only a very temporary function in the process of negotiating a peace treaty: to ensure good behavior in the time between the making of a truce and the ratification of a final peace accord.[264] For example, when Athens under Pericles suppressed the revolt of the Euboean cities, hostages were seized as a guarantee of submission, and remained in Athenian hands until a definitive agreement was reached.[265]

According to Amit's theory, hostages in ancient Greece were never exchanged as a guarantee for the subsequent performance of a treaty.[266] This conclusion is only contradicted by two instances, both of which have fairly been cited[267] for the Athenian practice of taking and retaining hostages beyond the time an actual treaty of peace was signed. Under the 446 BCE peace treaty between Athens and Chalcis,[268] Chalcidian hostages earlier taken[269] were to be retained until a later special agreement was made for their return.[270] In 441 BCE, after the Athenian intervention on Samos (on behalf of Miletos), 100 Samian children and adults, all from the oligarch class, were relocated to Lemnos to ensure the security of the newly installed democracy on the island.[271] These hostages may have been kept as security for the war reparations that the Samians were obliged to pay Athens after their later revolt.[272] In a sense, these isolated exceptions prove Amit's supposition about the virtual absence of any pattern in ancient Greece of hostage-taking to ensure treaty compliance.

---

[263] See Adcock and Mosley, *supra* note 124, at 197–98 (discussing Cythera's 424 BCE surrender to Athens, and 404 BCE surrender of Samos to the Spartans).

[264] See M. Amit, Hostages in Ancient Greece, 98 *Rivista di Filologia e di Istruzione Classica* 129, 130 (1970); Andreas Panagapoulos, *Captives and Hostages in the Peloponnesian War* (1978).

[265] See 1 Thucydides, *supra* note 118, at 189 (passage i.114.3). To a similar effect was the negotiation of the 409 BCE treaty between Athens and Selymbria. See Bengtson, *supra* note 132, No. 207 (for a related inscription). See also Amit, *supra* note 264, at 142.

[266] See Amit, *supra* note 264, at 132.   [267] See Adcock and Mosley, *supra* note 124, at 197.

[268] See Bengtson, *supra* note 132, No. 155.

[269] See 1 Thucydides, *supra* note 118, at 189 (passage i.114.3) and 3 Plutarch, *supra* note 133, at 67 (*Pericles*, passage xxiii) for more on that incident.

[270] See Bengtson, *supra* note 132, No. 155, at lines 49–52. See also 1 Arnold Wycombe Gomme, *A Historical Commentary on Thucydides* 343 (1945).

[271] See 1 Thucydides, *supra* note 118, at 191 (passage i.115.2–4).

[272] See 3 Plutarch, *supra* note 133, at 79 (*Pericles*, passage xxviii.1). See also Andrew Philip Bridges, The Athenian Treaty with Samos, ML 56, 100 JHS 185 (1980).

Treaty amendment and termination

Interrelated with questions concerning the enforcement of treaty terms in ancient Greece was the problem of modifying irrelevant or onerous obligations and of prescribing the ways in which an international agreement could be unilaterally ended. These concerns were amplified by the apparent Hellenic ambivalence towards the notion of "perpetual peaces," pacts that placed two or more cities on a permanent footing of friendship and cooperation. As previously discussed,[273] most Greek treaties were drafted with a clause specifying a limited duration. It is true that certain agreements did specify a perpetual term. The sixth-century treaty between the Serdaioi and Sybaris did so,[274] and in 478 BCE the members of the Delian League swore an oath of allegiance by hurling iron ingots into the sea, promising that their oaths held good until the iron floated upon the waves.[275] Once again, this was the exception. Between 550 and 400 BCE, the nearly universal practice of the Greek city-States was to make treaties for a limited term, never for more than a century.[276]

In fact, the actual duration of Greek treaties was rather shorter than the periods contemplated in their drafting.[277] As has been mentioned:

Members revolted from their perpetual alliance with Athens in the fourth century just as they had done in the fifth, and other alliances displayed the same degree of instability. Political subversion or a change in régime in one of the contracting states was a major factor in the breach or abrogation of treaties. There was no way to effectively obviate such tendencies except to incorporate some arrangement to guarantee the continued existence of the régime which secured the treaty. The longevity of a treaty generally depended on the will and determination as well as the sheer military strength of the leading party both to maintain its own obligations and to compel others to do so.[278]

In view of the extraordinary political volatility in Greek cities, it is hardly surprising that treaty modification or termination was a common feature on the landscape of Greek international relations. The question is, however, the extent to which legal rules influenced the claims and responses of cities wishing to cancel, change or retain treaty obligations.

---

[273] See *supra* notes 138–39 and accompanying text.
[274] See Bengtson, *supra* note 132, No. 120.
[275] See Adcock and Mosley, *supra* note 124, at 221. See also *ibid.* at nn. 589–90 (collecting other examples of perpetual treaties).
[276] See *ibid.* at 221–22. See also Martin, *supra* note 173, at 399–400 (arguing that limited duration of peace treaties was emblematic of continuing, residual distrust and particularism between different Greek city-States); Ténékidès, *supra* note 179, at 527–28.
[277] See, e.g., Adcock and Mosley, *supra* note 124, at 222.   [278] *Ibid.* at 222.

The Greeks entertained rather sophisticated notions about the amendment of treaty terms. Some agreements actually provided a mechanism
for modification: if, as in the words of the last article of the Peace of Nicias,
"anything be on either side forgotten, or shall be thought upon fair deliberations to be changed it shall be lawful for both [Athens and Sparta] to do
this as may be thought fit jointly by both parties."[279] In 407 BCE Neapolis
secured a revision (*epanorthosis*) of an earlier Athenian treaty.[280] The
process of mutual consent to change a treaty was also known as *epispon-
dai*, although the way that term was used by Thucydides[281] may also have
referred specifically to a truce during hostilities. Treaty revision, according to the ancient Greeks, was based on mutual consent freely given by all
the parties to the agreement.[282]

Much more problematic were unilateral attempts to cancel or alter the
obligations under a treaty. Such attempts implicated the most delicate
concerns of a rule of law in ancient Greek international relations. A party
seeking unilaterally to change the terms of an agreement, or to refuse subsequent performance, could rightly be charged with treaty breach and
perjury for violation of its ratification oaths. To deal with these diplomatic
crises, Greek city-States seemed to resort either to sophistic interpretations of treaties or to rules of Hellenic "custom" concerning specific
situations.

One such situation, considered by the Greeks to be relatively innocuous
and less threatening to the sanctity of treaties, was when the conclusion
of a later treaty directly or indirectly cast doubt on the continued validity
of an earlier agreement. Obviously, if both treaties were made by the same
sets of cities, this was merely a situation of treaty modification and not
forced termination. Also, it was possible for one city to have a defensive
alliance with two other polities at war with one another. The conclusion
of two such *epimachiai* would not constitute a conflicting obligation. These
were, in effect, treaty recognitions of a state of neutrality.[283]

---

[279] This translation is from 3 Thucydides, *supra* note 118, at 35–39 (passage v.18), as
    confirmed in Bengtson, *supra* note 132, no. 188.
[280] See Adcock and Mosley, *supra* note 124, at 225 n. 612.
[281] See 3 Thucydides, *supra* note 118, at 65 (passage v.32).
[282] See also Martin, *supra* note 173, at 487–90; 1 Phillipson, *supra* note 68, at 409–10.
[283] Xenophon recounted such when the Arcadians in 366 BCE sought an alliance with
    Athens. Arcadia was at war with Sparta. Sparta and Athens had a valid peace treaty and
    epimachia in force. Athens proceeded with the treaty with Arcadia, resolving that they
    could remain on good terms with both the Arcadians and Spartans, despite their
    promise to the Spartans that they have the same friends and enemies. See 2 Xenophon,
    supra note 119, at 291 (passage vii.4.2).

Polybius recounted one possible resolution in those cases where a later treaty seemed outright to contradict an earlier agreement: the pact that was more private and less general in character would be discarded in favor of the more solemn and more general convention. The situation suggesting this resolution arose when Acarnania approached Sparta seeking assistance in a war with Aetolia, pursuant to a standing *symmachia*. Yet the Spartans also had a pre-existing *epimachia* with the Aetolians. The orator Lyciscus, the Acarnanian envoy at Sparta, was reported to have said: "Which will be the graver breach of obligation . . . to neglect a private arrangement entered into with the Aetolians, or a treaty which has been inscribed on a column and solemnly consecrated in the eyes of the whole of Greece?"[284]

The first premise of Lyciscus' submission to the Spartans was surely correct: in ancient Greek practice a general treaty prevailed over a "private" arrangement. General peaces were held to cancel all outstanding networks of *symmachiai*. Athens' capitulation to Sparta after the end of the Peloponnesian War resulted in the end of the Delian League. Likewise, the King's Peace of 387 BCE resulted in Athens having to terminate its earlier alliance, concluded in 395 BCE, with the Boeotian League.[285] Finally, the Second Athenian Confederacy was dissolved in the aftermath of Philip of Macedon's victory at Chaeronea in 338 BCE.[286]

The problem with Lyciscus' submission was that it was by no means clear that Sparta's treaty with the Aetolians was somehow more "private" and inferior to the one contemplated with the Acarnanians. Lyciscus had, therefore, an alternative argument:

If the circumstances are the same now as at the time you made the alliance with the Aetolians, then your policy ought to remain on the same lines . . . But if they have been entirely changed, then it is fair that you should now deliberate on the demands made to you as on a matter entirely new and unprejudiced.[287]

This is rightfully regarded as the first invocation of the doctrine of *rebus sic stantibus* in international law – the principle that one party may unilaterally terminate a treaty because of an intervening, fundamental change of circumstances.[288] This doctrine was often used as a pretext by ancient

---

[284] See 4 Polybius, *supra* note 145, at 85 (passage ix.36).
[285] See Lysias 573 (W. R. M. Lamb transl. 1930) (Loeb Classical Library reprint 1988) (xxvi, *On the Scrutiny of Evandros*, passage 23).
[286] See 1 Pausanias, *supra* note 207, at 127–29 (Attica i, passage 25.3).
[287] 4 Polybius, *supra* note 145, at 87 (passage ix.37).
[288] See A. Vamvoukos, *Termination of Treaties in International Law: The Doctrine of Rebus Sic Stantibus and Desuetude* 5–6 (1985).

Greeks to allow a denunciation of a treaty on the flimsy grounds that there had been a change in government or regime in one of the cities. In 418 BCE the Argives, after the expulsion of the democratic party in the city, denounced their treaty with Athens and signed one with Sparta.[289] In 353 BCE, the Athenians promoted such treachery by encouraging the new government of the Arcadians to renounce their earlier treaty with Thebes.[290] It was not doubted, however, that a legitimate ground for changed circumstance could arise when one state conquered or absorbed another, thus having effects on the mutual treaty obligations of both the victor and vanquished.[291]

The failure of one party to observe the conditions of a treaty was considered by the ancient Greeks as grounds for its termination by another city. In 389 BCE, the Achaeans protested to the Spartans for their failure to render support under an earlier *symmachia*. They threatened to denounce the treaty unless the military support was forthcoming.[292] Interestingly, however, some treaties recognized that the penalty for one party's breach would be the payment of an established fine. This was the enforcement mechanism for the early treaty between the Eleans and Heraeans.[293] In the same fashion, the 400 BCE treaty between the Eritreans and Hestiaeans provided for the payment of a fine.[294] On other occasions, the city aggrieved by the alleged failure of its treaty partner to observe the treaty terms would register a formal protest by inscribing a record of the infraction on the pillar recording the text.[295]

So it was that the formal act of denouncing a treaty was usually accompanied by one country's destruction or defacing of the treaty inscription.[296] Such was the power of the written word in ancient Greek international relations. The Greeks gave such symbolic force to what they had "consecrated as inviolable to eternal remembrance, by records engraved in stone."[297] When, for example, Athens denounced the treaty with Leucon of the Bosporus, but left the *stelae* bearing the text intact, Demosthenes argued that those who would sully Athens' reputation for trust and probity would have grounds for additional aspersions.[298]

---

[289] See 3 Thucydides, *supra* note 118, at 144–45 (passage v.78).
[290] See 1 Demosthenes, *supra* note 135, at 455 (passage xvi.27).
[291] See Ernst H. Feilchenfeld, *Public Debts and State Succession* 17, 19 (1931).
[292] See 1 Xenophon, *supra* note 119, at 339 (passage iv.6.1).
[293] See *supra* note 247 and text.   [294] See Bengtson, *supra* note 132, No. 205.
[295] See 3 Thucydides, *supra* note 118, at 109 (passage v.56.3).
[296] See Adcock and Mosley, *supra* note 124, at 223 and nn. 598 and 599.
[297] See *supra* note 241 and accompanying text.
[298] See 1 Demosthenes, *supra* note 135, at 517 (passage xx.37).

Greek treaty texts emphasized secular, intellectual methods for ensuring compliance by the parties. These methods, coupled with the extraordinary diversity of treaty forms and relationships, placed Greek international relations on a legal footing entirely distinct fron ancient Near Eastern models. Indeed, as will be suggested below, they may have been largely more reasoned than the practices observed by the Romans and other western Mediterranean powers in antiquity.

Western Mediterranean departures in treaty-making

Patterns of treaty-making by Western Mediterranean cultures

Carthaginian practices

Any discussion of how the peoples of the ancient Western Mediterranean departed in their treaty practices from Hellenic paradigms should start with the international relations of the former Phoenician colonies, the leading one being Carthage. The reason to begin with the Carthaginians is that they were the direct recipient of many ancient Near Eastern forms and rituals of treaty-making. Yet evidence of Carthaginian treaty-making is scant. Some sources are neutral enough about Carthaginian treaty-making. Aristotle, in *The Politics*, said simply that: "Etruscans and Carthaginians, and all others with contractual obligations to each other . . . certainly . . . have trade agreements, non-aggression pacts, and written documents governing their alliance."[299] Much of the remaining evidence we have is undoubtedly colored by narration from Latin sources, Rome being Carthage's deadly rival for the period under review in this survey.

Punic diplomatic practices were drawn from the Syrian hinterland, which, in turn, was influenced by Hittite and Babylonian ways.[300] Polybius was adamant that Carthaginian treaty forms were distinctly Eastern Mediterranean; he noted that Carthage, alone among its neighbors, swore their treaties "by the gods of their ancestors."[301] The Punic covenants that are extant are virtually indistinguishable in form from Hittite parity or fealty agreements. It was routine in treaties made by Carthage that the ratification oaths would invoke the gods of both States parties, something

---

[299] Aristotle, *The Politics* 119 (T. A. Sinclair transl. 1969).
[300] See *supra* notes 98–99 and accompanying text. See also F. M. Heichelheim, New Evidence on the Ebro Treaty, 3 *Historia* 211 (1954–55).
[301] 2 Polybius, *supra* note 145, at 61 (passage iii.25).

Elias Bickerman has suggested was "alien to Greek and Roman . . . practice."[302]

Nevertheless, it seems that the Carthaginians were willing to compromise their ancient treaty forms when dealing with Greek outposts in Sicily and Italy, as well as the emerging power of Rome. It is known, for example, that Punic interests were substantially implicated in the Athenian invasion of Sicily during the Peloponnesian War. Athens regarded Carthage as a force to be reckoned with in the Western Mediterranean.[303] Tantalizing evidence exists regarding the negotiation of a *philia* between Athens and Carthage around 415 BCE. Thucydides made a reference to this negotiation.[304] Fragmentary inscription material suggests that the agreement was consummated.[305] It may have even been more than a simple friendship pact, having provided for mutual assurances of restraint and respect for the parties' own "spheres of influence" in southern Italy and Sicily.

The Punic *philia* with Athens was hardly unprecedented. Carthage had earlier concluded such agreements with the Agrigentines[306] and with Rome.[307] Moreover, substantial authority was given to Carthage's leaders in the field to conclude significant international agreements, subject only to nominal review by the Punic senate back at the capital. Hasdrubal, the governor-general of Punic Spain, gave a pledge to the Romans, prior to the Second Punic War, that the Carthaginians would not cross the Ebro for conquest.[308] While some modern critics[309] have been hard-pressed to understand this unilateral pledge, it becomes more comprehensible in view of the extraordinary delegation of powers to field commanders by

---

[302] Elias J. Bickerman, Hannibal's Covenant, 73 AJP 1, 5 (1952). See also R. Laqueur, Symbola, 71 *Hermes* 469 (1936).

[303] See 3 Thucydides, *supra* note 118, at 209 (passage vi.15.2), 245 (passage vi.34.2), 345 (passage vi.90.2). For other references, see 1 Aristophanes, *supra* note 227, at 249 (*Knights*, lines 1303–04), 477 (*Wasps*, line 700).

[304] See 3 Thucydides, *supra* note 118, at 339–41 (passage vi.88.6). For a gloss, see Bauslaugh, *supra* note 136, at 161 n. 40.

[305] See Bengtson, *supra* note 132, No. 208 (for the text of the badly mutilated Athenian decree naming two Carthaginian generals). See also B. D. Meritt, Athens and Carthage, in *Athenian Studies Presented to William Scott Ferguson* 247 (Cambridge 1940) (Harvard Studies in Classical Philology Supp. 1).

[306] See 5 Diodorus, *supra* note 126, at 361 (passage xiii.85.2).

[307] The first treaty between Rome and Carthage, mentioned in 2 Polybius, *supra* note 145, at 53 (passage iii.22.4) and recorded in Bengtson, *supra* note 132, No. 121, is dated to about 508 BCE. This will be considered further below, at notes 358–64 and the accompanying text.   [308] See 2 Polybius, *supra* note 145, at 65 (passage iii.27.9).

[309] See, e.g., G. de Sanctis, *Problemi di storia antica* 161–68 (Bari 1932); H. H. Scullard, *A History of the Roman World* 197–99 (London 1935).

the Carthaginian government, powers that would have been unheard of for comparable Greek military leaders.[310]

Indeed, one of the most famous treaties of antiquity – that between Carthage and Macedon, concluded in 215 BCE at the height of the Second Punic War – was made under the authority of Hannibal, a Punic general in the field. This treaty, narrated by Polybius,[311] was to have sealed the fate of Rome in that great war by bringing two of its most formidable (and implacable) foes into an effective alliance. It was a carefully drafted document, reflecting the most sophisticated legal terminologies and diplomatic artifices earlier employed in Greek inter-city relations. It also features some peculiarly Carthaginian features. These are all worthy of some attention here.

The treaty did follow ancient Near Eastern forms[312] by opening with an announcement of the titles and authority of the individuals negotiating the treaty – Hannibal on one side, and Xenophanes (emissary of Philip V of Macedon) on the other. The Carthaginian and Macedonian gods bearing witness to the covenant are then listed. The individuals taking the ratification oaths are then named. The preamble ends with the statement "Let us be friends, comrades and brethren on the following conditions."[313] The first two operative paragraphs of the treaty reflect a form of *epimachia* undertaken by co-equal sovereigns. King Philip and his allies agreed to "support the Carthaginians."[314] Likewise, Hannibal swore to "support" and "protect" the Macedonians and their Greek allies.[315]

---

[310] Cf. *supra* notes 226–32 and accompanying text.

[311] See 3 Polybius, *supra* note 145, at 421 (passage vii.9). Professor Bickerman makes a convincing argument that the text relied upon by Polybius was a Greek translation of a Punic document produced in Hannibal's chancellery. Bickerman doubts that the pact between Hannibal and Philip was originally drafted in Greek. See Bickerman, *supra* note 302, at 1–3. This would mean that the version that comes to us today is a translation of a translation. This is significant since the form and content of the treaty will reflect both Hellenic and Carthaginian traditions, which is precisely Bickerman's thesis. See also Wheeler, *supra* note 117, at 265–66.

[312] See *supra* notes 43–47 and accompanying text.

[313] For one English translation from Polybius, see Adcock and Mosley, *supra* note 124, at 262 (hereinafter "Carthage–Macedon Treaty"). For another, see 2 Phillipson, *supra* note 117, at 81–83. For more on the preamble in this treaty, see Bickerman, *supra* note 302, at 8–10. The express qualification of the oath of friendship on subsequent conditions was rare in Greek practice, but more common in Roman usage. See 2 Polybius, *supra* note 145, at 55 (passage iii.22.4) (first treaty between Rome and Carthage), 5 *ibid.* at 339 (passage xxi.43.1) (treaty between Rome and Antiochus III of Syria). See also M. L. Barré, *The God-List in the Treaty Between Hannibal and Philip V of Macedon* (1983).

[314] See Carthage–Macedon Treaty, *supra* note 313, at paragraph 1.

[315] See *ibid.* paragraph 2.

This duty to "support" and "protect" was typical of the *berit* form of ancient Near Eastern parity treaties.[316] It was surely a more complete obligation than a Greek *epimachia*, which was triggered only when the territory of one party was invaded by a third State. Likewise, under an *epimachia*, one city could give aid and comfort to its ally's enemy, so long as that enemy did not actually invade the territory of the treaty partner.[317] The treaty between Hannibal and Philip of Macedon was far more encompassing in its obligations than a typical Hellenic defensive alliance. Yet, while not an *epimachia*, it was too heavily qualified to be a *symmachia* in Greek practice.

The care that was taken to draft these clauses was evident from the inclusion of provisions extending the pact not only to the then-current allies of the respective parties, but also to any allies and subjects each might acquire in Italy afterwards.[318] This clause was needed because, while it was clear that an alliance leader could bind its confederates to an offensive arrangement, there was some doubt whether this could be applied prospectively. This very same controversy had arisen between Rome and Carthage regarding the proper construction of the peace treaty ending the first Punic War in 241 BCE. Each had agreed that "the allies of neither party should be attacked by the other."[319] Carthage had made what the Romans regarded as a sophistic interpretation of that earlier treaty by denying that it applied to subsequent allies. In other words, the Carthaginians seriously suggested that an after-acquired ally would be free to attack Rome or its confederate without engaging the international responsibility of Carthage. The Romans argued that if this had been the intent of the parties there would have been a clause in the 241 BCE treaty barring either side from acquiring any new allies. Polybius reported this Roman refutation of the Punic position.[320] The force of the Roman legal argument must have persuaded the Carthaginians, because by 215 BCE they had crafted a specific treaty provision to acknowledge this interpretation.

Yet, curiously enough, the covenant between Hannibal and Philip V stipulated that military aid (normally to be provided under the terms of a *symmachia*) "does not need to be furnished against allies of one's own who become enemies of the other partner."[321] This is a fair reading of the third and fourth stipulations of the compact which prescribes the duty "to be

---

[316] See *supra* notes 83–85 and accompanying text.

[317] See, e.g., 3 Herodotus, *supra* note 119, at 121 (passage v.99) (Athenians aiding Miletus against Persia). See also Bickerman, *supra* note 302, at 13 n. 26.   [318] See *ibid.*

[319] See 2 Polybius, *supra* note 145, at 63–64 (passage iii.27). See also *infra* note 364 and text.

[320] See *ibid.* at 67 (passage iii.29). See also Heichelheim, *supra* note 300, at 213–15.

[321] Bickerman, *supra* note 302, at 14.

enemies to the enemies [of the other party] saving those kings, cities, and tribes with which we have sworn agreements and friendships."[322] In short, if a later confederate of Carthage or Macedon was attacked by a third party, the other party would be obliged to give it support. But, if (say) an established ally of Macedon attacked a Carthaginian ally, then Macedon was under no duty to take up arms against that confederate. This is not what one would have expected under the terms of the *symmachia*, which meant, at a minimum, that the contracting parties had the same friends and the same enemies. This sort of "savings" clause for pre-existing treaty relationships (in both *symmachiai* and *epimachiai*) had precedents in both Near Eastern[323] and Greek[324] treaty practice.

Few details are provided for in the treaty about the nature of Carthaginian and Macedonian cooperation against Rome. The treaty, in its fifth stipulation, does say: "You [Philip V] will be allies to us in the war which we are now fighting against the Romans until such time as the gods give us and to you the victory: and you will assist us in all ways that may be needed and in whatsoever way we may mutually determine."[325] Hannibal's treaty was not, despite its careful drafting, intended to be an agreement specifying the precise modalities of a joint campaign by Carthage and Macedonian forces against Rome. No such auxiliary agreement was ever drafted because the tide of the war shifted too quickly against the Punic forces in Italy. This reflects another departure from the Greek model of treaty-making. If this had really been a *symmachia*, these questions would have been resolved.[326]

One possible explanation is that Hannibal's treaty with Philip was crafted to serve as an offensive alliance for the immediate future, and then to have been converted into a more conventional *epimachia* after the Roman threat was eliminated. That illuminates paragraph seven of the stipulations which said that "If ever the Romans make war on you or on us we will aid each other according to the need of either."[327] This is in the

[322] Carthage–Macedon Treaty, *supra* note 313, paragraphs 3, 4 and 8.
[323] See Bickerman, *supra* note 302, at 14 (discussing incident where Ben Hadad of Damascus entered into a covenant with Baasha of Israel, who then proceeded to attack Hadad's ally, Asa of Judah; Ben Hadad broke his covenant with Israel).
[324] See 10 Diodorus, *supra* note 126, at 407 (passage xx.99.3) and 4 Polybius, *supra* note 145, at 87 (passage ix.36). For example, in the *symmachia* between Miletus and Heracleia, the rights of Rhodes were reserved. See also Bickerman, *supra* note 302, at 14 n. 27.
[325] Carthage–Macedon Treaty, *supra* note 313, paragraph 5.
[326] See, e.g., 3 Thucydides, *supra* note 118, at 147 (passage v.79) (418 BCE alliance between Sparta and Argos provided for subsequent conclusion of specific agreements on auxiliary forces and their disposition).
[327] Carthage–Macedon Treaty, *supra* note 313, paragraph 7.

188 TREATY PRACTICES AMONGST ANCIENT PEOPLES

classic form of an *epimachia*, entirely open-ended and undefined except as
to the character of the likely threat. Yet, it is peculiar, coming after stipulation five acknowledging the state of war between Rome and Hannibal's
forces, and the promise of affirmative Macedonian help in that conflict.
If Hannibal agreed to only limited Macedonian help for the present war,
while reserving a general alliance for the future, it may have been that he
did not wish Philip's forces to join him as a principal ally.[328] It seems that
Carthage had no desire to allow Macedon into its sphere of influence. Of
course, this assumed that Hannibal would have been successful in bringing Rome to its knees in the Second Punic War.

As a carefully drafted legal text, the covenant between Hannibal and
Philip displays the usual panoply of anti-deceit clauses used by Greek city-
States in their treaty-making. There is the (fairly) usual provision[329] that
"[w]e will not make plots against, nor be in ambush for, each other; but in
all sincerity and good-will, without reserve or secret design, will be
[friends]."[330] Another significant provision was the limitation on
Hannibal's power to conclude a separate peace with Rome. As the principal alliance partner, Carthage was free to make peace with Rome, but only
if certain conditions were satisfied, prerequisites detailed in the treaty at
stipulation six.[331] The last provision of the treaty provided for subsequent
amendment by mutual agreement.[332]

What seems significant about the 215 BCE pact between Hannibal and
Philip V is the extraordinary detail and complexity of its provisions,
clauses which marry the strongest elements of Near Eastern and Greek
treaty-making patterns. It is as if, as Bickerman colorfully notes,
"Abraham suddenly should become the contemporary of Polybius. This
combining of new and of antique elements shows that the old-fashioned
form of the 'covenant' [*berit*] was adapted in Hellenistic Carthage to the
needs of a new time."[333]

Just as importantly, we have in this instrument the supple variation of
traditional treaty forms in the Greek tradition, in order to deal with a very
sensitive diplomatic situation. The combining of provisions common
with defensive and offensive alliances was surely considered awkward and

---

[328] See Bickerman, *supra* note 302, at 15 and n.30.
[329] See Wheeler, *supra* note 117, at 265–66.
[330] Carthage–Macedon Treaty, *supra* note 313, at paragraph 3.
[331] See *ibid.* at paragraph 6, which included "(a) that the Romans may never make war on
you, (b) that the Romans are not to have power over Corcyra, Apollonia, Epidamnus,
Pharos, Dimale, Parthini or Atitania, (c) that the Romans also restore to Demetrius of
Pharos all those of his friends now in the dominion of Rome."
[332] See *ibid.* paragraph 9.   [333] Bickerman, *supra* note 302, at 17.

challenging. Add to that a temporal context in which the treaty was to have accommodated the changing needs of the parties over time, and one has a very significant legal document. The fact that the alliance between Carthage and Macedon was doomed to failure does not matter. What does signify is the extraordinary union of different treaty-making modes in one instrument.

Roman treaty forms

Arthur Nussbaum has written that: "The comparatively infrequent treaties of the Romans were for the most part concluded under the Republic, and they are on the whole not good examples of international law. Most of them reflect in terse technical phraseology the Roman methods of political expansion."[334] In this regard, the two most characteristic forms of Roman treaty-making in the period of Rome's transmarine imperialism and consolidation, from 250 to 50 BCE, were the treaty of surrender (*deditio*) and the unequal alliance (*foedus iniquum*).

The *deditio*, by which a foreign community submitted itself unconditionally to Roman power, applied particularly to surrenders in war. It also could occur without any preceding military conflict with Rome, where the surrendering State was threatened by another, more powerful country and preferred to submit to the Romans.[335] In cases of military capitulation, the *deditio* was complete upon the subjugated state swearing a contractual, formal oath conveying all persons and property (whether sacred or profane) within its national territory to Romans.[336] The Roman representative would then declare his acceptance of the *deditio* in the name of the Roman people.[337] A *deditio* on these terms fully subjugated the conquered nation to Roman will, although the Romans were known to have granted rights and privileges to peoples so vanquished, including a measure of autonomy and the right to continue the observance of their laws and customs.[338] In cases where the *deditio* was made other than in a military conquest, it was usually followed by the conclusion of some form of treaty, usually a *foedus iniquum*.[339]

---

[334] See Nussbaum, *supra* note 11, at 11.   [335] See Scupin, *supra* note 23, at 138.
[336] The full formulary was "urbem, agros, aquam, terminos, delubra, utensilia, divina humanaque omnia." See 1 Livy, *supra* note 241, at 137 (passage 1.38), 2 *ibid.* at 353 (passage iv.30), 383 (passage vi.8), 4 *ibid.* at 5 (passage viii.1), 8 *ibid.* at 139 (passage xxviii.34), 12 *ibid.* at 127 (passage xl.41).
[337] See Nussbaum, *supra* note 11, at 11. See also Chapter 6, at notes 372–78 and text.
[338] See 4 Livy, *supra* note 241, at 243 (passage ix.20) (surrender of Capua).
[339] See Scupin, *supra* note 23, at 138.

The classification of Roman alliances has been the subject of much controversy among philologists. One might suppose that the basic distinctions were made between totally subjugated entities (*dediticii*), client States in some subordinate relationship to Rome, and nations with which Rome dealt on a level of perfect equality.[340] The Romans thus created a significant distinction between various forms of subordinate allies. A client State could be an *amicus* (friend) or a *foederatus* (ally), and the ruler of such states would be called by the Romans a king (*rex*) or phylarch or ethnarch.[341] In the late nineteenth century, Mommsen developed a scheme distinguishing between different Roman client State relations.[342] He identified three groups of states: (1) *amici*, who had no more than friendly relations with Rome; (2) *amici et socii*, those who in addition to friendly relations had a duty to send military contingents to Rome upon request; and (3) *socii*, who were virtually subordinated to Rome and were required to provide set military contingents on an annual basis.[343] Other scholars, including Bruno Paradisi, have speculated that the status of a *foedus* with Rome was quite distinct from that of an *amicitia*. The *amicus* relationship was premised on a renunciation of war; it was (in effect) the western equivalent of the Greek *philia*.[344]

For the application of these competing typologies, consider the following examples of Roman treaty-making. In 189 BCE, Rome vanquished the Aetolian League in Greece, after an abortive uprising abetted by Antiochus of Syria. The peace treaty that followed was a *socii* treaty, creating a virtually subordinate relation for the Greek cities to Rome. The Aetolians were

---

[340] Livy made this distinction in narrating the speech of Menippus, ambassador of Antiochus to Rome in 193 BCE. See 9 Livy, *supra* note 241, at 561 (passage xxxiv.57). To the same effect are 10 *ibid.* at 291 and 314 (passage xxxvii.1 and 8). See also Stephen Verosta, *International Law in Europe and Western Asia Between 100 and 650 AD*, 113 RCADI 484, 527 (1964-III). For more on the leagues that Rome entered into early in its history, including the Latin Confederation made around 492 BCE, see Arundell, *supra* note 200, at 364–65; 2 Phillipson, *supra* note 117, at 33–34. The terms of this confederation, likened to a Greek *symmachia* or *isopoliteia*, are rendered in 4 Dionysius of Halicarnassus, *Roman Antiquities* 137 (Ernest Cary and Edward Spelman transl. 1943) (Loeb Classical Library reprint 1986) (passage vi.95), and in 1 Livy, *supra* note 241, at 325 (passage ii.33). See also Donald Walter Baronowski, Roman Treaties with Communities of Citizens, 1 *Ancient Hist. Bull.* 43 (1987).   [341] See Verosta, *supra* note 340, at 527.
[342] See 3 T. Mommsen, *Römische Staatsrecht* 590, 645 (Berlin 1887) (W. P. Dickson transl. London 1894).
[343] See *ibid.* at 649, 663–65. See also Louise E. Matthaei, On the Classification of Roman Allies, 1 CQ 182, 184 (1907). For a classification of the later Roman Empire alliances, see Verosta, *supra* note 340, at 528. See also P. Catalano, *Linee del sistema sovrannazionale romano* 248–70 (1965).
[344] See Paradisi, *supra* note 156, at 350. See also *supra* notes 140–58 and accompanying text.

required to uphold the "empire and majesty (*maiestas*)" of Rome, and have the "same enemies as the people of Rome." A yearly tribute was imposed, as was the requirement that forty hostages be given into the care of the Roman consul for a period of six years.[345] This is considered by some writers to be the first *foedus iniquum*.[346] It was, in any event, to the Greeks more preferable than an outright *deditio* to Rome. It is interesting to note that the *maiestas* clause, essential in most Roman client treaties,[347] was coupled with a more traditional "same enemies" provision used by the Greeks. When Rome was negotiating with Antiochus of Syria in 193 BCE, and with Philip V of Macedon in 197 BCE, the same *maiestas* clause was imposed by Rome.[348]

Roman practice evolved in the last stages of its transmarine expansion into the eastern Mediterranean. In 160 BCE, for example, a treaty was made between Rome and Judas Maccabeus of Judea. The agreement, related in the Bible[349] and by Josephus,[350] was intended to supplant the harsh rule of Demetrius and Antiochus of Syria for Roman protection. The treaty was renewed in 139 BCE.[351] Both agreements were formalized by a *senatus consultum*, and both seemed to treat with Judea as a semi-independent entity.[352]

The pattern seemed to be that Rome would first make a treaty establishing peace and friendship with a polity on its periphery. This would be characterized as an *amicitia*, which, as Matthaei noted, "was not an

---

[345] The text of the treaty is recorded at 5 Polybius, *supra* note 145, at 311 and 373 (passage xxi.32 and xxii.13); 11 Livy, *supra* note 241, at 35 (passage xxxviii.11). See also M. James Mosovich, A Note on the Aetolian Treaty of 189 BC, in *Polis and Imperium: Studies in Honor of Edward Togo Salmon* 139 (J. A. S. Evans ed. 1979).

[346] See Larsen, *supra* note 142, at 439–40.

[347] The critical character of the *maiestas* clause, first used in the Aetolian Treaty of 189 BCE, was collected and recognized even in Justinian's *Digest*. See 4 *Digest of Justinian* 886 (Theodor Mommsen and Paul Krueger eds., Alan Watson transl. 1985) (49.15.7.1; Proclus, *Letters* 8). See also Larsen, *supra* note 142, at 440; Paradisi, *supra* note 156, at 345–46 n. 2. According to one authority, an entity which accepted a *maiestas* clause with Rome lost the legal position of a sovereign state, at least in relation to other States. See Scupin, *supra* note 23, at 137.

[348] See Matthaei, *supra* note 343, at 189; Paradisi, *supra* note 156, at 345–46 n. 2; 2 Phillipson, *supra* note 117, at 46–48. For more on the period of Roman expansion in Greece and Asia Minor, see R. Malcolm Errington, The Peace Treaty Between Miletus and Magnesia, 19 *Chiron* 279 (1989).   [349] 1 Maccabees 8:17–31.

[350] See 7 Josephus, *supra* note 114, at 7, 233 (*Antiquities*, passages xii.10.6 and xiii.9.2).

[351] See 1 Maccabees 15: 15–24.

[352] See Rosenne, *supra* note 105, at 143–44. For later treaty relations between Rome and Persia, see 3 Plutarch, *supra* note 133, at 365–421 (*Crassus*, passages 17–33) (treaty of 92 BCE invoked by Persia in 54 BCE to protest Crassus' invasion); Verosta, *supra* note 340, at 510–11.

alliance, it was rather a state of diplomatic relations, which [could] coexist with an alliance, or exist without it."[353] In this sense, it was fully like a *philia* in Greek practice.[354] The *amicitia* came, however, to be used as the form for Rome's later unequal treaties. These were instruments where all the advantages accrued to Rome: the subordinate state was under an obligation to come to Rome's aid upon request, but there was not necessarily a reciprocal duty. In contrast, the earlier form of the *foedus*, a perpetual offensive alliance contracted by Rome and a neighbor, came to be disfavored, and then nearly abandoned altogether.[355] Without question, the nature of Roman international relations, and territorial ambitions, changed during this period of legal transformation. The Romans simply had no wish to conclude *foedera* with their client states. A *foedus* was notionally perpetual; it could not have been terminated at will. Indeed, the only means for dissolving a *foedus* was the juridical "death" of the other contracting nation. A Roman declaration of war against a *foederatus* would not terminate the relationship; instead "it was merely an announcement that the other side had infringed some condition of the *foedus*, and an appeal to the arbitrament of the gods, to give victory to the side which kept the *foedus* unimpaired."[356] In contrast, an *amicitia* was terminable at will by a procedure known as *renuntiatio*, with striking private law analogues to termination of contracts.[357]

At least early in the period under review here, Rome made treaties on the basis of equality. The best and clearest examples of these are the three known agreements made with Carthage. The first was concluded in 509 BCE.[358] This instrument, considered elsewhere in this study,[359] has a definitive flavor of arranging the private, commercial relations of two powers whose interests were not yet in immediate conflict. The treaty, at least as reported by Polybius,[360] contained clauses establishing the respective spheres of influence of the parties and rules for the treatment of vessels and merchants of one nation finding themselves in the territory of the other. This instrument is properly to be considered an *amicitia*; no

---

[353] Matthaei, *supra* note 343, at 191.   [354] See *supra* notes 143–58 and accompanying text.

[355] See Matthaei, *supra* note 408, at 200–03.   [356] *Ibid.* at 190.

[357] See 4 Tacitus, *Annales* 203 (John Jackson transl. 1931) (Loeb Classical Library reprint 1956) (passage vi.29.3). See also 1 Cicero, *Verrine Orations* 389 (L. H. G. Greenwood transl. 1928) (Loeb Classical Library reprint 1978) (passage ii.2.36.89); and 1 Suetonius, *Lives of the Caesars* 407–09 (J. C. Rolfe transl. 1913) (Loeb Classical Library reprint 1989) (*Gaius Caligula*, passage iii.3) (on the notion of *renuntiatio*).

[358] For the controversy surrounding the dating of this treaty, see 2 Phillipson, *supra* note 68, at 74 n. 2.   [359] See Chapter 4, notes 287–92 and accompanying text.

[360] See 2 Polybius, *supra* note 145, at 53 (passage iii.22).

arrangements are made at all for military assistance to be extended between the parties.[361] Another treaty, made in 306 BCE and also reported by Polybius,[362] contained nearly an identical set of stipulations.

It was only in 279 BCE, on the eve of Pyrrhus' invasion into Italy, that Rome and Carthage had to confront the question of military cooperation as equals against a common foe. The treaty of the same year contained this key clause: "If they make a treaty of alliance with Pyrrhus, the Romans or Carthaginians shall make it on such terms as not to preclude the one giving aid to the other, if that one's territory is attacked."[363] This protocol also makes arrangements for the provision of Punic naval assistance to Rome, if required. Yet this alliance was quite tenuous. Each side simply wanted to ensure that the other would not make a separate peace with Pyrrhus, and, if need be, that certain limited naval cooperation would be forthcoming. This would be the end to any putative military alliance between these two growing powers. After Pyrrhus was vanquished, Rome and Carthage moved into a collision course culminating in the First Punic War, concluded in 241 BCE by a treaty which formalized the Carthaginian withdrawal from Sicily and Sardinia and the payment of a war reparation.[364]

It seems, then, that the Romans possessed a sophisticated understanding of different treaty forms. There has been an ongoing scholarly debate[365] as to whether the Romans were able to make the recognition, that had seemed to elude the Greeks,[366] of nations living in a perpetual state of peace. Pomponius, a later jurist, noted that the true state of nature between countries was "neither war nor friendship nor *hospitium* nor an alliance."[367] The evidence narrated above suggests that this recognition may have come early in the history of the Roman Republic's relations with its neighbors. Nonetheless, there is a strong element of these relationships being legally structured along lines conveying different nuances as to the relative power of Rome and its treaty partner. More so than in Greek treaty forms, even the hegemonic symmachy,[368] the Romans sought to

---

[361] See also M. David, The Treaties Between Rome and Carthage and Their Significance for our Knowledge of Roman International Law, in *Symbolae ad Jus et Historiam pertinentes Juliano Christiano Van Owen dedicatae* 231, 233–34 (M. David, B. A. van Groningen, E. M. Meijers eds. 1946); Leech, *supra* note 247, at 29–30.

[362] See 2 Polybius, *supra* note 145, at 57 (passage iii.24). See also David, *supra* note 361, at 233–34.   [363] See 2 Polybius, *supra* note 145, at 61 (passage iii.25).

[364] See 1 *ibid.* at 169 (passage i.62). See also William L. Carey, Nullus Videtur Dolo Facere: The Roman Seizure of Sardinia in 237 BC, 91 CP 203 (1996).

[365] See Scupin, *supra* note 23, at 137–38; Heichelheim, *supra* note 300, at 211.

[366] See *supra* note 123 and accompanying text.

[367] 4 *Digest*, *supra* note 347, at 886 (49.15.5.2; Pomponius, *Quintus Mucius* 37).

[368] See *supra* notes 181–95 and accompanying text.

develop treaty forms which powerfully conveyed different subordinate classifications. These were clearly intended also to be an imposition of legal status, culminating in the other treaty party losing all juridical personality.[369]

Formalities and enforcement of Roman treaties

Some aspects of Roman treaty oaths and oath-taking have already been considered in this study in the context of the sources of international legal obligation in antiquity.[370] Before considering the ways in which the Romans enforced treaties with their neighbors, it might be useful to summarize briefly the main points of Roman treaty negotiation and conclusion. In the Republican period, and certainly for the time considered here (up to 100 BCE), the Senate and the people of Rome still had substantial authority over the making of treaties.[371] The typical pattern of making a peace treaty followed along these lines. The army commander in the field would accept a vanquished (or near defeated) enemy's request for a truce, known as a *sponsio*. This suit for peace would be relayed back to Rome, upon which it might have been subject to a vote in the Senate and then to a plebiscite by the *comitia tributa*.[372] After the peace was ratified, it remained to negotiate the subsequent treaty to adjust the relationship between Rome and the other country. This might involve the movement of frontiers, the adoption of a *foedus iniquum*, or other measures. The Senate would usually appoint ten commissioners who, with the commander in the field, would negotiate the actual treaty with the former enemy.

When the treaty text was finalized, there was a definite event of ratification. It was this ceremony that was presided over by members of Rome's College of Fetials, a sacerdotal order already considered in this study.[373] The rite could be accomplished in Rome if there were duly accredited representatives of the foreign government in residence there.[374] In such a

---

[369] See 1 Phillipson, *supra* note 247, at 111.   [370] See Chapter 3.

[371] This seemed to be true also for the Rhodians and Carthaginians. See 2 Polybius, *supra* note 145, at 51 (passage iii.21) (Punic repudiation of General Hasdrubal's promise that Carthage would not march into Gaul), 6 *ibid.* at 95 (passage xxx.1) (ratification needed of Rhodian navarch's decision).

[372] See, e.g., 8 Livy, *supra* note 241, at 241, 529 (passages xxix.12, xxx.43), 9 *ibid.* at 345 (passage xxxiii.25), 10 *ibid.* at 461 (passage xxxvii.55) (negotiations surrounding 191 BCE treaty with Antiochus). See also Verosta, *supra* note 340, at 514–15.

[373] See Chapter 3 text with notes 140–59.

[374] See 10 Livy, *supra* note 241, at 461 (passage xxxvii.55).

case, the entire College would be present at the ceremony. Otherwise, a deputation of *fetials* – one of whom would be denominated the *pater patratus* – would be dispatched to the capital of the treaty partner. The officiating *fetial* carried to the foreign territory a rod (symbolizing his power and inviolability),[375] as well as sacred herbs and vessels for the treaty ratification ritual.[376]

The treaty rite apparently involved the sacrifice of a small animal, an anointment of herbs on the representatives of the States parties, and the uttering of a sacred oath.[377] Livy has the *pater patratus* declare:

> Hear, O Jupiter; hear, O pater patratus of the Alban people, and ye, Alban people, hear. As those conditions, from first to last, have been publicly recited from those tablets without deliberate fraud, and as they have been quite correctly understood here today, from those conditions the Roman people will not be the first to swerve. If they are the first to violate any of them deliberately by public concert, then on that day, O Jupiter, do thou strike down the Roman people, as I shall strike down this pig; and do thou strike them all the more as thou art more powerful.[378]

After the sacrifice, the generals and magistrates of both parties took an oath to uphold the terms of the treaty.[379] The *fetials* who presided over the ratification ceremony would convey the written text of the instrument back to Rome, after which the Senate and people of Rome would again ratify the instrument.[380]

Some modern scholars believe that the *fetials* played no serious role in lending legal authority to the conclusion of treaties, at least after 275 BCE and the defeat of Pyrrhus and the expansion of Roman power into southern Italy.[381] It appears that some sort of sacerdotal college, whether called *fetials* or something else,[382] existed in the communities close to Rome at the time of the kingship and early Republic. From Livy we know that the Alban people also had a *fetial* college, led by a *pater patratus*. The conclusion of many scholars is that the *fetial* institution was a Latin phenomenon,

---

[375] Livy refers to the rod as the scepter of Jupiter Feretrius, guarantor of treaties and oaths. See 1 *ibid.* at 83 (passage i.24), 8 *ibid.* at 531 (passage xxx.43). See also Chapter 4, at note 34 and text, for more on the ceremonial rod.

[376] See 1 *ibid.* at 83 (passage i.24). See also George E. Mendenhall, Puppy and Lettuce in Northwest-Semitic Covenant Making, 133 BASOR 26, 26–27 (February 1953); Alan Watson, *International Law in Archaic Rome: War and Religion* 8–9 (1993). See also Chapter 3, at notes 140–43 and accompanying text.

[377] For more details, see Georg Wissowa, *Religion und Kultus der Römer* 550–54 (Munich 1912).

[378] 1 Livy, *supra* note 241, at 85 (passage i.24).   [379] See *ibid.*

[380] See 4 Livy at 177 (passage ix.5). See also Christiane Saulnier, Le rôle des prêtres fétiaux et l'application du "ius fetiale" a Rome, 58 *Revue historique de droit français et étranger* 171, 181–83 (1980).   [381] See Matthaei, *supra* note 343, at 183.

[382] See Mendenhall, *supra* note 376, at 27 n. 6.

confined to a handful of cities in central Italy. As Rome grew in power and began to have consistent international relations with Greek and Punic out-posts in southern Italy and Sicily, the rigid sacerdotal forms of the college of *fetials* broke down. In the period of transmarine expansion, into Greece proper and into the Near East, the forms virtually vanished. The treaty cer-emonies, nonetheless, remained unchanged in form for centuries to come. The meaning and content of those forms was, however, conclusively altered.[383]

For example, the original idea of *foedus*, a perpetual peace and union, made sense when supervised by a *fetial* institution. After all, the *fetials* guaranteed the peace at the outset and also served as a neutral arbitrator in cases of dispute over whether one party had breached its duties.[384] One can even imagine a situation, as Livy narrates, of the Roman *pater patratus* consulting with his Alban counterpart in order to preserve the peace. The end of this notion of the *foedus* – and its replacement with various forms of unequal alliances[385] – paralleled the end of the legal role of the *fetial* institution in directing the viability of Roman alliances.

Another set of scholars have adopted a different viewpoint as to the role of the *fetials* in Roman treaty-making in the period between 250 and 100 BCE. They concede that, while the political influence of the college of *fetials* may have been on the wane, they have observed the extraordinary resilience of private law contract forms in the ratification ceremony pre-sided over by the *fetials*.[386] Their conclusion was that, while an enforce-ment mechanism based on the sacerdotal power of the *fetials* was in desuetude, a new form of obligation (based on contract) was being devel-oped.

Alan Watson in particular has speculated that the treaty ceremonial just described was a mutation of a *stipulatio*, bearing a strong resemblance to the oral contract used in Roman law, but with striking differences. The use of divine witnesses in treaty-making was one such distinction, and it is in this respect that the ceremony of *mancipatio* is relevant.[387] Likewise, it appears that divine witnesses may have also been considered parties to

---

[383] See Matthaei, *supra* note 343, at 182–83, 202.

[384] See Thomas Wiedemann, The Fetiales: A Reconsideration, 36 CQ 480, 488 (1987).

[385] See Matthaei, *supra* note 343, at 202. Professor Matthaei suggests that the Romans tried to use the *foedus* form in later relations with North African powers, but with mixed results. See *ibid.* (glossing Cicero, *supra* note 422, at 701 (*Pro Balbo*, passage xxiv)). See also Saulnier, *supra* note 380, at 182.

[386] See Watson, *supra* note 376, at 31–33.

[387] See *ibid.* at 32.

the treaty, making their role unique as both contractors and judges.[388] Another difference noted by Watson is that with the *stipulatio* it was always the person to whom the promise is being made who sets out the terms of the contract; "in the treaty it is the promisor."[389] Lastly, and most significantly, the phrasing of the *stipulatio* was always reciprocal, but with the Roman treaty form the promises being made by each country were "not technically linked."[390]

Watson puts substantial emphasis on the qualifying phrase used by the Roman *fetial* in the treaty ratification: promising Roman performance for the treaty terms "as they are today most correctly understood."[391] This precautionary phrase, Watson suggests, is "unparalleled in private law."[392] Such a qualification would be inappropriate, Watson believes, for a dispute that would arise before human judges, it being impossible to know with certainty how the terms of the treaty were correctly understood when recited. His whole point is that the deities invoked in Roman treaties served neither as passive witnesses nor as putative guarantors. They were, instead, taken to be real judges of the *bona fides* of the parties. In cases of a charge of subsequent treaty breach, the gods would have decided whether Rome was in default and then visited punishment on the Roman people.

But there is another interpretation of the caveat uttered by the Roman *fetials*. It may have been a simple recognition that treaty texts were subject to variant interpretations and that both parties were under an obligation to construe it in good faith. In this sense, the *fetial's* utterance was no more than a form of anti-deceit clause as used by the Greeks.[393] In view of the modern perception[394] that the Romans were sticklers for treaty performance, one might wonder why the *fetials* felt the need for such a qualification. The truth is, of course, that substantial uncertainty exists as to whether the Romans were so scrupulous. The evidence is simply ambivalent on this point.

---

[388] Professor Watson expressed some doubts whether there was enough evidence to suggest that deities served as actual guarantors of the terms of the treaty. See *ibid.* at 33. See also Semitic Influences in Early Rome, in *Daube Noster* 343 (Alan Watson ed. 1974).

[389] Watson, *supra* note 376, at 32. See also Alan Watson, *Roman Law and Comparative Law* 122 (1991).

[390] *Ibid.* See also *ibid.* at 61. But see Scupin, *supra* note 23, at 139 (who suggests that the oaths are "corresponding").   [391] 1 Livy, *supra* note 241, at 85 (passage i.24).

[392] Watson, *supra* note 376, at 32.   [393] See *supra* notes 253–59 and accompanying text.

[394] See Walker, *supra* note 202, at 47 ("The infraction of formally contracted treaties was deemed by all right thinking Romans a breach of the most sacred of religious obligations and a particular cause of divine resentment.").

Some have seriously suggested that the Romans regarded all treaties as *nudae pactiones* as in private law,[395] creating only moral commitments but not civil, binding obligations.[396] The better view, and the one consistent with the most recent scholarship,[397] is that treaties did have some kind of status as a binding contract. The question was how the Romans regarded the contract to be enforced. Aside from the well-known problem of making ransom agreements with pirates or marauders,[398] the Romans tended to regard a treaty made with an enemy as binding.[399] There are well-known instances in which the Romans made sophistic interpretations of treaties. In one such case (undoubtedly apocryphal), the Roman general Quintus Fabius Labeo made peace with King Antiochus of Syria, in which the King agreed to forfeit half of his fleet to Rome. It is reported that Labeo cut each Syrian galley in half, thus denying Antiochus the use of all his fleet.[400]

More credible was the situation involving the peace treaty between Rome and the Aetolians of 197 BCE.[401] This agreement had been intended to be a *foedus* between Rome and the Greeks to break Philip V of Macedon's power. The Romans promised the Aetolians that all lands and conquered towns in Macedon would go to them. The Greeks, though, proved feckless and defected to Macedon in the ensuing conflict. When the Aetolians returned to alliance with Rome in the last stages of the conflict with Macedon, they claimed their right under the earlier treaty to occupy Thessaly which had surrendered to the Roman army. The Roman general Quinctius refused the Greek request, first noting that the Aetolians had breached the treaty by earlier defecting to Macedon. And, besides, because the Thessalian cities had surrendered to Rome, and had not been "conquered" (*captae*), as the treaty required, there was no obligation by Rome to hand them over.[402]

---

[395] See 1 Phillipson, *supra* note 117, at 380–81 (ascribing this view to Mommsen).

[396] See 1 *Digest*, *supra* note 347, at 63 (2.14.7.4; Ulpian, *Edict* 4) ("Nuda pactio obligationem non parit").

[397] See the views, for example, of Alan Watson, *supra* notes 387–92 and accompanying text.

[398] See 21 Cicero, *supra* note 357, at 387 (*De Officiis*, passages iii.22, 27–32), who argues that a promise to pay ransom to a pirate is unenforceable since a pirate is not to be considered a public enemy, but, rather, as an outlaw. For commentary on this, see Alfred P. Rubin, *The Law of Piracy* 5–13 (1988).

[399] See Henry Wheaton, *History of the Law of Nations in Europe and America* 22–23 (New York 1845).

[400] See Robert Ward, *An Enquiry into the Foundation and History of the Law of Nations in Europe* 192 (London 1795) (quoting *Valerius Maximus*, passage 1.7.c.3).

[401] See 9 Livy, *supra* note 241, at 309 (passage xxxiii.13). See *supra* notes 345–47 and accompanying text for more on subsequent treaties.   [402] See *ibid.*

Quinctius' interpretive exercise was hardly necessary; surely it was legally sufficient that the Greeks had broken the 197 BCE alliance with Rome. The Roman college of *fetials* had been consulted when the Greeks' perfidy became clear. They advised that Rome could immediately terminate the state of friendship (*amicitia*) that existed between the two states. The college also advised that the Aetolians had to make an overt hostile act before the *foedus* could notionally be terminated and the war commenced.[403] This pattern[404] was repeated in the Third Macedonian War against Perseus in 172 BCE[405] and the conflict with Prusias.[406] There may have also been occasions where treaty termination was allowed where there had been a fundamental change of circumstances between the parties.[407]

The Aetolians again feature in Roman concerns about the enforcement of treaties. Knowing the Greeks to be untrustworthy, when the Romans finally subjugated them in 189 BCE they imposed a harsh *foedus iniquum*, as has already been discussed.[408] Among the provisions was the transfer of forty hostages, between the ages of ten and forty, who remained in Rome for six years.[409] Hostage-taking was a favored tactic in Roman power diplomacy, particularly as Rome expanded into the Eastern Mediterranean. Many *foedera iniqua* contained a requirement of tender of hostages to Rome.[410] The Romans, in fact, often considered the sending of hostages not so much as security for treaty performance, but rather as symbolic that the sending state did not treat with Rome on a footing of equality.[411]

Hostages were well treated at Rome – so long as the underlying treaty was faithfully kept by the other party. Such individuals enjoyed great freedom and access to the highest ranks of Roman citizens, as Antiochus (King of Syria) later recalled of his time as a hostage.[412] In contrast, the

---

[403] See 10 Livy, *supra* note 241, at 163, 181 (passages xxxvi.3 and 8).
[404] For more on which, see Matthaei, *supra* note 343, at 189–90.
[405] See 7 Livy, *supra* note 241, at 361 (passage xlii.25.1).
[406] See 6 Polybius, *supra* note 145, at 279 (passage xxxiii.12.5).
[407] See Vamvoukos, *supra* note 288, at 5–11.
[408] See *supra* notes 345–47 and accompanying text.
[409] See 5 Polybius, *supra* note 145, at 313 (passage xxi.32).
[410] For a collection of these circumstances, see 1 Phillipson, *supra* note 117, at 399–400. See also Mosovich, *supra* note 345, at 139–42; M. James Mosovich, Hostage Regulations in the Treaty of Zama, 23 *Historia* 417 (1974/75).
[411] See 12 Livy, *supra* note 241, at 407 (passage xlii.39) ("Nec tam in pignus fidei obsides desiderati erant quam ut appareret sociis nequaquam ex dignitate pari congredi regem cum legatis"). See also Oleg I. Tiunov, Pacta Sunt Servanda: The Principle of Observing International Treaties in the Epoch of the Slave-Owning Society, 38 *Saint Louis University Law Journal* 929, 935–36 (1994).   [412] See 12 Livy, *supra* note 241, at 309 (passage xlii.6).

Carthaginians and Gallic tribes were known to be brutal to their cap-tives.[413] If a war did break out between Rome and a state the nationals of which it held hostage, those persons were considered prisoners of war and classed with ordinary captives.[414] Interestingly, the noble hostages held by a state with which Rome was at war were considered to be enemy captives, and were not granted any special immunities (even if Rome were at peace with their country of origin).[415]

Hostages played a critical role also in Rome's fulfillment of its own *bona fides* since they were a necessary part of the conclusion of truces or *sponsio*. Ensuring the terms of such a truce, as prefatory to the conclusion of a lasting treaty, was a perennial problem in ancient international relations. As a matter of necessity, great diplomatic authority was extended to mil-itary commanders in the field. The difficulty arose when a *sponsio* or similar agreement made by a military leader was later repudiated by the civil authorities of that state. The Romans were preoccupied by this problem, as were other Mediterranean polities.[416] If, for example, a Roman commander demanded (and received) hostages upon the negotiation of a *sponsio*, he was obliged to return those hostages unharmed if the Senate back in Rome refused to ratify his actions.[417] Roman commanders were usually instructed to add a condition to any *sponsio* they made in the field that it was subject to later ratification.[418]

But a *sponsio* was considered really as a personal covenant, entered into by the general on his own authority. If a *sponsio* was later disavowed by Rome, the only recourse that could be had by the aggrieved nation was against the military leader who sponsored the agreement.[419] This is the rule which gave rise to the Roman practice of noxal surrender (or *deditio*) of individuals who had made a *sponsio* which was later repudiated. The

---

[413] See 4 Polybius, *supra* note 145, at 147 (passage x.18); Julius Caesar, *The Gallic War* (H. J. Edwards transl. 1921) (Loeb Classical Library reprint 1986) (passage v.27).

[414] See 9 Livy, *supra* note 241, at 551 (passage xxxiv.52) (Greek captives in Rome in 194 BCE). See also N. Ivanov, *Kharacteristika Mezhdunarodnikh Otnoshenij i Mezhdunarodnovo Prava v Istoricheskom Razvitii* [The Characteristics of International Law and International Relations in Historical Development] 77 (Kazan 1874).

[415] See 8 Livy, *supra* note 241, at 403 (passage xlv.42) (Roman occupation of Macedon and treatment of Thracian hostages held there).

[416] See 1 Phillipson, *supra* note 117, at 384–85 (describing Carthaginian and Rhodian practice on this point).

[417] See 5 Polybius, *supra* note 145, at 173 (passage xviii.39) (four months' armistice between Rome and Macedon in 197 BCE provided for return of hostages if Senate did not confirm agreement).

[418] See 10 Livy, *supra* note 241, at 403 (passage xxxvii.45).

[419] See 4 *ibid.* at 197 (passage ix.9) ("sponsio . . . neminem praeter sponsorem obligat"). See also J. Rubino, *Untersuchungen über römische Verfassung und Geschichte* 264 (Cassel 1839); Tiunov, *supra* note 411, at 933–34.

first, and most famous, of these incidents was the affair at the Caudine Forks.[420]

Occurring in 321 BCE, at the time of Rome's expansion into central Italy, a Roman army (under the command of two consuls, Postumius and Veturius) was compelled to surrender to a Samnian general, Caius Pontius. In the misplaced belief that generosity would seal a peace between the Samnites and Romans, Caius Pontius agreed to spare the lives of the Roman army if the consuls and men would agree to the conclusion of a treaty between Rome and the Samnites, requiring Rome to withdraw from territory taken. Postumius and Veturius took an oath before both hosts and then ordered the Roman legions to pass under a trellis of spears, symbolic of Samnian supremacy and mercy. Not fully trusting Roman scruples, the Samnians required that 600 hostages be kept as surety.

The Senate and people of Rome promptly disavowed the peace treaty. Speaking before the Senate, Postumius suggested that he and Venturius

> be surrendered to [the Samnites] by the fetials, naked and in chains. Let us thus liberate the people from an obligation we may have had cause of imposing on them; so that there may be no hindrance to your re-entering on the war without violating either religion or justice.[421]

Thereupon, the generals were conveyed by a delegation of *fetials* to Caudium, the Samnite capital, stripped of their clothes, hands bound. The *pater patratus* declared: "Inasmuch as these men became sureties for a treaty, without the sanction of the Roman people, and thus rendered themselves criminally liable, I hereby surrender them into your hands, in order that the Roman people may thereby be absolved from the impious offense."[422] But the Samnite chief would have none of this nonsense. He returned the consuls and 600 hostages, declaring that, if Rome wished to observe its *bona fides*, it could either adhere to the treaty or return its legions to the mercy of Samnite power. The Samnites were even less impressed with Postumius' subsequent conduct: having declared himself a Samnite (by virtue of his *deditio*), he kicked a Roman *fetial* in the groin in order to give the Romans a pretext for restarting the war.[423]

---

[420] The story is narrated in 4 Livy, *supra* note 241, at 193 (passage ix). See also Husack, *supra* note 216, at 17–19 (for a felicitous rendition).

[421] 4 Livy, *supra* note 241, at 191 (passage ix.8).   [422] 4 *ibid.* at 201 (passage ix.10).

[423] Postumius' attack on the *fetial* may have been a version of the Roman civil procedure of *de vi armata*, by which one party would symbolically attack the other in order to establish which was the plaintiff, and which the defendant. The procedure is referred to in 9 Cicero, *supra* note 357, at 99 (*Pro Caecina*, passage ii). See also Bruce W. Frier, *The Rise of the Roman Jurists* 78 (1985). This procedure was probably a dead letter by Livy's time. See Wiedemann, *supra* note 384, at 490 n. 41.

The *deditio* was Roman legal formalism at its best. Few treaty partners accepted the Roman offer of a sacrificial hostage. In 236 BCE, Claudius Clineas made a treaty with the Corsicans which was then violated. Like the Samnians, the Corsicans declined to accept his *deditio*.[424] Likewise, the Celtiberians of Numantia in 137 BCE refused to accept the noxal surrender of Hostilius Mancinus, after he waged a disastrous campaign against them and was forced to conclude a *sponsio*.[425] By the time Rome repudiated the two *sponsiones* with Jugurtha in 111 and 110 BCE, they did not seem much troubled with legal niceties. No *deditio* of the Roman officials was even offered to the North Africans.[426] Although the authorities disagree,[427] the best view seems to be that, by the first century BCE, the Romans no longer viewed *deditio* as being a necessary remedy for the violation of a *sponsio*.[428]

Despite this, the Romans continued to demand (and give) noxal surrender as a penalty for violating other, more binding, treaty obligations. *Deditio* of individuals charged with the abuse or mistreatment of foreign diplomats has already been considered.[429] Private violations of treaty obligations, particularly *amicitia*, were also liable to be satisfied via a demand and surrender of the malefactor. *Deditio* was often used with conspirators or instigators of rebellion.[430] At least early in the Republic, the Romans were more often in the position of granting *deditio* of treaty violators than they were of demanding it. The Romans' heavy emphasis on personal surety and responsibility in the enforcement of treaty values was at striking variance with Greek precedents, but probably in line with ancient Near Eastern methods.

Ancient treaty-making: enforcement, sophistication, tradition, and universality

Enforcement was always a difficult issue of making faith in antiquity. For early Near Eastern polities there were consistent concerns about crafting

---

[424] See Zonaras viii.18; Valerius Maximus iii.3.3.
[425] See 21 Cicero, *supra* note 357, at 387 (*De officiis*, passage iii.30); 3 *ibid.* at 127 (*De orat.*, passage i.40).
[426] See Sallust, *The Jugurthine War* 219 (J. C. Rolfe transl. 1921) (Loeb Classical Library reprint 1985) (passage xxxix).
[427] For an historiography, see 1 Phillipson, *supra* note 117, at 373–74.
[428] See also consideration of Roman practice at the time of Julius Caesar's conquest of Gaul. Wiedemann, *supra* note 384, at 489–90 and n. 38.
[429] See Chapter 4, at notes 175–76 and accompanying text.
[430] See 1 Phillipson, *supra* note 117, at 367–69.

treaty terms that were truly reciprocal and recognized as equally binding on both sets of parties. For both cultures, the act of treaty-making was viewed as a unilateral act: the sovereign of one nation pledged his troth on the assumption (although without the certainty) that the treaty partner was doing the same.[431] The idea that treaty- making was an inherently reciprocal exercise – indeed, that it had no meaning otherwise – appeared only later in the ancient Near Eastern tradition, with the covenant between Rameses II and Hattusili III being exemplary.[432]

Once the notion of reciprocity was embraced by ancient cultures, they could then confront the problem of internal and external means of treaty enforcement. This chapter has suggested a dynamic tension between these two approaches. An "internal" way of enforcing an international agreement emphasized background rules of good faith, reasonable interpretation, and faithful observance over time. "External" means implicated personal surety and responsibility in the enforcement of treaty values. These included hostage-taking and noxal surrenders.

Every ancient culture surveyed in this study vigorously debated the question of how to coerce treaty faith. This argument was typically conducted in the form of a disquisition of the morality (or at least the political wisdom) of accepting hostages as treaty guarantors. And, indeed, while commentators condemned the practice, it was followed with more or less regularity by every State system reviewed here, with the notable exception of the Greek city-States. As just recounted, even the Romans, despite their strong sense of *bona fides* in treaty observance, took hostages. The Greeks sought, instead, to put their reliance in a whole panoply of structural solutions to ensure treaty fidelity: anti-deceit clauses,[433] rules of treaty interpretation,[434] and refined doctrines of treaty termination.[435] The Greek approach to treaties was, in a very real sense, a legal one.

The Romans conceived treaties in a legal sense of obligation as well, but their vision was formalistic. The elaborate charade of noxal surrender following a repudiated *sponsio* was emblematic of (largely) empty Roman legal forms. It also says much about Roman (and, for that matter, ancient Near Eastern) ambivalence about observing international obligations for the simple reason that they reflect a rational exchange of promises and an expectation of subsequent certainty in political and diplomatic relations.

[431] See *supra* notes 34–35, 63–65 and accompanying text.
[432] See *supra* notes 69–92 and accompanying text.
[433] See *supra* notes 253–55 and accompanying text.   [434] See *supra* notes 259–62 with text.
[435] See *supra* notes 283–95 and accompanying text.

There may well be a correlation between the character of the State system in which diplomacy (and treaty-making) is being conducted and the preferred mode of treaty enforcement. "Dynamic" State systems (those with more than five major actors) may well have resorted to more "internal" means of enforcement. Greek multi-polarism was exemplary of this. Alliances were extraordinarily fluid in these State systems, and so "external" (and usually more coercive) means of enforcement were likely not to have been employed with substantial success. The more "static" State systems that prevailed during much of the ancient Near East and the period of Roman expansion, having (typically) fewer than four or five Great Powers, were more brittle. Treaties seemed to matter for less, were drafted at a higher level of abstraction, and, yet, ironically, were more often enforced by coercive, "external" means, including hostage-taking and personal pledges of surety.

Problematic enforcement of international agreements did not seem, however, to interfere with the process of developing legal sophistication. A signal aspect of every State system reviewed here is that, as time went on, treaties became more diverse in the subject-matters of substantive provisions, more precise in the structuring of those clauses, and (generally) more complex in the interrelation of these obligations. Treaties like the 1280 BCE instrument between Egypt and the Hittites, or the 215 BCE agreement between Hannibal and Macedon, are models both of complexity and precision.

Both were treaties of alliance *and* friendship, capturing all the ambiguity and difficulty that those relationships entailed for the two treaty partners. Every legal culture considered in this study had to confront the issue of how to narrate and control diverse kinds of alliance statuses between two or more polities. Sovereign equality was always problematic, and although Greek alliance typology was certainly the most nuanced in antiquity,[436] Roman conceptions of different kinds of affiliations were complex,[437] and so too were Hittite and Assyrian treaty forms.[438] Alliance configurations culminated in extraordinarily complicated league patterns.

The most convincing evidence that ancient peoples conceived of international links as legal relations was that they committed their treaties to writing. The power of the written word was not to be underestimated in antiquity. The emphasis – one might say the obsession – of ancient States

---

[436] See *supra* notes 159–99 and accompanying text.
[437] See *supra* notes 340–64 and accompanying text.
[438] See *supra* notes 36–58 and accompanying text.

in properly keeping and revering treaty texts[439] was symbolic of the power and authority of the written word to convey legal meanings for international relations.

Ancient treaty-making also had a strong universalist flavor. By this I mean two distinct things. The first is that there was a single ancient tradition in treaty-making, an inherent unity of conception in the way that treaties were made and observed. There were, of course, some variations in these forms, but what is surprising is the commonality. The basic Hittite treaty form, a secular contract formed out of solemnized oaths, was adopted (with some changes) by the Assyrians, Egyptians, and ancient Israelites. It was, in turn, transmitted into the Greek and Hellenistic worlds, and thence into the western Mediterranean region of Rome and her neighbors.

The proof lies in those agreements made by nations at the temporal and spatial intersections of these different State systems – such as that between Rameses II and Hattusili,[440] or that between Macedon and Carthage,[441] or that between Rome and the Aetolians.[442] In each of these instances, pre-existing forms were (to be sure) altered. It may have been the dropping of elaborate preambular passages, or the inclusion of specific legal terms or provisions (such as *maiestas* clauses or qualifications regarding after-acquired allies). Regardless, there was always a synthesis of forms and motifs of legal expression in treaties, never an outright repudiation of old forms.

As developed in the ancient Near East, treaties narrated a story of relations between two or more States, and purported to tell also a story of their peaceful relations for all time to come. Although the elaborate preambular statements used by the Hittites were not replicated even in all ancient Near Eastern texts – and certainly not in Roman, Greek or Egyptian instruments – there was still a strong element of historic narration and structure to these later treaties. All political cultures reviewed here had to struggle with the fundamental dilemma of State relations: did the conclusion of treaties necessarily mean that relations with another polity could be based on the notion of perpetual peace?

There seems no doubt that ancient peoples regarded treaties as the chief means of regulating peaceful relations between States. The institutions of private hospitality and the public reception of emissaries could assist in this process, but, ultimately, it was up to States to pledge their

---

[439] See *supra* notes 39–40, 234–40 and accompanying text.
[440] See *supra* notes 46–47 with text.   [441] See *supra* notes 318–24 and accompanying text.
[442] See *supra* notes 345–52 with text.

faith to each other. This act of making faith could have many forms. It could have been a simple recognition of friendship existing between nations. Or it could be a conclusion of some sort of political alliance. Greek and Roman statecraft understood a distinction between *philia* and *symmachia*, *amicitia* and *foedus*;[443] they also knew that the alternative to peace was a state of war or enmity. The next chapter considers whether hostilities marked the end to a rule of law in ancient international relations.

---

[443] See *supra* notes 138–39, 365–69 and accompanying text.

6 Making war: the commencement and conduct of hostilities in ancient times

Having explored how ancient States made friends through diplomacy, and how they made faith through treaties, it is now time to turn to the questions of how the rule of law influenced the manner in which war was declared by ancient peoples and whether there were any legal restraints on the conduct of hostilities in antiquity. On first consideration, it would seem fanciful to suggest that ancient States deemed themselves bound by definitive rules of State behavior in wartime. Such an intimation seems counter-intuitive precisely at moments in ancient international relations that values associated with peaceful coexistence between ancient polities were being discarded in favor of notions of national particularism, imperial conquest, or ethnic self-preservation.

This chapter offers, therefore, a second look at the seeming oxymoron of an ancient law of war. The discussion here is divided into two broad themes. The first is how ancient States commenced hostilities with each other. This topic subsumes such matters as what justifications were considered as sufficient to begin a war with another State. Moreover, this part will look at the procedures that ancient States employed to formally declare war. Last to be discussed is how ancient States viewed the legal consequences attendant on a condition of war.

The second theme of the chapter will be the extent to which ancient States observed rules in the actual conduct of warfare. This part will explore general principles of restraint in war, as well as the immunities that were enjoyed by certain places and persons during the course of war. Finally, the legal repercussions coming with the conclusion of hostilities will also be examined, particularly the effects of surrender and occupation.

The broad thematic scope of this chapter is consistent with its purpose in finding a law of nations that was present in ancient polities' decisions to commence hostilities and to prosecute a war with another State. Sometimes that adherence to a rule of law will be difficult to detect, but, as I suggest here, there is enough evidence to suggest that there were certain rules of conduct in warfare that were consistently observed by ancient States. Moreover, those rules were congruous with the basic ideas of international law already considered in this study – the ancient world's concern for regulating friendship and trust between peoples of different cultures.

Declarations of war

Justifications for commencing hostilities

As has already been considered in this study, the act of declaring war was a solemn and significant one for an ancient State. Even if Michael Rostovtseff was correct when he said that "[t]he sole deciding force [in ancient international relations] was might,"[1] ancient States were still anxious to ensure that the religious formalities of declaring war were satisfied. As was suggested in Chapter 3, these religious rituals often had legal aspects to them. Contemporary literary and inscription evidence shows that when ancient States seriously considered the reasons for engaging in war they were often assessing the legal justifications for recourse to armed conflict. This subtle transformation of religion and ritual into discourse on legal reason is a singular feature of the ancient international law of war.

It is not only, as Arundell said, that "[t]he declaration of war . . . is manifestly the hinge upon which the whole system of the law of nations turns."[2] The initiation of war marked the transition from an (arguably uneasy) condition of peace in ancient State relations to the atavistic and particularistic footing of war, whether culminating in conquest or defeat. There is also no doubt that in antiquity war was considered to be the unique prerogative of the State, a social phenomenon of legitimized violence between polities.[3] At the same time, ancient States sought to

---

[1] Michael Rostovtseff, International Relations in the Ancient World, in *The History and Nature of International Relations* 43 (E. Walsh ed. 1922).

[2] Lord Arundell of Wardour, *Tradition Principally with Reference to Mythology and the Law of Nations* 386 (1872).

[3] See Maurice Rea Davie, *The Evolution of War: A Study of its Role in Early Societies* 5, 9 (1929); G. L. Dickinson, *The Causes of International War* 7 (1920).

regulate conflict – both in preventing its outbreak, and, once commenced, mitigating its horrors. As Joachim von Elbe considered in the context of a doctrine of just war in antiquity, "[t]he civilization of antiquity is to be credited with serious attempts to overcome the natural state of war by institutionalizing it as part of religious and philosophical systems, and even to subject it to legal principles."[4] Or, as Wegner wrote, "[w]e notice everywhere in the sources of Antiquity that the ancients conceived war and its extent as instituted by Divine command. In this conception, war is raised above the stage of blind passion: it has become a legal institution."[5]

The thrust of these writers' views is that belief and ritual and law commingled in the ancient State's appreciation of the decision to proceed with hostilities. Von Elbe and Wegner both speak of "institutionalizing" this solemn moment in State relations. In each of the three State systems considered in this study – the ancient Near East, the Greek city-States, and the period of Roman expansion – rituals and institutions were a signal feature of State practice in declaring war. The ideas surrounding these ceremonials and social structures remained fairly constant in antiquity, even while the specific rites and institutions may have changed with time and circumstance. This consistency in the idea of the proper way a State should declare war transcended stereotypes in these ancient cultures. There were, for sure, strong elements of divine and scriptural command in ancient Israelite practices, of political philosophy and rhetoric in Greek custom, and of formalism in Roman usages.[6] As will be seen, the underlying value to be protected in the proper formalities to be observed in initiating hostilities was to protect the State's superior moral position in the ensuing conflict.

The Israelite distinction between obligatory and optional war

The central concept of justification in the ancient Israelite law of war was the divine command that certain military campaigns were ordained by God. In Hebrew, this form of obligatory war was known as *mitzva*. It was only in a colloquial sense a "holy" war, although there was very much the belief that Jehovah fought on behalf of his people, the Israelites, and that the enemy was consecrated to the divinity.[7] "Optional" war (*reshut*) has

---

[4] Joachim von Elbe, The Evolution of the Concept of the Just War in International Law, 33 AJIL 665 (1939).   [5] R. Wegner, *Geschichte des Völkerrechts* 35 (1936).
[6] See von Elbe, *supra* note 4, at 666.   [7] See M. Hengel, *Die Zeloten* 277–95 (2nd ed. 1976).

also been referred to in the Talmudic literature as "authorized" or "permitted" war.[8] "Optional" wars were those undertaken to increase territory or "to diminish the heathens so that they shall not march."[9] Shabtai Rosenne has maintained, though, that the distinction between *mitzva* and "secular" wars was a legal (*halachic*) one, "in the sense that different legal rules or legal consequences applied according to the nature of the war, which itself was determined by the law."[10]

The law which mandated *mitzva* was the Pentateuch itself. The scriptures contained in Deuteronomy prescribed that:

> in the cities of these peoples that the LORD your God gives you for an inheritance, you shall save alive nothing that breathes, but you shall utterly destroy them, the Hittites and the Amorites, the Canaanites and Per'izzites, the Hivites and Jeb'usites, as the LORD your God has commanded.[11]

Milhemit mitzva – obligatory wars – were essentially military campaigns for national existence and self-defense. The selection of the neighboring Canaanite kingdoms as being the only legitimate subjects for war was no mistake. The historic sense must have been that a politically and militarily viable Israel must imperatively have had to dominate these neighboring, rival powers. The surest way of domination was the utter destruction and annihilation of the enemy.[12]

The premise of holy war was rooted in the ancient wilderness experience of the Israelites.[13] It must have been perceived that *mitzva* was not a human enterprise like the wars fought by kings with trained soldiers and impressive arrays of cavalry and chariots. Rather, it was a conflict fought

---

[8] See Michael J. Broyde, Fighting the War and the Peace: Battlefield Ethics, Peace Talks, Treaties, and Pacifism in the Jewish Tradition, in *War and its Discontents: Pacifism and Quietism in the Abrahamic Traditions* 13 and n. 22 (J. Patout Burns ed. 1996). *Reshut* was a term later derived in the Rabbinic sources to describe the countervalent of *mitzva*.

[9] See the Sotah Talmud 44b. See also the codification of Jewish law by Maimonides, the great jurist who lived from 1135 to 1204 CE. See *The Code of Maimonides Laws of Kings* 5:1 (reprinted 1949).

[10] Shabtai Rosenne, The Influence of Judaism on the Development of International Law, 5 Netherlands ILR 119, 139 (1958). See also Rabbi Eliezer Berkovits, *Not in Heaven: The Nature and Function of Halakha* (1983).

[11] Deuteronomy 20:16–18. Reference is made to the remaining Canaanite nation, the Girgashites, and to Amalek, at Deuteronomy 7:11 and at 25:19.

[12] See 1 Samuel 23:9. But see Commentary of Maimonides on Mishna (transl. of J. Kapach) Mishnah Sotah 8:7 (suggesting that an offensive war cannot be justified unless a prior state of belligerency existed).

[13] See Deuteronomy 2:33–35, 3:3–7, 3:18–22, 7:1–5, and 11:22–25. See also Prosper Weil, Le Judaïsme et le Développement du Droit International, 151 RCADI 253, 290–91 (1976–III).

by Jehovah himself in which his people responded with fanatical zeal.[14] That devotion was tested in each Israelite combatant, and the fearful and the fainthearted were sifted from the host.[15] Neutrality, the idea that one could abstain from conflict, was not an option with *mitzva*.[16] Other aspects which distinguished the conduct of *mitzva* from secular war will be considered below.[17]

There were notable restrictions on the grounds for declaring *reshut*, or optional war. The most important of these was the requirement that "[w]hen you approach a city to do battle with it you should call to it in peace."[18] This seemed to have compelled the ancient Israelites at least to enunciate to the enemy the military objectives of their campaign.[19] There has been scholarly disagreement as to whether the duty to "demand peace" was also an element of *mitzva*, but that seems unlikely since such wars were pre-ordained and could not be limited in their military objectives.[20]

It is important to note here that this distinction between *mitzva* and *reshut* only obtained in Israelite practice in the period considered in this study under the rubric of the ancient Near East. Indeed, by the time of kings David and Saul, by 966–700 BCE,[21] the practice of *mitzva* was on the wane.[22] Some scholars have suggested that by the tenth century BCE, warfare had become entirely secularized for the Israelites,[23] and that by the Hellenistic period the actual practice of *mitzva* was considered legendary.[24] Indeed, by the end of the seventh century BCE, Jeremiah could even write of God fighting against Israel for its chastisement,[25] something that would have been unthinkable if the notion of *mitzva* had still been embraced at that time. And even though the original concept of holy war was partially revived in the Maccabean struggle of the second century

---

[14] See Deuteronomy 20:1–4.
[15] See Deuteronomy 20:8. See also Broyde, *supra* note 8, at 24–25.
[16] This point was made by Alfred P. Rubin, The Concept of Neutrality in International Law, 16 *Denver Journal of International Law and Policy* 353, 353 (1988). See also Weil, *supra* note 13, at 292–93.   [17] See *infra* notes 216–39 and accompanying text.
[18] Deuteronomy 20:10.
[19] See Numbers 21:21–24, where the Israelites promised to limit their military objectives in return for peaceful passage through the lands of Sichon.
[20] See Maimonides, *Law of Kings* 6:1. See also Broyde, *supra* note 8, at 18.
[21] For more on this period, see Chapter 2, at notes 77–88 and accompanying text.
[22] See Roland De Vaux, *Ancient Israel: Its Life and Institutions* 265 (1961), and 8 *Encyclopedia Judaica* 347 (1973–95).   [23] See Rosenne, *supra* note 10, at 140.
[24] See A. J. Holloday and M. D. Goodman, Religious Scruples in Ancient Warfare, 36 CQ 160, 165 (1986).   [25] See Jeremiah 21:5.

BCE, and in the revolt against Rome in the first century CE, no claim was made of direct divine intervention in the conflict.[26] At that point, the Israelites were fighting for God, and not the other way around.[27]

Greek grounds for declaring war and the problem of neutrality

Of what were regarded by the ancient Greeks as legitimate grounds for declaring war we know relatively little. In epic Greece, according to Homer, there was apparently some recognition of the idea that hostilities could not be commenced without an appropriate cause, and that it was the duty of the city-State feeling aggrieved to make a demand for redress.[28] It was as much the failure to make amends, as it was the original offense, which provided the justification for war. As a consequence, in *The Iliad*, Agamemnon is recorded as being concerned that upon the death of Menelaus, the Greek demand for the return of the kidnapped Helen would be mooted, and the justification for the war against Troy would be over.[29]

The truth was that in the historic period of Greek international relations, the necessity of making a formal demand for redress was not often recognized. That is not to say that certain kinds of offensive conduct did not lead to an immediate outbreak of hostilities. The Persian defilement of Greek temples in Asia Minor was cited as the reason for the offensive war against Xerxes, at least according to Thucydides,[30] whom we have no reason to doubt on this point. Polybius, writing much later of course, had cause to suggest that the Greeks frequently authorized reprisals in lieu of, or preliminary to, a declaration of actual war.[31] Indeed, as Adcock and Mosley have suggested:

---

[26] See Hengel, *supra* note 7, at 289–93. See also 1 Maccabees 5:68.

[27] See De Vaux, *supra* note 22, at 262.   [28] See Arundell, *supra* note 2, at 375.

[29] 1 Homer, *The Iliad* 165 (A. T. Murray transl. 1921) (Loeb Classical Library reprint 1929) (passage iv.160–62). See also Peter Karavites, *Promise-Giving and Treaty-Making: Homer and the Near East* 175–78 (1992).

[30] See 1 Thucydides, *History of the Peloponnesian War* 251–53 (C. F. Smith transl. 1919) (Loeb Classical Library reprint 1980) (passage i.144). See 4 Herodotus, *Histories* 313–15 (A. D. Godley transl. 1920) (Loeb Classical Library reprint 1969) (passage vii.9) (Persian attitudes about Greek provocations).

[31] See 1 Polybius, *The Histories* 383–85 (W. R. Paton transl. 1922) (Loeb Classical Library reprint 1975) (passage ii.58) (discussing Achaean reprisals against Aetolian raiders, as well as Eleutheran authorization of reprisals against Rhodes upon hearing a rumor that a Rhodian admiral had executed one of their citizens). See also Thomas A. Walker, *A History of the Law of Nations* 52 (1899).

[i]t was possible for [Greek] states to drift into war in a sequence of hostile events, none of which in themselves was sufficient justification or pretext for war. It was equally possible in such a situation that either or both sides wished to escape the actual responsibility for declaring war.[32]

An excellent example of this arose in the diplomatic maneuverings involved in Athens' support for the break-away Corinthian colony of Corcyra. As has already been narrated,[33] Athens sought to play a delicate game in which it provided support to the Corcyraeans (going so far as concluding a defensive alliance with them),[34] while, at the same time, observing the letter of their peace treaty with Corinth and Sparta. According to Thucydides,[35] a confrontation was inevitable, insofar as Corinth was actively attempting to suppress the Corcyraeans.

A curious stand-off occurred in the harbor at Sybota, in which an Athenian naval force was, in essence, screening the Corcyraean rebels from a superior expeditionary force from Corinth. The frustrated Corinthians finally decided to put a group of armed soldiers in a row-boat, unaccompanied by a herald, and challenged the Athenians to treat them as enemies if Athenian intentions were deliberately hostile towards Corinth. The Athenians refused to respond to this provocation, saying merely that they were there to defend Corcyra against attack, but would not, in any other fashion, hinder the Corinthians.[36] So it was that the Athenians attempted to adhere to the letter of two contradictory treaties, one with Corcyra, and the other with Corinth and Sparta. Again, as previously recounted, this incident led directly to the outbreak of the Peloponnesian War.[37]

Two vital matters are suggested by this account. The first involves the use of heralds. Although more will be said later about their role in the Greek process of declaring war,[38] the important point to be noted here is

---

[32] Sir Frank Adcock and D. J. Mosley, *Diplomacy in Ancient Greece* 202 (1975).

[33] See Chapter 5, at notes 260–62 and accompanying text.

[34] See Rubin, *supra* note 16, at 355.

[35] See 1 Thucydides, *supra* note 30, at 78–79, 91 (passages i.44 and i.53).

[36] 1 *ibid.* at 91 (passage i.53). For another interpretation of this incident, see Adcock and Mosley, *supra* note 32, at 153–54 (suggesting that the Corinthians sent their delegation in a row-boat with a herald's *ensign*, but without an actual herald, in order precisely not to convey the impression that they regarded themselves at war with Athens). Curiously, Professor Mosley (writing alone) made the interpretation I make here. See D. J. Mosley, *Envoys and Diplomacy in Ancient Greece* 84 and n. 42 (1973).

[37] See Adcock and Mosley, *supra* note 32, at 202–03.

[38] See *infra* notes 125–36 and accompanying text.

that the Corinthians deliberately provoked an Athenian response by placing combatants in a (possibly) hostile setting without the protection of a herald. And, indeed, in the months that followed after the confrontation at Sybota, contacts between the Athenians and Corinthians occurred without the use of heralds.[39] It was only later still, after relations between the two sides had utterly degenerated, that Thucydides noted that "the starting point of the war between the Athenians and the Peloponnesians [was when] they no longer made contacts without heralds."[40]

Manifestly, a Greek city-State did not wish to have it appear that it was the one initiating hostilities.[41] The incident at Sybota was emblematic of a kind of Greek morality in which the appearance of aggression in international relations was to be avoided. So, even though there may have been little Greek law suggesting the permissible grounds for recourse to armed conflict, there was an evident legal concern associated with being the party that actually declared the war. These concerns may have been implicated in both the procedures for declaring war and the legal consequences of a condition of belligerency (both of which will be considered presently).

But there is probably an additional consideration at work here. This may be plainly stated as the problem of neutrality. As was discussed in Chapter 2, the State system of the ancient Greek cities was multi-polar and dynamic. The Greek city-States were quite unlike the more static sovereignties of the ancient Near East, and very different from the thrusting imperialism of Rome and her rivals. The key characteristic of ancient Greek international relations was the sheer number of polities and the many combinations in which they formed for the purposes of offense and defense, and of hegemonic and balance-of-power diplomacy.

The diversity of these alliance relationships, as well as their international legal consequences, has been intensively considered in this study.[42] What has not so far been considered is the reciprocal of alliance – neutrality. By neutrality, I mean the idea of a status that gives political freedom and legal immunities to those polities abstaining from a conflict.[43] Some

---

[39] See 1 Thucydides, *supra* note 30, at 255 (passage i.146).   [40] 1 *ibid.* at 259 (passage ii.1).

[41] See Peter Karavites, *Capitulations and Greek Interstate Relations* 99–106 (1982).

[42] See Chapter 2, at notes 116–18 and accompanying text; Chapter 4, pp. 120–35; and Chapter 5, pp. 154–83.

[43] I am indebted to the outstanding scholarship of my colleague, Professor Robert A. Bauslaugh, and his superb work, *The Concept of Neutrality in Classical Greece* (1991). For his definition of neutrality in ancient Greece, see *ibid.* at 250–51. For alternative definitions of the political concept of neutrality, see S. Séfériadès, La Conception de la Neutralité dans l'ancienne Grece, 16 *Revue de droit international et de legislation comparée* 641, 644–45

historians of public international law have vigorously maintained that the Greeks could not have recognized such a concept.[44] Other scholars have concluded that such a status, while "not clearly and juridically defined, did confer some protection."[45] And still other writers have maintained that neutrality was definitively a legal conception in ancient Greece,[46] especially in the period between the conclusion of the Persian Wars (479 BCE) and the beginning of the Peloponnesian War (431 BCE).[47]

It is beyond the scope of this study to review fully the evidence of neutrality in ancient Greece, but some observations need to be made here concerning the impact of a city-State's neutral status as grounds for another State's declaration of war against it. The first point is that the concept of neutrality was hotly disputed in the ancient Greek world. For the major hegemonic powers – Athens, Sparta, and Thebes – recognition of the rights of smaller *poleis* to remain neutral in their great-power machinations and struggles would have meant the end to an effective system of offensive and defensive alliances.[48] States such as Megara and Corinth,

---

(1935). This present study has already compared the concept of neutrality, with the notion of *philia* (friendship) in ancient Greece (see Chapter 5, at notes 150–53 and accompanying text). See also Adcock and Mosley, *supra* note 32, at 207 ("On other occasions 'friendship' meant little, if anything, more than neutrality.").

[44] See 1 R. Kleen, *Lois et usages de la neutralité* 2 (1898); Hannis Taylor, *Treatise on International Public Law* 617 (1901). See also 2 Coleman Phillipson, *The International Law and Custom of Ancient Greece and Rome* 305 (1911) (writing that: "The constant practice of establishing alliances and confederations, the keen solicitude to prevent the inordinate aggrandizement of this or that State, and to maintain a balance of power militated considerably against the full development of the doctrine of neutrality.").

[45] See Adcock and Mosley, *supra* note 32, at 207.

[46] See, e.g., Bauslaugh, *supra* note 43, at 250–51.

[47] See *ibid.*, at 250–51. The period of the Persian Wars was a difficult one for the concept of neutrality. A few Greek city-States attempted to remain neutral and not to contribute to the Greek forces defending against the Persian invasion of Xerxes. Among these were far-away Crete, Thebes, and the city of Argos. The abstention of Argos may actually have been sanctioned by the Delphic Oracle. See *ibid.* at 96. Professor Bauslaugh has suggested that this sanctioning of neutrality on the part of a few, selected Greek city-States was intended as a means to protect the Delphic sanctuary from violation from (what was expected to be the victorious) Persian host. See *ibid.* at 97–98. See also C. Hignet, *Xerxes' Invasion of Greece* 439–47 (1963). After Xerxes' defeat, the Spartans made a motion in the Delphic Amphictyony (for more on which, see Chapter 4, notes 200–24 and accompanying text) to expel the neutral cities. This proposal was defeated. See 2 Plutarch, *Lives* 57 (B. Perrin transl. 1917) (Loeb Classical Library reprint 1968) (*Themistocles*, passage xx.3). See also 4 Herodotus, *supra* note 30, at 71 (passage viii.73) (suggesting that neutrality in the Persian Wars was treasonous); Karavites, *supra* note 41, at 120–22.

[48] See Bauslaugh, *supra* note 43, at 74–75. See also 2 Xenophon, *Collected Works* 183 (Carleton L. Brownson transl. 1921) (Loeb Classical Library reprint 1932) (*Hellenica*, passage vii.4.7) (suggesting that the policy behind neutrality was "so that they might make peace with those who wanted it; and those who wished to make war to do so").

which were able to remain neutral for long periods of time (at least for decades in the period between 479 and 400 BCE), posed a profound threat to the Greek international public order of hegemony and dynamic balancing-of-power.[49]

More than this obvious political reality of ancient Greek inter-city relations, there was a more subtle issue of whether a city could abstain, or disassociate itself, from the political life of the Greek world by claiming a neutral status. As A. W. H. Adkins has noted, the central value in Greek political culture and public life was a competitive spirit.[50] Such a sense of competitiveness – of engagement in a common enterprise (whether it be a social group, the *polis*, or relations between Greek cities)[51] – was inimical to abstention. In short, the very dynamism of the multi-polar Greek diplomatic world meant that those States that were neutral were not doing their part in either repelling external threats or in maintaining an internal balance of power. Abstention was a virtual renunciation of what it meant, quite fundamentally, to be Greek.[52]

It was also perceived to be a moral abdication of responsibility. This was seen especially to be true in the context of declarations of war, and was discussed in the submissions made to the Camarinaeans, a small Sicilian city-State which sought to remain neutral in the middle of the Athenian campaign against Syracuse in 415 BCE. Both sides courted Camarinaean support. The Syracusan delegate, Hermocrates, made this speech:

> Nor should that precaution – to assist neither side on the excuse of being allies of both – be considered by anyone to be either fair to us or safe for you; for it is not fair in fact as the plea of right represents it. For if by not taking sides, the one who is suffering shall be defeated and the conqueror prevail, what else have you done but failed to aid one party to be saved and not prevented the other from doing wrong?[53]

Hermocrates was making a moral appeal for active resistance to an aggressor, the Athenians. Inaction, in the face of aggression, was considered ethically infirm. Nor was it considered a moral justification for neutrality that the neutral State would actively pursue a role as mediator in the conflict, pursuing an objective of resolving the disputes between the belligerents and thus bringing the conflict (and the suffering it engendered) to an end. There is no recorded instance of a neutral Greek city-State playing

[49] See, e.g., J. B. Salmon, *Wealthy Corinth: A History of the City to 338 BC*, at 380–81 (1984).
[50] See A. W. H. Adkins, *Merit and Responsibility: A Study in Greek Values* (1960).
[51] See L. B. Carter, *The Quiet Athenian* 1–25 (1986).
[52] See Karavites, *supra* note 41, at 122–24.
[53] 3 Thucydides, *supra* note 30, at 323–25 (passage vi.80).

such a role.[54] It has been suggested that this was consistent with the attitude of neutral States in seeking only self-preservation through passive resistance to hegemony, as well as profiting by trade with both sides.[55]

There is a second point to be made about neutrality as a legal concept implicated in the Greek conception of the legitimacy of armed conflict: how it evolved in its expression in treaties. In the period before the Persian Wars, it was probably thought that a city-State's declaration of neutrality was not to be automatically respected by belligerents. Instead, the neutral city was obliged to have its neighbors acknowledge, by oath, its abstention and to promise not to violate that status.[56] At this stage in ancient Greek international relations, neutrality was a status that could only be achieved by the affirmative consent of the belligerents.

The first general recognition of a neutral status for particular Greek city-States was found in the Peace of Nicias, made in 422 BCE as what turned out to be a temporary truce in the Peloponnesian War.[57] The fifth provision of the treaty recognized that the cities of Argilua, Stagirus, Acanthus, Stolus, and Olynthus were all to be recognized as neutral in the conflict between Athens and Sparta.[58] The best interpretation of this provision was that it was intended to give a measure of protection to these five Thracian cities, all of which had revolted from their tributary relationship with Athens during the first stage of the Peloponnesian

---

[54] This could have (ostensibly) been a basis for Argive abstention in the Persian Wars, especially to the extent that such neutrality was sanctioned by the Delphic Oracle. See *supra* note 47 and accompanying text. But there is no indication that this was, in fact, the intent of allowing those States to be neutral.

[55] See Bauslaugh, *supra* note 43, at 252–53. Bauslaugh draws this observation of Greek political life from such sources as Hartvig Frisch, *Might and Right in Antiquity* (C. C. Martindale transl. 1949); S. Perlman, Panhellenism, the Polis and Imperialism, 25 *Historia* 1 (1976). Argos during the Archidamian War (431–421 BCE) shamelessly profited in its trade with both sides. This fact was even parodied in 2 Aristophanes, *Plays* 45 (Benjamin Bickley Rogers transl. 1924) (Loeb Classical Library reprint 1961) (*Peace*, lines 475–77). For additional parodies of Argive conduct, see the notations in Bauslaugh, *supra* note 43, at 71 n. 2.

[56] For examples, see the fourth-century decree of many Greek city-States that they would remain neutral in Persia's war against its rebellious satraps, as long as the Persian king refrained from interfering in Greek internal affairs. See 1 M. N. Tod, *A Selection of Greek Historical Inscriptions* No. 145 (1933). There was also the 420 BCE treaty made between Athens, Argos, Mantinea, and Elis, by which all of the contracting parties bound themselves to refuse passage by land and by sea to any force proceeding under arms with hostile intent, unless all the parties unanimously consented. See 2 H. Bengtson, *Die Staatsverträge des Altertums* No. 193 (1962); 3 Thucydides, *supra* note 30, at 93–95 (passage v.47.5). See also Bauslaugh, *supra* note 43, at 34–35, 81–82, 156–58.

[57] See Chapter 5, at notes 128–30 and accompanying text.

[58] See 3 Thucydides, *supra* note 30, at 35–37 (passage v.18.5).

War.[59] The five cities were to resume paying tribute to Athens, but they were to be accorded autonomy,[60] and they would be respected as neutrals unless they themselves decided to return to an alliance with Athens. Bauslaugh has construed this provision as being an unprecedented coupling in Greek practice of an autonomous relationship (although requiring a tributary obligation) with a treaty-based recognition of neutrality.[61]

It was not until 371 BCE and the Common Peace of that year that a general multilateral recognition of the right of neutrality was made. The Common Peace ended the long, desultory conflict between Athens and her allies and the Spartan confederation (which had been aided by Persian influence).[62] The Athenian and Lacedaemonian hegemonies had simply exhausted themselves after nearly sixty years of intermittent conflict, and no city on either side wished to continue the war, especially if that meant renewed and growing Persian dominance.[63] The neutrality stipulation in the Common Peace read: "If any state should act in violation of this agreement, it was provided that any which so desired might aid the injured cities, but that any which did not so desire was not under oath to be the ally of those who were injured."[64] Athens had cynically intended this provision as a way to remain on the sidelines when Sparta launched a campaign against the newly emerging hegemon of Thebes. Ironically, Thebes quickly vanquished Sparta at the battle of Leuctra, and the Athenians found themselves in the posture of abandoning neutrality and taking up the fight against the Thebans.[65] Despite this political miscalculation, the treaty grant of neutrality was repeated in the Common Peace concluded among the Greek city-States in 362 BCE.[66]

The third detail to be considered here is how, exactly, considerations of

---

[59] See 3 A. W. Gomme, *An Historical Commentary on Thucydides* 668–72 (1956); F. J. Fernandez Nieto, *Los Acuerdos bélicos en la antigua Grecia (época arcaica y clásica)* (1975).

[60] See generally Martin Ostwald, *Autonomia, Its Genesis and Early History* (1982).

[61] See Bauslaugh, *supra* note 43, at 137–40.

[62] See 2 Xenophon, *supra* note 48, at 49–51 (*Hellenica*, passage vi.3.18). See also G. E. Underhill and E. C. Marchant, *Commentary on Xenophon's Hellenika* 236–37 (1906); T. T. B. Ryder, Athenian Foreign Policy and the Peace Conference at Sparta in 371 BC, 13 CQ 237 (1963).   [63] See Chapter 5, at note 137 and accompanying text.

[64] This text is indicated in 2 Xenophon, *supra* note 48, at 49–51 (*Hellenica*, passage vi.3.18). The passage is virtually repeated in 7 Diodorus Siculus, *History* 91–93 (C. H. Oldfather, C. L. Sherman, C. Bradford Welles and F. R. Walton transl.) (Loeb Classical Library reprint 1946) (passage xv.50.4–6), and in 5 Plutarch, *supra* note 47, at 77–81 (*Agesilaus*, passage xxviii).

[65] See Aeschines, *The Speeches of Aeschines* 185 (Charles Darwin Adams transl.) (Loeb Classical Library reprint 1919) (*On the Embassy*, passage xxxii). See also John Buckler, *The Theban Hegemony, 371–362 BC*, at 68 (1980); Ryder, *supra* note 62.

[66] See Bauslaugh, *supra* note 43, at 211–14, who carefully glosses the inscription evidence of this later provision. See also 2 Bengtson, *supra* note 56, at No. 292; Tod, *supra* note 56, at No. 145.

neutrality affected a Greek city-State's decision to commence hostilities. The historical evidence strongly suggests that claims of neutrality did not deter aggression. The most famous example of this failing in the neutrality principle was, of course, the Melian Dialogue of 416 BCE, recounted by Thucydides.[67] Melos was a small island which had been linked politically to Sparta, but which had sought to maintain its neutrality in the Peloponnesian War. The Athenians demanded that the Melians submit to their hegemony, and the Athenians rejected all Melian contentions of neutrality. The Athenian response was premised on an assumption shared by many Greeks: that it was the natural condition that the strong would dominate the weak,[68] and that a legal status of neutrality could not frustrate the fulfillment of that condition.[69] Against this grim embrace of might, the Melian argument that a recognition of neutrality was based on conventional justice (in Greek, *to dikaion*)[70] proved unavailing.

The Melian Dialogue is the literary source which most condemns international law to irrelevance in ancient Greece. The Athenian submission to the Melians is really that force and power and might are what dictate the actual behavior of States.[71] Many scholars have examined the Dialogue for notions of realpolitik in ancient Greek thought, and they are sure to find them.[72] Fewer writers have given hard thought to the legal conception of neutrality in the Athenian response to Melian claims of justice.[73] There were two legal rebuttals that Athens made to the Melian claim. The first was that the Melians had not really ever been neutral and that, by virtue of their association with Sparta, they were invested with an enemy character and not entitled to neutrality. It is not entirely clear, however, that the Athenians actually believed that the Melians were seriously to be considered as enemies.[74]

The more pertinent riposte made by the Athenians was that, if the Melian claim of neutrality was respected, it would encourage other Athenian allies, those on the mainland and closer to the theater of operations of the war, to defect to neutrality and sap the strength of the Athenian alliance against Sparta. The Athenians were as much as saying that the doctrine of neutrality was not well developed enough doctrinally

---

[67] See 3 Thucydides, *supra* note 30, at 155–77 (passage v.84–114).

[68] See *ibid.* at 159 (passage v. 89) ("[T]he powerful exact what they can, while the weak yield what they must."). See also *supra* note 50 and accompanying text.

[69] See also Rubin, *supra* note 16, at 356.

[70] See 3 Thucydides, *supra* note 30, at 157, 159, 163, 167 (passages v.86, 90, 98, 104).

[71] See *ibid.* at 159, 163, 167–69 (passages v.89, 97, 105).

[72] See, e.g., Peter R. Pouncey, *The Necessities of War: A Study of Thucydides' Pessimism* 83–104 (1980).   [73] But see Bauslaugh, *supra* note 43, at 142–45.   [74] See *ibid.* at 114–15.

in order to distinguish a State like Melos (which may have legitimately had a claim to independence and neutrality) from those being Athenian tributaries (which had no such claim).[75] In short, it was necessary that the Melians be made an example of.

The sequel to Thucydides' measured account of the negotiations between Melos and Athens is horrific enough. Athens invaded and conquered the island in 416 BCE, killed all men of military age, enslaved the Melian women and children, and colonized the island with 500 Athenian settlers. This event was reminiscent of the fate of the Plataeans, who were condemned by the Spartans in 427 BCE.[76] The Athenians were simply according the same treatment to a "neutral" that the Lacedaemonians extended.[77] Admittedly, the Melians had a better claim to neutrality than the Plataeans did. As Thucydides seemed to conclude, the Plataeans had been the consistent allies of Athens.[78] They had rejected repeated offers by Sparta (along with its (then) junior confederate, Thebes) for a "true" neutrality in which Plataea promised not to aid Athens.[79]

Despite these extraordinary narrations, there is additional evidence that, if a State's neutral status was at least initially acknowledged, it was subsequently respected. And the converse was true as well: neutrals did observe the international custom of not providing direct aid to a belligerent.[80] The most signal way that neutrality affected the outbreak of hostilities was that a belligerent force had to first get the permission of a neutral

[75] See 3 Thucydides, *supra* note 30, at 161, 163–65 (passages v.91, 96, 99).

[76] See Chapter 3, at note 23 and accompanying text.

[77] See Adcock and Mosley, *supra* note 32, at 207–08.

[78] See 1 Thucydides, *supra* note 30, at 391 (passage ii.72.1). See also C. W. MacLeod, Thucydides' Plataean Debate, 16 GRBS 227 (1977).

[79] See 1 Thucydides, *supra* note 30, at 391 (passage ii.72.1) (Sparta proposed that "[a]nd if not [alliance with Sparta], then remain at peace, as we have previously proposed, enjoying your own possessions; and be not with either side; but receive both as friends, while neither for hostile purpose; and this will satisfy us"); 2 *ibid.* at 123 (passage iii.68.1). See also W. R. Connor, *Thucydides* 91–95 (1984). Hostile forces often took hostages in neutral territories, in order to ensure the passivity of the inhabitants. See 1 Thucydides, *supra* note 30, at 181 (passage i.108.3) (Athenian *strategos*, Myronides, took 100 hostages from the Opuntian Locrians in 457 BCE); 4 *ibid.* at 195–97 (passage viii.3) (Spartan King Agis demanded hostages of the Thessalians). See also M. Amit, Hostages in Ancient Greece, 98 *Rivista di Filologia e di Istruzione Classica* 129, 137–38 (1970).

[80] Direct aid meant outright support for an enemy's host. Neutrals could, apparently, trade with and supply a belligerent without losing neutral status. See 3 Thucydides, *supra* note 30, at 263–65 (passage vi.44), 4 *ibid.* at 23–25 (passage vii.14.3). See also 10 Diodorus, *supra* note 64, at 115 (passage xix.103.4–5); 9 Plutarch, *supra* note 47, at 81 (*Demetrius*, passage xxxiii.3). On whether a neutral could pay tribute to a belligerent and maintain its status, see Bauslaugh, *supra* note 43, at 148–50.

before it crossed the neutral's territory or anchored in its harbors.[81] If a neutral gave its permission to one combatant party to cross its territory,[82] or to recruit soldiers within its domains,[83] it was expected that the other could as well. Athens respected Croton's neutrality in 413 BCE, and an Athenian army under Demosthenes was obliged to detour around it.[84] In another *cause célèbre*, the Spartan general Brasidas' march through Thessaly, during the Archidamian War (431–421 BCE), was challenged for want of advance permission.[85]

The problem of neutrality gave a sharp focus to the Greek conception of the proper grounds for starting a war. On the one hand, there was a moral reluctance shared by Greek city-States in being the aggressor in a conflict. Cities would go to substantial lengths not to be the party to initiate hostilities. This rectitude was, however, balanced with a dynamic and divisive international political culture in which diplomatic offense and geopolitical advantage were frequently discerned and responded to. This competitive spirit in ancient Greek international relations not only made

[81] See 3 Thucydides, *supra* note 30, at 263–65, 271–73, 293 (passages vi.44.2–4; vi.50.1; vi.62.2). The custom appeared to be that a belligerent could visit a neutral port with only one vessel at a time. See 1 *ibid.* at 271 (passage ii.7.2), 2 *ibid.* at 179 (passage iii.71.1), 3 *ibid.* at 275 (passage vi.52.1). See also D. J. Mosley, Crossing Greek Frontiers Under Arms, RIDA 161 (1973); Séfériadès, *supra* note 43, at 655. See also 8 Livy, *History of Rome* 71–79 (Frank G. Moore, Evan T. Sage and Alfred C. Schlesinger transl. 1922) (Loeb Classical Library reprint 1967) (passage xxviii.17 and 18) (when Punic and Roman naval forces simultaneously arrived at a neutral harbor of the Numidians, they both abstained from combat).

[82] See 1 Thucydides, *supra* note 30, at 391 (passage ii.72.1) (Archidamus demanded that Plataeans allow both him and Athens access to their city). See also Mosley, *supra* note 81, at 167–68.

[83] See 1 *ibid.* at 63 (passage i.35.3) (Corcyrans demanded that if the Athenians allow Corinth to recruit mercenaries in their city, Corcyra should be allowed also to do the same). See also H. B. Leech, Ancient International Law, 43 *Contemporary Review* 264 (1883). For a later such claim, see 8 Livy, *supra* note 81, at 523–29 (passage xxx.42) (Macedonian request to Rome to release their mercenaries captured while in the service of Carthage; Rome refused, noting that it was a violation of neutrality).

[84] See 4 Thucydides, *supra* note 30, at 67 (passage vii.35.2). So well known was this convention of going around neutral territory that it was parodied in 2 Aristophanes, *supra* note 55, at 147 (*Birds*, lines 188–89). See also 2 Plutarch, *supra* note 47, at 457 (*Cimon*, passage xvii.2).

[85] See J. A. O. Larsen, *Greek Federal States: Their Institutions and History* 143 (1968). See also 3 Gomme, *supra* note 59, at 541–43. It was not expected that a neutral could demand payment for its permission to cross its territory. See 6 Diodorus, *supra* note 64, at 91 (passage xiv.27.7) (in 388 BCE, Dionysius of Syracuse accused Rhegium of a violation of neutrality by permitting him to cross its territory, but not allowing him to provision his troops); 5 Plutarch, *supra* note 47, at 43 (*Agesilaus*, passage xvi.1) (King Agesilaus marched across territory of the Trallians without paying their toll).

neutrality a difficult concept to embrace, it sometimes obscured the sub-stantial legal grounds for resorting to armed force.[86] The conventional justice (*to dikaion*) of norms in international relations may not always have been respected, but they were perceived and pleaded in ancient Greece.

Roman just war and *casus belli*

It is received wisdom that, unlike the Greeks, the Romans scrupulously observed the principle that there had to be a just cause in order for the Roman Republic to initiate hostilities against another State.[87] The great Roman orator and statesman, Marcus Tullius Cicero,[88] said as much in *De Re Publica*, his political testament for an ideal State, where he noted that not only were the formalities to be observed in declaring war but that it was necessary that Rome's participation in the conflict rest upon a *iusta causa* or *pium*. Such a just cause could only be had where the war was waged to avenge a wrong suffered at the hands of an enemy or in self-defense.[89] Cicero said that "[t]he only excuse . . . for going to war is that we may live in peace unharmed . . . [N]o war is just, unless it is entered upon after an official demand for satisfaction has been submitted, or warning has been given and a formal declaration made."[90]

It hardly matters whether Cicero was writing extravagantly about Roman restraint and *bona fides*, because the classical literature is replete with references to Roman leaders embracing the rhetoric of *iusta causa* as being the basis of Roman moral and military superiority. Scipio Africanus, for example, is said to have told the Carthaginian general, Hannibal, on the eve of the decisive battle of Zama, that the gods had given the Romans the strength to vanquish Carthage, even when Hannibal's host had

---

[86] See generally 1 Virgilio Ilari, *Guerra e Diritto nel Mondo Antico* 38–73 (1980).

[87] See, e.g., Henry Wheaton, *History of the Law of Nations in Europe and America* 21 (New York 1845); Hans-Ulrich Scupin, History of the Law of Nations: Ancient Times to 1648, in 7 *Encyclopedia of Public International Law* 132, 138 (Rudolph Bernhardt ed. 1984); Stephen Verosta, *International Law in Europe and Western Asia Between 100 and 650 AD*, 113 RCADI 484, 502 (1964–III).

[88] For more on whom, see Christian Habicht, *Cicero the Politician* (1990); W. K. Lacey, *Cicero and the End of the Roman Republic* (1978); Thomas N. Mitchell, *Cicero, the Senior Statesman* (1991); Thomas N. Mitchell, *Cicero, the Ascending Years* (1979); Torsten Petersson, *Cicero: A Biography* (1962); Elizabeth Rawson, *Cicero: A Portrait* (1975); D. R. Shackleton Bailey, *Cicero* (1971).

[89] 16 Cicero, *De Re Publica* 211–13 (Clinton Walker Keyes transl. 1928) (Loeb Classical Library reprint 1988) (passage iii.23) ("extra ulciscendi aut propulsandorum hostium causam bellum geri iustum nullum potest").

[90] Cicero, *De Officiis* 37–39 (Walter Miller transl. 1913) (Loeb Classical Library reprint 1956) (passage i.11.34–36).

appeared at the gates of Rome.[91] Livy's report of a conversation between the Greek leader, Lycortas, and a Roman embassy in 184 BCE is also strongly suggestive that the Romans had an honest belief that a *iusta causa* would ensure Roman victory in any conflict.[92] Indeed, during the period of Roman transmarine expansion considered here, there was a consistent Roman penchant for declaring that their wars were justly fought.[93]

Perhaps the best historical account of the Roman concept of just war can be found in Livy's narration of the Second Samnite War (c. 321 BCE), fought by Rome in its early stages of expansion in central Italy. The affair of the Caudine Forks, already recounted here,[94] occurred during that conflict. Livy places the blame for starting the war on the Samnites. A *foedus* had been in force between Rome and the Samnites since 341 BCE.[95] The Samnites, it seems, had consistently violated it by interfering in the conflict with Palaipolis.[96] The Romans demanded restitution, and even went so far as to offer to submit the dispute to arbitration by a third party, something they were not normally inclined to do.[97] In any event, the Samnites refused and the Romans declared war. At first, the war went badly for the Samnites, and they scrambled to make amends to Rome. They offered to give up as a *deditio*[98] the body of their dead leader, Brutulus Papius, in full satisfaction of the broken *foedus*.[99] The Romans, sensing advantage, refused to grant the Samnites peace except under the harshest terms.[100]

[91] See 4 Polybius, *supra* note 31, at 481 (passage xv.8.2).
[92] See 11 Livy, *supra* note 81, at 333 (passage xxxix.36.12) ("pro vobis igitur iustum piumque bellum suscepimus"). We may assume that this discussion was faithfully reported. Livy's account comes from Polybius. Lycortas was Polybius' father. See Jurgen Deininger, *Der politische Widerstand gegen Rom im Griechenland, 217–86 v. Chr.*, at 123 and n. 28 (1971).
[93] See William V. Harris, *War and Imperialism in Republican Rome, 327–70 BC*, at 269 (1979); William L. Carey, Nullus Videtur Dolo Facere: The Roman Seizure of Sardinia in 237 BC, 91 CP 203, 215–16 (1996).
[94] See Chapter 5, at notes 420–23 and accompanying text. For some revisionist accounts of the Second Samnite War, see E. T. Salmon, *Samnium and the Samnites* 224–30 (1967) (who suggests that much of Livy's account of the events at the Caudine Forks was fabricated, but in order to imitate a later incident in 137 BCE, where a Roman leader (Hostilius Mancinus) was given as *deditio* to the Numantines when a cowardly truce he arranged was repudiated). For more on this, see Ö. Wikander, Gaius Hostilius Mancinus and the Foedus Numantium, 11 *Opuscula Romana* 84, 87–100 (1976).
[95] See 4 Livy, *supra* note 81, at 5–7 (passage viii.2.1–4).
[96] See 4 *ibid.* at 87 (passage viii.23.1).
[97] See Louise E. Matthaei, The Place of Arbitration and Mediation in Ancient Systems of International Ethics, 2 CQ 241, 251–53 (1908).
[98] For more on *deditio* as the means of satisfying a treaty breach, see Chapter 5, at notes 420–30 and accompanying text.
[99] See Chapter 5, at notes 340–69 and accompanying text.
[100] See 4 Livy, *supra* note 81, at 153–55, 163 (passages viii.39.10–14 and ix.1.1–2).

It was at this point that the moral advantage of the war shifted to the Samnites. Although not wanting to continue the conflict, they did so, ultimately luring a Roman army into a trap and forcing it to surrender at the Caudine Forks. Livy says that the Romans, by refusing the *deditio* offered by the Samnites, had been guilty of undue harshness and pride, *superbia*.[101] This had been amply punished by the Roman humiliation at the Caudine Forks. But Livy was very careful to say that the Roman hubris in rejecting the Samnite settlement did not invalidate the original just cause of the war. The Samnites, Livy as much as said, were condemned to ultimate defeat because of their infraction in refusing arbitration before the war broke out. Nothing the Samnites could do subsequently would deny the Romans the *iustum piumque* which they had possessed at the outbreak of hostilities.[102] And, of course, the sequel to the Caudine Forks was that the Romans themselves renounced the truce (*sponsio*) granted by the Samnite leaders, and offered up the Roman generals as a *deditio*. When the Samnites refused this offer of atonement, the war continued on its original footing with the moral balance once again (at least in Livy's view)[103] restored to the Romans. Roman victory was thus inevitable.[104]

Aside from an adversary's refusal to offer up the person who had given offense to Rome,[105] there were many other forms of international law breaches that provided the basis of a *iustum piumque* in a conflict. Indignities directed against Roman ambassadors were a common enough *casus belli*.[106] Indeed, the Romans believed deeply that a violation of the personal sanctity of an ambassador was an obvious violation of the *ius gentium*. This has already been discussed,[107] but the literary sources

---

[101] See also 1 Appian, *Roman History* 65–67 (Horace White transl. 1912) (Loeb Classical Library reprint 1988) (*Res. Samn. fr.* iv.2).

[102] See 4 Livy, *supra* note 81, at 165 (passage ix.1.10).   [103] See *ibid.* at 191 (passage ix.8.6).

[104] See Matthaei, *supra* note 97, at 251–53, for the debate between Livy and the even earlier Roman annalist literature that was sharply critical of Roman conduct in the Second Samnite War. The annalists believed, as Livy acknowledged (see 4 Livy, *supra* note 81, at 177–79 (passage ix.5.1)), that Rome had violated a *foedus* with the Samnites, when the Roman Senate refused to enforce the terms that the Roman generals made upon surrender at the Caudine Forks. Violation of a *foedus* would have automatically stripped Rome of any *iusta causa*. But the later view came to be, as Livy reported, that what was concluded at the Caudine Forks was a "mere" *sponsio*, or truce, which Rome was free to repudiate, as long as they offered up the leaders who made the *sponsio* as a *deditio*. See also Cicero, *De Officiis*, *supra* note 90, at 387 (passage iii.30.109).

[105] For another example, see 3 Livy, *supra* note 81, at 383 (passage vii.9).

[106] See Chapter 4, at notes 166–67 and accompanying text.

[107] See Chapter 4, at notes 150–67 and accompanying text.

reserved special vehemence for the observation that this was one of the gravest transgressions that a State could commit against Rome.[108]

In a similar category were breaches of treaties. Especially as Rome grew more powerful after she vanquished Carthage (at the end of the Second Punic War in 202 BCE), Roman insistence on absolutely faithful performance by her treaty-partners became a *sine qua non*.[109] Likewise, if a State that was a *foederatus* to Rome defected to the enemy, that was instant grounds for war. By the same token, and in contrast to some Greek city-States,[110] the Romans took care never to be in the position of owing inconsistent obligations to different States. In 340 BCE the Romans and Samnites were in alliance, and were at war with the Volscians. The Campanians sought an alliance with Rome in order to defend themselves against the Samnites. The Romans refused this entanglement:

Campanians, the senate considers you deserving of aid. But it is meet that friendship be so established with you that no prior friendship and alliance be violated. The Samnites are united to us by compact; therefore we are bound to refuse you arms against the Samnites, for to assist you would be a violation of duty, on the one hand, to the gods, and, on the other, to men. But we will, as divine law and human law require, despatch ambassadors to our allies and friends to entreat them that no violence be committed against you.[111]

However, when Rome had made a *foedus* with another State, an attack on that other polity's territory was considered as an attack on Rome,[112] and was a cause for war. In 300 BCE, Rome demanded that the Samnites withdraw from the territory of the Lucanians,[113] and in 201 BCE, the Romans declared war on Macedon after it had made a (probably justified) reprisal against the Athenians.[114]

---

[108] In Livy's narration of the Roman response to the Veientians' execution of four Roman ambassadors in 436 BCE, he has Rome declare war immediately and a Roman tribune challenges the Veientian king to personal combat, shouting "Is this the breaker of human treaties, the violator of the law of nations? This victim I will now slay – if it is the wish of the gods that there should be anything sacred on earth – and I will offer him up to the shades of the ambassadors." See 2 Livy, *supra* note 81, at 319 (passage iv.19). See also 4 *ibid.* at 399–401 (passage x.12) (for a later incident with the Samnites).

[109] See 4 Polybius, *supra* note 31, at 463–67 (passage xv.1) (Rome remonstrates with Carthage after truce made in 203 BCE was broken).

[110] See the example of Athenian relations with both Corcyra and Corinth, *supra* notes 33–37 and accompanying text.   [111] 3 Livy, *supra* note 81, at 465 (passage vii.31).

[112] See 2 Phillipson, *supra* note 44, at 189–90 (collecting examples of when an attack on Rome's territory, an *incursio hostilis*, was an obvious just cause for war).

[113] See 4 Livy, *supra* note 81, at 401 (passage x.12).

[114] See 8 *ibid.* at 523 (passage xxx.42). The Athenians had hastily executed two citizens of Acarnania, allies of Macedon.

Like the Greeks, the Romans often had little truck with claims of neutrality.[115] In 360 BCE, the Tiburtians were neutral in Rome's war with the Hernicans and shut their gates to a Roman force, even after the Roman generals had made solemn pledges that the city would be safe from reprisals. According to Livy, the Romans had other grievances against the Tiburtians, but their "abuse" of neutrality was the *ultima causa* for the war.[116] During the life-and-death struggle in the Second Punic War, just as in the Peloponnesian War, neutrality was either impossible or came at a very high price. The Carthaginians routinely sacked cities which claimed neutrality.[117] After their victory over Hannibal, the Romans methodically inserted clauses into their new treaties with their unreliable Hellenic allies that the Greeks could not opt out of aiding Rome by declaring their neutrality.[118]

By the same token, the Romans could be sticklers if an ostensibly neutral city did not live up to its obligations, as the Faliscans learned in 356 BCE when they gave material aid to the Tarquinians.[119] The Macedonians had professed neutrality in Rome's war against Hannibal, but actually had been in league with the Carthaginians since 215 BCE.[120] They were later called to account for their perfidy,[121] whereupon Rome declared war on Macedon. The Romans did, however, respect the neutrality of Ptolemaic Egypt in its war against Carthage, and, likewise, the Egyptians admirably kept their impartiality.[122]

Roman rhetoric and actual practice were sometimes difficult to reconcile. The Romans clearly valued the moral high ground that a proper *casus belli* granted to them. They regarded it as a signal feature of their international relations and what made them special as a State. Roman *bona fides* was very much caught up in their appreciation that the Roman State never went to war without good cause, and, just as importantly, the legitimacy of Roman military might was part and parcel of the favor the gods extended to Rome when they acted in accordance with *iustum piumque*. Nevertheless, there were occasions when Roman conduct was something

---

[115] See generally Louise E. Matthaei, On the Classification of Roman Allies, 1 CQ 182, 192–94 (1907).   [116] See 3 Livy, *supra* note 81, at 383 (passage vii.9).

[117] See 5 Diodorus, *supra* note 64, at 361–63 (passage xiii.85), in which the Carthaginians besieged Agrigentum in Sicily.

[118] The first such treaty was the 211 BCE agreement with the Aetolians, which the Greeks proceeded to break and recant no fewer than three or four times. See 7 Livy, *supra* note 81, at 93 (passage xxvi.24.12), 9 *ibid.* at 369 (passage xxxiii.34.7), 10 *ibid.* at 237 (passage xxxvi.27.5).   [119] See 3 *ibid.* at 409 (passage vii.16).

[120] See Chapter 5, at notes 311–33 and accompanying text.

[121] See 8 Livy, *supra* note 81, at 523–27 (passage xxx.42).

[122] See 1 Appian, *supra* note 101, at 127 (*Res Sic.*, passage i).

less than exemplary and scrupulous, although perhaps not to the degree that the Greeks were prepared to tolerate.

It would be inconceivable for us to imagine a Roman interlocutor in the Melian Dialogue.[123] The Roman mentality was different. The Romans very much self-consciously framed their decisions on recourse to war on legal notions of right and wrong: a *foedus* violated, a *deditio* refused, an ambassador defiled. Creative thinking could provide a convenient legal pretext for war where one did not really exist. The point, as also manifested in other parts of the Melian Dialogue, and in the other evidence of Greek and Roman practices, was that legal justification seemed to matter. What remains to be considered is what procedures were used to ritualize and institutionalize those justifications.

The rituals for starting a war and the legal consequences of an outbreak of hostilities[124]

Ancient Greek practice

As has already been intensively reviewed, ancient Greek city-States made extensive use of heralds as facilitators of diplomatic contact.[125] At no time was this as imperative as in events leading up to a rupture of relations and in the actual declaration of war and its prosecution.

The legendary accounts of the conduct of heralds, particularly in the Homeric texts, emphasize the role of heralds in seeking to obtain redress for injuries prior to an outbreak of hostilities.[126] Likewise, it was the heralds in the epic texts who aroused the warriors on the battlefield and selected the actual ground upon which the clash was to take place.[127] In

---

[123] See *supra* notes 67–75 and accompanying text.

[124] Very little is known of ancient Israelite rituals for declaring war. All that is understood has to do with the process for declaring an "optional" war against nations other than those mentioned in Deuteronomy. See *supra* notes 7–12 and accompanying text. The Talmud prescribed that there were three ritual requirements for declaring such a war. The first was the consent of the Parliament, or *Sanhedrin*, a legislative assembly known to the ancient Israelites. See Torah Sanhedrin 29b. The second requirement was the presence of the king or ruler. See *ibid.* at 20a. The third requisite was that consultation be made with a mystical ornament, the *urim ve-tumim*, worn by the High Priest. See *ibid.* at 16b. For alternative views, see Rabbi David J. Bleich, Arms Sales, in 3 *Contemporary Halakhic Problems* 10 (1983); Broyde, *supra* note 8, at 14 n. 26.

[125] See Chapter 4, at notes 48–53 and accompanying text.

[126] See 1 Homer, *Iliad, supra* note 29, at 181, 253 (passages iv.384 and v.803).

[127] See *ibid.* at 83 (passages ii.437 and 446). See also Chapter 4 at note 37 and accompanying text. See also Arundell, *supra* note 2, at 398–99.

the single combat arranged between Hektor and the representative of the Achaeans, each side elected a herald, "both men of good counsel,"[128] who, in essence, served as the seconds for the duel. Indeed, the combatants heeded the advice of the heralds to cease their combat at nightfall. Later, the heralds resolved the challenge through the peaceful exchange of gifts. The Trojan War continued, of course, but as a general mêlée and not a battle of champions. As for the heralds' role in the Greek epic text, the fighters were, in principle, free to ignore or reject their advice, but, as Peter Karavites noted, "the ultimate compliance of the duelists with the heralds' judgement exemplifies the importance ascribed to heralds in Homeric times."[129]

In the historic period, heralds were central in the process by which one city-State declared war on another. Herodotus clearly believed that some sort of formal declaration was required.[130] Typically, the city-State desiring to declare war passed a decree to that effect, and that promulgation was transmitted to the enemy.[131] So when the Corinthians finally had enough of Corcyraean duplicity, they had a herald travel to Corcyra and make an announcement.[132] On the other hand, some States dispensed with the requirement of giving notice in order to launch a surprise attack. There is evidence that Aegina began hostilities with Athens, early in the fifth century BCE, without a formal announcement.[133] In the third century BCE, Sparta began a campaign against Messenia, without either declaring war or specifically renouncing the *philia* in force between the two cities.[134] The tables were turned a few years later on the Lacedaemonians when the Epirote general, Pyrrhus, made a sneak attack. The Spartans alleged a violation of the Greek law of nations, to which Pyrrhus replied that "[w]e know well that neither do you Spartans tell any one beforehand what you

---

[128] 1 Homer, *Iliad, supra* note 29, at 173 (passage ii.276).

[129] Peter Karavites, Diplomatic Envoys in the Homeric World, 34 RIDA (3rd ser.) 41, 52 (1987). See also Donald Lateiner, Heralds and Corpses in Thucydides, 71 *Classical World* 97, 100 (1977).

[130] See 3 Herodotus, *supra* note 30, at 313 (passage vii.9.2). See Lateiner, *supra* note 129, at 103 (who collects the four examples in Thucydides of heralds declaring war: at the outsets of the Plataean affair and the Ten Years' War, at the Archidamian siege of Plataea, and the Sicilian expedition).

[131] See Mosley, *supra* note 36, at 84. See also Karavites, *supra* note 41, at 99–106.

[132] See 1 Thucydides, *supra* note 30, at 53 (passage i.29). See also *ibid.* at 221 (passage i.131).

[133] See 3 Herodotus, *supra* note 30, at 89–91 (passage v.81). See also Mosley, *supra* note 36, at 85–86; J. L. Myres, 57 *Classical Review* 66 (1943) (glossing this text in Herodotus).

[134] See 2 Pausanias, *Description of Greece* 195 (W. H. S. Jones transl. 1935) (Loeb Classical Library reprint 1979) (Messenia iv, passage 5.3).

mean to do."[135] But, once again, when a declaration of war was made it was done by a herald.[136]

A simple declaration of war by a Greek city-State, without more, did not really affect the lives of enemy or neutral nationals living within the frontiers of a belligerent. Of course, the signal distinction of being a stranger in any Greek polity was that one could be subject to reprisals at any time for any personal grievance. The practice of *androlepsia*, "man seizure," which has already been considered here,[137] would have been particularly vicious during war time. But, as we have also seen, the Greek city-States were obliged to reach an accommodation on this atavistic practice, and this they achieved through networks of exemptions from *androlepsia* given to valued aliens living in their territory (*asylia*)[138] or to the entire citizenry of another *polis* (agreements called *isopoliteiai*).[139]

What seems clear is that a declaration of war did not *ipso facto* terminate either a grant of an *asylia* to an individual, nor a pre-existing *isopoliteia* concluded with the enemy. A decree which promulgated a state of war could also terminate or suspend an *isopoliteia*, but it was not considered logically inconsistent that two cities might be at war and yet that their citizens were protected from private vengeance under the terms of the *isopoliteia*.[140] In any event, it was considered exceptional for a warring State to terminate a grant of *asylia* to a particular individual resident in the city, even if he was a citizen of an enemy State.

All of this applied with especial force to the citizens of neutral States. It was considered by some contemporary writers a grave breach of the common law of nations in Greece to execute neutral merchants, even when they were engaged in trade with the enemy.[141] So, when Diodorus

---

[135] 9 Plutarch, *supra* note 47, at 437 (*Pyrrhus*, passage xxvi.11).

[136] Oftentimes, though, a Greek city-State in adopting the decree which declared the conflict would announce that the war would be conducted without the use of heralds. This so-called notion of "heraldless" war will be considered *infra* at notes 310–17 and accompanying text. The role of heralds as facilitators of truces and the burial of the dead will be considered at pp. 257–60 below.

[137] See Chapter 4 at notes 216–18 and accompanying text.

[138] See Chapter 4, at notes 224–31 and accompanying text.

[139] See Chapter 4, at notes 237–40 and accompanying text.

[140] See 4 Demosthenes, *Collected Works* 285, 295 (A. T. Murray transl. 1939) (Loeb Classical Library reprint) (*Lacrit.*, passages xiii and xxvi) (reporting terms of an agreement between the Phaselites and Athenians). See also 2 Phillipson, *supra* note 44, at 355, 357–59.

[141] See, e.g., 3 Demosthenes, *supra* note 140, at 379 (*Timoc.*, passages xi–xii); 1 Xenophon, *supra* note 48, at 377 (*Hellenica*, passage iv.8.33).

recounts the Carthaginian seizure and mutilation of Athenian traders at Syracuse in 312 BCE, he reports it as an obvious criminal act which was the cause of later divine retribution against the Punic State.[142] Likewise, Plutarch's description of how Demetrius Poliorcetes seized a merchant ship (bringing grain to Athens during his siege of the city in 297 BCE), and his decision to execute the vessel's officers, indicates that the writer regarded Demetrius' behavior as unrestrained and unlawful.[143] When at the beginning of the Peloponnesian War Sparta executed merchants doing business with Athens, the Lacedaemonian defense was that they regarded their objectives and military interests as being threatened by continued trade with Athens. This was soundly repudiated by Thucydides.[144] Indeed, he specifically referred to that outrage as a violation of Greek customary international law (*nomoi Hellenes*).[145]

There was a delicate balance in the Greek conception of the proper comportment of neutral traders in wartime and the apparent immunities they enjoyed. Argive overreaching and avarice in the Archidamian War earned the scorn of playwrights[146] and historians[147] alike. On the other hand, numerous practices attempted to ensure the safety of private citizens during wartime. Safe conducts were routinely issued.[148] Official labels were affixed to goods in order that they not be treated as contraband.[149]

So, in these very real ways, Greek war was not "total," at least in the sense of embroiling belligerent (and even neutral) civilians. "War did not extend to everyone. Rules applied."[150] We will return to this theme – how Greek particularism in war was balanced with humanity and restraint –

---

[142] See 9 Diodorus, *supra* note 64, at 151–57 (passage xx.4–5).

[143] See 9 Plutarch, *supra* note 47, at 81 (*Demetrius*, passage xxxiii.3).

[144] See 1 Thucydides, *supra* note 30, at 381–83 (passage ii.67.4).

[145] See *ibid.* For more on this concept, see Chapter 2, at notes 133–49 and accompanying text. See also Ilari, *supra* note 86, at 192–218.   [146] See *supra* note 55.

[147] Thucydides referred to Argive conduct as reaping a harvest of profits from the War. See 3 Thucydides, *supra* note 30, at 55 (passage v.28). In fact, the word that Thucydides used was *ekkarpōsamenoi*, a rarely used construction which appears only one other place in the canon, in 4 Euripides, *Collected Plays* 83 (Arthur S. Way transl. 1912) (Loeb Classical Library reprint 1971) (*Ion*, line 815), where it has been commonly translated as "having children by another woman"! I am grateful for Robert Bauslaugh's insight on this usage. See Bauslaugh, *supra* note 43, at 71 n.3.

[148] See *Aeneas the Tactician* 55 (Illinois Greek Club transl. 1928) (Loeb Classical Library reprint 1986) (passage x.8). See also Phillippe Gauthier, *Symbola, les etrangers et la justice dans les cités Grecques* 75–76 (1972).

[149] See B. R. MacDonald, The Import of Attic Pottery to Corinth and the Question of Trade During the Peloponnesian War, 102 JHS 113 (1982).

[150] Bauslaugh, *supra* note 43, at 70.

in the next part. But it is worth remembering here that, although rudimentary and (sometimes) poorly observed, Greek procedures for declaring war did have the effect of insulating large parts of the populace from the most virulent effects of conflict.

The Roman *ius fetiale* and its significance

Any discussion of the Roman procedures for declaring war must proceed on a number of different levels. The method of exposition adopted here is, first, to recount the traditional *fetial* procedure, as handed down in the literary sources. The next step is then to consider the origins and nature of the *fetial* institution as it developed to provide legitimacy for Roman declarations of war. Although the College of Fetials has already been considered in this study (in the context of how the Romans received diplomats and how they made treaties),[151] it is with initiating hostilities that the *ius fetiale* reached its apotheosis. But, as with many rituals in antiquity, and especially those that implicated the State's conduct and legitimacy in international affairs, the *fetial* procedure changed with time, and so did its authentic legal character. This process will also be explored here, as will the ways in which modern historians have interpreted the overall significance of the *fetial* procedure as being integral to the Roman understanding of the nature of legal restraints on warfare.

It is wise to begin, therefore, with a composite picture of the "classical" Roman procedure for declaring war against another State.[152] When Rome had a grievance against a foreign State,[153] the first step was to make a demand for satisfaction, what was known in Latin as a *rerum repetitio*.[154]

---

[151] See Chapter 4, at notes 170–76 and accompanying text; Chapter 5, at notes 373–94 and accompanying text.

[152] A short narration of this procedure appears in Chapter 3, at notes 141–43 and accompanying text.

[153] It is important to indicate that the *fetial* procedure for declaring war was *not* used "against a body of people not regularly organized as a State, in the proper sense of the term." 2 Phillipson, *supra* note 44, at 344. Justinian's *Digest* specifically noted that a declaration of war need not be made against pirates or brigands. See 4 *Digest of Justinian* 892 (Theodor Mommsen and Paul Krueger eds., Alan Watson transl. 1985) (49.15.24; Ulpian, *Institutes* 1).

[154] For the use of this phrase in the classical sources, see 2 Livy, *supra* note 81, at 87 (passage iii.25), 357 (passage iv.30), 3 *ibid.* at 373–77 (passage vii.6), 4 *ibid.* at 87 (passage viii.22), 345–49 (passage ix.45), 11 *ibid.* at 153–57 (passage xxxviii.45); Valerius Maximus ii.2; Macrobius, *Saturnal.* i.16. In later periods, the phrase *clarigatio* was also used for such a demand for reparation. See Servius, *Ad Aeneida (commentarii)* ix.53 and x.14. For more on the usages and distinctions between *rerum repetitio* and *clarigatio*, see 2 Phillipson, *supra* note 44, at 329–30.

According to Livy, the head of the College of Fetials (the *pater patratus*) would be dispatched to the offending city's territory, where he would utter the formula:

Hear, O Jupiter, hear, ye territories [naming the country in question], let the law of heaven hear. I am the state envoy of the Roman people; I come, as their ambassador, in all justice and piety, and let my words gain credence. [Whereupon the specific request for reparation was made.] If I unjustly or impiously demand those persons or those things to be given up to me [in cases of a request for extradition or cession of territory], as the messenger of the Roman people, then never permit me to enjoy my native country.[155]

This combined demand and oath was made by the *pater patratus* when he crossed the frontier, when he met the first man within the enemy's territory, when reaching the city gate of the capital, and upon addressing the forum of the enemy's assembly.[156]

After making the demand for reparation, the *fetial* withdrew to Rome and waited thirty-three days for an answer. If satisfaction was forthcoming from the offending State, that was the end of the matter. If no reply was made, or if settlement was refused, the *pater patratus* again made his way to the transgressor's territory. Once there, he uttered this shorter, and more ominous, formula:

Hear, O Jupiter, and thou Janus Quirinus, and all ye gods of heaven, ye of earth, and ye beneath the earth, give ear! I call you to witness that this nation [naming it] is unjust, and does not act agreeably to law; but we will take counsel with the elders in our own country concerning these matters, and by what means we may obtain our rights.[157]

At this time, the Senate and people of Rome could elect to declare war against the State that had failed to give appropriate satisfaction to Rome's legal demand. Upon the decree (*rogatio*) declaring war being formalized, the *pater patratus* again donned his traveling garb, in order to deliver the final, magical incantation of the *fetial* ritual. He made his way again to the frontier, and, in the presence of three adult enemy males, he said:

Inasmuch as [your] State and people have transgressed against the Roman people, the senate and people of Rome have resolved, agreed, and voted that there should be war against [you]; whereupon I and the Roman people declare and make war on [you].[158]

[155] 1 Livy, *supra* note 81, at 115–17 (passage i.32.6–14). See also J. W. Rich, *Declaring War in the Roman Empire in the Period of Transmarine Expansion* 58 (1976) (Collection Latomus No. 149).   [156] See 1 Livy, *supra* note 81, at 115–17 (passage i.32.6–14).
[157] 1 *ibid.* at 117 (passage i.32.10).   [158] *Ibid.* at 113–19 (passage i.32).

With these words he threw within the enemy's territory a spear, pointed with steel, or burnt at the end and dipped in blood (*hastam ferratam aut praeustam sanguineam*).[159] At that moment, a formal, and regularly declared (*bellum indicere*), state of war existed between that nation and Rome.[160]

There are many aspects of this legendary account of the *fetial* procedure that bear close scrutiny. We can begin with Cicero's observation that "as for war, human laws touching it are drawn up in the *fetial* code of the Roman people under all guarantees of religion."[161] This statement is strongly suggestive of the combined legal and religious character of the College of Fetials, and of the war-declaring ritual that they oversaw. As was begun in an earlier chapter,[162] what needs to be considered here is how religion and law mixed in a ritual institution which purported to restrain recourse to use of force in ancient international relations.

There seems to be substantial agreement today that the *fetial* institution grew out of the practices of the small, Latinate city-States (which included Rome) in central Italy in the period 750 to 400 BCE.[163] The basic unit of organization of all of these communities was the family, and at the head of each family was the *paterfamilias*. The beginning of social order was groupings of families into larger and larger aggregations. Families, clans (*agnati*), tribes (*gentes*), and cities were in inevitable competition with one another, and these rivalries were often manifested in raiding expeditions launched against neighbors, whether for food or forage or women. Within a clan or tribe, it would be the role of the *paterfamilias* to negotiate solutions to these disputes. As between political entities of the magnitude of a city-State, it was logical that a sacerdotal college, part religious and part secular, would develop to carry out the same role.[164] In short,

---

159 *Ibid.*
160 Livy's account of the *fetial* procedure is substantively identical with that in Servius' *Ad Aeneida* ix.53. See 2 Phillipson, *supra* note 44, at 339. See also Christiane Saulnier, Le rôle des prêtres fetiaux et l'application du "ius fetiale" à Rome, 58 *Revue historique du droit français et étranger* 171, 186–87 (1980).
161 Cicero, *De Officiis*, *supra* note 90, at 37–39 (passage i.11.34–36).
162 See Chapter 3 at notes 144–59 and accompanying text.
163 See 1 Dionysius of Halicarnassus, *Roman Antiquities* 235–41 (Ernest Cary and Edward Spelman transl. 1943) (Loeb Classical Library reprint 1986) (passage ii.72). See also 3 Theodor Mommsen, *Römisches Staatsrecht* 1157–58 (1969); Arthur Nussbaum, *A Concise History of the Law of Nations* 10–11 (rev. ed. 1954); Alan Watson, *International Law in Archaic Rome: War and Religion* 6–7 (1993); T. R. S. Broughton, Mistreatment of Foreign Legates and the Fetial Priests: Three Roman Cases, 41 *Phoenix* 50, 58 and n. 27 (1987).
164 See Kurt Latte, *Römische Religionsgeschichte* 121–24 (1960); E. Rawson, Religion and Politics in the Late Second Century BC in Rome, 28 *Phoenix* 193 (1974).

the *pater patratus* of the College of Fetials served the same function as the *paterfamilias* in a family unit. He was the personification of his people.[165]

In Rome, *fetial* procedure was probably guided by custom, although both Livy and Cicero suggested that there may have been a law on such procedure, promulgated in the time of Tullus Hostilius.[166] According to Dionysius of Halicarnassus, the seventh part of the Sacred Laws of Rome was devoted to the College of Fetials, a class of priests chosen from the best families in Rome.[167] And, make no mistake, the *fetial* institution must have begun as a sacerdotal college, a keeper of religious mysteries and rituals. There are records of such archaic practices as the *fetials* using flint stones (*silices*) and sacred (*sagmina*) herbs and roots. The flint stone was probably a vestige of a pre-Iron Age form of animal sacrifice.[168] As for the plants, which are vaguely reminiscent of the objects used in Syrian treaty rituals a millennium before,[169] the thought is that the *fetials* believed that their life-giving force protected them as they traversed through enemy territory, a sort of magical talisman which reinforced their diplomatic immunities.[170]

It is hard to discern a legal institution from these aspects of Roman religion and (almost) magical belief.[171] But there was one. As Coleman Phillipson said:

The imputation that the *fetials* belonged entirely to a religious sphere is not really valid. In the first place . . . a religious connection does not necessarily militate against . . . juridical significance, and in the second place, the college of *fetials* was not exclusively a religious body.[172]

---

[165] See Thomas Wiedemann, The Fetiales: A Reconsideration, 36 CQ 480, 487 (1987).

[166] See 1 Livy, *supra* note 81, at 83–85 (passage i.24). Cicero said that Tullus Hostilius actually decreed a law on the *fetial* procedure. See 16 Cicero, *supra* note 89, at 139 (*De Re Publica*, passage ii.17).

[167] See 1 Dionysius of Halicarnassus, *supra* note 163, at 521–27 (passage ii.72). For a gloss on this passage, see Watson, *supra* note 163, at 1–3.

[168] See Servius, *Ad Aeneida* i.448. See also Georg Wissowa, *Religion und Kultus der Römer* 30 (1912).

[169] See Chapter 3, at note 53 and accompanying text.

[170] This is actually implied in Justinian's *Digest*. See 1 *Digest*, *supra* note 153, at 25 (1.8.8.1; Marcian, *Rules* 1) ("Sunt autem sagmina quaedam herbae, quas legati populi Romani ferre solent, ne quis eos violaret, sicut legati Graecorum ferunt ea quae vocantur Kerykia."). See also Latte, *supra* note 164, at 121. For an alternative theory, see Wiedemann, *supra* note 165, at 485–86.

[171] See generally, Georges Duméz, *La religion romaine archaique* (1970); Warde Fowler, *The Religious Experience of the Roman People* (1911); Herbert Jennings Rose, *Ancient Roman Religion* (1948); Alan Watson, *The State, Law and Religion: Pagan Rome* (1992).

[172] See 1 Phillipson, *supra* note 44, at 115–16.

Cicero was not being extravagant when he referred to the *fetial* procedure as being a part of the "human laws . . . drawn up in the *fetial* code."[173] The primary function of the *fetials* was to safeguard the public faith of the Roman people, the *fides publica*, or, as Varro said, "*fidei publicae inter populos praeerat.*"[174] Again, as Cicero wrote, in its function to determine whether a war was just or unjust (*bellum nullum nisi iustum*), the *fetials* enjoyed great independence; they were the judges of that issue.[175]

The emphasis on the word *iustum* was not accidental in these passages.[176] The Latin word implies both justice and regularity, fairness and procedural uniformity. Now, obviously, the ritual of declaring war (the incantations and spear-throwings) lent itself to a literal Roman vision of *iustum*. It is more difficult to establish whether the *fetials* applied a sense of legal restraint in advising the Senate and People of Republican Rome on whether a conflict would be *iustum piumque*.

Some of the evidence is circumstantial. There were, for example, very strong private law analogies to the entire *ius fetiale* and war-declaring procedure. Coleman Phillipson was among the first to suggest that the *rerum repetitio* bore a very strong resemblance to the civil law procedure of *legis actio sacramentum*, with its requirement of notice and thirty-three days' repose before proceeding before a *praetor* for a formulary writ of action.[177] Even the final declaration of war uttered by the *pater patratus* is structurally similar to that made by the plaintiff in beginning the formal action (the *manus iniectio*).[178] Of course, the civil law analogies can be taken too far, and some scholars probably have.[179]

Not surprisingly, much of the historiographic debate about the *fetial*

---

[173] Cicero, *De Officiis, supra* note 90, at 37–39 (passage i.11.34–36).

[174] 1 Varro, *De lingua Latina* 83 (Roland G. Kent transl. 1938) (Loeb Classical Library reprint 1993) (passage v.15.86).

[175] See 16 Cicero, *supra* note 89, at 395 (*De legibus,* passage ii.9) ("belli oratores fetiales iudicesque sunto"). See also 1 Plutarch, *supra* note 47, at 347–51 (*Numa,* passage xii).

[176] See Harris, *supra* note 93, at 168–69 (carefully examining the textual basis for the idea that the *fetial* procedure was considered as *ius* by the Romans). See also Latte, *supra* note 164, at 5, 37–38, 121.

[177] See 2 Phillipson, *supra* note 44, at 200–01, who relies upon Gaius' *Institutes* for his conclusions. See Gai. Inst. iv.12 and 18. For a gloss on Gaius, see 2 F. de Zulueta, *The Institutes of Gaius* 274 (1953). For more on the thirty-three-day period of repose, see Code Th. 9.40.13, reprinted in *The Theodosian Code* 257 (Clyde Pharr transl. 1952). See also Watson, *supra* note 163, at 21–24; Wiedemann, *supra* note 165, at 487.

[178] Compare Gai. Inst. iv.16 and 21 and 1 Livy, *supra* note 81, at 113–19 (passage i.32).

[179] Compare H. A. A. Danz, *Der sacrale Schutz in römischen Rechtsverkehr* 179 (1857) (who suggests a complete correspondence between the two procedures), and Guido Fusinato, *Dei feziali e del diritto feziale,* 13 *Atti Della Reale Accademia dei Lincei* (ser. 3) 520 (1883–84) (who rejects that view, calling it "artificial" and in "error").

institution has been precisely over how far its war-declaring procedures embraced a legal restraint on recourse to war. In short, how much did the *fetials* really judge the *fides publica* of Rome? Early scholarship on this issue could probably be considered to be uncritical. Robert Ward wrote in 1795 that the *ius fetiale* "would do honour to the wisest and most polished of the modern Nations."[180] Many writers in the nineteenth and early twentieth centuries were of the opinion that the *fetials* had to deliberate on the equity or intrinsic justice of the proposed conflict, before they would proceed to make a *rerum repetitio.*[181]

Maine's 1861 publication, *Ancient Law*, changed the tenor of this debate. In that work, Maine argued that the Roman sense of a law of nations was entirely subsumed in the doctrines surrounding the *ius fetiale*, what he described as the "law of negotiation and diplomacy."[182] Other writers have been guilty of this conflation of *ius gentium* and *ius fetiale.*[183] In part, this confusion is understandable since the classical sources themselves place a great deal of emphasis on the other international law consequences of declarations of war. Private rights of reprisals were supposed to be regulated by whether there was a state of war in existence between two States.[184] Declarations of war likewise figured in problems of private hospitality and immunities, as in the story (narrated by Livy) of the Roman Titus Quintius Crispinus' initial refusal to engage in individual combat with his Campanian host, Badius, even after war had been declared between the two cities.[185] Lastly, the Roman civil law was itself exceedingly exact about the private law consequences of an outbreak of hostilities, the disabilities imposed on Roman citizens taken as prisoners of war, and the correlative right of *postliminium.*[186]

In any event, there was an expected backlash against the claim that there had been a general Roman law of war. But many classicists pointed

---

[180] 1 Robert Ward, *An Enquiry into the Foundation and History of the Law of Nations in Europe* 184 (London 1795).

[181] See, e.g., R. Müller-Jochum, *Die Geschichte des Völkerrechts im Altertum* 155 (1848); Tenney Frank, *Roman Imperialism* 7–12 (1914); Leo Strisower, *Der Krieg und die Völkerrechtsordnung* 42 (1919); Alfred Vanderpol, *La doctrine scholastique du Droit de guerre* 44 (1919); J. Vogt, *Vom Reichsgedanken der Römer* 130–31 (1942).

[182] Henry S. Maine, *Ancient Law* 53 (1861) (reprinted 1986).

[183] See 1 Phillipson, *supra* note 44, at 98 (collecting these sources, including Zouche, Wheaton, and Calvo).

[184] See 2 Polybius, *supra* note 31, at 57–59 (passage iii.24) (discussing provision of the second treaty between Rome and Carthage, dated from 306 BCE, and discussed in Chapter 5, at note 362). See also Watson, *supra* note 163, at 21 and nn. 5–6.

[185] See 6 Livy, *supra* note 81, at 411–15 (passage xxv.18). See also Valerius Maximus v.1.3.

[186] An entire chapter of the post-classical *Digest* of Justinian is devoted to this subject. See 4 *Digest*, *supra* note 153, at 885–92 (49.15).

out the narrow scope of the *ius fetiale* as only one branch of a wider Roman law governing foreigners in their relations with the State and citizens of the Republic (what is properly called the *ius gentium*).[187] This debate resulted in a shift of thinking about the significance of the *fetial* procedure for declaring war. Writers came to the conclusion that the *fetial* procedure was "'merely' designed to invest a war with the character of a formally correct action."[188] Some writers challenged that the *fetial* procedure was a magnificent facade intended to cover Roman aggression and hypocrisy.[189]

Based on this approach, contemporary philologists have returned to the literary texts to check on how the paradigmatic *fetial* declaration of war, described above, changed during the period of Roman transmarine expansion, precisely the time considered in this study.[190] The hypothesis of many of these classicists is that, as Rome expanded and became an unambiguously imperial power, both the ability to adhere to ritual war-declaration forms, and the willingness to do so, decreased.

The first aspect of this was the change in the spear-throwing ritual, the *bellum indicere*, which culminated the *fetial* procedure.[191] Around 281 BCE, Rome was obliged to declare war against the Epirote mercenary, Pyrrhus.[192] The problem was that Pyrrhus' domain was across the Adriatic. In a very real sense, this was Rome's first transmarine war. Wishing to begin offensive operations immediately, the Fetial College arranged a clever bit of legal fiction to resolve the problem of how to throw the spear across the sea. We have a snippet from Servius' *In Vergilii Aeneida*:

Thirty-three days after they demanded restitution from the enemy, the *fetials* threw the spear. Subsequently when in the time of Pyrrhus the Romans were about to wage war against an overseas enemy, and found no place where they might perform the solemnity of declaring war through the fetials, they devised this scheme that one of Pyrrhus' soldiers was captured, and they compelled him to buy

---

[187] See Arundell, *supra* note 2, at 373–74; H. B. Leech, *An Essay on Ancient International Law* 18 (1877). This is discussed in Chapter 3, at notes 179–86 and accompanying text.

[188] Von Elbe, *supra* note 4, at 666–67 n. 14. For writers embracing this notion, see 3 Sir Robert Phillimore, *Commentaries Upon International Law* 79 (1879); Giuseppe Salvioli, *Le concept de la guerre juste* 13 (1918); Frederic Buret, *Le droit de la guerre chez les Romains* 16 (1888); Louis Le Fur, Guerre juste et juste paix, 26 RGDIP 9 (1919).

[189] See 3 F. Laurent, *Histoire du droit des gens et des relations internationales* 17–18 (1870); Michel Revon, *L'arbitrage international* 96–97 (1892).

[190] See Enrico Besta, Il Diritto Internazionale nel Mondo Antico, in 2 *Communicazione e studi dell' Istituto di Diritto Internazionale e Straniero dell' Università di Milano* 9, 15 (1946); R. M. Ogilvie, *A Commentary on Livy, Books 1–5*, at 110– 12, 127–36 (1965). This theory can properly be attributed to F. W. Walbank, Roman Declarations of War in the Third and Second Centuries, 44 CP 15 (1949).

[191] See Rich, *supra* note 155, at 103–04.   [192] See generally, Harris, *supra* note 93, at 267–69.

land in the Circus Flaminius so that they might carry out the law of declaring war as if in enemy territory. Later, in that place, in front of the temple of Bellona a column was consecrated.[193]

Revisionists have fallen on this account like wolves on the fold. As Thomas Wiedemann has pungently noted, there are three things about the story that make it fictitious, an "aetiological myth intended to explain a particular ritual."[194] The first is that the story implies that war had already broken out, for how else could the soldier have been captured? This raises the concern that the Romans may have (properly) given dispensation from the formalities of the *ius fetiale* when they were, themselves, the victims of an outright attack.[195] Still, the question is raised why (if they had been the victims of an attack) they had to proceed with a formal declaration.

The second problem was that Roman law prohibited a non-citizen, much less an enemy, from owning real property.[196] To have allowed the Epirote prisoner to have made this transaction, he would have had to have been manumitted, and then given Roman citizenship. All of this would have meant that the property he would have bought would not have been invested with enemy character. The third problem with Servius' account of the change in *fetial* procedure in 281 BCE was that, technically speaking, Rome did not declare war against Pyrrhus; they opened hostilities against the King of Tarentum, for whom Pyrrhus was hired as a mercenary. Throwing a spear into Tarentine territory should have been an easy matter.

For all of these reasons, many writers have speculated that there may

---

[193] Servius, *Ad Aeneida Commentarii* ix. 52. This translation was provided in Watson, *supra* note 163, at 56. The story of the forced sale of land at the Circus Flaminius was repeated in Ovid, *Fasti* 333–35 (Sir James George Frazer transl.) (Loeb Classical Library reprint 1951) (passage vi.206–08). See also Latte, *supra* note 164, at 122 and n. 3.

[194] See Wiedemann, *supra* note 165, at 481 and n. 13.

[195] In 191 BCE, the Romans were attacked by Antiochus of Macedon and his Aetolian confederates (who were supposed to be in alliance with Rome). The College of Fetials advised that there was no need for a declaration under such circumstances. See 10 Livy, *supra* note 81, at 163–65 (passage xxxvi.3). See also S. I. Oost, 75 AJP 147 (1954) (on whether war was properly declared against Jugurtha). And, as previously mentioned (*supra* note 153), a declaration of war was unnecessary in cases of conflict with pirates or brigands, or in cases of civil war. See 4 *Digest*, *supra* note 153, at 886 (49.15.7.1; Proclus, *Letters* 8); 4 *ibid.* at 891 (49.15.21.1; Ulpian, *Opinions* 5). William V. Harris has read Cicero as implying that the *fetial* procedure need not be used "if the enemy was not especially daunting." See Harris, *supra* note 93, at 166–67 (glossing Cicero, *De Officiis*, *supra* note 90, at 39 (passage i.11.36)).

[196] See Wiedemann, *supra* note 165, at 481 and n. 13.

not have existed a spear-throwing ritual at all.[197] Others have adopted the more moderate suggestion that the war-initiating procedures simply changed around the year 280 BCE.[198] After all, as J. W. Rich noted, the *bellum indicere* "was often used not to denote any specific formal act, but to mean something like 'to make public, or publicly make a war decision'."[199] The spear-throwing was simply an element of ritual magic that was replaced, with time,[200] by more secular ways to proclaim war to the enemy.[201]

Still other scholars have combined evidence of the desuetude of the spear-throwing ritual with documented changes in the manner in which a *rerum repetitio* was demanded. Harris has written that *fetials* were replaced with *legati* as bearers of demand for restitution,[202] and there is a certain appeal to the notion. It would mean that in Rome (as in Greece) a small, elite, quasi-religious group of functionaries were replaced in their duties by politically appointed and directed emissaries.[203] In the Roman case, the transition would be even more attractive, because the Roman *fetials* represented a sacerdotal college that was less universally respected than the heralds of Greece. This point ignores that the *fetials* were a common institution of central Italian polities in the centuries before 300 BCE. It also neglects the point made in this study that heralds and diplomats operated side-by-side in ancient Greece, each with their own duties. The parallel between Roman *fetials* and Greek heralds has a symmetry to it, but it is one that can be taken too far, thus blurring important differences and similarities.

What may, in fact, be more significant is the evidence which insinuates that the Romans only very rarely expected that a *rerum repetitio* addressed to another State would be satisfied. And, it has been noted that there was always a bit of blackmail in the demands made by the Romans to avert

---

[197] See, e.g., E. Rawson, 63 *Journal of Roman Studies* 167 (1973).
[198] See Mary Beard and Michael Crawford, *Rome in the Late Republic* 29, 37 (1985); Harris, *supra* note 93, at 166.   [199] Rich, *supra* note 155, at 106.
[200] In truth, the spear-throwing rite was rehabilitated by Octavian Augustus in 32 BCE, in declaring war against Cleopatra. See also R. J. Goar, *Cicero and the State Religion* 10 (1972); M. H. Lewis, *The Official Priests of Rome for the Julio-Claudians* 114–15, 138–40, 155–59 (1955); Broughton, *supra* note 163, at 61–62. The classic *fetial* procedure was also used by the Emperor Marcus Aurelius in declaring war against the Quadi in CE 178. See 9 Dio Cassius, *Roman History* 56–59 (Herbert Baldwin Foster transl. 1905) (Loeb Classical Library reprint 1980) (passage lxxii.33.3).
[201] See J. Bayet, *Croyances et rites dans la Rome antique* 9–43 (1971).
[202] See Harris, *supra* note 93, at 166–67.
[203] For more on the office of *legatus*, see Rich, *supra* note 155, at 102.

war. As already discussed, the demand made was either the surrender of key territory or the *deditio* of political leaders, neither of which was expected to be easily granted.[204] In fact, there may have only been one instance that a State averted war with Rome by acceding to her demands: Carthage's agreement in 238 BCE to transfer Sardinia to the Roman orbit of influence and the payment of a reparation of an additional 1,200 talents.[205]

Of course, it may have been that when Roman demands were less ambitious – or more negotiable – a diplomat (given full powers) was sent to deliberate.[206] In fact, consistent with the functional affinity between *fetials* and heralds, the use of the *pater patratus* may have been reserved precisely for those situations where Rome's demands were so outrageous that it was necessary to cloak the bearer of those demands with the most sacred of characters. Because it was not expected that a *fetial* would negotiate, the *pater patratus*' function was precisely the same in these circumstances as a Greek herald in declaring war.

That leaves for consideration Alan Watson's tantalizing thesis that the *fetial* procedure was one in which the Roman gods were asked to be the judges, not the witnesses, of the *fides publica* of Rome.[207] The key passage for Watson from the classical ritual is the one I have emphasized here, where the *fetial* returns to the enemy's frontier and remonstrates that the adverse State has failed to respond to the *rerum repetitio*. What the *pater patratus* says, in pertinent part, is that "I call you [the gods, Jupiter and Janus Quirinus] to witness that this nation [naming it] is unjust, and does not act agreeably to law."[208] Watson maintains that the phrase, "ego vos testor" is properly translated as asking the gods to judge, and not to witness.[209]

For Watson, the distinction is important. The gods never served as guarantors of Roman treaties, nor as sureties that Rome would be successful

---

[204] For demands of territory, see 4 Livy, *supra* note 81, at 401 (passage x.12.1–3) (demand that Samnites leave Lucania); 5 Polybius, *supra* note 31, at 75 (passage xvi.34.3) (demand in 200 BCE that Philip V forswear territorial claims in Greece). For demands of surrenders of individuals, see 1 Appian, *supra* note 101, at 79 (*Samnites*, passage vii.2) (the demand actually made to Tarentum in 281 BCE); 2 Polybius, *supra* note 31, at 51 (passage iii.20.6–10) (demand that Carthage surrender Hannibal in 218 BCE).

[205] See Harris, *supra* note 93, at 167–68.   [206] See Rich, *supra* note 155, at 103–04.

[207] See generally, Watson, *supra* note 163, *passim*. See also Chapter 3, at notes 149–55 and accompanying text.

[208] See 1 Livy, *supra* note 81, at 117 (passage i.32.10). For the full passage, see *supra* note 157 and text.

[209] See Watson, *supra* note 163, at 10–11. Cf. Max Kaser, *Das altrömische Ius* 21 (1949).

in a war declared with *iustum piumque*. As in the civil law, enforcement of a judgment was the litigant's responsibility; it did not directly implicate the Roman State.[210] So, too, in international relations. It was up to the Romans to enforce and vindicate their rights through war.[211] If they lost, that was not the fault of the gods, nor (and this is a point that I imply from Watson) would it ever be construed that, in such situations, the gods would abandon Rome to its enemies. This was especially important, Watson speculates, in the early years of Roman expansion when it absorbed political cultures, very similar to its own, of city-States that also had *fetial* colleges. Watson concludes his argument by noting that: "The *fetial* system was devised to keep the peace or, if all else failed, to ensure the gods declared a legal verdict in favor of the Romans before fighting began."[212]

If Watson is correct in his premise that the gods invoked by the *pater patratus* would not punish a faithless Roman offer of war by abandoning Rome to its enemies, one is left wondering what institutional role it had in restraining Roman recourse to war. The point must be that, at least by the period under consideration here, the *fetial* procedure was largely secularized, stripped even of its (obviously popular) drama and ritual. Gone was the magic. Gone was the religion. Gone even was the implied threat of a social sanction if the *fetials*, and (by implication) the Roman State, violated its *fides publica*.

The process of secularization – revealed in the reform of the spear-throwing *bellum indicere* and the use of *legati* in making the demand of *rerum repetitio* – shows an emergence of a distinctively legal approach to the process of declaring war. When Cicero, writing at the end of this period of transmarine expansion, spoke of the *fetial* institution, he saw it as part of "human laws," but "under all guarantees of religion."[213] There was an element of reason to be found in observing the old forms, Cicero believed, and in ensuring that there was regularity in the manner in which "an official demand for satisfaction has been submitted, [and] warning has been given and a formal declaration made."[214] The ritual had value as a procedure, even if the substantive limitation on Rome's freedom of action in declaring war may have dissipated as it rose to power.

---

[210] See Watson, *supra* note 163, at 25–26 (glossing Gai. Inst. 4.21).   [211] See *ibid.* at 28.
[212] *Ibid.* at 29–30.   [213] Cicero, *De Officiis, supra* note 90, at 37–39 (passage i.11.34–36).
[214] *Ibid.*

Laws of war

Restraint in warfare

A notable commonality among the ancient cultures discussed in this study is that they all recognized the distinction, in both language[215] and practice, between private enemies and public foes. This contrast has already been mentioned here, particularly in the manner in which ancient peoples extended hospitality and the effects of war on the continuation of that relationship between host and guest. In the context of the laws of war, the rules that ancient States observed in the actual conduct of hostilities, the distinction between enemy and foe takes on a slightly different meaning and importance.

Indeed, the difference is one that intimates a pattern to study the violent relations of nations in antiquity. The key is understanding the extent to which the ancient State recognized the need for restraint in the way that war was prosecuted against a public foe. One would normally expect that the distinction between private enemy and public foe in antiquity would simply be a license for unrestrained hostilities between nations, that when war was declared it was a "total war" in every sense of that phrase. While the State had an inherent interest in restraining private conflict between its citizens, there would be (one might speculate) no such interest when the State was in conflict with other nations. Yet, the historical evidence suggests quite the opposite: that the enemy–foe distinction tended to privilege public combatants, and that that extended to deeply observed restraints on the conduct of hostilities.

To begin the proof of this supposition, one must confront the most difficult historical evidence first: the practices of the ancient Israelites in pursuing obligatory war, *mitzva*.[216] Israelite particularism has been consistently reviewed in this study,[217] and it enters with a vengeance here. The distinction in Hebrew between *soneh* and *ojeb*, private enemy and public foe,[218] was employed in times of *mitzva* as an invitation to abandon all restraint in warfare. While the ancient Israelites recognized that not all

---

[215] In Hebrew, the word for private adversary was *soneh*, while that for public enemy was *ojeb*. See Exodus 23:4. The distinction between *soneh* and *ojeb* may have been shaped in later Rabbinic glosses on the Talmud. In Greek, enemy was *echthrós*, while foe was *polémios*. Finally, in Latin, the word for a private enemy is *inimicus*, while that for a public foe is *hostis*. See George Schwab, Enemy or Foe: A Conflict of Modern Politics, 72 *Telos* 194, 194–95 (1987).   [216] See *supra* notes 7–12 and accompanying text.
[217] See Chapter 3, at notes 32–34 and accompanying text.   [218] See Leviticus 19:18.

peoples could be classified as either clan member or "foreigner," as friend or foe,[219] the distinction in Deuteronomy was stark: those belonging to the indicated tribes[220] were to be exterminated.

These were the holy wars, the obligatory wars of the Old Testament,[221] and the biblical accounts of the excesses of these conflicts were legendary. Quarter was refused on the battlefield,[222] women and children captured in war were slaughtered or enslaved,[223] and bodies were multilated.[224] The enemy's land was laid to waste.[225] In the words of Deuteronomy, the Israelites:

shall save alive nothing that breathes, but [they] shall utterly destroy them . . . ; that they may not teach you to do according to all their abominable practices which they have done in the service of their gods, and so to sin against the LORD your God.[226]

A Canaanite city was thus put under a sacrificial ban, as a holy offering to Jehovah,[227] and no booty or prisoners could be taken.[228] All had to be destroyed. It has been pointed out, of course, that the Israelites' conduct of *mitzva* was no better or no worse than that of their Canaanite neighbors.[229]

Obviously, if the only way that the ancient Israelites practiced war was under the conditions of *mitzva*, it would be very difficult to make any argument that the idea of restraint in conflict was recognized. But the Pentateuch's commands for the conduct of *mitzva* may, in fact, be the exception that proves the rule that even ancient Near Eastern peoples recognized that there were certain norms to be respected in limiting the atrocities of war. When the Israelites were engaging in "optional" war, outside the realm of territory prescribed as the Israelite inheritance in

---

[219] See Benjamin N. Nelson, *The Idea of Usury: From Tribal Brotherhood to Universal Otherhood* xv (1949).

[220] See *supra* note 11 and accompanying text. See also Broyde, *supra* note 8, at 13 and n. 24.

[221] See generally, D. Gerhard von Rad, *Der heilige Krieg im Alten Testament* (1951).

[222] See Numbers 31; 1 Samuel 15:3 and 33 (war against Amalek); 2 Samuel 8:2 (Moab).

[223] See Numbers 31; Joshua 6–7, 10–11.

[224] See Judges 1 (thumbs and toes of Adonibezek); 1 Samuel 18:27 (David taking trophies of slain Philistines).

[225] See 1 Samuel 15:3. In Israel's war against the revolted tributary King of Moab, around 895 BCE, Elisha instructed that the Israelites "should beat down the cities, and on every good piece of land cast every man his stone, and filled it; and they stopped all the wells of water and felled all the good trees." 2 Kings 3:25–27.   [226] Deuteronomy 20:16–17.

[227] See also Deuteronomy 13:12–18.   [228] See also Joshua 7.

[229] See Walker, *supra* note 31, at 35–36 (glossing biblical texts at Amos 1:3 and 13; Judges 1:7; 1 Samuel 31:9–10).

Deuteronomy, the restraints were more notable. When Israel had to decide the fate of Syrian captives taken in Samaria, Elisha ruled that they had to be released.[230]

Even more pertinently, there is the text of Deuteronomy itself, which prescribes the rules for conducting "optional" war. These included the idea that when the Israelite host drew near to an enemy city they were to make an offer of peace, and, if it was accepted, the inhabitants' lives should be spared (although all could be made to do forced labor).[231] If they refused to surrender, the male defenders could be put to the sword, but the women and children were to be spared. Indeed, a passage prescribes that a captive woman can properly be made a wife, upon conditions of perfect equality.[232] Lastly, there is this passage:

> When you besiege a city for a long time, making war against it in order to take it, you shall not destroy its trees by wielding an axe against them; for you may eat of them, but you shall not cut them down. Are the trees in the field men that they should be besieged by you? Only trees which you know are not trees for food you may destroy and cut down that you may build siegeworks against the city that makes war with you, until it falls.[233]

Although there is dispute about this passage,[234] it seems that in context with the balance of the rules for optional wars, there was a clear idea of restraint in ancient Israelite warfare.

Some writers have gone so far as to suggest that the ancient Israelites themselves chose not to apply the strict rules of *mitzva*, even in conflicts with Canaanite nations. When Joshua entered Canaan, he made a "call for peace" which allowed the inhabitants to emigrate, to make peace, or to make war.[235] This biblical text was interpreted to mean that when Israelite forces were investing a city, they were obliged to leave open an avenue for civilians to flee from the town unhindered.[236] In this fashion Israelite law managed to distinguish combatants from innocents.[237] All who elected to remain in a town once it was invested could be treated as hostile, as *ojeb*,

---

[230] See 2 Kings 6:22.   [231] See Deuteronomy 20:10. See also Weil, *supra* note 13, at 299.
[232] See Deuteronomy 21:10–14.   [233] Deuteronomy 20:19–20.
[234] Compare the *Standard Oxford Bible* 240–41 (which suggests that this is a qualification on the total war rule of *mitzva*) with Rosenne, *supra* note 10, at 139–40 (who considers it as part of the rules for optional war) and Weil, *supra* note 13, at 296–97.
[235] See Joshua 11:19 and Maimonides, *Law of Kings* 6:5. See also Weil, *supra* note 13, at 293.
[236] See Maimonides, *Law of Kings* 6:7. See also Bradley Artson, The Siege and the Civilian, 36 *Judaism* 64 (1987).
[237] See Rabbi David J. Bleich, Preemptive War in Jewish Law, 3 *Contemporary Halakhic Problems* 251, 277 (1989); Broyde, *supra* note 8, at 21.

public enemies. And so, by the time of the Maccabees,[238] there was a "general tendency to modify the strictness of the legal regime of the war for religious duty [*mitzva*] by assimilating it to optional war."[239]

Greek particularism was every bit as strong as that of the ancient Israelites. As has already been considered, as a matter both of political philosophy and religious exclusion, the Greeks regarded those beyond the Hellenic pale as barbarians.[240] The Greeks were not, however, a unified political entity, and so local fractiousness and competition was also a feature of Greek international life. Indeed, external threats by powers such as Persia and (later) Macedon were not usually considered to be as grave as those presented by a *polis*'s immediate neighbors or nearby hegemons. In fact, like the Romans, the Greeks made distinctions between competing powers solely on the basis of whether they were sufficiently organized politically as to merit equal treatment in diplomacy or worthy of a formal declaration of war.[241]

In the epic texts this is apparent. The Achaeans' war against Troy was hardly a holy war carried out against ostensible barbarians. It barely had much sanction by the gods, who seemed (at times) to equally favor the heroes on both sides. There were excesses, of course: prisoners were sacrificed to the gods,[242] corpses mutilated,[243] mercy refused to children and the infirm,[244] and wild talk of blood and slaughter.[245] Nevertheless, there

---

[238] For more on the Israelite observance of a prohibition of war in Sabbatical years, see Holloday and Goodman, *supra* note 24, at 166. The Pentateuch does not, apparently, require such abstention, but later documents (from the first century BCE) suggest it was still followed. See *ibid.* at n. 10. See also Weil, *supra* note 13, at 297–98.

[239] Rosenne, *supra* note 10, at 140.

[240] See Chapter 2, at notes 119–32 and accompanying text. See also Schwab, *supra* note 215, at 195–96.   [241] See 3 Herodotus, *supra* note 30, at 313–15 (passage vii.9.2).

[242] See 2 Homer, *Iliad*, *supra* note 29, at 507 (passage xxiii.175). These may be the only occasions where there is a specific mention of human sacrifice to a deity, as opposed to a "mere" slaughter of combatants. By 371 BCE, if any such practice had existed, it was repudiated. The Thebans, on the eve of the battle of Leuctra, would not make a human sacrifice of a prisoner, deeming it barbarous and impious. See 5 Plutarch, *supra* note 47, at 391–95 (*Pelop.*, passages xxi and xxii). See also Walker, *supra* note 31, at 42–43 (who suggests that the Athenians immolated Persian prisoners before the battle of Salamis in 480 BCE, as an offering to Bacchus the Devourer).

[243] See 1 Homer, *Iliad*, *supra* note 29, at 491 (passage xi.145–47), 2 *ibid.* at 17 (passage xiii.203).

[244] See 4 Ovid, *Metamorphoses* 259 (F. J. Miller transl.) (Loeb Classical Library reprint 1984) (passage xiii.415–17) (Ulysses' execution of Astyanax, son of Hector and Andromache, by throwing him from a tower).

[245] See 2 Homer, *Iliad*, *supra* note 29, at 353 (passage xix.213) (speeches of Achilles after the death of his comrade, Patroclus).

was restraint evidenced in these texts. Hospitality was respected, even among enemies. Suppliants were spared, truces were granted for the burial of the dead,[246] and, as related in the *Odyssey*, limitations on the use of dangerous weapons were proclaimed by the gods.[247]

By the time of Greek recorded history (c. 750 BCE), there was a well-established ethic that there were restraints in war to be universally respected. Diodorus Siculus, writing later, said that every war, even when prosecuted in such a manner as to offend against human law, nevertheless observed laws of some kind.[248] Xenophon was emphatic on this point; he described the laws of war as being the "law established for all time among all men."[249] And so Xenophon depicts his ideal king as a warrior who makes an agreement with his foe that the laborers of the land should be let alone on either side, and the operations of war confined to those bearing arms.[250] Polybius also had this to say about the conduct of war:

> [W]hereas the taking and demolishing of an enemy's forts, harbors, cities, men, ships, and crops, and other such things, by which our enemy is weakened, and our own interests and tactics supported, are necessary acts according to the laws and rights of war; to deface temples, statues, and such like erections in pure wantonness, and without any prospect of strengthening oneself, or weakening the enemy, must be regarded as an act of blind passion and insanity.[251]

Greek city-States even made treaties in which it was agreed that if war were to occur between them, certain kinds of weapons (particularly long-range missiles) would not be used.[252]

The proof that there developed in the period of the Greek city-State a definite and universal law of war is that historians went to great lengths to elaborate excuses of necessity when these norms were not observed. This would not have been necessary if there had not also been perceived some notion that the conduct of hostilities had to be restrained. So it was

---

[246] This will be examined in great detail, *infra* at notes 341–51 and accompanying text.

[247] See 1 Homer, *The Odyssey* 23 (A. T. Murray transl. 1919) (Loeb Classical Library 1919) (passage i.261–63) (Ilus of Ephyra refused to give to Odysseus a deadly drug for smearing on arrows, saying that the gods would not sanction such an act). See also Eugène Audinet, Les traces du droit international dans l'Iliade et dans l'Odyssée, 21 RGDIP 29, 55 (1914).   [248] See 11 Diodorus, *supra* note 64, at 303 (passage xxx.18.2).

[249] 2 Xenophon, *supra* note 48, at 293 (*Cyropaedia*, passage vii.5.73).

[250] 2 *ibid.* at 81 (*Cyropaedia*, passage v.4.24).

[251] 3 Polybius, *supra* note 31, at 31 (passage v.11).

[252] See 1 *Translated Documents of Greece and Rome: Archaic Times to the End of the Peloponnesian War* 9–10 (Charles W. Fonora transl.) (2nd ed. 1983) (discussing a fragment of a *stela* found at Amarysia and treaty between Chalcis and Eretria). See also 2 F. W. Walbank, *A Historical Commentary on Polybius* 416 (1957).

that the Athenians, after they had drawn water from the sacred well at Delium, argued that such a course was necessary in the face of Boeotian aggression.[253] In the later period, when Greece vacillated in the face of Roman expansion, Aristaenus' final switch to Roman allegiance (and his betrayal of Macedonian forces) was approved by Polybius on grounds of necessity.[254]

In contrast to the professed universality of the laws of war practiced by the Greeks, Roman attitudes towards their *ius in bello* were always conditioned by the outrageously bad manners and barbarism of the peoples they fought against. In the early war between Rome and the Falerii, narrated both by Livy and Cicero,[255] the moral is readily apparent. A traitorous tutor, who had charge of the sons of the leading citizens of the Falerii, led his charges into the camp of the besieging Romans, commanded by Camillus. Camillus refused to accept the offer of these hostages, and, instead, put the traitor in chains and had the Falerii youths drive him back to the city with rods. Camillus is said to have uttered that "there are laws of war as well as of peace; and we have learned to enforce them not less justly than bravely."[256] Impressed by Roman *publica fides*, the Falerii made peace.

Again and again, Roman good faith in war was contrasted with treachery by the enemy. The Samnites tortured and then executed the men of a town weakened by famine.[257] The Lucanians mutilated the body of the slain king of Epirus.[258] The Gauls of Northern Italy used the skull of a murdered Roman consul as a libation cup,[259] and Rome's most implacable enemy, Carthage, was also the most brutal and senseless in its violations of the laws and customs of war. Partly attributed to the large numbers of mercenaries in its forces,[260] the Punic army was notorious for the *crudelitas* (in the words of the Roman annalists)[261] of its leaders. Hannibal ordered pontoon bridges erected with corpses.[262] At Agrigentum, men were dragged from the temples and put to death.[263] Passing through

---

[253] See 2 Thucydides, *supra* note 30, at 379–83 (passage iv.98).

[254] See 5 Polybius, *supra* note 31, at 111–15 (passage xviii.13 and 14).

[255] See 3 Livy, *supra* note 81, at 93–97 (passage v.27); Cicero, *De Officiis*, *supra* note 90, at 39 (passage i.11.36).   [256] See 3 Livy, *supra* note 81, at 97–99 (passage v.28).

[257] See 4 *ibid.* at 281 (passage ix.31).   [258] See 4 *ibid.* at 97 (passage viii.24).

[259] 4 *ibid.* at 459–61 (passage x.26); 6 *ibid.* at 83 (passage xxiii.24).

[260] This was the observation in 1 Polybius, *supra* note 31, at 175 (passage i.65–67), and 215–33 (passage i.80–86).

[261] See 5 Livy, *supra* note 81, at 37–43 (passage xxi.13–14); Eutropius, *Brev. hist. Rom.* iii.11.

[262] See 6 Livy, *supra* note 81, at 17 (passage xxiii.5).

[263] See 5 Diodorus, *supra* note 64, at 283 (passage xiii.57).

Umbria and Picenum, Hannibal ordered all men slaughtered, which (as Polybius noted) was customary only after storming a defended town.[264] Although some of the stories recounted by the historians were manifestly apocryphal,[265] the Roman sense of moral superiority in war was certainly not. A Roman citizen was proud to inveigh against *Punica fides*.[266]

With this in mind, it is unlikely that those Roman historians and statesmen who referred to a law of war were merely indulging in rhetoric or propaganda, although both could be (and were) achieved by such statements. Polybius considered the rules of conduct in warfare as the "laws of war," the "common law of mankind," and the "well-settled rules of human right."[267] Cicero was careful to say that:

there are certain peculiar laws of war also, which are of all things most strictly to be observed . . . And as we are bound to be merciful to those whom we have actually conquered, so should those also be received into favor who have laid down their arms . . . Our good forefathers were most strictly just as to this particular, the custom of those times making him the patron of a conquered city or people who first received them into the faith and allegiance of the people of Rome.[268]

Also, the Romans on occasion could be harsh in judgment of their own military leaders. Both Sallust and Livy were critical of the conduct of Marius in leading the sack of the Numidian town of Capsa, which had surrendered without giving resistance to the Roman host during the Jugurthine War.[269] His actions were, simply enough, declared *contra ius belli*.

All of this has been meant as exposition for the proposition that ancient people observed restraint in their international conflicts. Public war against a common foe was not, at least notionally, a license for the suspension of the norms of human decency. Excesses, atrocities, and outrages were to be expected. But that was very different from imagining that they were to be the norm in warfare. Even the Israelite tradition of compulsory war, pursued with the single-minded purpose of exterminating the enemy without any restraints on the means or objectives of conflict, gave way to

---

[264] See 2 Polybius, *supra* note 31, at 213 (passage iii.86).

[265] See 2 Phillipson, *supra* note 44, at 207 n. 3; Walker, *supra* note 31, at 57.

[266] See 5 Livy, *supra* note 81, at 11 (passage xxi.4); Sallust, *The Jugurthine War* 371 (J. C. Rolfe transl. 1921) (Loeb Classical Library reprint 1985) (passage 108).

[267] See 1 Polybius, *supra* note 31, at 259 (passage ii.8), 283–85 (passage ii.58), 2 *ibid.* at 309–13 (passage iv.6).

[268] Cicero, *De Officiis, supra* note 90, at 39 (passage i.11.36). See also *ibid.* at 391–93 (passage iii.31.111).

[269] See Sallust, *supra* note 266, at 331–33 (passage 91). See also 10 Livy, *supra* note 81, at 351–53 (passage xxxvii.21), 11 *ibid.* at 225–29 (passage xxxix.4) (discussing other incidents, including Philip of Macedon's sack of Attica and destruction of temples).

something different over time. Greek and Roman practices, although by no means uniform or civilized, showed the same progression.

Immunities in warfare

Having established that the ancient mind could actually conceive of a law of war, a *ius in bello* as the Romans said, it remains now to give content to at least some of those rules. I have largely grouped them here under two headings. This first title, immunities in warfare, speaks to the simple idea that certain places, persons, and times should be *hors de combat* and sheltered from the effects of warfare. This section will examine, therefore, how sacred places and persons were immunized, as well as how the rights of neutrals were spared. Secondly, the important topic of how truces were negotiated and enforced will be considered. Thirdly, I will discuss the extent to which quarter was granted on the battlefield and how prisoners were treated. Lastly, the distinctive ancient practices regarding burial rites will be narrated.

The sacred and the neutralized

The Greeks clearly acknowledged that certain localities and structures were sacred and inviolable (*asylia*), and that to destroy or harm them in any way was to invite divine vengeance. Accounts of such human folly and the (inevitable) punishments of the gods are cheerily reported by the Greek historians.[270] Herodotus relates that madness seized Cleomenes because when he had invaded Eleusis he cut down the sacred grove of Demeter and Persephone.[271] Alyattes of Lydia accidentally burned down the shrine of Athena at Assesos; he was deathly ill until he ordered the temple rebuilt.[272] Antiochus and Prusias suffered similar fates for their transgressions.[273] Oftentimes, after a war, the parties would arrange for the restoration of sacred objects, as in the peace signed at Nicaea in 197 BCE between Macedon and Pergamus.[274]

---

[270] For an examination of the epic texts on this point, see Audinet, *supra* note 247, at 54–55.

[271] See 3 Herodotus, *supra* note 30, at 223–25 (passage vi.75).

[272] See 1 *ibid.* at 23–25 (passage i.19–22).

[273] See 6 Polybius, *supra* note 31, at 181–83 (passage xxxi.11) (Antiochus for plundering the temple of Artemis), 257 (passage xxxii.15) (Prusias for robbing a temple).

[274] See 5 Polybius, *supra* note 31, at 87–89 (passage xviii.2). See also 9 Livy, *supra* note 81, at 367 (passage xxxiii.33). See also Elie Bikerman, La trêve de 423 av. J.-C. entre Athènes et Sparte, RIDA 199, 208 (1952), who discusses a provision regarding the Delphic Temple in the 423 BCE treaty between Athens and Sparta.

Generally speaking, observance of the rules of immunity of sacred places was widely respected. "Piety was a powerful force that influenced the collective behavior of Greek communities just as it did individuals."[275] In the vicious Athenian sack of Syracuse in 414 BCE, the temple of the Olympian Zeus was spared.[276] The Spartan king, Agesilaus, also respected temples, even those belonging to barbarians.[277] It is true that in 424 BCE, in the eighth year of the Peloponnesian War, the Athenians occupying Boeotia did commit some transgressions at Delium, for which they were charged with violating the universally recognized customs of Greece.[278] The Athenians confessed error, although noting that while they occupied Boeotia its temples were under their charge and that they would, consistent with the necessities of the war, show them "customary reverence."[279] Even the Macedonians, at the time of their conflict with Rome in Greece, acknowledged that it was part of the "laws and rights of war" to punish those that defaced temples.[280]

With the recognition of there being sacred places, it was an obvious corollary that there were individuals cloaked with a sacred or inviolable character. The priests of the temples were one obvious example. In the *Iliad*, Agamemnon had committed an outrage against Chryses, a priest of Apollo, for which act a pestilence descended on the Greek camp.[281] When Alexander the Great destroyed Thebes, he carefully spared the lives of the priests.[282] Aside from priests, individuals participating in religious festivals and public games were supposed to be immune from attack.[283] Individuals who had taken refuge in Greek temples were also to be spared.[284] Complaint was made in 322 BCE against Antipater's cruel conduct in dragging men from the altars and temples for execution.[285]

---

[275] Bauslaugh, *supra* note 43, at 38.
[276] See 4 Pausanias, *supra* note 134, at 529 (passage x, Phocis, 28.3). See also Séfériadès, *supra* note 43, at 645–46 (discussing sacred temple at Elis).
[277] See 7 Xenophon, *supra* note 48, at 125 (*Agesilaus*, passage x.1); Cornelius Nepos 200–01 (John C. Rolfe transl. 1929) (Loeb Classical Library reprint 1994) (*Agesilaus*, passage iv.7).
[278] See 2 Thucydides, *supra* note 30, at 379 (passage iv.97).
[279] *Ibid.* at 379–83 (passage iv.98).
[280] See 3 Polybius, *supra* note 31, at 31–33 (passage v.11). See also Walker, *supra* note 31, at 52–54.   [281] See 1 Homer, *Iliad*, *supra* note 29, at 37 (passage i.442–45).
[282] 7 Plutarch, *supra* note 47, at 25–55 (*Alexander*, passage xi).
[283] See 2 Phillipson, *supra* note 44, at 271 and n. 2 (discussing inscription evidence of the Aetolian protection granted to musicians and actors of the Dionysian festival). See also Audinet, *supra* note 247, at 39–40.
[284] See 2 Plutarch, *Moralia* 463–67 (F. C. Bobbitt transl. 1928) (Loeb Classical Library reprint 1962) (*De superst.*, passage iv). See also 7 Diodorus, *supra* note 64, at 279 (passage xvi.14).
[285] See 4 Polybius, *supra* note 31, at 67–69 (passage ix.29). See 2 *ibid.* at 385–87 (passage iv.35) (calling a similar outrage a gross act of sacrilege).

Proxenoi were often granted protection from attack both by their city of origin and adopted *polis*.[286] Lastly, as has already been considered in substantial detail in this study,[287] heralds were given virtual immunity from harm, even while the more secular class of envoys were not given such expansive protections.

There are thus two explanations for the Greek respect of sacred places and persons in wartime. The first, as suggested by Bauslaugh[288] and Séfériadès,[289] is that the protection of certain sanctuaries was critical to the existence of civilized life in Greece. This was notorious even to barbarian States, including the Persians, who were desirous on occasion to gain propaganda advantages by making shows of respecting Greek sanctuaries.[290] Transgressions against the immunities of the pan-Hellenic shrines were met often with the declaration of sacred wars, initiated by the members of the *amphictyony* of cities which protected the sanctuary.[291]

The second explanation is more subtle, and connects with the earlier discussion in this chapter of the Greek conception of neutrality. Sanctuaries such as those at Delphi and Elis, also served secular purposes that have already been mentioned in this study. These included the preservation and judicial enforcement of treaties,[292] the occasional arbitration of international disputes,[293] and the giving of supposedly impartial advice regarding international acts. Religious shrines thus served important functional purposes for the Greek international community, and thus were neutralized in a secular sense.

From this, it was but a short step for the Greeks to recognize, by

---

[286] See W. Dittenberger, *Sylloge Inscriptionum Graecarum* No. 110 (3rd ed. 1915–25) (Rhodian decree of c. 410 BCE granting *proxenoi* this right). See also Chapter 4, at notes 259–85 and accompanying text.   [287] See Chapter 4, at notes 113–47 and accompanying text.

[288] See Bauslaugh, *supra* note 43, at 39.

[289] See Séfériadès, *supra* note 43, at 647–48. See also W. Kolbe, Neutrality of Delos, 50 JHS 20 (1930); M. M. W. Tarn, The Political Standing of Delos, 44 JHS 141 (1924).

[290] See 3 Herodotus, *supra* note 30, at 249 (passage vi.97.2) (where Datis, general of Darius, says to the priests of Delos that "the King's command to me [is] to do no harm to the land in which the two gods were born, neither to the land itself or the inhabitants").

[291] As has been previously mentioned, see Chapter 5, at notes 213–16 and accompanying text, three Sacred Wars were fought to protect the Delphic shrine. See L. H. Jeffrey, *Archaic Greece: The City-States, c. 700–500*, at 73–74 and 81 (1976) (for the First Sacred War in the sixth century); 1 H. W. Parke and D. E. W. Wormell, *The Delphic Oracle* 184–86, 216–32 (1956).

[292] See Chapter 5, at note 238 and accompanying text. See also P. Siewert, L'autonomie de Hyettos et la sympolitie thespienne dans les Helleniques d'Oxyrhynchos, 90 *Revue des études Grecques* 463 (1977).

[293] See Chapter 3, at notes 170–73 and accompanying text. See also 1 L. Piccirilli, *Gli arbitrati interstatali greci: Dalle origini al 338 aC*, No. 8 (1973) (documentary fragment showing Delphic temple's use as an arbitrator).

treaty, that certain secular locales were to be perpetually neutralized and protected from military assault. These designations were different from the recognition of "occasional" neutrality already considered in this chapter. Instead, the idea was that cities could be lastingly immunized from the effects of war. Alalcomenae, an unfortified town in Boeotia which had Athena as its tutelary deity, was given this status.[294] The territory around Teos in Asia Minor was neutralized by a treaty concluded with neighboring cities. The precincts of the town of Teos were declared inviolable and immune from pillage, its citizens free from reprisal, and their goods exempt from confiscation.[295] The Romans even adhered to this agreement in 193 BCE.[296]

Truces

Having considered the immunities in war associated with places and persons, the next issue is the extent to which temporary lulls in hostilities were made and respected. This already has been the subject of intense consideration in this study, because the process for negotiating and enforcing truces was part and parcel of the dynamic of making faith in antiquity. The great *causes célèbres* of classical treaties – the broken *sponsio* at the Caudine Forks[297] and the shattered Peace of Nicias of 421 BCE[298] – were both, in fact, truces.

In Greece, the concept of temporal immunities in wartime, of general truces operating throughout the Greek domain, can be traced to the great pan-Hellenic festivals.[299] When the time of the festival of games approached, truce-bearers (*spondophoroi*) were dispatched to proclaim the sacred truce in all of the affected communities,[300] and once the proclama-

[294] See 4 Strabo, *The Geography* 331–33 (H. L. Jones transl. 1927) (passage ix.2.36).

[295] An extant inscription records the terms of this agreement; see C. Michel, *Recueil d'inscriptions grecques* No. 68 (1900).

[296] See 2 A. Boeckh, E. Curtius, A. Kirchoff and H. Roehl, *Corpus inscriptionum Graecarum* no. 3046, at 633 (1877).   [297] See Chapter 5, at notes 420–23 and accompanying text.

[298] See Chapter 5, at notes 128–32 and accompanying text. See also Bikerman, *supra* note 274, at 209. For the terms of the Peace, see the passage in 2 Thucydides, *supra* note 30, at 395–99 (passage iv.118).

[299] There were many local festivals observed only by those cities that shared the same cult or temple or hearth. In 367 BCE, the Athenians, for example, declared a fifty-five-day truce to celebrate the Greater Eleusinian Mysteries, an Attic tradition. See 2 Tod, *supra* note 56, at No. 137 (inscription recording this proclamation).

[300] Curiously, *spondophoroi* may have not been accorded the treatment due to heralds. The Athenians proclaiming the truce for the Eleusinian Mysteries were seized by the citizens of Trichoneia. They were released, however, when a herald made a demand upon the Aetolian League. See Adcock and Mosley, *supra* note 32, at 199–200.

tion was made, combatants were obliged to desist from hostilities for the sacred month (*hieromenia*).[301]

This rule was what gave rise to one of the many disputes between Plataea and Thebes, a conflict which culminated in the massacre of the Plataean garrison. One of the submissions made by the Plataean deputies was that the Thebans "came not only in time of peace, but at a holy season, and attempted to seize our city; we righteously and in accordance with universal law defended ourselves and punished the aggressor."[302] The Thebans concurred that if they had done such an act it would have been a grave breach of Hellenic custom; they simply denied that they had made any offensive move against Plataea during the holy truce.[303] Likewise, the Spartans were disqualified from participating in the Olympic Games in 420 BCE, because, in an earlier olympiad, they had violated the truce. The only defense raised by the Lacedaemonians was that the truce had not yet been proclaimed at Sparta when they made the attack.[304]

There were occasions when one side attempted cynically to induce a holy truce in order to gain a respite from conflict.[305] In 388 BCE, the Argives attempted to forestall an imminent Spartan attack by declaring an ancestral truce, supposedly recognized by all Dorian cities. Undeterred, the Lacedaemonians went to the Delphic Oracle for a determination whether such a truce was to be recognized. The Oracle declared that there was no authority for such an observance, and Spartan offensive operations against Argos promptly resumed.[306]

The vast majority of truces occurring in conflicts engaged in by the Greeks or Romans had nothing to do with observing a religious festival.[307] These were negotiated out of political or military necessity. On some occasions, a truce was used as a preliminary to negotiating a general

---

[301] See 2 Thucydides, *supra* note 30, at 97–99 (passage iii.56), 115–17 (passage iii.65), 3 *ibid.* at 107 (passage v.54). This rule applied even when the Greeks were engaged in a war against outsiders, such as Persia. It was reported that the observance of the Carnean and Hyacinthian festivals in 480 BCE resulted in Greek delays in defending against the Persian attack. See 3 Herodotus, *supra* note 30, at 523 (passage vii.206), 4 *ibid.* at 169 (passage ix.11). For an analogy to the Jewish observance of the Sabbatical Year, see *supra* note 238. For more on the timing and duration of Greek festivals, see H. Popp, *Die Einwirkung von Vorzeichen, Opfern und Festen auf die Kriegführung der Griechen im 5. und 4. Jahrhundert v. Chr.* 75–144 (1957).

[302] See 2 Thucydides, *supra* note 30, at 91–125 (passage iii.56.2).

[303] See *ibid.* at 115–17 (passage iii.65).   [304] See *ibid.* at 99 (passage v.49).

[305] See Holloday and Goodman, *supra* note 24, at 153–54.

[306] See 1 Xenophon, *supra* note 48, at 349 (*Hellenica*, passage iv.7.2).

[307] See Adcock and Mosley, *supra* note 32, at 199–202.

peace,[308] as in the abortive Peace of Nicias.[309] This use of truces posed, however, a problem to military commanders, fearful of mutiny or flagging morale. As a consequence, there developed, in ancient Greece at least, the concept of "heraldless war." This phrase, as noted by Mosley, was given various meanings in the literary texts, including a conflict begun without declaration.[310]

But "heraldless war" typically referred to a situation where a military force would not entertain discussions with heralds coming from the enemy in order to negotiate truces.[311] There was, for example, concern among the generals of the Ten Thousand, the Greek expeditionary force operating against Persia, that the barbarians would attempt to induce dissent and mutiny when they came to negotiate. The leaders thus declared that, while in enemy territory, they would not entertain Persian heralds.[312] When in 432 BCE, the Megarians murdered the Athenian herald, Anthemocritus, Athens declared that there would be a heraldless war against them.[313] A declaration of "heraldless war," while certainly indicating that it would be conducted implacably, as Aeschines and Plutarch wrote,[314] did not mean that an enemy herald would be killed. He simply would not be allowed to negotiate.[315]

The practice of "heraldless" or "truceless" war was vigorously opposed by Greek intellectuals as being political folly in having the effect of putting envoys at risk.[316] Mosley describes such declarations as having

---

[308] See 2 Thucydides, *supra* note 30, at 237 (passage iv.15.2) (Athens and Sparta after Battle of Pylos), 3 *ibid.* at 115 (passage v.59.5) (Sparta and Argos). See also M. James Moscovich, Hostage Regulation in the Treaty of Zama, 23 *Historia* 417, 422–23 (1974–75); Karavites, *supra* note 41, at 27–30.

[309] One provision of that Peace allowed for the "safe-conduct both by sea and land for a herald, with envoys, and any number of attendants which may be agreed upon, passing to and fro between the Peloponnesus and Athens, to make arrangements about the termination of the war and about the arbitration of disputed points." 2 Thucydides, *supra* note 30, at 413 (passage iv.118).

[310] See Mosley, *supra* note 36, at 85–86 (discussing the incident of Aegina's attack on Athens, discussed *supra* at note 133 with text).

[311] See 2 Demosthenes, *supra* note 140, at 191–93 (*De Corona*, passage xviii.262).

[312] See 3 Xenophon, *supra* note 48, at 217–19 (*Anabasis*, passage iii.3.5).

[313] See 2 Plutarch, *supra* note 47, at 87 (*Pericles*, passage xxx.3).

[314] See Aeschines, *supra* note 65, at 189 (passage ii.37); 3 Plutarch, *supra* note 47, at 87 (*Pericles*, passage xxx).

[315] This occurred with the Ten Thousand, after their announcement of heraldless war. See 3 Xenophon, *supra* note 48, at 293 (*Anabasis*, passage iv.4.4). But see the Athenian decree of Charinus, passed after Anthemocritus' murder, which is strongly suggestive that a Megarian herald would be executed if he entered Attica. See 3 Plutarch, *supra* note 47, at 87 (*Pericles*, passage xxx.2). See also Mosley, *supra* note 36, at 87 (interpreting this passage).   [316] See Aeschines, *supra* note 65, at 219–21 (passage ii.80).

"more emotional than legal or diplomatic significance."[317] The Romans, in any event, did not appear to have any analogue to the concept.

Granting quarter and taking prisoners

No area of the ancient law of war was more controversial than whether a victorious host should spare the lives of enemy soldiers that laid down their arms in surrender. It is impossible, really, to draw any conclusions on this point. As has already been suggested, the Israelites had a partially developed sense that in certain situations it was possible to give quarter to those that had surrendered without a fight.[318]

Euripides has a character in *Heraclidae* condemn the practice of not granting quarter to prisoners by saying: "It is not possible for you to put [the prisoner] to death . . . not anyone they have taken alive in battle."[319] The Speech of the Plataean Deputies, discussed as a narrative in Chapter 3,[320] has as its central theme the answer to the Plataean proposition "that we surrendered ourselves, and stretched out our hands to you; the custom of Hellas does not allow the suppliant to be put to death."[321] But, remember, the Plataeans had been less than scrupulous in dealing earlier with the Theban vanquished, and the Boeotians demanded that the Spartans "[m]aintain . . . the common Hellenic law which [the Plataeans] have outraged, and give to us, who have suffered contrary to law, the just compensation of our zeal in your cause."[322] In short, both the Plataeans and the Thebans agreed on the content of the unwritten Greek law of war. The only question was whether the Plataeans, by virtue of their earlier offense, were any longer entitled to beneficial treatment. The Spartans ruled that they were not.

---

[317] Mosley, *supra* note 36, at 87.

[318] See Deuteronomy 20:10. See also Weil, *supra* note 13, at 299.

[319] 3 Euripides, *Collected Plays* 329 (Arthur S. Way transl. 1912) (Loeb Classical Library reprint 1971) (*Children of Hercules*, lines 965–71).

[320] See at note 23 and accompanying text. It is worth summarizing here Thucydides' historical narrative involving Plataea. In 431 BCE, a Theban force entered Plataea (arguably during a religious festival) in order to provoke a coup against the ruling regime. This was repulsed, and the Theban force was taken captive and executed, despite attempts by an Athenian herald to stop the killings. See 1 Thucydides, *supra* note 30, at 269 (passage ii.6.2). Two years later, in 429 BCE, the Thebans and Spartans invested Plataea. The siege lasted a year. Although part of the Plataean garrison escaped, the remainder starved and then surrendered, upon assurances by the Spartans that none would be unjustly condemned. 2 *ibid.* at 91 (passage iii.52.2–3).

[321] 2 Thucydides, *supra* note 30, at 103–05 (passage iii.58).

[322] *Ibid.* at 117–19 (passage iii.66). See also Karavites, *supra* note 41, at 85–90 (for more on mercy in Greek warfare).

Roman practice was also mixed. Notionally, if the surrender of a city occurred before the Roman battering ram touched the principal wall, the lives even of the male population were to be spared. So it was when, in 209 BCE, Scipio the Elder captured Nova Carthago in Spain.[323] However, in 107 BCE, Marius did slaughter the defenders at Capsa, conduct which Sallust regarded as *contra ius belli*.[324] Roman atrocities occurred at the sieges of Ausona in 314 BCE,[325] at Saepinum in 293 BCE,[326] at Henna in 214 BCE,[327] at Tarentum in 209 BCE,[328] at Antipatrea in 200 BCE,[329] and at Corinth in 146 BCE.[330]

If combatants were spared, they were subject to being held hostage or made slaves. This was the practice in Greece since epic times.[331] In the Trojan War, according to Homer, the Achaeans routinely enslaved the populations they vanquished.[332] According to the *Iliad*, some Trojan soldiers became the hostages of those that had defeated them in combat, while women and children were enslaved to serve the needs of the army.[333] Despite the legitimacy given by the epic texts to the practice of making laborers of Greek prisoners, it was subject to harsh criticism by later philosophers. Plato strongly opposed the enslaving of Hellenes by people of the same race.[334]

In the historic period, prisoners of war could be returned unconditionally after peace was negotiated,[335] ransomed for money,[336] or kept as slaves.[337] During the course of the war, prisoners could be used as hostages

---

[323] See Scupin, *supra* note 87, at 138.   [324] Sallust, *supra* note 266, at 333 (passage 91).

[325] See 4 Livy, *supra* note 81, at 259 (passage ix.25).   [326] See *ibid.* at 535 (passage x.45.14).

[327] See 6 *ibid.* at 299–301 (passage xxiv.39.6) (against an unarmed allied population suspected of disloyalty to Rome).   [328] See 7 *ibid.* at 275 (passage xxvii.16.5–7).

[329] See 9 *ibid.* at 81 (passage xxxi.27.4) (all young men killed).

[330] See 3 Pausanias, *supra* note 134, at 259 (vii, Achaia, passage 16.8).

[331] See 1 Homer, *Odyssey*, *supra* note 247, at 31–33 (passage i.398).

[332] See 2 Homer, *Iliad*, *supra* note 29, at 457 (passage xxii. 44–45).

[333] See Audinet, *supra* note 247, at 42–43 (for a close textual analysis of key passages in the *Iliad*).

[334] See 1 Plato, *Republic* 499–501 (Paul Shorey transl. 1930) (Loeb Classical Library reprint 1982) (passage v.471).

[335] See, e.g., 8 Diodorus, *supra* note 64, at 83 (passage xvi.87.3) (after the battle of Chaeronea in 338 BCE, Philip released all Greek prisoners without ransom). See also Onasander, *The General* 489 (Illinois Greek Club transl. 1928) (Loeb Classical Library reprint 1986) (passage xxxv.4–5) (a manual for military leaders). See also Moscovich, *supra* note 308, at 417.

[336] See, e.g., 4 Thucydides, *supra* note 30, at 177–79 (passage vii.87) (Athenian prisoners at Syracuse); 3 Herodotus, *supra* note 30, at 87 (passage v.77) (Euboeans).

[337] During the Sicilian War, Athenian prisoners were kept in a camp in a Syracusan quarry, where conditions were horrific. See 4 Thucydides, *supra* note 30, at 177–79 (passage vii.87.1–2). See also P. Ducrey, *Le Traitement des prisonniers de guerre dans la Grèce antique, Des origines à la conquête Romaine* (1968).

in order to compel the enemy to come to terms.[338] Prisoner exchanges during truces or after treaties of peace were quite common.[339] The Peace of Nicias of 421 BCE had such a provision.[340]

Burial rites

One of the peculiar immunities in war recognized by the ancient Greeks was corpse retrieval. Indeed, the literature on the subject is vast, far out of the proportion that one might expect for the topic. It is critical to examine how the Greeks came to endow this subject with such signifi-cance, an importance that was not replicated either in ancient Near Eastern societies or in Western Mediterranean cultures.

The beginnings must be traced to the *Iliad*. Stories of corpse retrieval litter the narrative, and although there remains scholarly dispute about many of the passages,[341] broad patterns can be detected. Most of the war scenes in the *Iliad* feature a victor desiring to acquire the armor from the body of his vanquished enemy. For example, when Menelaus made his speech enumerating the violations of the Trojans, he stripped only the armor from the Trojan he had just killed.[342] An earlier battle sequence elaborates the efforts made to recover the armor of the dead as war spoils: "[H]e dropped, and the armor elaborate with the bronze clashed about him, and Teukros ran up, eager to strip the armor . . . Then Hektor charged in to tear the helm of great-hearted Amphimachos from his head where it fitted close on the brows."[343]

These passages indicate only that the custom was that to the victor went the spoils. But in the duel between the Achaean, Patroklos, and the Trojan, Sarpedon, the behavior of the combatants began to diverge from the

---

[338] See Amit, *supra* note 79, at 146 (glossing 2 Thucydides, *supra* note 30, at 283 (passage iv.40) (fate of the Spartans surrendered at Sphacteria in 425 BCE)).

[339] See Aristotle, *Nicomachean Ethics* 313 (H. Rackham transl. 1926) (Loeb Classical Library reprint 1990) (passage v.10 (1134b)) (discussing such a prisoner transfer and ransoming between Athens and Sparta, in 408 BCE).

[340] See 3 Thucydides, *supra* note 30, at 37 (passage v.18.7). The Romans and Carthaginians exchanged prisoners towards the end of the First Punic War, in 242 BCE, and in the Second Punic war with Hannibal. See 5 Livy, *supra* note 81, at 279 (passage xxii.23.6).

[341] The dispute has been largely between Lateiner, *supra* note 129, at 99–101 (who argues that there was an obligation not to mutilate the dead, or take them as trophies, and the affirmative obligation to observe truces to bury the dead) and Audinet, *supra* note 247, at 43–44 (who argues that the corpses of the enemy received no respect, were routinely defiled, and, in fact, victory in epic Greece would not be complete without such acts).   [342] See 2 Homer, *Iliad*, *supra* note 29, at 51 (passage xiii.640–42).

[343] *Ibid.* at 17 (passage xiii.181–89).

norm. When Patroklos slayed Sarpedon, he allowed the Trojan's body to be carried into the Greek camp. When Hektor, in turn, killed Patroklos, the Trojans attempted to take Patroklos' body and use it as a means to force the Achaeans to return Sarpedon's corpse.[344] The cycle of revenge was completed when Achilles killed Hektor in the ultimate duel of the book, and then ordered the defilement of Hektor's body: "Hektor was dragged, his dark hair was falling about him, and all that head that was once so handsome was tumbled in the dust; since by this time Zeus had given him over to his enemies, to be defiled in the land of his fathers."[345]

This act, a sin "against the most sacred international law of Greece" and "principles universally accepted,"[346] nearly brings divine retribution. Apollo says that "Great as [Achilles] is, let him take care not to make us angry; for see, he does dishonor to the dumb earth in his fury."[347] Ultimately, Zeus intervenes and suggests that Priam give gifts to the Achaean camp, and Hektor's body is returned.[348] A truce is called, and both sides agree to abide by the duty to return the bodies of warriors fallen in battle. Order is restored. It is no surprise, therefore, that ancient Greeks, as Adrastus noted in Euripides' play, *The Suppliants*,[349] equated the rules regarding burial of war dead with "Hellenism and Panhellenic morality itself."[350] Those who prevented the proper respect for the dead were criminals who confounded and destroyed Hellenic customs.[351]

Greek accounts of battlefield deeds must be read in this epic context.[352] Military commanders were under an obligation to seek to recover the bodies of their soldiers after battle. A hasty retreat, in which this duty was

---

[344] *Ibid.* at 243 (passage xvii.156–63) (the Trojans say: "If [Patroklos] dead man though he be, could be brought into the great city of lord Priam, if we could tear him out of the fighting, the Argives must at once give up the beautiful armor of Sarpedon, and we could carry his body inside Ilion.").   [345] *Ibid.* at 485 (passage xxii.401–04).

[346] 6 George Grote, *History of Greece* 393–95 (1864). Compare Karavites, *supra* note 41, at 23–24 (glossing Herodotus ix.78–79), with Leonard A. Curchin, The Unburied Dead at Thermopylae, 9 *Ancient History Bull.* 68 (1995) (who questions the universality of the custom of burying the dead on the battlefield) (analyzing Pausanias x.21.6).

[347] 2 Homer, *Iliad*, *supra* note 29, at 565–67 (passage xxiv.40–54).

[348] *Ibid.* at 569 (passage xxiv.75–76).

[349] 3 Euripides, *supra* note 319, at 525, 541, 553 (*Suppliants*, lines 312–13, 524–27, 537–40, 670–72).

[350] Lateiner, *supra* note 129, at 99. See also Isocrates, *Panath.* line 170 (where Thebans' refusal to allow burial of fallen enemies was regarded as a violation of "Greek common law").   [351] 3 Euripides, *supra* note 319, at 525 (*Suppliants*, line 311).

[352] See J. K. Anderson, *Military Theory and Practice in the Age of Xenophon* 3–4 (1970); 2 W. K. Pritchett, *The Greek State at War* 251 (1974); P. Ducrey, Aspects juridiques de la victoire et du traitement des vaincus, in *Problèmes de la guerre en Grèce ancienne* 231 (J.-P. Vernant ed. 1968).

forgotten, could lead to censure or condemnation back home.[353] Once again, the role of the heralds was positively crucial in facilitating the conclusion of a truce after a battle, in order that the respective belligerents could recover, identify, and bury their war dead. Of the thirty-three times that heralds are mentioned in Thucydides, eleven occasions involve their making a request for a truce to bury the dead.[354] Indeed, it has been noted that there is a definitive progression in Thucydides' narratives of burial rites during the Peloponnesian War. Essentially the story is of the Athenian descent into defeat and barbarity.

After the Battle of Delion between Athens and Thebes in 424 BCE, there was a legal stand-off. The Athenian offensive was blunted at Delion, decisively ending that phase of the Ten Years War.[355] Although defeated on the battlefield, the Athenians sought to retain a key fortification astride the Boeotians' lines of communication and advance. The problem was that it was a temple. The Boeotians refused, therefore, to allow the Athenians to recover the bodies of their fallen comrades until they withdrew from the temple precincts. The ensuing negotiation was conducted between two heralds, one from each side, which was (apparently) a unique occurrence.[356] Each side argued that the other's transgression was the worse sacrilege (*to asebein*). All of this was clearly a cover for military advantage.

Nevertheless, the language used by the heralds of the two sides was essentially legal; both argued consistently as to the legality of occupying shrines or of refusing to return corpses.[357] A few weeks later, the Thebans ejected the troublesome Athenian force in the temple, and, later, an Athenian herald was allowed to collect the bodies.[358] In the meantime, they had badly decomposed. This incident started a trend by which sacred acts became the subject of meaningless debate. The Athenians met with disaster in the Sicilian War, and, with each military reverse, they became more and more callous about their war dead. They were overcome by

---

[353] See 1 Xenophon, *supra* note 48, at 67–69 (*Hellenica*, i.7) (prosecution of Athenian generals after battle of Arginusae).

[354] See Lateiner, *supra* note 129, at 99. Some of these mentions of heralds and corpses in Thucydides are purely literary. See 2 Thucydides, *supra* note 30, at 199–201 (passage iii.113.1 and 5) (Ambraciote herald stunned at seeing the bodies heaped on the field at Idomene). See also 5 Dio Chrysostom 247 (H. Lamar Crosby transl. 1951) (Loeb Classical Library reprint 1985) (*On Law*, lxv. 9) (noting role of heralds in burial of dead).

[355] See 2 Thucydides, *supra* note 30, at 365–79 (passages iv.89–97).

[356] *Ibid.* at 379 (passage iv.97.3).

[357] See 3 Gomme, *supra* note 59, at 570. See also Onasander, *supra* note 335, at 491 (passage xxxvi).

[358] See 2 Thucydides, *supra* note 30, at 385 (iv.101.1). See also Mosley, *supra* note 36, at 84–85.

ataphos, a situation in which (according to Thucydides) their spirit was crushed so much, so "overwhelmed by their evils, [they began] to ignore both divine and human concerns."[359]

After the war

Burial rites in ancient Greek war practice were a constant reminder that the condition of man was not to engage in hostilities with his neighbors. Many of the laws of war just considered, including the granting of truces and immunizing heralds, must have been intended to facilitate reconciliation. It is a point that needs to be tested, at least in the context of how ancient States made the transition from war back to peace. This examination has already been done in the setting of peace treaties,[360] but it is worth considering (however briefly) the actual laws of war which governed the conclusion of hostilities and legal status of the victor and vanquished.

It was, for example, the custom of the Greeks that a trophy could be erected by the victor at the site of a great battle.[361] The trophy was usually dedicated to the patron deity of the successful city, and, as a monument, could not be defaced or demolished. By the same token, the trophy could not be made with stone or bronze, only wood, and could not be repaired or rebuilt when it decayed.[362] When the Thebans raised a brass plaque to commemorate their victory over the Spartans, the Lacedaemonians laid a complaint before the Amphictyonic Council saying that it violated Hellenic custom.[363] The standard rationale for this quaint practice was that to allow permanent commemorations of victory would be "to perpetuate the memory of a conflict, [and] that the descendants of the conquered [would] be denied due amnesty."[364]

In Greece, the capitulation of an enemy city could be had either by treaty or by force of arms. A surrender could be arranged by agreement, the only question being the terms that the victor would accede to. An arranged capitulation usually had the advantage, as already suggested

[359] 1 *ibid.* at 351 (passage ii.52.3).
[360] See Chapter 4, at notes 59–92, 123–39, 358–69 and accompanying text.
[361] See 3 Euripides, *supra* note 319, at 417 (*Phoenician Maidens*, line 853); 2 Pausanias, *supra* note 134, at 547 (v, Elis, passage 27.7). Aside from the erection of triumphal arches, the Romans also erected trophies on the battlefields. See 1 Tacitus, *Annales* 415 (John Jackson transl. 1931) (Loeb Classical Library reprint 1956) (passage ii.22).
[362] See 4 Plutarch, *Moralia, supra* note 284, at 63–65 (*Quaest. Rom.* 37); 5 Diodorus, *supra* note 64, at 189 (passage xiii.24). See also Arundell, *supra* note 2, at 376 n. 1.
[363] See 2 Cicero, *supra* note 89, at 235 (*De Inventione*, passage ii.23.69).
[364] 2 Phillipson, *supra* note 44, at 296–97. For evidence of archaic Roman practice, see 1 Livy, *supra* note 81, at 135 (passage i.37.5) (trophy of victory over Sabines).

here, that the affected populace would not be enslaved by the successful occupiers.[365] Some Greek writers, including Andocides and Xenophon, assumed that such a promise made in an agreement to capitulate was legally binding.[366] With the exception of the Plataean garrison, there was no other instance in Thucydides where a city was razed and its population enslaved when it had made an affirmative treaty of capitulation.

Even the agreed capitulation of a city did not, however, protect the property of the vanquished from being taken as war booty.[367] A surprising amount of attention is given by Thucydides to record instances of disagreement among allies in dividing the spoils after a successful siege or campaign.[368] There were even recorded instances where the victor in a conflict established a tribunal to pass in judgment on the acts of individuals in the occupied city. With the exception of the Spartan judges of the Plataean garrison, these tribunals were not intended to condemn those that had violated the Greek laws of war. More typically, they were used to redistribute power and wealth between factions in the cities under enemy control, or to determine the territorial claims of competing cities affected by the war.[369]

---

[365] See 1 Thucydides, *supra* note 30, at 53 (passage ii.29.4); Onasander, *supra* note 335, at 497 (passage xxxviii.1–6), 519–21 (passage xlii.18–22). But see 21 Aristotle, *supra* note 339, at 25 (*Politics*, passage i.2.16–18 (1255a)) (arguing the contrary). See generally, W. L. Westermann, The Slave System of Greek and Roman Antiquity, 40 *Memoirs of the American Philosophical Society* (1955).

[366] See 1 Andocides, *Minor Attic Orators* 507 (K. J. Maidment transl. 1941) (Loeb Classical Library reprint 1982) (*On the Peace*, passage xi); 2 Xenophon, *supra* note 48, at 227 (*Cyropaedia*, passage vii.1.44). See also Elie Bikerman, Remarques sur le droit des gens dans la Grèce classique, 4 RIDA (ser. 3) 99, 106–07 (1950).

[367] See 2 Xenophon, *supra* note 48, at 293 (*Cyropaedia*, passage vii.5.73). See also 10 Plato, *supra* note 334, at 7–11 (*Laws*, i.626).

[368] See Bikerman, *supra* note 366, at 119–20 (glossing a number of passages). See also the treaties between Knossos and Tylissos (c. 450 BCE); and the agreement between Malla and Lyttos (c. 221 BCE) on division of spoils, reprinted in 1 *Fontes Historiae Iuris Gentium* 142–44 (Wilhelm G. Grewe ed. 1992). This was a constant source of tension between Rome and her unreliable Greek allies in the war against Macedon. Roman *amici* were supposed to have the right of participating in any peace negotiations with an enemy, and to receive a fair share of the war booty. See 9 Livy, *supra* note 81, at 253–65 (passage xxxii.33–36) (Roman–Aetolian negotiations with Macedon). See also E. Badian, *Foreign Clientelae, 264–70 BC* (2nd ed. 1984); Larsen, *supra* note 85, at 367–68; A. Aymard, Le partage des profits de la guerre dans les traités d'alliance antiques, 217 *Revue historique* 233 (1957); Peter Karavites, *Promise-Giving and Treaty-Making: Homer and the Near East* 156–70 (1992) (on ancient Near East and Homeric literature on taking and sharing of booty).

[369] See 1 Thucydides, *supra* note 30, at 93 (passage i.55), 313 (passage ii.30), 2 *ibid.* at 123–25 (passage iii.68), 297 (passage iv.49). See also Bikerman, *supra* note 366, at 110–12. The Roman practice of the *recuperatores* could be considered in this context. See T. J. Haarhoff, *The Stranger at the Gate: Aspects of Exclusiveness and Co-operation in Ancient Greece and Rome* 151–52 (1938).

Greek attitudes about the proper respect to be accorded to the vanquished did influence Roman practice. Polybius was clear that, while certain kinds of movable property were legitimate booty for the victor and could be taken "right and fair by the laws of war," it was impermissible for the conqueror willfully to destroy the structures and sanctuaries of the defeated city.[370] For the Romans, such acts of wanton destruction were uncommon, if for no other reason than that the property of a surrendered city was formally transferred to the Republic.[371]

The form of capitulation (also known as *deditio* in Latin) was established as early as 616 BCE, when King Tarquin of Rome engaged in a surrender colloquy with envoys from Collatia.

KING TARQUIN: Are you ambassadors and deputies sent by the people of Collatia to surrender yourselves and the people of Collatia?
DEPUTATION OF COLLATIANS: We are.
TARQUIN: Are the people of Collatia their own masters?
COLLATIANS: They are.
TARQUIN: Do you surrender yourselves and the people of Collatia, their city, lands, water, boundaries, temples, utensils, and everything sacred or profane belonging to them, into my power, and that of the Roman people?
COLLATIANS: We do.
TARQUIN: Then I receive them.[372]

As archaic as this passage appears, this was the standard form of surrender used by the Romans well into the first century BCE. We have a tablet excavated from Alcántara in Spain, on which is recorded the capitulation of the town of Seano in 104 BCE.[373] The only difference, as discussed by Watson, is that, whereas in the archaic period and the early Republic a *fetial* might be involved in accepting the *deditio* of a defeated town, that was not the case during the period of transmarine expansion.[374]

Watson also suggests that there was a difference recognized in Roman law between a vanquished people making a capitulation to the dominion of Rome (*deditio in dicionem*, or, alternatively, *deditio in potestatem*)[375] and one made in trust to Rome (*deditio in fidem*). The distinction was

---

[370] See 3 Polybius, *supra* note 31, at 25–27 (passage v.9). See also Karavites, *supra* note 41, at 124–27, 130–31 (on relative infrequence in Greek history of destruction of vanquished cities).

[371] But see Maine, *supra* note 182, at 204–05 (who suggests the property of a surrendered polity was considered as *res nullius*).   [372] 1 Livy, *supra* note 81, at 137 (passage i.38).

[373] See Dieter Nörr, *Aspekte des römischen Völkerrechts; Die Bronzetafel von Alcántara* 18–23 (1989).   [374] See Watson, *supra* note 163, at 49–50.

[375] Cf. 11 Livy, *supra* note 81, at 391 (passage xxxix.54.6) (Gallic legates in 183 BC) (*potestatem*).

previously thought to be rhetorical only.[376] Watson, glossing a text from Valerius Maximus,[377] suggests, instead, that the difference went to the matter of how the Romans could treat the vanquished people, their lands, and property.[378] A surrender *in fidem* implied limitations on Roman power.

Managing conflict in antiquity

The ancient preoccupation with war focused on applying rationality to a fundamentally irrational endeavor. The goal was nothing less than managing conflict. To the extent that ancient societies developed religious, ritual, and rational strictures on declaring war and initiating hostilities, there must have been some manifest belief that war was an exception to the normal course of international relations, an aberration in the way that peoples dealt with each other.

The nearly universal conscience of peoples in antiquity was that it was never desirable to be branded the aggressor in a conflict.[379] There was a moral advantage to be won in exercising restraint before entering a condition of belligerency, or at least in appearing to do so. It was this fact that led to the development of rules for neutrality, which depended for their vitality on a status being given to those polities that chose to abstain from conflict. And if the regime of neutrality was never widely, nor absolutely, recognized, it was an epitome of a legal status used in ancient State relations.

As for rules governing the conduct and prosecution of hostilities, one might wonder whether there was even a need actually to manage ancient warfare. Ancient conflict was usually a desultory affair, synchronized with the turn of the seasons, limited by great distances, imperfect communications, and difficult logistics. There were battles fought and towns besieged, for sure, but the structure of ancient warfare was such that a campaign could end very easily with a decisive engagement or a stormed city. Civilians were usually left alone, if for no other reason than that if armies killed peasants and burned fields, soldiers would probably starve before the inhabitants of the district did. Total war was virtually unheard of. Notwithstanding the Israelite doctrine of *mitzva*,[380] and the dramatic,

---

[376] See W. Dahlheim, *Struktur und Entwicklung des römischen Völkerrechts im dritten und zweiten Jahrhundert vor Chr.*, at 25–28, 43 (1968); Nörr, *supra* note 373, at 28.

[377] Valerius Maximus vi.5.1.   [378] See Watson, *supra* note 163, at 51–52.

[379] See *supra* notes 18–20, 36–40 and accompanying text.

[380] See *supra* notes 7–12 and accompanying text.

life-and-death struggles of the Peloponnesian and Second Punic Wars, the very process of war in antiquity succeeded in limiting its effects.

Ancient wars were fought for territory – and for glory. Most ancient States were socially organized on a footing that facilitated the marshaling of resources for armed conflict. These resources were finite. Blood and treasure came in limited supplies. The Israelites, the Greeks, and the Romans all came to understand that war depleted social and economic capital so quickly that the very integrity of the State was jeopardized. All ancient belligerents had an incentive, therefore, to make war quick and cheap. Warring nations feared defeat, but they trembled more in the face of *ataphos*, the death of the human spirit that the conditions of war produced. In antiquity, war was (at once) the great legitimizer of the State, and its greatest threat.

To respond to the challenges that war presented to the State, religion and ritual and reason were called upon to sanction and give order to life in belligerency. These mixed and produced a distinctively legal vision of how ancient States initiated hostilities and how they conducted them. The mechanism by which religious values were transformed into rituals and thence into legal rules was achieved in two different ways, both hastened by war itself. The first was in the creation of distinctive social institutions, whether sacerdotal colleges like the *fetials* or the Israelite high priests. Religious values, often expressed in virulently nationalist forms, were maintained and applied by these institutions. Their primary goal was to preserve the legitimacy of the State against both internal and external challenge. These institutions kept the mysteries of the State religion and carried on a discourse with the national gods concerning the State's place in the world. The key element in the legitimacy of these institutions were the rituals they managed on behalf of the State and its people.

The second mechanism was simply the process of secularism. Religion and ritual, after time, could not succeed in sustaining State values or legitimacy. *Mitzva*, as a command for divine, obligatory war, gave way to a rational notion of "optional" war.[381] The spear-throwing ritual of the fetials, as the dramatic *bellum indicere*, was modified as time and international conditions changed.[382] It was replaced, as I have suggested here, by the language and rhetoric of law and legal rules of obligation. *Halachic* (legal) thinking influenced and moderated the Israelite approach to war. The

---

[381] See *supra* notes 21–27 and accompanying text.
[382] See *supra* notes 191–201 and accompanying text.

Greeks, strongly disposed to philosophy and rhetoric already, consistently referred to the norms of conduct in warfare as a common law of mankind. After all, the final, winning argument of the Thebans was that they had "suffered contrary to law" because of the Plataeans' previous violations of those customs.[383] The Romans, from their earliest period of organized political history, claimed legal right as the basis for their moral and military superiority. Remember the words of the *pater patratus* when he remonstrated against the enemy that had failed to do right. "Let the law of heaven hear"; the enemy, he said, was "unjust, and does not act agreeably to law."[384]

It was not just that ancient peoples had a sense of legal obligation in warfare. The Greek *to dikaion* and the Roman *ius ad bellum* and *ius in bello* had actual, substantive content. In part this can be seen in the many dualities that were part of the ancient law of war. Ancient States made a distinction between enemies and foes.[385] This was the central concept of restraint and proportionality in conflict. Without the idea that public wars had to be treated differently from private feuds, there could be no rule of law in wartime, since conflict presumably dissolved all bonds of hospitality.

Ancient States also saw a difference between just and unjust, lawful and unlawful wars. Sometimes this was a matter only of internal, scriptural significance (as in the Israelite contrast of *mitzva* and *reshut*), but it could also extend to broader notions of justification. Lastly, all ancient States saw the need for limitations and immunities to be impressed on the conduct of warfare. These were the most specific, and literal, of the norms governing armed conflict. And although there were only a handful of rules of conduct in warfare, these were generally observed and respected, to a degree that was startling for a time that was supposed to be barbaric and lawless.

Whether there was a law of war in antiquity is the ultimate test of whether there was a cohesive idea of a law of nations at all in ancient times. I have argued here that there indeed was a common core of ideas leading to the exercise of restraint by ancient States in armed conflict. As with all of the themes considered in this study, the sources of legal obligation in ancient State relations were multivalent, and this is nowhere

---

[383] See 2 Thucydides, *supra* note 30, at 117–19 (passage iii.66).
[384] See 1 Livy, *supra* note 81, at 115–17 (passage i.32.6–10).
[385] See *supra* note 215 and accompanying text.

more evident than in the ancient law of war. The final chapter places all of the issues considered so far – the sources of international legal obligation and the ancient mind's engagement with the problems of transnational friendship, faith, and friction – in a single inquiry of the meaning of community and civilization.

7 Civilization and community in the ancient mind

This study has explored the assertion that an ancient law of nations had the traits of a primitive legal system. After considering the sources of international legal obligation in antiquity, I have reviewed the three essential areas in which law influenced ancient State relations: (1) the reception of envoys and the protection of aliens living in ancient States; (2) the making and enforcement of treaties; and (3) the rules governing the declaration of war and the actual conduct of hostilities. I have not merely sought to catalogue instances where ancient States apparently recognized these doctrinal features of a law of nations. Instead, the object has been to establish recurrent patterns of thinking and practice concerning these doctrines.

This study has thus scrupulously avoided the conclusion that there was a single, cohesive body of rules for a law of nations, recognized by all States in antiquity or that such rules were proximate to those that we regard today as being part of "modern" international law. Instead, I conclude that there was a common *idea* held in antiquity that international relations were to be based on the rule of law. The embrace of that idea, and not any particular structure of process or doctrine, is what qualifies ancient international law as something more than "primitive."

It remains to elaborate these points by responding to the two most prevalent critiques of the idea that ancient international relations were based on a rule of law. The first criticism is an objective dissection of ancient international law as a putative legal system, supposedly lacking key ingredients and attributes. The second attack takes the form of a subjective deconstruction of the rhetoric of legality in the international relations of ancient times. This jurisprudential epilogue will answer these appraisals, while offering its own conclusions on the idea of a law of nations in antiquity.

I

Ancient international law is twice accursed. It is, first of all, posited as a law governing independent, sovereign nations – polities that would otherwise recognize no superiors, no sanctions, and no rules. As H. L. A. Hart said, international law has a "doubtful" claim to being a legal system.[1] He would have likely suggested that the law of nations in antiquity was also, by virtue of its pre-Modern historical setting, quintessentially primeval. It is this combination of "historical" antiquity with "doctrinal" primitiveness that gives the ancient law of nations its doubly ambiguous character. Ignored by historians of ancient or primitive law, and forsaken by contemporary international law publicists, the ancient law of nations would appear to be an obvious oxymoron, unworthy of serious scholarly attention.

The indictment that ancient international law was not really law in any modernly understood way is typically presented through two sets of counts. One group criticizes ancient international law for its antiquity; the other for its claim to manage international relations under a rule of law.

A

In the first set of criticisms, the "ancient" character of the system is emphasized in its true, primitivist sense. These charges would include that an ancient law of nations was based on religion as its sole sanction. Moreover, even to the extent that custom was a source of obligation (itself a sign of a primitive legal system) there were no consistent rules of customary State behavior. This attack on ancient international law focuses on the inherent weakness in the sources of obligation in rules of conduct in ancient societies, quite apart from the special challenge posed by rules of State conduct in ancient international relations.

This critique of the primitive sources of ancient international law would be recognized as being a restatement of Hart's assertion that in primitive legal cultures there are no "secondary" rules. These "secondary" norms are of three types. The first is guidance in recognizing the legitimacy of legal standards, which is necessary to counter uncertainty as to legal expectations in primitive cultures. The second are rules for change, to remedy the static nature of such systems. The third grouping of "secondary" norms are those for the allowance of adjudication, to handle the

---

[1] H. L. A. Hart, *The Concept of Law* 2 (2nd ed. 1994).

social inefficiencies in applying the "primary" rules of primitive societies.[2] These rules of recognition, change, and adjudication roughly correspond with the notion that the central features of any modern legal system are institutions and processes which make law, which interpret and apply norms, and which enforce sanctions.

In assessing the sources of an ancient law of nations, the signal defect which has been mentioned is that which is supposedly common to all primitive legal systems: that religion, and not reason, provided the basis of obligation and the critical determinant for recognizing a "legal" norm. This study has gone to great lengths to dispel this assertion for the ancient law of nations. It is undeniable that deeply held religious beliefs may have accounted for compliance with some of the essential, "primary" rules of State behavior considered in this study: protecting ambassadors, keeping treaties, observing formalities in declaring war, and avoiding excesses on the battlefield. Envoys were cloaked with the character of religious immunity. Oaths invoking deities guaranteed treaties. Religious sanctuaries were protected from the ravages of war. National gods were called upon to witness or judge the justness of a war properly declared. It would be easy to trace all the primary rules of obligation in ancient international law back to a religious command, divorced from a sense of custom which gives full expression to the practices of a people or a sense of reason which gives voice to human rationality.

It would be easy to do this for an ancient law of nations – and quite wrong. It would be error insofar as it imposes a peculiarly modern vision of human impulses, segregating rationales for human behavior as those inspired by faith and those directed by reason. It would also ignore the reality that ancient peoples mixed idioms of obligation. To take as just one example, consider statements made in antiquity as to why murdering an envoy was a bad thing. Xerxes, King of Persia, is quoted by a Greek historian as saying that such an act would "make havoc of all human law."[3] Cato the Younger denounced Caesar's slaughter of tribal envoys in Gaul, fretting that "the pollution of his crime [would] fall upon the city."[4] Each of these extracts refers both to secular and religious concerns. The Greek word "havoc," placed in the Persian king's mouth by Herodotus, was meant as an imprecation of divine vengeance, though invoked in the

---

[2] See *ibid.* at 92–93, 95–96.

[3] 3 Herodotus, *Histories* 435–39 (A. D. Godley transl. 1920) (Loeb Classical Library reprint 1969) (passage vii.133–36).

[4] 8 Plutarch, *Lives* 359 (B. Perrin transl. 1917) (Loeb Classical Library reprint 1968) (*Cato Minor*, passage li.1).

transgression of "human law." Likewise, the "polluting" act referred to by the younger Cato is both religious sacrilege and secular "crime."

The manichean preoccupation with religion and reason as bases for legal obligation also distorts the important effects of custom and ritual and practice in any legal system. As used in this study, custom has been considered as a discrete impulse in the ancient mind's engagement with rules of conduct. It was one thing to fear direct divine intervention for breaking a treaty, mutilating corpses on the battlefield, or killing an envoy. It was quite another to court adverse public opinion, as the Plataean deputies admonished. Somewhere in between was the concern that a breach of an international legal obligation would undermine the very structure, cohesion, and legitimacy of the ancient State.

The sources of a law of nations in antiquity, as well as its instruments of coercion and enforcement, were subtle and multivalent. Divine sanctions, actuated by oaths, brought direct retribution against the wrongdoer. Using reasoned statements as arguments for obeying the law gave diplomatic, political, and moral advantage to those who did right and denied the same for those who did wrong. Social sanctions for violations of customary norms were enforced by depriving essential State institutions of their legitimacy.

Together these sources of obligation produced consistent results in law compliance. Recall, for example, how ancient polities confronted the problem of enforcing treaty obligations. For some ancient State systems, particularly those that were not so multi-polar, treaty compliance mechanisms were "external." Hostages might be exchanged, to be detained or killed in the event of one party's breach. Treaty-makers would give their personal bond that their nation would fulfill the promises made, or else they would be handed back to the aggrieved polity. There even may have been an expectation that the surety gods of the "oath-fulfilling pledges" would actually punish the transgressor nation. We might view these enforcement mechanisms with distaste, and decide that they are not really "legal" sanctions at all. But I think that would be a mistake. The alternative form of compliance mechanism, more "internal" in nature, was to use sophisticated and detailed provisions of substantive obligation, to create reasoned rules for interpreting treaty texts, to devise anti-deceit clauses, to prescribe monetary punishments for breach, and to arrange for disputes of treaty performance to be settled by arbitration. These methods for enforcing good faith we would instantly prefer as being more secular in character, more reasoned, and (of course) more lawyerly. These internal means of compliance were more commonly employed among Greek city-States, although they were by no means absent from ancient Near Eastern or Western Mediterranean State practice. Still, the conclusion drawn in this study is that the best conditions for faithful treaty compliance were achieved when both sets of enforcement mechanisms were used in tandem.

State systems in antiquity thus appeared to have some institutions and processes that H. L. A. Hart might acknowledge as "secondary" rules of conduct. They were not, I concede, very well developed within any single, ancient State system, nor universally followed in the three time periods surveyed here. Formalized, judicial settlement of disputes was unknown outside of Greece. There were few rules of adjudication, at least within Hart's meaning, available to ancient peoples. But, I would maintain, there were principles of "recognition" ready for identifying rules of State behavior in antiquity, and this factor, standing alone, conferred at least one critical element of legal legitimacy on an ancient law of nations.

B

As Hart wrote, "international law not only lacks the secondary rules of change and adjudication which provide for legislature and courts, but also a unifying recognition specifying 'sources' of law and providing general criteria for the identification of its rules."[5] Those who critique ancient international law from the perspective of historical primitiveness have wrongly attempted to portray the source of the law of nations in antiquity as religion, hoping that that association would alone disqualify it as a real legal system. I have attempted to refute that assertion not only by disclaiming its factual predicate (religion was not the only source of international obligation in antiquity), but also by making the obvious point that even if such *were* true, it would not matter. Faith (and belief) is a perfectly legitimate source for rules of State behavior.

Then there are those who would criticize the ancient law of nations as simply the distant ancestor of an enfeebled, contemporary international law. These critics level the same charges against ancient international law as they would against its modern equivalent. They merely assume that the doctrinal primitiveness that they claim for modern international law must have been especially apparent in ancient times. Current international law publicists have colluded in this attack, joining Hart's observation that "[i]n form, international law resembles . . . a regime of

[5] Hart, *supra* note 1, at 214.

primary rules, even though the content of its often elaborate rules are very unlike those of a primitive society, and many of its concepts, methods and techniques are the same as those of modern municipal law."[6] The doctrinal sophistication of modern international law, even though accompanied by nagging questions about the sources of those "elaborate rules" and how they are enforced, can still be compared favorably with the international law of antiquity which had relatively few substantive norms and no apparent way to supplement (legislate) those rules of State behavior.

I readily concede that an ancient law of nations had but a handful of primary obligations. But those rules of State behavior, the doctrines considered in this study, are fundamental to international relations being based on a rule of law. Protection of envoys meant that relations of friendship could subsist between States of very different ethnic and political characters. Recognitions of status for foreigners living within a polity permitted the building of commerce and culture, the prime objective of peaceful relations between States. Rules facilitating the making of agreements and their subsequent fulfillment gave scope for atomistic sovereignties being able to cooperate with one another over a wide spectrum of diplomatic, political, economic, and legal concerns. Formalities concerning recourse to war could help to preserve peace, by at least permitting certain kinds of disputes between States to be resolved. And, finally, limits and restraints in the conduct of hostilities not only advanced humanitarian interests, but also had the effect of easing States back into a condition of harmony.

That ancient international law was limited in its substantive doctrines to these fundamental norms meant that other "secondary" rules were not so necessary. I would go further and say that many of these primary rules of obligation also had a secondary or procedural character. Rules regarding diplomatic activity, treaty-making, and war-declaring were intended not so much as substantive limitations on the ancient State's freedom to act, as they were designed to promote the process of communication, cooperation, and dispute settlement between polities in antiquity.

The ancient law of nations confounded primary and secondary rules of obligation (utilizing Hart's idiom), as well as the sources, processes, and doctrines of a legal system (the metaphor used elsewhere in this study). Whether this confusion between process and doctrine exists in today's

---

[6] *Ibid.* at 227.

international law is beyond the scope of this study, although it is certainly the issue that Hart takes up with Hans Kelsen's theory explicating those "basic norms" in public international law.[7]

Just because an ancient law of nations had only a small nucleus of primary rules of obligation in State relations should not disqualify it from enjoying the status of an authentic legal system. Moreover, the historical record surveyed here strongly suggests that ancient State systems were capable of developing needed changes to those norms over time. In the 150-year period from 500 to 350 BCE, Greek city-States elaborated the rules of conduct between them in all of the doctrinal fields considered here (and many others not reviewed in this book). The diversity of legal terminology governing diplomatic activity, treaty forms, friendship statuses, arbitration of disputes, and war-fighting limitations was simply astounding. How did this occur? Through extraordinarily deep contacts within an intensely competitive State system. In short, the custom of States (and here I am referring to custom in the sense of the repeated practices of ancient polities) gave rise to new international norms of conduct.

The more dynamic and multi-polar the State system in antiquity, the quicker the tempo of customary international law formation. Each of the periods surveyed here exhibited just such a characteristic, although admittedly none to such a degree as the Greek city-States. Nevertheless, periods of intense diplomatic activity in the ancient Near East – the fractious discord of the Sumer cities or Egyptian and Hittite competition in Palestine – produced notable advances in statecraft, and in the elaboration and refinement of the rules of international relations. Likewise, the period of Rome's transmarine expansion and contact with other great powers (including the already legally sophisticated Greek cities) produced changes in international law practices as varied as the substantive provisions of treaties, the formulas for declaring war, and the immunities to be accorded envoys.

C

Common to both sets of critics of ancient international law have been some observations as to the nature of international relations in antiquity. For example, the assertion has been made that because ancient States did

---

[7] Compare *ibid.* at 233–34, with Hans Kelsen, *General Theory of Law and State* 110–24, 369–73 (1945).

not conceive of themselves as sovereign polities, they could not possibly have embraced a system of rules governing State conduct.

This is a peculiar, paradoxical observation. It is, first of all, belied by the political and international history narrated in this volume. Ancient States had a self-perception of sovereignty. Indeed, ancient States may have had a too-robust sense of self: ethnic, linguistic, religious, and cultural particularism defined ancient States. These factors of separation – of "differentness" – impelled the creation, expansion, and death of ancient polities. The great Near Eastern empires, the Greek *poleis*, and the Western Mediterranean States all embraced these particularistic features. And they all were capable, by virtue of political centralization, economic wealth, and military might, of concentrating power to manage relations with other polities. If sovereignty is simply the power and willingness to exclude others from a national territory, ancient States were, most certainly, sovereign.

The emphasis on sovereignty is, in any event, a two-edged sword for those who would attack an ancient law of nations for its primitiveness. The lack of sovereignty would imply, for one set of critics, an obvious failing in the conception of the ancient State. After all, if there was no such thing as an ancient State, there could not possibly have been ancient State *systems* – groupings of autonomous, sovereign States seeking to order their relations on the basis of a rule of law. For the other set of critics (those who focus on the putative claim of international law to manage international relations), it is precisely because there are sovereign States that it is impossible to imagine those independent polities acquiescing in a system of exogenous rules to govern their behavior.

The more powerful claim, and the one that both sets of critics concur in, is that even if there were ancient States, there was no sense of community in the ancient mind. Ancient States may have had the sentience we today call sovereignty, but they did not have that extra ingredient, that desire to live in peace among their neighbors and to order relations amongst themselves based on rules and expectations of conduct, as opposed to brute force. This, I conclude, along with Hedley Bull and Wolfgang Preiser,[8] is the essence of an authentic State system.

Ancient states created rules of law for their international relations because such rules served their interests. The entities which participated in the State systems reviewed in this study were all able to conceive

---

[8] See Hedley Bull, *The Anarchical Society: A Study of Order in World Politics* 13 (1977); Wolfgang Preiser, History of the Law of Nations: Basic Questions and Principles, in 7 Rudolph Bernhardt, *Encyclopedia of Public International Law* 126, 128–29 (1984).

relationships between polities which transcended war and peace, vanquishment or belligerence. The dynamic State systems considered here, especially the city-States of Greece and Mesopotamia, certainly used balance-of-power and hegemonic diplomacy, through which they developed legal expectations to fashion and maintain those relations.

Just as significantly, the more static State systems reviewed in this study fashioned both dependency relationships and positions of neutrality. Hittite and Assyrian fealty treaties indicated that polities could acquire a status of subordination or association with a central empire, and not just mere subjugation. Abstention from conflict was a possible (although difficult) posture to maintain in each of the time periods reviewed here. The most persuasive evidence that ancient States could accept a condition of peace with their neighbors were the paradigmatic parity treaties of antiquity: the Egyptian–Hittite agreement of 1280 BCE and the covenant between Hannibal and Philip V of Macedon of 215 BCE. Both instruments showed remarkable technical sophistication directed toward precise political and diplomatic ends.

II

Ancient peoples manifested a genuine appreciation that legal principles and relationships could govern international affairs. The bulk of this study has been the collection and presentation of evidence to support that conclusion. The historical record indicates that the twin "primitivist" attacks on international law – its religious source of obligation and its lack of doctrinal sophistication – are unsupportable. That still leaves the question of whether, quite apart from the accretions of State practice (the indicia of conduct in diplomacy, the treatment of foreigners, the making of treaties, and the waging of war), ancient peoples had a single idea of a law of nations.

So, even though an "external," objective evaluation of ancient international law (such as might be advocated by Hart) fails to convince, a critic might still wonder whether a vision of the ancient law of nations satisfies a more subjective, "internal" analysis. Hart's descriptive legal theory might give way to a more interpretive approach, such as that suggested by Ronald Dworkin.[9] In responding to this second jurisprudential method, I argue here that ancient peoples had a distinct legal rhetoric surrounding international relations. It is worth reviewing the language and metaphor

---

[9] See Ronald Dworkin, *Law's Empire* 13–14, 102, 410 (1986); Ronald Dworkin, *A Matter of Principle* 148 (1985).

of legal obligation in ancient State affairs, while also considering the evidence of a single, common law of nations tradition in antiquity.

A

Ancient peoples consistently spoke of a law of nations. At times, however, the vernacular of references to such a law was obscure and opaque. Where such was the case, this study has respected that rhetorical ambivalence, and has not attempted to argue that the ideas conveyed in the words used by ancient peoples meant more than was likely to have been intended. But a major conclusion of this book is that legal idioms pervaded the conduct of ancient international relations. Ancient States manifested a wish that relations between polities be predictable, be rational, and be governed by a set of neutrally discernible rules. Ancient international relations were still motivated by force, might, and authority. What is remarkable is the degree to which the language of law got mixed with the profanity of power.

The task of identifying the rhetoric of ancient international law has been complicated by the ancient ability to conceive of very different sources of legal obligation: religious, social, and rational. One must not dismiss, as irrelevant and primitive, sources of international legal obligation not based in reason. If that mistake is avoided, the pattern of ideas in ancient writings about a law of nations becomes more readily apparent.

The essence of an ancient rhetoric of international law is evident in one observation: ancient States were very reluctant to characterize their own conduct as lawless. Realpolitik was no doubt a motive force of all State relations in ancient times, as it is today. The question is, however, the extent to which objective and neutral rules of international affairs modify the behavior of nations. My conclusion is that each polity considered within the three ancient State systems sought to exploit a sense of legality for its own conduct, while also disclaiming the conduct of its rivals and enemies as lawless and illegitimate.

When ancient States engaged in violations of clearly established norms of international conduct, they still sought to explain their comportment in legal language, or offer what might be considered a legal defense, whether framed as justification or as necessity. It was never considered sufficient to claim that an international law violation was permitted because the perpetrator was strong and the victim weak. Not even in the infamous Melian Dialogue, nor in Demosthenes' speech on the Rhodians, did the Athenians exclusively rely on such arguments, preferring, instead, to balance statements of diplomatic bluster with carefully crafted legal arguments as to why Melian or Rhodian neutrality was really a sham. In many cases, ancient States recognized that an earlier offense against the law of nations was the cause of later punishment directed against the offender. Whether it was the Plague Prayers of King Mursilis, the Fable of Fabius, the murder of Darius' Heralds, or the Speech of the Plataean Deputies, the offender always got what was due.

In the sphere of war, no ancient State ever gladly claimed the role of aggressor. Even the earliest of ancient peoples sought to avoid such a stigma, while the Greeks and Romans went through elaborate legal rituals to disavow that status. We might today regard those rituals as legal formalism, or, even worse, as charades covering naked lawlessness. But that does not explain why ancient peoples regarded such observances as being essential to State integrity and legitimacy. The reason must have been that the basic rules of State conduct considered in this study were taken quite seriously in antiquity. The fulfillment of those objective norms was seen, for whatever reason, as being integral to the ancient State.

The language of international law was replete in all ancient cultures. It was clear when Hammurabi spoke of "touching his throat" when making a treaty. A more sophisticated sense resided in the Greek concept of an unwritten law governing all Hellenes, the *agraphos nomos*, as well as in the Roman *ius gentium*. Finally, it was palpable in the angry words of the *pater patratus* spat across the frontier: "this nation does not act agreeably to law."

When properly read and understood, the language of law in ancient international relations was both absolute and conditional. The content of the basic norms of State relations was clear and beyond question. What *was* contingent in ancient State relations was power and expediency. An exercise of power might give rise to a claim or defense, but it did not excuse or disavow the rule itself. When ancient States broke the law of nations, they tended to explain, rationalize, and even to apologize. That very intellectual act of explanation, of rationalization, and of apology is, at its core, the idea for international law.

B

But was there a single idea of a law of nations in ancient times? This study has examined three State systems in antiquity and has identified two distinct traditions of international relations. The earlier one was formed in the ancient Near East out of Mesopotamia, and transmitted to the

Assyrian and Hittite empires, and thence to Egypt and the Mediterranean cultures. Its primary characteristic was a static empire system, although punctuated by complicated and subtle fealty arrangements between sovereignties of different strengths. Great empires subsisted with narrow, particularistic religions. This tradition of international relations produced a set of international laws that would be recognizable throughout antiquity: the institution of diplomacy, the conclusion and sanctity of treaties, and some limited restraints on warfare.

The second tradition of State relations was birthed in Greece. Intensely competitive and multi-polar, the Greek city-States transformed the rigid and hierarchical rules of war, diplomacy, and alliance used in the ancient Near East and created a vast array of power and friendship relations, all with some sort of legal significance. Ancient Greek diplomacy was, at once, more and less particularistic than those in the Near East. Religion did not divide the Hellenes, but politically they were more fractious and ungovernable. Much of the language and terminology of the law of nations was reformulated by the Greeks. It would be easy to speak of a Greek tradition of international relations and law, one that supplanted the old forms from the Near East. But this study has suggested that those older constructs did not disappear. They co-existed in the Hellenistic world with Greek forms. They were retained by Ptolemaic Egypt and transmitted to Carthage.

Most astonishingly, they were adopted by the Romans in equal measure with their own, indigenous traditions (such as the *fetial* institution) and with Greek diplomatic and treaty practices. In the more intense and challenging periods of Roman expansion in Italy and in the Western Mediterranean, the Romans tended to cleave to Greek customs. With time and success, Roman diplomacy itself became more settled, and as Republic evolved into Empire, the old Near Eastern forms crept back.

So we have two well-defined traditions of statecraft in antiquity, each generating some special features for a law of nations. There were commonalities in these traditions, enough similarities so that it is sensible to speak of a single idea of international law in antiquity. The substantive content of the norms was strikingly similar. While further nuances on the rules of diplomatic contact, treaty-making, and war-making were developed as time went on, the essential contours of the norms did not change: envoys were not to be killed, treaties were to be kept in good faith, aggression was not to be rewarded, and basic restraints in warfare were to be observed.

Finally, both traditions tended to perpetuate themselves through balance-of-power diplomacy and hegemonic alliances. The only difference was the relative size, stability, and duration of the empires and alliances in each system, with those in ancient Greece tending to be more precarious. The fact that both models of statecraft worked in the same way (although with different results) meant that the objectives of a system of State relations based on rules were also the same.

III

The norms of international law thus had the same purpose throughout antiquity: to promote predictability and stability, to adequately channel State conduct in ways that were conducive to maintaining power relations, and to nourish the internal legitimacy and sovereignty of polities. Despite my occasional use of the term "international law" in this study, the ancient law of nations was conceived only as an instrument of State relations. It had virtually no regard for other values such as human rights or dignity, the protection of common resources, or the advancement of some exogenous ideology or philosophy. The law of nations in antiquity was, first and foremost, an expression of the ancient mind's desire for *order*.

To achieve international society meant that a delicate balance had to be struck with the internal, political and religious order of individual States. This was the singular task of the law of nations in antiquity, one that it accomplished to a surprisingly effective degree. Ancient States were particularistic. Their internal political order depended on exclusion, on aggression, and on difference. The rules of State relations in ancient times managed to transform this particularism into cooperation. *Friendship* was achieved through the translation of hospitality practices into the institutions of diplomacy. Likewise, the ancient State was made *tolerant* by rules of conduct which permitted the movement of people, goods, and services across boundaries. *Trust* was made possible through the rituals and forms of making faith through treaties and alliances. Finally, *restraint* came to be exercised by ancient States even in wartime as a consequence of self-interest and concern for order.

We do not speak of these values today in modern international law. Perhaps we should. These are the essential ingredients of community, a notion and principle which is at the theoretical center of the modern law of nations. This book has, in large measure, been the story of the creation of a nascent community, one with a political structure and legal sensibility. Ancient State systems may have little to teach us about today's global world order, and they may not have much to instruct as to the substantive content of essential doctrines of international law, but the history narrated in this volume has substantial bearing on the creation of legal communities which aspire to universality.

The law of nations sought to civilize ancient States, and thereby to create order. It gave voice to reason, even while it extolled faith. As Cicero wrote: "there will not be different laws at Rome and at Athens, or different laws now and in the future, but one eternal and unchangeable law will be valid for all nations and for all times."[10]

---

[10] Cicero, *De re publica* 211 (Clinton Walker Keyes transl. 1928) (Loeb Classical Library reprint 1988) (passage iii.22.33).

Topical bibliography

Rendered below is full bibliographic information for the major sources consulted for, and cited in, this study. The bibliography is arranged topically, with divisions for primary and secondary sources. For the secondary materials, separate listings are provided for (1) more general sources of ancient statecraft, law, religion, warfare, and historiography, and (2) works detailing specific issues or doctrines in ancient international law. Books, manuscripts, articles, and other materials are arranged alphabetically by author (or editor) within each topic.

Primary sources

Inscription and archeological materials

Archives Royales de Mari: Correspondance de Samsi-Addu (vol. 1) (Georges Dossin transl.), Paris: Impr. Nationale, 1950

Archives Royales de Mari: Lettres Diverses (vol. 2) (Charles François Jean transl.), Paris: Impr. Nationale, 1950

Archives Royales de Mari: Correspondance de Iasmah-Addu (vol. 5) (Georges Dossin transl.), Paris, Impr. Nationale, 1950

Archives Royales de Mari: Correspondance de Bahdi-Lim (vol. 6) (Jean Robert Kupper transl.), Paris: Impr. Nationale, 1954

Barbeyrac, Jean, *Histoire des anciens traitéz*, Amsterdam: Chez les Janssons a Waesberge, Wetstein Smith, 1739

Bengtson, Hermann, *Die Staatsverträge des Altertums*, Munich: C. H. Beck, 1962

Boeckh, August, Ernst Curtius, Adolph Kirchhoff and Hermann Roehl, *Corpus inscriptionum graecarum*, Hildesheim and New York: G. Olms, 1977

Cauer, Paul, *Delectus inscriptionum graecarum*, Leipzig: S. Hirzel, 1883

Dareste de la Chavanne, Rudolph, Bernard Haussoullier and Theodore Reinach, *Recueil des inscriptions juridiques grecques*, Paris: E. Leroux, 1891

Dittenberger, Wilhelm, *Sylloge inscriptionum graecarum* (3rd ed.), Leipzig: S. Hirzel, 1915–24

Fornara, Charles W. (ed. and transl.), *Translated Documents of Greece and Rome: Archaic Times to the End of the Peloponnesian War*, New York and Cambridge: Cambridge University Press, 1983

Grewe, Wilhelm G. (ed.), *Fontes Historiae Iuris Gentium*, Berlin and New York: W. De Gruyter, 1992

Harper, Robert Francis, *Assyrian and Babylonian Letters*, Chicago: University of Chicago Press, 1902

Hicks, Edward Lee and George Francis Hill, *A Manual of Greek Historical Inscriptions*, Oxford: Clarendon Press, 1901

Inscriptiones Graecae (2nd ser.), Berlin, 1925

Pritchard, James B. (ed.), *Ancient Near Eastern Texts Relating to the Old Testament*, Princeton, NJ: Princeton University Press, 1969

Roehl, Hermann, *Inscriptiones Graecae antiquissimae*, Berolini: G. Reimerum, 1882

Scala, Rudolph von, *Die Staatsverträge des Altertums*, Leipzig: B. G. Teubner, 1898

Schmitt, Hatto Herbert, *Die Staatsverträge des Altertums*, Munich: Beck, 1969

Sherk, Robert K. (ed.), *Rome and the Greek East to the Death of Augustus*, New York and Cambridge: Cambridge University Press, 1984

Tod, Marcus Niebuhr, *A Selection of Greek Historical Inscriptions*, Oxford: Clarendon Press, 1948

Ventris, Michael and John Chadwick, *Documents in Mycenaean Greek*, Cambridge: Cambridge University Press, 1956

Wickersham, John and Gerald Verbrugghe, *The Fourth Century BC: Greek Historical Documents*, Toronto: Hakkert, 1973

Literary materials

All citations in this section are to the Loeb Classical Library editions published by Harvard University Press at Cambridge, Massachusetts.

Aeneas the Tactician (Illinois Greek Club transl. 1928), Loeb Classical Library reprint, 1986

Aeschines, *Speeches* (Charles Darwin Adams transl. 1919), Loeb Classical Library reprint, 1988

Andocides, *Minor Attic Orators* (K. J. Maidment transl. 1941), Loeb Classical Library reprint, 1980

Appian, *Roman History* (Horace White transl. 1912), Loeb Classical Library reprint, 1982

Aristophanes, *Plays* (Patric Dickinson transl.), Loeb Classical Library reprint, 1970

Aristotle, *The Art of Rhetoric* (J. H. Freese transl. 1926), Loeb Classical Library reprint, 1982

The Athenian Constitution (H. Rackham transl. 1935), Loeb Classical Library reprint, 1981

Nicomachean Ethics (H. Rackham transl. 1926), Loeb Classical Library reprint, 1990

Politics (H. Rackham transl. 1932), Loeb Classical Library reprint, 1990

Athenaeus, *The Deipnosophists* (C. B. Gulick transl. 1927), Loeb Classical Library reprint, 1969

Caesar, Julius, *The Gallic War* (H. J. Edwards transl. 1921), Loeb Classical Library reprint, 1986

Cicero, *De Officiis* (Walter Miller transl. 1913), Loeb Classical Library reprint, 1990

De Re Publica (Clinton Walker Keyes transl. 1928), Loeb Classical Library reprint, 1988

Letters (E. O. Winstedt transl. 1912), Loeb Classical Library reprint, 1980

Demosthenes, *Collected Works* (J. H. Vince transl. 1930), Loeb Classical Library reprint, 1989

Dio Cassius, *Roman History* (Herbert Baldwin Foster transl. 1905), Loeb Classical Library reprint, 1980

Dio Chrysostom, *Collected Works* (H. Lamar Crosby transl. 1951), Loeb Classical Library reprint, 1985

Diodorus Siculus, *History* (C. H. Oldfather, C. L. Sherman, C. Bradford Welles and F. R. Walton transl. 1946), Loeb Classical Library reprint, 1989

Dionysius of Halicarnassus, *Roman Antiquities* (Ernest Cary and Edward Spelman transl. 1937), Loeb Classical Library reprint, 1990

Euripides, *Collected Plays* (A. S. Way transl. 1912), Loeb Classical Library reprint, 1979

Herodotus, *Histories* (A. D. Godley transl. 1920), Loeb Classical Libary reprint, 1969

Homer, *The Iliad* (A. T. Murray transl. 1921), Loeb Classical Library reprint, 1971

The Odyssey (A. T. Murray transl. 1919), Loeb Classical Library reprint, 1919

Isocrates, *Orations* (George Norlin transl. 1929), Loeb Classical Library reprint, 1982

Josephus, *Antiquities* (Ralph Marcus transl. 1963), Loeb Classical Library reprint, 1990

Livy, *History of Rome* (B. O. Foster transl. 1929), Loeb Classical Library reprint, 1982

Lysias, *Orations* (W. L. Lamb transl. 1930), Loeb Classical Library reprint, 1988

Nepos, Cornelius, *Great Generals of Foreign Nations* (John C. Rolfe transl. 1929), Loeb Classical Library reprint, 1984

Onasander, *The General* (Illinois Greek Club transl. 1928), Loeb Classical Library reprint, 1986

Ovid, *Fasti* (Sir James George Frazer transl.), Loeb Classical Library reprint, 1951

Metamorphoses (F. J. Miller transl.), Loeb Classical Library reprint, 1984

Pausanias, *Description of Greece* (W. H. S. Jones transl. 1935), Loeb Classical Library reprint, 1979

Plato, *Laws* (R. G. Bury transl.), Loeb Classical Library reprint, 1984

Plutarch, *Lives* (B. Perrin transl. 1914), Loeb Classical Library reprint, 1968
  Moralia (Frank Cole Babbitt transl. 1936), Loeb Classical Library reprint, 1972
Polybius, *The Histories* (W. R. Paton transl. 1922), Loeb Classical Library reprint, 1975
Sallust, *The Jugurthine War* (J. C. Rolfe transl. 1921), Loeb Classical Library reprint, 1985
Seneca, *Moral Essays* (John W. Basore transl. 1928), Loeb Classical Library reprint, 1985
Strabo, *The Geography* (H. L. Jones and J. R. Sitlington Sterrett transl. 1927), Loeb Classical Library reprint, 1989
Suetonius, *Lives of the Caesars* (J. C. Rolfe transl. 1913), Loeb Classical Library reprint, 1989
Tacitus, *Annales* (John Jackson transl. 1931), Loeb Classical Library reprint, 1979
Thucydides, *History of the Peloponnesian War* (C. F. Smith transl. 1919), Loeb Classical Library reprint, 1980
Varro, *De lingua Latina* (Roland G. Kent transl. 1938), Loeb Classical Library reprint, 1993
Xenophon, *Hellenika, Anabasis, Cyropaedia* (Carleton L. Brownson transl.), Loeb Classical Library reprint, 1932
  Scripta Minora (E. Marchant transl. 1925), Loeb Classical Library reprint, 1984

Scriptural and legal materials

Cohen, Abraham and Isidore Epstein (eds.), *Sotah Talmud*, London: Soncino Press, 1985
The Code of Maimonides, New Haven: Yale University Press, 1949
Maimonides, Moses, *Law of Kings*, New York: Moznaim Publishing Corporation
Mommsen, Theodor and Paul Kruger (eds.), *The Digest of Justinian* (Alan Watson transl.), Philadelphia: University of Pennsylvania Press, 1985
The Theodosian Code (Clyde Pharr transl.), Princeton: Princeton University Press, 1952
Torah Sanhedrin (new ed.), London: Soncino Press, 1987

Secondary works

General works

Ancient states and statecraft

Adams, Robert McCormick, Developmental Stages in Ancient Mesopotamia, in *Irrigation Civilizations: A Comparative Study*, Washington, DC: Pan American Union Department of Cultural Affairs, 1955
  The Evolution of Urban Society, Chicago: Aldine Publishing Co., 1966

Adkins, Arthur W. H., *Merit and Responsibility: A Study in Greek Values*, Oxford: Clarendon Press, 1960

Ahlström, Gösta W., *The History of Ancient Palestine*, 1993

Alföldi, Andreas, *Early Rome and the Latins*, Ann Arbor: University of Michigan Press, 1964

Amit, M., *Great and Small Poleis* (Collection Latomus No. 134), Brussels: Latomus, 1973

Badian, Ernst, *Foreign Clientelae (264–70 BC)*, Oxford: Clarendon Press, 1958
    Roman Imperialism in the Late Republic, Pretoria: University of South Africa, 1967

Beard, Mary and Michael Crawford, *Rome in the Late Republic*, London: Duckworth, 1985

Bengtson, Hermann, *Introduction to Ancient History* (6th ed.) (Richard Ira Frank and Frank Daniel Gilliard transl.), Berkeley: University of California Press, 1970

Buckler, John, *The Theban Hegemony, 371–362 BC*, Cambridge, MA: Harvard University Press, 1980
    Thebes, Delphoi, and the Outbreak of the Third Sacred War, in *Le Béotie Antique* 237 (P. Roesch and G. Argoud eds., Lyon: Saint-Etienne, 1985)
    The Actions of Philip II in 347 and 346 BC: A Reply to N.G.L. Hammond, 46 CQ 380 (1996)

Busolt, Georg and Heinrich Swaboda, *Griechische Staatskunde*, Munich: Beck, 1926

Carneiro, Robert L., A Theory of the Origin of the State, 169 *Science* 733 (1970)

Cary, Max, *History of the Greek and Roman World: 323 to 146 BC* (2nd ed. rev.), London: Methuen, 1963

Catalano, P., *Linee del sistema sovrannazionale romano*, Turin, 1965

Chadwick, John, *The Mycenaean World*, Cambridge and New York: Cambridge University Press, 1976

Claessen, Henri J. M., Despotism and Irrigation, 129 *Bijdragen tot de Taal-, Land-, en Volkenkunde* 70 (1973)

Claessen, Henri J. M. and Peter Skalník, The Early State: Theories and Hypotheses, in *The Early State* (Henri J. M. Claessen and Peter Skalník eds.), The Hague: Mouton, 1978

Colin, G., *Rome et la Grèce de 200 à 146 avant JC*, Paris: Fontemoing, 1908

Contenau, Georges, *La Civilisation des Hittites et des Mitanniens*, Paris: Payot, 1934
    La Civilisation d'Assur et de Babylon, Paris: Payot, 1937

Coote, Robert B. and Keith W. Whitelam, *The Emergence of Early Israel in Historical Perspective*, 1987

Cowley, Arthur Ernest, *The Hittites*, London: British Academy, 1926

Croix, Geoffrey Ernest Maurice de Ste, *The Origins of the Peloponnesian War*, Ithaca, NY: Cornell University Press, 1972

Deininger, Jurgen, *Der politische Widerstand gegen Rom im Griechenland, 217–86 v. Chr.*, Berlin and New York: De Gruyter, 1971

Dellaporte, Louis, *Les Hittites*, Paris: La Renaissance du Livre, 1936

Desborough, Vincent Robin d'Arba, *The Greek Dark Ages*, London: Benn, 1972

Detienne, Marcel and Jean-Pierre Vernant, *Cunning Intelligence in Greek Culture and Society* (J. Lloyd transl.), Hassocks, Sussex: Harvester Press, 1978

Dorey, Thomas Alan and Donald Reynolds Dudley, *Rome Against Carthage*, London: Secker and Warburg, 1971

Dunbabin, Thomas James, *The Western Greeks: The History of Sicily and South Italy from the Foundation of the Greek Colonies to 480 BC*, Oxford: Clarendon Press, 1948

Dupont-Sommer, André, *Les Araméens*, Paris: A. Maisonneuve, 1949

Ehrenberg, Victor, *The Greek State*, Oxford: Blackwell, 1960

Erman-Ranke, Adolph, *Aegypten und ägyptisches Leben* (Charles Mathien transl.), Paris: Payot, 1952

Errington, Robert Malcolm, *The Dawn of Empire: Rome's Rise to World Power*, Ithaca, NY: Cornell University Press, 1972

Falkenstein, Adam, *The Sumerian Temple City* (Maria deJ. Ellis transl.), Los Angeles: Undena Publications, 1974

Finley, Moses I., *Economy and Society in Ancient Greece*, London: Chatto and Windus, 1981

    Politics in the Ancient World, Cambridge and New York: Cambridge University Press, 1983

    The Ancient Economy, Berkeley: University of California Press, 1973

    The World of Odysseus, London: Chatto, 1956

Francotte, Henri, *La polis grecque*, Paderborn: F. Schoningh, 1907

Frank, Tenney, *Roman Imperialism*, New York: Macmillan, 1914

    The Impact of the Fetial Institution, 7 CP 335 (1912)

Frankfort, Henri, *Kingship and the Gods*, Chicago: University of Chicago Press, 1948

Freeman, Edward Augustus, *History of Federal Government in Greece and Italy* (2nd ed.), London and Cambridge: Macmillan, 1893

Frick, Frank S., *The Formation of the State of Ancient Israel*, Sheffield: Almond, 1985

Fried, Morton H., *The Evolution of Political Society*, New York: Random House, 1967

Friedrich, Johannes, *Hethitisches Wörterbuch*, Heidelberg: C. Winter, 1952

Frisch, Hartvig, *Might and Right in Antiquity* (C. C. Martindale transl.), New York: Hafner, 1949

Gadd, Cyril John, *Ideas of Divine Rule in the Ancient East*, London: British Academy, 1948

Garstang, John, *The Land of the Hittites*, London: Constable, 1910

Giraud, Paul, *La propriété foncière en Grèce jusqu'à la conquête romaine*, Paris: Impr. Nationale, 1893

Gjerstad, Einar, *Early Rome*, Lund: C. W. K. Gleerup, 1953–73

Gomme, Arnold Wycombe, *The Population of Athens in the Fifth and Fourth Centuries BC*, Oxford: Basil Blackwell, 1933

Gottwald, Norman, *All the Kingdoms of Earth: Israelite Prophecy and International Relations in the Ancient Near East*, New York: Harper and Row, 1964

Grant, Elihu (ed.), *The Haverford Symposium on Archaeology and the Bible*, New Haven, CT: American School of Oriental Research, 1938

Green, Peter, *Alexander to Actium: The Historic Evolution of the Hellenistic Age*,
    Berkeley: University of California Press, 1990
Griffeth, Robert and Carol G. Thomas (eds.), *The City-State in Five Cultures*, Santa
    Barbara, CA: ABC-CLIO, 1981
Grote, George, *History of Greece*, London: Murray, 1872
Gsell, Stéphane, *Histoire ancienne de l'Afrique du Nord*, Paris: Hachette, 1920
Haarhoff, Theodore Johannes, *The Stranger at the Gate: Aspects of Exclusiveness and
    Co-operation in Ancient Greece and Rome*, London and New York: Longmans,
    Green and Co., 1938
Hammond, Nicholas G. L., *A History of Greece to 322 BC* (2nd ed.), Oxford:
    Clarendon Press, 1967
    Philip's Actions in 347 and Early 346 BC, 44 CQ 367 (1994)
    Plataea's Relations to Thebes, Sparta and Athens, 112 JHS 143 (1992)
Harle, Vilho, *Ideas of Social Order in the Ancient World*, Westport, CT: Greenwood
    Press, 1998
Harris, William V., *War and Imperialism in Republican Rome, 327–70 BC*, Oxford:
    Clarendon Press, 1979
Herman, Gabriel, *Ritualised Friendship and the Greek City*, Cambridge and New York:
    Cambridge University Press, 1987
Heurgon, Jacques, *The Rise of Rome* (James Willis transl.), Berkeley: University of
    California Press, 1973
Hignet, Charles, *Xerxes' Invasion of Greece*, Oxford: Clarendon Press, 1963
Hooker, J. T., *Mycenaean Greece*, London and Boston: Routledge and Kegan Paul,
    1976
Hume, David, On the Balance of Power, in 1 *Essays* 348 (T. H. Green and T. H.
    Grose ed.), London: Longmans, Green, and Co., 1875
Jeffrey, Lilian Hamilton, *Archaic Greece: The City-States c. 700–500 BC*, New York: St.
    Martin's Press, 1976
Kagan, Donald, *The Outbreak of the Peloponnesian War*, Ithaca, NY: Cornell
    University Press, 1969
Kessler, Josef, *Isokrates und die panhellenische Idee*, Paderborn: Druck von Ferdinand
    Schoningh, 1911
Kohler, Josef and Arthur Ungnad, *Assyrische Rechtsurkunden*, Leipzig: E. Pfeiffer,
    1913
Koschaker, Paul, *Babylonische–Assyrisches Bürgschaftsrecht*, Leipzig: B. G. Teubner,
    1911
Krader, Lawrence, *Formation of the State*, Englewood Cliffs, NJ: Prentice-Hall, 1968
Kramer, Samuel Noah, *The Sumerians*, Chicago: University of Chicago Press, 1963
Larsen, Jakob Aall Ottesen, *Greek Federal States: Their Institutions and History*,
    Oxford: Clarendon Press, 1968
    Representative Government in Greek and Roman History, Berkeley: University of
    California Press, 1955
Larsen, Mogens Trolle, *The Old Assyrian City-State and its Colonies*, Copenhagen:
    Akademisk Forlag, 1976

Levêque, Pierre, *Pyrrhos*, Paris: E. de Boccard, 1957

Lorton, David, *The Juridical Terminology of International Relations in Egyptian Texts through Dynasty XVIII*, Baltimore: Johns Hopkins University Press, 1974

Lowie, Robert H., *The Origin of the State*, New York: Harcourt, Brace and Co., 1927

Magie, David, *Roman Rule in Asia Minor*, Princeton, NJ: Princeton University Press, 1950

Maspero, Gaston, *The Struggle of Nations, Egypt, Syria and Assyria*, New York: D. Appleton and Co.. 1897

Matthews, Victor H. and Dan C. Benjamin, *The Social World of Ancient Israel, 1250–587 BCE*, Peabody, MA: Hendrickson, 1993

Meiggs, Russell, *The Athenian Empire*, Oxford: Clarendon Press, 1972

Meissner, Bruno, *Babylonien und Assyrien*, Heidelberg: C. Winter, 1920–25

Meritt, B. D., Athens and Carthage, in *Athenian Studies Presented to William Scott Ferguson* 247, Cambridge: Harvard Studies in Classical Philology Supp. 1, 1940

Miller, J. Maxwell and John H. Hayes, *A History of Ancient Israel and Judah*, Philadelphia: Westminster Press, 1986

Momigliano, Arnaldo, *Alien Wisdom: The Limits of Hellenization*, Cambridge and New York: Cambridge University Press, 1975

Morris, Ian, *Burial and Ancient Society: The Rise of the Greek City-State*, Cambridge and New York: Cambridge University Press, 1987

Numelin, Ragnar, *The Beginnings of Diplomacy*, New York: Philosophical Library, 1950

Olmstead, Albert Ten Eyck, *A History of Palestine and Syria to the Macedonian Conquest*, New York and London: C. Scribner's Sons, 1931

History of Assyria, New York and London: C. Scribner's Sons, 1923

Oppenheimer, Franz, *Der Staat*, 1909

Orlin, Louis Lawrence, *Assyrian Colonies in Cappadocia*, The Hague: Mouton, 1970

Ostwald, Martin, *Autonomia: Its Genesis and Early History*, Chico, CA: Scholars Press, 1982

From Popular Sovereignty to the Sovereignty of Law, Berkeley: University of California, 1986

Was There a Concept of *Agraphoi Nomoi* in Classical Greece? in *Exegesis and Argument: Studies in Greek Philosophy Presented to Gregory Vlastos* 70 (E. N. Lee, A. P. D. Mourelatos and R. M. Rorty eds.), Assen: Van Gorcum, 1973

Pais, Ettore, *Storia di Roma durante le grandi conquiste Mediterranee*, Turin: Unione tipografica editrice torinese, 1931

Perlman, S., Panhellenism, the Polis and Imperialism, 25 *Historia* 1 (1976)

Picard, Gilbert Charles and Colette Picard, *The Life and Death of Carthage*, London: Sidgwick and Jackson, 1968

Plescia, John, *Oath and Perjury in Ancient Greece*, Tallahassee: Florida State University Press, 1970

Redfield, Robert, *The Primitive World and Its Transformations*, New York: Penguin, 1968

Rey, Relations internationales de l'Egypte ancienne du XVe au XIIIe siècle avant Jésus-Christ, 48 RGDIP 35 (1941–45)

Roeder, Gunther, *Ägypter und Hethiter*, Leipzig: J. C. Hinrichssche Buchhandlung, 1919

Roux, George, *L'Amphictionie, Delphes et le temple d'Apollon au IVe siècle*, Lyon, 1979

Salmon, Edward Togo, *Roman Colonization*, London: Thames and Hudson, 1969
  Samnium and the Samnites, Cambridge: Cambridge University Press, 1967

Salmon, J. B., *Wealthy Corinth: A History of the City to 338 BC*, Oxford: Clarendon Press, 1984

Sayce, Archibald Henry, *The Hittites* (3rd ed.), London: Religious Tract Society, 1903

Schmidt, Hatto H., *Rom und Rhodos*, Munich: Beck, 1957

Scullard, Howard Hayes, *A History of the Roman World, 753–146 BC* (3rd ed.), London: Methuen, 1961
  From the Gracchi to Nero, New York: F. A. Praeger, 1959
  Scipio Africanus and the Second Punic War, Cambridge: Cambridge University Press, 1930

Sealey, Raphael, *A History of the Greek City-States ca. 700–338 BC*, Berkeley: University of California, 1976

Service, Elman R., *Origins of the State and Civilization: The Process of Cultural Evolution* (1st ed.), New York: Norton, 1975

Sherwin-White, Adrian Nicholas, *Roman Citizenship* (2nd ed.), Oxford: Clarendon Press, 1973
  Roman Foreign Policy in the East, 168 BC to AD 1 (1st ed.), Norman: University of Oklahoma Press, 1983

Sickler, Martin, *Judaism, Nationalism and the Land Borders of Israel*, Boulder: Westview Press, 1992

Snodgrass, Anthony M., *The Dark Age of Greece*, Edinburgh: University Press, 1971

Spaeth, John William, *A Study of the Causes of Rome's Wars from 343 to 265 BC*, Princeton: Princeton University dissertation, 1926

Steward, Julian H., *Theory of Cultural Change*, Urbana: University of Illinois Press, 1955

Thureau-Dangin, François, *Die Sumerischen und Akkadischen Königsinschriften*, Leipzig: J. C. Hinrichs, 1907
  Rituels Accadiens, Paris: E. Leroux, 1921

Turner, Ralph, *The Great Cultural Traditions: The Ancient Cities* (1st ed.), New York and London: McGraw-Hill, 1941

von Lyenden, Wolfgang, *Aristotle on Equality and Justice: His Political Argument*, New York: St. Martin's Press, 1985

Walbank, Frank William, *Philip V of Macedon*, Cambridge: Cambridge University Press, 1940

Westermann, William Linn, The Slave System of Greek and Roman Antiquity, in 40 Memoirs of the American Philosophical Society, Philadelphia: American Philosophical Society, 1955

Wiseman, Donald John, The Alalakh Tablets, London: British Institute of Archaeology at Ankara, 1953

The Vassal-Treaties of Esarhaddon, London: British School of Archaeology in Iraq, 1958

Wittfogel, Karl A., Oriental Despotism: A Comparative Study of Total Power, New Haven: Yale University Press, 1957

Woolley, C. Leonard, The Sumerians, New York: W. W. Norton, 1965

General works on ancient international law

Adcock, Sir Frank and Derek J. Mosley, Diplomacy in Ancient Greece, London: Thames and Hudson, 1975

Ago, Roberto, The first International Communities in the Mediterranean World, 53 BYIL 213 (1982)

Arundell of Wardour (Lord), Tradition Principally with Reference to the Mythology of the Law of Nations, London: Burns and Oates Ltd., 1872

Audinet, Eugène, Les traces du droit international et dans l'Iliade et dans l'Odyssée, 21 RGDIP 29 (1914)

Barré, Michael L., The God-List in the Treaty Between Hannibal and Philip V of Macedon, Baltimore: Johns Hopkins University Press, 1983

Bauslaugh, Robert A., The Concept of Neutrality in Classical Greece, Berkeley: University of California Press, 1991

Besta, Enrico, Il Diritto Internazionale nel Mondo Antico, 2 Comunicazione e studi dell' Istituto di Diritto Internazionale e Straniero dell' Università di Milano 9 (1946)

Bibikov, Petr Alekseevich, Ocherk Mezhdunarodnaya Prava v Gretsii [The Feature of International Law in Greece], 1852

Bikerman, Elie, Remarques sur le droit des gens dans la Grèce classique, 4 RIDA 99 (1950)

Chauveau, A., Le droit des gens dans les rapports de Rome avec les peuples de l'antiquité, 4 Nouvelle Revue historique de droit français et étranger 393 (1891)

Dahlheim, Werner, Struktur und Entwicklung des römischen Völkerrechts im dritten und zweiten Jahrhundert vor Chr., Munich: C. H. Beck, 1968

David, Martin, The Treaties Between Rome and Carthage and Their Significance for our Knowledge of Roman International Law, in Symbolae ad Jus et Historiam pertinentes Juliano Christiano Van Owen dedicatae 231 (Martin David, Bernard Abraham van Groningen, Edward Maurits Meijers eds.), Leiden: Brill, 1946

Fensham, F. Charles, Common Trends in Curses of the Near Eastern Treaties and Kudurru-Inscriptions Compared with Maledictions of Amos and Isaiah, 75 Zeitschrift für die Alttestamentliche Wissenschaft 155 (1963)

Heffter, August Wilhelm, *Das Europäische Völkerrecht der Gegenwart* (F. H. Geffcken ed.), Berlin: E. H. Schroeder, 1881

Hillers, Delbert R., *Treaty Curses and the Old Testament Prophets*, Rome: Pontifical Biblical Institute, 1964

Hosack, John, *On the Rise and Growth of the Law of Nations* (originally published in London in 1882), Littleton, CO: F. B. Rothman, 1982

Ivanov, N., *Kharakteristika Mezhdunarodnikh Otnoshenii i Mezhdunarodnovo Prava v Istoricheskom Razvitii* [The Characteristics of International Law and International Relations in Historical Development], Kazan: Universitetskaia, 1874

Karavites, Peter, *Capitulations and Greek Interstate Relations*, Göttingen: Vandenhoeck and Ruprecht, 1982 (Hypomnemata No. 71)

Karavites, Peter, with Thomas Wren, *Promise-Giving and Treaty-Making: Homer and the Near East*, Leiden: E. J. Brill, 1992

Kestemont, Guy, *Diplomatique en droit international en Asie Occidentale (1600–1200 av. J. C.)*, Louvain-la-Neuve: Université Catholique de Louvain, Institut Orientaliste, 1974

Laurent, Francois, *Histoire de droit des gens* (volumes 1 and 2), Ghent: L. Hebbelynck, 1850–1870

Leech, H. Brougham, *An Essay on Ancient International Law*, Dublin: University Press, 1877

Levin, David Bentsionovich, *Istoriya Mezhdunarodnovo Prava* [A History of International Law], Moskva: Izd-vo In-ta mezhdunarodnykh otnoshenii, 1962

Martin, Victor, *La vie international dans la Grèce des cités*, Paris: Recueil Sirey, 1940

McCarthy, Dennis J., *Treaty and Covenant*, Rome: Pontifical Biblical Institute, 1963

Mendenhall, George, *Law and Covenant in Israel and the Ancient Near East*, Pittsburgh: Presbyterian Board of Colportage of Western Pennsylvania, 1955

Mosley, Derek J., *Envoys and Diplomacy in Ancient Greece*, Wiesbaden: Steiner, 1973

Munn-Rankin, J. M., Diplomacy in Western Asia in the Early Second Millennium BC, 18 *Iraq* 68 (1956)

Paradisi, Bruno, L'amitié internationale: les phases critiques de son ancienne histoire, 78 RCADI 325 (1951–I)

Due aspetti fondamentali nella formazione del diritto internazionale antico, in 1 *Civitas Maxima, Studi di storia del diritto internazionale* 173 (1974)

Phillipson, Coleman, *The International Law and Custom of Ancient Greece and Rome*, London: Macmillan and Co., 1911

Pirenne, Jacques, *Histoire de la Civilisation*, Neuchatel: La Baconnière, 1961

Les Grands Courants de l'histoire universelle, Neuchatel: Editions de la Baconnière, 1959

L'Organization de la paix dans le Proche-Orient aux 3ᵉ et 2ᵉ millénaires, 14 *Recueil de la Société Jean Bodin* 200 (1962)

Preiser, Wolfgang, Die Epochen der antiken Völkerrechtsgeschichte, 23–24 *Juristenzeitung* 737 (1956)

History of the Law of Nations: Basic Questions and Principles, in 7 *Encyclopedia of Public International Law* 126 (Rudolph Bernhardt ed. 1984)

Zum Völkerrecht der vorklassischen Antike, 4 *Archiv des Völkerrecht* 257 (1954)

Redslob, Robert, *Histoire des Grands Principes du droit des gens: Depuis l'antiquité jusqu'à la veille de la grande guerre*, Paris: Rousseau et cie, 1923

Rosenne, Shabtai, The Influence of Judaism on the Development of International Law, 5 *Netherlands International Law Review* 119 (1958)

Rostovtseff, Michael, International Relations in the Ancient World, in *The History and Nature of International Relations* (Edmund Walsh ed.), New York: Macmillan & Co., 1922

Scupin, Hans-Ulrich, History of the Law of Nations: Ancient Times to 1648, in 7 *Encyclopedia of Public International Law* 132 (Rudolph Bernhardt ed. 1984)

Taube, Le Baron Michel de, *Istoriya Zarozhdeniya Sovremennovo Mezhdunarodnovo Pravo* [The History of the Conception of Contemporary International Law], St. Petersburg: P. I. Shmidt, 1894

L'inviolabilité des traités, 32 RCADI 292, 301–02 (1930–II)

Ténékidès, G. M., Droit International et Communautés Fédérales dans la Grèce des Cités, 90 RCADI 469 (1956–II)

La Notion Juridique de l'Indépendance et la Tradition Hellénique, Athens: Institut français d'Athènes, 1954

Théodoridès, Aristide, Les relations de l'Egypte pharaonique avec ses voisins, 23 RIDA 87 (1975)

Thompson, John Arthur, *The Ancient Near Eastern Treaties and the Old Testament*, London: Tyndale Press, 1964

Tiunov, Oleg I., Pacta Sunt Servanda: The Principle of Observing International Treaties in the Epoch of the Slave-Owning Society, 38 *Saint Louis University Law Journal* 929 (1994)

Verosta, Stephen, International Law in Europe and Western Asia Between 100 and 650 AD, 113 RCADI 484 (1964–III)

Vinogradoff, Sir Paul, *Outlines of Historical Jurisprudence* (vol. 1), London and New York: Oxford University Press, 1920

Walbank, Michael B., *Athenian Proxenies of the Fifth Century BC*, Toronto and Sarasota, FL: Samuel Stevens, 1978

Walker, Thomas A., *A History of the Law of Nations*, Cambridge: Cambridge University Press, 1899,

Ward, Robert, *An Enquiry Into the Foundation and History of the Law of Nations in Europe*, London: J. Butterworth, 1795

Watson, Alan, *International Law in Archaic Rome: War and Religion*, Baltimore: Johns Hopkins University Press, 1993

Weil, Prosper, Le Judaïsme et le Développement du droit International, 151 RCADI 253 (1976–III)

Ziegler, Karl-Heinz, Das Völkerrecht der römischen Republik, in 1 *Aufstieg und Niedergang der römischen Welt* 68 (H. Temporini ed. 1972)

Ziskind, Jonathan Rosner, Aspects of International Law in the Ancient Near East, Ann Arbor, MI: University Microfilms International, 1983

General works on international law

Bonfils, Henry, *Manuel de droit international public* (4th ed.), Paris: Arthur Rousseau, 1905

Bos, Maarten, *A Methodology of International Law*, Amsterdam and New York: Elsevier Science Pub. Co., 1984

Brierly, James, *The Basis of Obligation in International Law and Other Papers* (Hersch Lauterpacht and Claude Humphrey Meredith Waldock eds.) (originally published in 1958), Aalen: Scientia Verlag, 1977

Franck, Thomas, Legitimacy in the International System, 82 AJIL 705 (1988)

Fur, Louis Le, Guerre juste et juste paix, 26 RGDIP 9 (1919)

Guggenheim, Paul, Contribution à l'Histoire des Sources du Droit des Gens, 94 RCADI 1 (195–II)

Lauterpacht, Hersch, *The Function of Law in the International Community*, Oxford: Clarendon Press, 1933

Nussbaum, Arthur, *A Concise History of the Law of Nations* (rev. ed.), New York: Macmillan, 1954

Oppenheim, Lassa, *International Law* (vol. 1) (7th ed.), London and New York: Longmans, Green, 1948

Paradisi, Bruno, *Storia del diritto internazionale del Medio Evo*, Milan: A. Giuffre, 1940

Phillimore, Sir Robert, *Commentaries Upon International Law*, London: Butterworths, 1879

Rubin, Alfred P., The Concept of Neutrality in International Law, 16 *Denver Journal of International Law and Policy* 353 (1988)

Salvioli, Giuseppe, *Le concept de la guerre juste*, Paris: Editions Bossard, 1918

Schwarzenberger, George, International Law in Early English Practice, 25 BYIL 52 (1948)

Scott, James Brown, *Law, the State and the International Community*, New York: Columbia University Press, 1939

Vanderpol, Alfred, *La doctrine scholastique du Droit de guerre*, Paris: A. Pedone, 1919

Wheaton, Henry, *History of the Law of Nations in Europe and America*, New York: Gould, Banks, 1845

International law as a primitive legal system

Austin, John, *The Province of Jurisprudence Determined* (originally published in 1832) (H. L. A. Hart ed.), London: Weidenfeld and Nicolson, 1954

Barkun, Michael, *Law Without Sanctions: Order in Primitive Societies and the World Community*, New Haven, CT: Yale University Press, 1968

Bryce, James, *Studies in History and Jurisprudence*, Oxford: Clarendon Press, 1901
Bull, Hedley, *The Anarchical Society: A Study of Order in World Politics*, New York:
    Columbia University Press, 1977
Diamond, Arthur Sigismund, *Primitive Law Past and Present*, London: Methuen,
    1971
Dias, Reginald Walter Michael, *Jurisprudence* (5th ed.), London: Butterworths,
    1985
Dinstein, Yoram, International Law as a Primitive Legal System, 19 *New York
    University Journal of International Law and Politics* 1 (1986)
Gluckman, Max, *Politics, Law and Ritual in Tribal Society*, Chicago: Aldine, 1965
Hart, H. L. A., *The Concept of Law*, Oxford: Clarendon Press, 1961
Hartland, Edwin S., *Primitive Law*, London: Methuen, 1924
Hoebel, Edward Adamson, *The Law of Primitive Man*, Cambridge, MA: Harvard
    University Press, 1954
Kennedy, David W., Primitive Legal Scholarship, 27 *Harvard International Law
    Journal* 1 (1986)
Luard, Evan, *Conflict and Peace in the International System*, Boston: Little, Brown,
    1968
Maine, Sir Henry, *Ancient Law* (1861 ed.), Tucson: University of Arizona Press,
    1986
    Village-Communities in the East and West, Oxford: Oxford University Press, 1871
Masters, Roger D., World Politics as a Primitive Political System, 16 *World Politics*
    595 (1964)
Verzijl, Jan H. W., *International Law in Historical Perspective* (vol. 1), Leyden: A. W.
    Sijthoff, 1968
Wight, Martin, *International Theory: The Three Traditions* (Gabriele Wight and Brian
    Porter eds.), New York: Holmes and Meier for the Royal Institute of
    International Affairs, 1992

Ancient laws

Alt, Albrecht, *Die Urspruenge des israelitischen Rechts*, Leipzig: S. Hirzel, 1934
Cohen, Edward E., *Ancient Athenian Maritime Courts*, Princeton: Princeton
    University Press, 1973
Driver, Godfrey Rolles and John C. Miles, *The Babylonian Laws*, Oxford: Clarendon
    Press, 1960
Francotte, Henri, *De la condition des étrangers dans les cités grecques*, Louvain: C.
    Peeters, 1903
Frier, Bruce W., *The Rise of the Roman Jurists*, Princeton: Princeton University Press,
    1985
Gagarin, Michael, *Early Greek Law*, Berkeley: University of California Press, 1986
Gruen, Erich S., *Roman Politics and Criminal Courts, 149–78 BC*, Cambridge, MA:
    Harvard University Press, 1968

Herzog, Isaac, *The Main Institutions of Jewish Law* (2nd ed.), London: Soncino Press, 1965

Huffman, Herbert B., The Covenant Lawsuit in the Prophets, 78 *Journal of Biblical Literature* 285 (1959)

Jacobsen, T., Note, 2 JNES 171 (1943)

Kaser, Max, *Das altrömische Ius*, Göttingen: Vandenhoeck and Ruprecht, 1949
Das römische Zivilprozessrecht, Munich: C. H. Beck, 1966

Kelly, John Maurice, *Studies in the Civil Judicature of the Roman Republic*, Oxford: Clarendon Press, 1976

Latte, Kurt, *Heiliges Recht*, Tübingen: J. C. B. Mohr, 1920

Mommsen, Theodor, *Römische Geschichte* (W. P. Dickson transl.), New York: C. Scribner's Sons, 1895
Römische Staatsrecht (originally published in 1899), Basel: B. Schwabe, 1952

Noth, Martin, *Geschichte Israels* (2nd ed.), Göttingen: Vandenhoeck and Ruprecht, 1954

Plescia, Joseph, *The Oath and Perjury in Ancient Greece*, Tallahassee, FL: Florida State University Press, 1970

Poste, Edward, *Gaii institutiones juris civilis*, Oxford: Clarendon Press, 1890

Schmindlin, Bruno, *Das Rekuperatorenverfahren*, Freiburg, Schweiz: Universitätsverlag, 1963

Visscher, Fernand de, *Le Régime romain de la noxalité*, Brussels: A. de Visscher, 1947

Watson, Alan, *The Law of Persons in the Later Roman Republic*, Oxford: Clarendon Press, 1967

Whitehead, D., *The Ideology of the Athenian Metic*, 4 Cambridge Philological Proceedings Supplement (Cambridge 1977)

Zulueta, Francis de, *The Institutes of Gaius*, Oxford and New York: Clarendon Press, 1953

Ancient religions

Bayet, Jean, *Croyances et rites dans la Rome antique*, Paris: Payot, 1971
Histoire politique et psychologique de la religion romaine (2nd ed.), Paris: Payot, 1969

Bentwich, Norman, *The Religious Foundations of Internationalism* (2nd ed.), New York: Bloch, 1959

Berkovits, Rabbi Eliezer, *Not in Heaven: The Nature and Function of Halakha*, New York: Ktav Publishing House, 1983

Dumézil, Georges, *Archaic Roman Religion* (originally published in 1966) (Philip Krapp transl.), Chicago: University of Chicago Press, 1970

Falkenstein, Adam and Wolfram von Soden, *Sumerische und Akkadische Hymnen*, Zurich: Artemis-Verlag, 1953

Fowler, William Warde, *The Religious Experience of the Roman People*, London: Macmillan and Co., 1911

Frank, Tenney, The Import of the Fetial Institution, 7 CP 335 (1912)

Gernet, Louis, Anthropologie de la Grèce antique (originally published in 1968) (John Hamilton and Blaise Nagy transl.), Baltimore: Johns Hopkins University Press, 1981

Goar, Robert Jefferson, Cicero and the State Religion, Amsterdam: Hakkert, 1972

Gunkel, Hermann and Joachim Begrich, Einleitung in die Psalmen, Göttingen: Vanderhoeck and Ruprecht, 1933

Hengel, Martin, Die Zeloten (2nd ed.), Leiden: Brill, 1976

Hillers, Delbert R., Treaty Curses and the Old Testament Prophets, Rome: Pontifical Biblical Institute, 1964

Hirzel, Rudolf, Der Eid: ein Beitrag zu seiner Geschichte, Leipzig: S. Hirzel, 1902

Latte, Kurt, Römische Religionsgeschichte, Munich: Beck, 1960

Lewis, Martha Wilson Hoffman, The Official Priests of Rome for the Julio-Claudians, Rome: American Academy in Rome, 1955

Maury, Louis-Ferdinand-Alfred, Histoire des religions de la Grèce antique, Paris: Librairie Philosophique de Ladrange, 1856–59

McCarthy, Dennis J., Treaty and Covenant, Rome: Pontifical Biblical Institute, 1963

Mendenhall, George E., Puppy and Lettuce in Northwest-Semitic Covenant Making, 133 BASOR 26 (February 1953)

Mercer, Samuel, The Oath in Babylonian and Assyrian Literature, 1927

Murawaka, K., Demiurgos, 6 Historia 385 (1957)

Nilsson, Martin P., Greek Folk Religion, New York: Harper, 1961

Parke, Herbert William and David Ernest Wilson Wormell, The Delphic Oracle, Oxford: Blackwell, 1956

Popp, Harald, Die Einwirkung von Vorzeichen, Opfern und Festen auf die Kriegführung der Griechen im 5. und 4. Jahrhundert v. Chr., West Germany, 1957

Rawson, E., Religion and Politics in the Late Second Century BC in Rome, 28 Phoenix 193 (1974)

Rose, Herbert Jennings, Ancient Roman Religion, London and New York: Hutchinson's University Library, 1948

Vaux, Roland De, Ancient Israel: Its Life and Institutions, New York: McGraw-Hill, 1961

Waele, Ferdinand Joseph M. De, The Magic Staff or Rod in Graeco-Italian Antiquity, Ghent: Drukkerij Erasmus, 1927

Watson, Alan, The State, Law and Religion: Pagan Rome, Athens, GA: University of Georgia Press, 1992

Weinfeld, M., Covenant Terminology in the Ancient Near East and its Influence on the West, 93 JAOS 190 (1973)

   The Covenant of Grant in the Old Testament and in the Ancient Near East, 90 JAOS 184 (1970)

Wissowa, Georg, Religion und Kultus der Römer (2nd ed.), Munich: C. H. Beck, 1912

Ziebarth, Erich, Der Fluch im griechischen Recht, 30 Hermes 57 (1895)

Ancient warfare

Anderson, John Kinloch, *Military Theory and Practice in the Age of Xenophon*, Berkeley: University of California, 1970

Curchin, Leonard A., The Unburied Dead at Thermopylae, 9 *Ancient History Bulletin* 68 (1995)

Davie, Maurice Rea, *The Evolution of War: A Study of its Role in Early Societies*, New Haven: Yale University Press, 1929

Dickinson, Goldsworthy Lowes, *The Causes of International War*, New York: Harcourt, Brace and Howe, 1920

Garlan, Yvon, *La guerre dans l'antiquité*, Paris: 1972

Lonis, Raoul, *Guerre et religion en Grèce à l'époque classique*, Paris: Les Belles Lettres, 1979

  Les usages de la guerre entre grecs et barbares, Paris: Les Belles Lettres, 1969

Pritchett, William Kendrick, *The Greek State at War*, Oxford: Oxford University Press, 1979

Seckel, Emil, *Über Krieg und Recht in Rom*, Berlin: Norddeutschen Buchdruckerei und Verlagsanstalt, 1915

Strauss, Barry S. and Josiah Ober, *The Anatomy of Error: Ancient Military Disasters and Their Lessons for Modern Strategists* (1st ed.), New York: St. Martin's Press, 1990

Vernant, Jean Pierre, *Problèmes de la guerre en Grèce ancienne*, The Hague: Mouton, 1968

Historiography and the ancient craft of history

Bury, John Bagnell, *The Ancient Greek Historians*, London: Macmillan, 1909

Camerer, Luitgard, *Praktische Klugheit bei Herodot*, Tübingen: Doctoral dissertation, 1965

Cochrane, Charles Norris, *Thucydides and the Science of History*, London: Oxford University Press, 1929

Connor, Walter Robert, *Thucydides*, Princeton: Princeton University Press, 1984

Gomme, Arnold Wycombe, *The Greek Attitude to Poetry and History*, Berkeley: University of California Press, 1954

Gomme, Arnold Wycombe, Antony Andrewes and Kenneth James Dover, *A Historical Commentary on Thucydides*, Oxford: Clarendon Press, 1945–81

Griffith, G. T., Some Habits of Thucydides when Introducing Persons, 187 PCPhS 21 (1961)

Macleod, C. W., Thucydides' Plataean Debate, 16 GRBS 227 (1977)

Ogilvie, Robert Maxwell, *A Commentary on Livy, Books 1–5*, Oxford: Clarendon Press, 1965

Page, Denys Lionel, *History and the Homeric Iliad*, Berkeley: University of California Press, 1959

Palmer, Leonard Robert, *Interpretation of Mycenaean Greek Texts*, Oxford: Clarendon Press, 1963

Pouncey, Peter R., *The Necessities of War: A Study of Thucydides' Pessimism*, New York: Columbia University Press, 1980

Powell, John Enoch, *The History of Herodotus*, Cambridge: Cambridge University Press, 1939

Romilly, J. de, Fairness and Kindness in Thucydides, 28 *Phoenix* 95 (1974)

Sheets, George A., Conceptualizing International Law in Thucydides, 115 *American Journal of Philology* 51 (1994)

Underhill, G. E. and E. C. Marchant, *Commentary on Xenophon's Hellenika*, Cambridge: Cambridge University Press, 1906

Walbank, Frank William, *Historical Commentary on Polybius*, Oxford: Clarendon Press, 1957

Works detailing specific issues or doctrines in ancient international law

Diplomacy

Beckman, Gary M., *Hittite Diplomatic Texts*, Atlanta: Scholar's Press, 1996

Boak, A. E. R., Greek Interstate Associations and the League of Nations, 15 AJIL 375 (1921)

Broughton, T. R. S., Mistreatment of Foreign Legates and the Fetial Priests: Three Roman Cases, 41 *Phoenix* 50 (1987)

Bruce, I. A. F., Athenian Embassies in the Early Fourth Century BC, 15 *Historia* 272 (1966)

Greene, John T., *The Role of the Messenger and the Message in the Ancient Near East*, Atlanta: Scholar's Press, 1989

Jones, Christopher P., *Kinship Diplomacy in the Ancient World*, Cambridge, MA: Harvard University Press, 1999

Karavites, Peter, Diplomatic Envoys in the Homeric World, 34 RIDA 41 (1987)

Kolbe, W., Neutrality of Delos, 50 JHS 20 (1930)

Mitchell, Margaret M., New Testament Envoys in the Context of Greco-Roman Diplomatic and Epistolary Conventions: The Example of Timothy and Titus, 111 *Journal of Bibilical Literature* 641 (1992)

Robert, L., Adeimantos et la Ligue de Corinthe, 2 *Hellenica* 15 (1946)

Ryder, T. T. B., Athenian Foreign Policy and the Peace Conference at Sparta in 371 BC, 13 CQ 237 (1963)

Siewert, P., L'autonomie de Hyettos et la sympolitie thespienne dans les Helléniques d'Oxyrhynchos, 90 REG 463 (1977)

Tarn, M. M. W., The Political Standing of Delos, 44 JHS 141 (1924)

Walker, E. M., The Confederacy of Delos, 478–463 BC, 5 *Cambridge Ancient History* (1970)

Wéry, Louise M., Le fonctionnement de la diplomatie à l'époque homérique, 14 RIDA 195 (1967)

  Le meutre de hérauts de Darius en 491 et l'inviolabilité du heraut, 35 *L'antiquité classique* 468 (1966)

Treaties

Andrewes, A., The Peace of Nicias, 77 JHS 177 (1957)

Baltrusch, Ernst, *Symmachie und Spondai: Untersuchungen zum griechischen Völkerrecht der archaischen und klassischen Zeit*, Berlin: de Gruyter, 1994

Baltzer, Klaus, *The Covenant Formulary*, D. E. Green transl., Philadelphia: Fortress Press, 1971

Baronowski, David Walter, Roman Treaties with Communities of Cities, 1 *Ancient History Bulletin* 43 (1987)

Barré, Michael, L., *The God-List in the Treaty Between Hannibal and Philip V of Macedon*, Baltimore: Johns Hopkins University Press, 1983

Bickerman, Elias J., Hannibal's Covenant, 73 AJP 1 (1952)
    La trêve de 423 av. J.-C. entre Athènes et Sparte, RIDA 199 (1952)

Blamire, A., Epilycus' Negotiations with Persia, 29 *Phoenix* 24 (1975)

Bridges, Andrew Philip, The Athenian Treaty with Samos, ML 56, 100 JHS 185 (1980)

Buckler, John, Theban Treaty Obligations in IG II² 40: A Postscript, 20 *Historia* 506 (1971)

Bürgel, Heinrich, *Die pylaeisch-delphische Amphiktyonie*, Munich: Theodore Ackermann, 1877

Errington, R. Malcolm, The Peace Treaty Between Miletus and Magnesia, 19 *Chiron* 279 (1989)

Fensham, Charles F., Notes on Treaty Terminology in Ugaritic Epics, 11 *Ugarit-Forschungen* 265 (1979)

Gauthier, Philippe, *Symbola, les étrangers et la justice dans les cités grecques*, Nancy: Université de Nancy, 1972

Gomme, A. W., The Treaty of Callias, 65 AJP 332 (1945)

Greenfield, J. C., *Some Aspects of Treaty Terminology in the Bible*, Jerusalem: World Union of Jewish Studies, 1967 (Fourth World Congress of Jewish Studies No. 117)

Gurney, O. R., The Treaty with Ulmi-Tesub, 43 *Anatolian Studies* 13 (1993)

Heichelheim, F. M., New Evidence on the Ebro Treaty, 3 *Historia* 211 (1954–55)

Hopper, R. J., Interstate Juridical Agreements in the Athenian Empire, 63 JHS 35 (1943)

Jacobson, Howard, The Oath of the Delian League, 119 *Philologus* 256 (1975)

Kalluveettil, P., *Declaration and Covenant*, Rome: Pontifical Biblical Institute, 1982 (Analecta Biblica No. 88)

Korosec, V., Hethitische Staatsverträge: Ein Beitrag zu ihrer juristischen Wertung, 60 *Leipziger Rechtswissenschaftliche Studien* 23 (1931)

Langdon, S. and Alan H. Gardiner, The Treaty of Alliance Between Hattusili, King of the Hittites, and the Pharaoh Rameses II of Egypt, 6 *Journal of Egyptian Archaeology* 179 (1920)

Laqueur, R., Symbola, 71 *Hermes* 469 (1936)

Lee, Rhonda, *On Treaties Between Greece and Rome*, PhD dissertation, Newcastle upon Tyne, 1993

Matthaei, Louise E., On the Classification of Roman Allies, 1 CQ 182 (1907)

Merrill, William P., To P LETHOS in a Treaty Concerning the Affairs of Argos, Knossos, and Tylissos, 41 CQ 16 (1991)

Monceaux, Paul, *Les proxénies grecques*, Paris: E. Thorin, 1885

Mosley, D. J., Who "Signed" Treaties in Ancient Greece?, 7 *Proceedings of the Cambridge Philological Society* (ns) 59 (1961)

Oliver, J. H., The Peace of Callias and the Pontic Expedition of Pericles, 6 *Historia* 254 (1957)

Raubitschek, Anthony E., The Treaties Between Persia and Athens, 5 GRBS 151 (1964)

Smith, Vincent A., Asoka Notes (IV): Consular Officers in India and Greece, *India Antiquary* 200 (September 1905)

Thompson, J. A., *The Ancient Near Eastern Treaties and the Old Testament*, London: Tyndale Press, 1964

Wheeler, Everett L., Sophistic Interpretations and Greek Treaties, 25 GRBS 253 (1984)

Wikander, Ö., Gaius Hostilius Mancinus and the Foedus Numantium, 11 *Opuscula Romana* 84 (1976)

International arbitration

Ager, Sheila L., *Interstate Arbitration in the Greek World, 337–90 BC*, Berkeley: University of California Press, 1996

Bérard, Victor, *De arbitrio inter liberas Graecorum civitates*, Paris: E. Thorin, 1894

Martin, Victor, *La Vie Internationale dans la Grèce des Cités* (originally published in 1940), New York: Arno Press, 1979

Matthaei, Louise E., The Place of Arbitration and Mediation in Ancient Systems of International Ethics, 2 CQ 241 (1908)

Piccirilli, Luigi, *Gli arbitrati interstatali greci: dalle origini al 338 aC*, Pisa: Marlin, 1973

Raeder, Anton Henrik, *L'arbitrage international chez les Hellènes*, New York: G. P. Putnam's Sons, 1912

Ralston, Jackson H., *International Arbitration from Athens to Locarno*, Palo Alto, CA: Stanford University Press, 1929

Revon, Michel, *L'arbitrage international*, Paris: A. Rousseau, 1892

Taube, Baron Michel de, Les Origines de l'Arbitrage International: Antiquité et Moyen Age, 32 RCADI 1 (1932–IV)

Tod, Marcus Niebuhr, *International Arbitration Amongst the Greeks*, Oxford: Clarendon Press, 1913

Westermann, W. L., International Arbitration in Antiquity, 2 *Classical Journal* 197 (1906–07)

The laws of war

Amit, M., Hostages in Ancient Greece, 98 *Rivista di Filologia e di Istruzione Classica* 129 (1970)

Artson, Bradley, The Siege and the Civilian, 36 *Judaism* 64 (1987)

Aymard, A., Le partage des profits de la guerre dans les traités d'alliance antiques, 217 *Revue historique* 233 (1957)

Bikerman, Elie, Remarques sur le droit des gens dans la Grèce classique, 4 RIDA 99 (1950)

Bleich, Rabbi David J., Preemptive War in Jewish Law, 3 *Contemporary Halakhic Problems* 251 (1989)

Broyde, Michael J., Fighting the War and the Peace: Battlefield Ethics, Peace Talks, Treaties, and Pacifism in the Jewish Tradition, in *War and its Discontents: Pacifism and Quietism in the Abrahamic Traditions* (J. Patout Burns ed.), Washington: Georgetown University Press, 1996

Buret, Frederic, *Le droit de la guerre chez les romains*, Paris: A. Rousseau, 1888

Carey, William L., Nullus Videtur Dolo Facere: The Roman Seizure of Sardinia in 237 BC, 91 CP 203 (1996)

Danz, August Heinrich Emil, *Der sacrale Schutz in römischen Rechtsverkehr*, Jena: F. Mauke, 1857

Ducrey, P., Aspects juridiques de la victoire et du traitement des vaincus, in *Problèmes de la guerre en Grèce ancienne* 231 (Jean-Pierre Vernant ed.), The Hague: Mouton, 1968

   Le Traitement des prisonniers de guerre dans la Grèce antique, Des origines à la conquête romaine, Paris: E. de Boccard, 1968

Elbe, Joachin von, The Evolution of the Concept of the Just War in International Law, 33 AJIL 665 (1939)

Fusinato, Guido, Dei feziali e del diritto feziale, 13 *Atti Della Reale Accademia dei Lincei* (ser. 3) (1883–84)

Holleaux, M., Etudes d'historique hellénistique: Remarques sur les décrets des villes de Crète relatifs à l'*asylia* de Téos, 13 *Beiträge zur alten Geschichte* (1913)

Holloday, A. J. and M. D. Goodman, Religious Scruples in Ancient Warfare, 36 CQ 150 (1986)

Ilari, Virgilio, *Guerra e Diritto nel Mondo Antico*, Milan: A. Giuffre, 1980

Lateiner, Donald, Heralds and Corpses in Thucydides, 71 *Classical World* 97 (1977)

Lécrivain, Charles, Le droit sur se faire justice soi-même et les représailles dans les relations internationales de la Grèce, 9 *Mémoires de l'Académie de Toulouse* 277 (1897)

Lonis, Raoul, Les otages dans les relations internationales en Grèce classique, in *Mélanges offerts à Léopold Sédar Senghor* 215, Dakar: Nouvelles Editions africaines, 1977

MacDonald, B. R., The Import of Attic Pottery to Corinth and the Question of Trade During the Peloponnesian War, 102 JHS 113 (1982)

Michel, J.-M., L'extradition du général en droit romain, 39 *Latomus* 675 (1980)

Mishulin, A., Obyavleniye Voini i Zaklucheniye Mira oo Drevnik Rimlyan [The Declaration of War and the Conclusion of Peace in Ancient Rome] 10–11 *Historical Journal* 106 (1944)

Moscovich, M. James, A Note on the Aetolian Treaty of 189 BC, in *Polis and Imperium: Studies in Honor of Edward Togo Salmon* 139 (J. A. S. Evans ed.) Toronto: Hakkert, 1974

Hostage Regulations in the Treaty of Zama, 23 *Historia* 417 (1974–75)

Mosley, D. J., Crossing Greek Frontiers Under Arms, 21 RIDA 161 (1973)

Nieto, F. J. Fernandez, *Los Acuerdos bélicos en la antigua Grecia (época arcaica y clásica)*, Santiago de Compostela: Secretariado de Publicaciones de la Universidad de Santiago, 1975

Nörr, Dieter, *Aspekte des römischen Völkerrechts: Die Bronzetafel von Alcántara*, München: Verlag den Bayerischen Akademie den Wissenschaften, 1989

Panagopoulos, Andreas, *Captives and Hostages in the Peloponnesian War*, Athens: Grigoris, 1978

Rad, D. Gerhard von, *Der heilige Krieg im alten Testament*, 1951

Rich, J. W., *Declaring War in the Roman Empire in the Period of Transmarine Expansion* (Collection Latomus No. 149), 1976

Saulnier, Christiane, Le rôle des prêtres fétiaux et l'application du "ius fetiale" à Rome, 58 *Revue historique du droit français et étranger* 171 (1980)

Schlesinger, E., *Die griechische Asylie*, Giessen, 1913

Schwab, George, Enemy or Foe: A Conflict of Modern Politics, 72 *Telos* 194 (1987)

Séfériadès, S., La Conception de la Neutralité dans l'ancienne Grèce, 16 *Revue de droit international et de législation comparée* 641 (1935)

Vogt, Joseph, *Vom Reichsgedanken der Römer*, Leipzig: Koehler and Amelang, 1942

Walbank, F. W., Roman Declarations of War in the Third and Second Centuries, 44 CP 15 (1949)

Wiedemann, Thomas, The Fetials: A Reconsideration, 36 CQ 480 (1987)

Index

CAMBRIDGE STUDIES IN INTERNATIONAL AND COMPARATIVE LAW

Books in the series